Lecture Notes in Computer Science 8965

Commenced Publication in 1973
Founding and Former Series Editors:
Gerhard Goos, Juris Hartmanis, and Jan van Leeuwen

T0214376

Tarek Abdelzaher   Nuno Pereira
Eduardo Tovar (Eds.)

Wireless Sensor Networks

12th European Conference, EWSN 2015
Porto, Portugal, February 9-11, 2015
Proceedings

 Springer

Volume Editors

Tarek Abdelzaher
University of Illinois at Urbana Champaign
Department of Computer Science
Urbana, IL 61801, USA
E-mail: zaher@illinois.edu

Nuno Pereira
Eduardo Tovar
CISTER/INESC TEC, ISEP - Instituto Superior de Engenharia do Porto
Rua Dr. António Bernardino de Almeida, 431, 4200-072 Porto, Portugal
E-mail: {nap, emt}@isep.ipp.pt

ISSN 0302-9743   e-ISSN 1611-3349
ISBN 978-3-319-15581-4   e-ISBN 978-3-319-15582-1
DOI 10.1007/978-3-319-15582-1
Springer Cham Heidelberg New York Dordrecht London

Library of Congress Control Number: 2015930358

LNCS Sublibrary: SL 5 – Computer Communication Networks
and Telecommunications

Typesetting: Camera-ready by author, data conversion by Scientific Publishing Services, Chennai, India

Printed on acid-free paper

Springer is part of Springer Science+Business Media (www.springer.com)

Preface

This volume contains the proceedings of EWSN 2015, the 12th European Conference on Wireless Sensor Networks. The conference took place in Porto, Portugal, during February 9–11, 2015.

This edition of EWSN featured an updated scope, which resulted in a diverse program covering a wide range of topics grouped into five sessions: Services and Applications, Mobility and Delay-Tolerance, Routing and Data Dissemination, and two sessions on Human-centric Sensing. We also introduced a short-paper presentation session for validated early ideas that can be described as a concise contribution. These contributions are included in the proceedings with a shorter (8 pages) paper format.

EWSN 2015 received 85 paper submissions. In the full-paper category, it received a total of 65 papers, of which 14 were selected for publication and presentation as a full paper, yielding an acceptance rate of 21.5%. In the short paper category, nine papers were selected for publication and presentation.

EWSN 2015 adopted a double-blind review process. A total of 318 reviews were written. All papers were evaluated by at least three independent reviewers, and most received four reviews. Following the written reviews, the papers were selected after a very active weeklong online discussion.

The conference program also included two keynote talks, an industry session, and a poster and research demonstration session. The latter attracted numerous submissions for which separate proceedings are available.

We would like to thank everyone who contributed to EWSN 2015. In particular, we would like to thank the 36 members of the Technical Program Committee for their reviews and active participation in the discussions. We would like to thank the entire Organizing Committee, and particularly the general chair, Eduardo Tovar, for all the support provided. Finally, we would also like to thank the local organization team, Filipe Pacheco, Inês Almeida, Sandra Almeida, André Ribeiro, and Cristiana Barros, for their help.

February 2015

Tarek Abdelzaher
Nuno Pereira

Organization

General Chair

Eduardo Tovar   CISTER, ISEP, Porto, Portugal

Program Chairs

Tarek Abdelzaher   University of Illinois at Urbana Champaign,
                                     USA
Nuno Pereira   CISTER, ISEP, Porto, Portugal

Local Chair

Filipe Pacheco   CISTER, ISEP, Porto, Portugal

Demo and Poster Chairs

Vlado Handziski   TU Berlin, Germany
Raja Jurdak   CSIRO, Autralia
Ricardo Severino   CISTER, ISEP, Porto, Portugal

Publicity Chairs

Simon Duquennoy   SICS, Sweden
Anis Koubaa   CISTER, ISEP, Porto, Portugal

Industry and Sponsor Co-chairs

Luís Ferreira   CISTER, ISEP, Porto, Portugal
Martin Kubisch   Airbus Group, Germany

Web and Social Media Chair

Vikram Gupta   CISTER, ISEP, Porto, Portugal

Technical Program Committee

Table of Contents

Services and Applications

PyFUNS: A Python Framework for Ubiquitous Networked Sensors   1
    Stefano Bocchino, Szymon Fedor, and Matteo Petracca

On Target Counting by Sequential Snapshots of Binary Proximity
Sensors   19
    Tongyang Li, Yongcai Wang, Lei Song, and Haisheng Tan

Detecting and Avoiding Multiple Sources of Interference in the 2.4 GHz
Spectrum   35
    Venkatraman Iyer, Frederik Hermans, and Thiemo Voigt

Human-Centric Sensing I

Extracting Human Behavior Patterns from Appliance-level Power
Consumption Data   52
    Alaa Alhamoud, Pei Xu, Frank Englert, Andreas Reinhardt,
    Philipp Scholl, Doreen Boehnstedt, and Ralf Steinmetz

SocialSense: A Collaborative Mobile Platform for Speaker and Mood
Identification   68
    Mohsin Y. Ahmed, Sean Kenkeremath, and John Stankovic

Discovering Latent Semantic Structure in Human Mobility Traces   84
    Budhaditya Deb and Prithwish Basu

Mobility and Delay-Tolerance

Mind the SmartGap: A Buffer Management Algorithm for Delay
Tolerant Wireless Sensor Networks 104
    Pehr Söderman, Karl-Johan Grinnemo, Markus Hidell,
    and Peter Sjödin

A Knapsack-Based Message Scheduling and Drop Strategy for
Delay-Tolerant Networks 120
    En Wang, Yongjian Yang, and Jie Wu

Integrating Mobility in RPL 135
    Cosmin Cobârzan, Julien Montavont, and Thomas Noel

Human-Centric Sensing II

Limited-Memory Warping LCSS for Real-Time Low-Power Pattern
Recognition in Wireless Nodes 151
    *Daniel Roggen, Luis Ponce Cuspinera, Guilherme Pombo, Falah Ali,
    and Long-Van Nguyen-Dinh*

Sensor-Based User Authentication................................. 168
    He Wang, Dimitrios Lymberopoulos, and Jie Liu

Routing and Data Dissemination

Improving the Performance of Trickle-Based Data Dissemination in
Low-Power Networks 186
    *Milosh Stolikj, Thomas M.M. Meyfroyt, Pieter J.L. Cuijpers,
    and Johan J. Lukkien*

Featurecast: Lightweight Data-Centric Communications for Wireless
Sensor Networks 202
    Michał Król, Franck Rousseau, and Andrzej Duda

RoCoCo: Receiver-Initiated Opportunistic Data Collection and
Command Multicasting for WSNs.................................. 218
    Andreas Reinhardt and Christian Renner

Short Papers

Implementation and Experimentation of Industrial Wireless
Sensor-Actuator Network Protocols 234
    Mo Sha, Dolvara Gunatilaka, Chengjie Wu, and Chenyang Lu

Recycling Corrupt Packets over Multiple Hops 242
    *Muhammad Hamad Alizai, Muhammad Moosa Khattak, Dong Han,
    Omprakash Gnawali, and Affan A. Syed*

On the Scalability of Constructive Interference in Low-Power Wireless
Networks 250
    *Claro A. Noda, Carlos M. Pérez-Penichet, Balint Seeber,
    Marco Zennaro, Mário Alves, and Adriano Moreira*

LibReplay: Deterministic Replay for Bug Hunting
in Sensor Networks.. 258
    Olaf Landsiedel, Elad Michael Schiller, and Salvatore Tomaselli

If You Can't Take the Heat: Temperature Effects on Low-Power
Wireless Networks and How to Mitigate Them 266
    Florian Schmidt, Matteo Ceriotti, Niklas Hauser, and Klaus Wehrle

A Software Approach to Protecting Embedded System Memory from
Single Event Upsets 274
    Jiannan Zhai, Yangyang He, Fred S. Switzer, and Jason O. Hallstrom

Revealing Protocol Information and Activity from Energy
Instrumentation in Wireless Sensor Network 283
    Dong Han, Omprakash Gnawali, and Abhishek B. Sharma

Is RPL Ready for Actuation? A Comparative Evaluation in a Smart
City Scenario 291
    Timofei Istomin, Csaba Kiraly, and Gian Pietro Picco

Adaptive Packet Size Control for Bulk Data Transmission in IPv6 over
Networks of Resource Constrained Nodes 300
    Yang Deng, Zhonghong Ou, and Antti Ylä-Jääski

Author Index 309

PyFUNS: A Python Framework
for Ubiquitous Networked Sensors

Stefano Bocchino[1], Szymon Fedor[2,*], and Matteo Petracca[3]

[1] Scuola Superiore Sant'Anna, Pisa, Italy
s.bocchino@sssup.it
[2] United Technologies Research Centre Ireland, Ltd. Cork, Republic Of Ireland
[3] National Inter-University Consortium for Telecommunications, Pisa, Italy

Abstract. In recent years Wireless Sensor Networks (WSNs) have been
deployed in wide range of applications from the health and environment
monitoring to building and industrial control. However, the pace of prevalence of WSN is slower than anticipated by the research community due
to several reasons including required embedded systems expertise for developing and deploying WSNs; use of proprietary protocols; and limits in
scalability and reliability. In this paper we propose PYFUNS (Python-
based Framework for Ubiquitous Networked Sensors) to address these
challenges. PYFUNS handles low level and networking functionalities,
using the services provided by Contiki, and leaves to the user only the
task of application development in the form of Python scripts. This approach reduces required expertise in embedded systems to develop WSN
based applications. PYFUNS also uses 6LoWPAN and CoAP standard
protocols to enable interoperability and ease of integration with other
systems, pursuing the Internet of Things vision. Through a real implementation of PYFUNS in two constrained platforms we proved its feasibility in mote devices, as well as its performance in terms of control
delay, energy consumption and network traffic in several network topologies. As it is possible with PYFUNS to easily compare performance of
different deployments of distributed application, PYFUNS can be used
to identify optimal design of distributed application.

1 Introduction

Research in Wireless Sensor Networks (WSNs) has started over a decade ago with
great enthusiasm and community expectations to revolutionize our daily life. In
those years WSNs have been described as "distributed systems of numerous
smart sensors and actuators connecting computational capabilities to the physical world which have the potential to revolutionize a wide array of application
areas by providing an unprecedented density and fidelity of instrumentation".
Since the first testbeds, numerous deployments of WSNs have been described
for a wide range of applications (e.g., climatic monitoring, structural monitoring

---

* Szymon Fedor is currently affiliated with MIT Media Lab.

T. Abdelzaher et al. (Eds.): EWSN 2015, LNCS 8965, pp. 1–18, 2015.

of building), with the aim of introducing enhancements, and underlining open issues in the WSNs research field.

After numerous deployments in research projects, WSNs are nowadays reaching the industrial and consumer markets for large scale deployments. As matter of example it is possible to cite the GINSENG and SmartSantander projects where the potential of WSNs have been proved through real large scale deployments. Distributed smart sensors able to interact with the physical world exchanging data through wireless communications are nowadays considered the key components in the envisioned Smart City scenario.

However, to reach a wide adoption of the WSNs in several domains still several limitations persist. In this respect some of the main issues are: interoperability, ease of reprogramming and reliability. New generation of standards for WSN enables interoperability with Internet world (using IP and HTTP-type of protocols) and they need to be adopted in future smart sensors in order to reduce required effort for integration of WSN with other systems. The ease of reprogramming is a main requirement to be taken into account in large scale systems where the application logic must be changed remotely and without physical access to nodes. Network reliability is another key point to consider, in fact, this issue affects the real capability of the WSN to sense and interact with the physical world. Single point of failure must be avoided in order to prevent the possibility of losing data from several devices deployed in the field.

In respect of the above mentioned issues some progress has been made in WSN interoperability. In particular, it has been improved by adopting low level standard protocols (e.g., IEEE802.15.4), and by adapting IPv6 to the WSN scenario, thus really enabling the so called Internet of Things (IoT) vision. The IPv6 for WSN (i.e., 6LoWPAN) is only the first step towards a global interoperability, further improvements have been reached by enabling HTTP-based transactions in WSNs. CoAP is nowadays a standard protocol solution to enable the RESTful architecture in IoT-based WSNs. Progress has also been made in facilitating nodes reprogramming and programming although the proposed approaches are either not so easy, limited to a specific scope, and not really suitable for constrained devices such as those used in WSNs. In this direction a very promising and challenging approach is that following a virtual machine based design where Python scripts can be installed through RESTful transactions.

To address all the above mentioned issues we propose PyFUNS, a Python framework for ubiquitous sensor networks. By leveraging on IoT-based protocols (i.e., 6LoWPAN and CoAP) PyFUNS guarantees a higher interoperability and reliability with respect to old-style WSNs. Moreover, PyFUNS enables ease of reprogramming by introducing a virtual machine design based on Pymite, a reduced Python virtual machine for embedded systems.

The rest of the paper is structured as follows. Related works are described in Section 2, followed by the design of PyFUNS framework in Section 3. In Section 4 PyFUNS performance is presented in various network topologies and distributed application configurations. Section 5 concludes the paper.

2   Related Work

PYFUNS provides a number of features and several relevant solutions which have been described in WSN literature. We have divided them into (i) techniques for remote reprogramming, and (ii) frameworks enabling easier programming.

2.1   Techniques for Remote Reprogramming of WSNs

System Reprogramming. Such a method consists of replacing the node full firmware. It is very inefficient because even a minor application change requires reloading node binary image. Therefore they require more power and time to reprogram a node than other approaches in which only a reduced set of modules or functions is modified. Moreover, during the updating process, the new firmware must be stored in an external flash memory before being copied into the internal flash memory when the system restarts. Therefore, the nodes must have available external flash to store full software image. System level reprogramming technique are used in some existing WSN monolithic operating systems (e.g., TinyOS [HC1]) in which the whole application consists of a single image file.

Modular Reprogramming. According to this approach the node application is composed of independent, re-loadable modules. Contiki [DG1] is an example of a modular system which consists of two main components: system core and loaded program. The Contiki Core, with the boot loader exception, is a non-reprogrammable component. Therefore, any change in the code of the kernel, program loader, symbol table and communication interfaces is not supported. However, enhanced functionalities (e.g., file system support, shell support, power management) are loaded modules and are reprogrammable. The modular reprogramming is suitable for over-the-air reprogramming. Unlike the monolithic method, any system change is local, only the updated modules need to be transmitted. However, a large-memory footprint and slow system execution are disadvantages of any modular system. There are also other solutions implementing modular reprogramming (e.g., Dynamic TinyOS [MA1], LiteOS [CA1], RETOS [HS1]), similarly to Contiki their use requires embedded system experts.

Virtual Machine. In Virtual Machine (VM) based WSN, every node runs an instance of the virtual machine. The VM is used for the execution of both on-network applications and byte code instructions. In the literature there are several VM based approaches proposed for WSN [LC1][SC1]. Mate [LC1] is a VM built on TinyOS which uses the concept of capsules - a small set of high level primitives of up to 23 bytes. Mate-based applications are composed of several capsules which can propagate throughout the network to deliver an objective. Another VM for WSN is Squawk [SC1], a scale-down version of Java VM that runs without an OS on memory constrained devices. Squawk allows deployment and execution of multiple, isolated applications on a node. The use of a VM-based approach requires sensor nodes with improved resources with respect to well-known target platforms. This is because the virtual machine could be demanding in terms of CPU and memory. Considering the general trend in providing sensor nodes with higher performance at lower costs, the VM approach can be nowadays considered an effective and powerful solution in WSNs.

Differential. The use of a differential reprogramming is mainly based on the use of code patches: a patch is generated using the difference between the old and the updated program. Rsync [TM1] is a differential update scheme, and its functionalities has been demonstrated in WSNs [JC1]. As working principle, Rsync divides the program into different blocks and calculates their hash values. The evaluated hash values are then matched to determine the block insertion, deletion, or modification. There are many other examples of differential reprogramming systems [KP1][RL1], and in general it has been shown that the size of the deltas produced by the differential-based approaches is very small compared to the full binary image. However, most of them poorly perform when there is a change of both program and variable layout. This is because such update requires full flash memory writing, and large amount of additional external flash memory. Differential solutions can be easily used only by embedded system experts.

2.2   Frameworks Enabling Easier Programming of WSN

Many solutions for enabling an easier WSN programming have been described in the literature [MP1]. They were designed with different objectives, including energy-efficiency, scalability, failure-resilience or collaborative data processing. In this respect it must be underlined that one of PyFUNS main goals is to reduce required expertise in embedded systems for programming WSNs, as this has been previously identified by domain experts [MD1] as one of the major barriers for deploying WSNs. In that study the authors implemented the BASIC programming language for sensor networks and conducted a user study with novice programmers. Half of users with no previous programming experience of any kind were able to program simple network tasks using developed BASIC programs while only 0-17% could do so in TinyScript. Therefore the authors concluded that current WSN languages require knowledge of either very low-level systems development (including the details of sensor hardware and embedded system design), or high-level programming concepts and abstractions that are not obvious to most application domain experts. And because application domain experts have little programming experience, most of which is with simple single-threaded imperative programming models, the authors have ported a small BASIC interpreter to a WSN platform. Authors motivations are coherent with ours although our solution provides more features (e.g., interoperability due to IP and CoAP protocols) and is based on Python interpreter.

Recently several publications [AP1][C1] described solutions to program WSNs in Python language, due to its popularity and ease-of-use. In fact, according to [P1], Python requires no more than half as much time as writing in C, and it appears to be more intuitive with respect to C for new students [F1]. Regarding previously cited Python-based solutions, they must be considered at the early stage of development and incomplete to be used nowadays in real applications, though the most promising in this respect is T-Res. In fact, T-Res enables programming of the node to execute simple data-processing tasks performing the following actions: (i) monitoring one or more resources, (ii) executing some processing on their values, and (iii) sending the resulting output to other resources. The main lack of T-Res is in the possibility of monitor resources only: a method to retrieve the current resource state by using Python scripts is not supported.

3   PyFUNS Design

Having identified the limitations of literature of systems aiming at enabling remote reprogramming and an easier programming in WSNs, we have designed PyFUNS, a framework that can be used in a easy way to reprogram WSNs. Our framework leaves to the user only the application development task in the form of Python scripts, while abstracting low level and networking functionalities.

3.1   Dynamic Services over WSN

Traditional WSNs enable the development and deployment of pervasive networks aiming at providing many simple services, such as the environmental monitoring or the basic actuation control through basic operations. With the introduction of the IPv6 over Low power Wireless Personal Area Networks (6LoWPAN) protocol and Constrained Application Protocol (CoAP), following the IoT vision, WSNs have acquired enough resources to accomplish more complex services, such as the capability of exposing equipped sensors in Internet to perform automatic control operations. The next natural step in the WSNs domain is to build a smart management of dynamic services, thus enabling the possibility of remotely reprogramming the services provided by an IoT-based WSN.

In general terms a service provided by a WSN is a set of operations to be performed to accomplish a specific task. For instance, a service can be the automatic light control in a room and the operations to be performed are: (i) check the light value periodically, (ii) check the presence of people in the room, (iii) switch on the lamp while setting the power according to the desired light value, and (iv) switch off the lamp when people leave the room.

As previously stated, PyFUNS enables the management of dynamic services in WSNs. In the rest of paper we follow the aforementioned definition of service (i.e., a set of operations) calling the operations to be performed applications.

3.2   Application Components

An application deployed on a sensor node has several components:

- *Name:* string of characters that uniquely identifies the application;
- *Period:* it is related to the periodicity of the application execution. Values bigger than zero mean periodicity, equal to zero is for one time executions, while less than zero mean application blocked waiting for an answer. Application flow changes based on the Period value;
- *Timer:* used for periodic applications, it fires when executing the application;
- *State:* indicates the current state of the application in its internal Finite State Machine (FSM);
- *Script:* it contains the Python byte code performing the specific task which the application has to provide;
- *Variables:* list of variables required to store data to be exchanged among different scripts of the same application or among different applications;
- *Requests:* list of active requests. A request is used to retrieve the current representation of a resource through network messages. Each request is associated to both a callback function, called when a reply is received, and a variable, which is used to store the received data.

To the end of building an abstract framework that allows to implement applications able to perform data communication through the network (e.g., request/reply paradigm), we decomposed the application in three sub-scripts: *PreScript* (optional), *MainScript* (mandatory) and *PostScript* (optional). *PreScript* allows to send data request messages to a specific node in the network, and the answer will be processed in the *MainScript*. Moreover, it allows to set up the application environment (e.g., to create the variables required), and to retrieve the resource representation. *PostScript* is executed when the application has been stopped, and is mainly used to clean the application environment (e.g., to delete active requests). *PreScript* runs once at the application start, whereas *PostScript* runs once at the application stop. *MainScript* is the only mandatory byte code to be installed on the nodes, and represents the application core. It can be run once or several times according to the Period value. The *MainScript* execution can be triggered by a periodic event, the expiration of a timer, or by a sporadic event, the reception of a message. Fig. 1.a illustrates the script flow for an application using all the three described scripts.

3.3   Application Life-Cycle

The FSM model has been used to implement the application life-cycle, that can be dynamically installed, started, stopped, updated and uninstalled. To enable the aforementioned operations, five different states have been defined: (i) NEW, all the memory required to store the application structure has been allocated successfully; (ii) INSTALLED, scripts have been installed on the node; (iii) RESOLVED, application is ready to execute; (iv) RUNNING, application is active

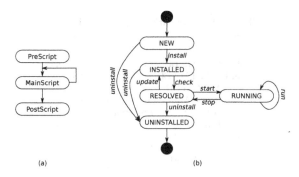

Fig. 1. (a) Scripts flow chart. (b) Application finite state machine.

and performs its operations; and (v) UNINSTALLED, the application structure has been deleted and the memory has been released. Fig. 1.b depicts the
application life-cycle and the possible transitions among states.

The application life starts in the NEW state, in which the necessary memory
is allocated to store the components described in Section 3.2. All the components are set to a default value, except for the name which is filled when the
application is created. In the NEW state it is possible to install *PreScript*, *Main-
Script* and *PostScript* on the node. As previously stated *MainScript* is mandatory
for each application and installing it implies a change of state to INSTALLED.
In the NEW state it has been enabled the possibility to uninstall the application through a defined uninstall event. In the INSTALLED state all necessary
components for the application are set, even though they are still waiting for
a control check aiming at verifying the compatibility among scripts (e.g., check
scripts version). The check is triggered by a defined check event, and in case all
the tests are passed, the state changes to RESOLVED. Also in the INSTALLED
state it is possible to trigger an uninstall event to delete the application. Once
the application reaches the RESOLVED state it has been successfully checked
and it is ready to be executed. Three different events can be triggered from this
state: (i) start, to run the application, *PreScript* is executed in case it is present,
otherwise *MainScript* is interpreted, as result the state moves to RUNNING; (ii)
update, to perform any changes concerning the scripts (e.g., install, update or
delete scripts on the node), in this case the state moves to INSTALLED and
the check compatibility on the new installed scripts must be redone; and (iii)
uninstall, to remove the whole application and release the memory used by the
application, next triggered state is UNINSTALLED. In RUNNING state the application can be executed one or many times according to the Period, and can be
stopped through a dedicated stop event. *PostScript*, if present, is executed during
the transition from RUNNING to RESOLVED. Last state is UNINSTALLED
where the application is deleted from the node. Table 1 summarizes the state
transitions of the above described FSM.

Table 1. Application state transition

CurrentState	Input	fNextState	Output
NEW	install	INSTALLED	At least *MainScript* has been installed
	uninstall	UNINSTALLED	Application deleted
INSTALLED	check	RESOLVED	Application ready to execute
	uninstall	UNINSTALLED	Application deleted
RESOLVED	start	RUNNING	*PreScript* executed, if installed
	update	INSTALLED	Changes in installed scripts
	uninstall	UNINSTALLED	Application deleted
RUNNING	run	RUNNING	None
	stop	RESOLVED	*PostScript* executed, if installed

3.4 Application Flow

As mentioned in Section 3.2, the application flow, in particular when *Main-Script* is executed, depends on the value of the application period. Two different period categories have been defined: period equal to zero when *MainScript* runs one time, and period not equal to zero when *MainScript* can run zero, one or many times. Fig. 2 shows different flow chart depending on the value of period, Fig. 2.a is for the first category, while Fig. 2.b and Fig. 2.c for the second.

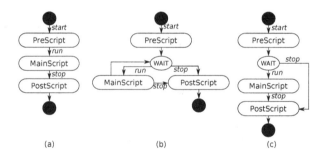

Fig. 2. Script flow chart for period equal to zero (a), period not equal to zero (b) and period less than zero, particular implementation (c)

In case of period equal to zero (Fig. 2.a), the application goes from *Pre-Script* to *PostScript* directly, running *MainScript* one time. It is not possible to stop the application once it is started. This setting of period is useful for applications changing the resource representation only one time.

With period not equal to zero (Fig. 2.b), after *PreScript*, the application waits for an event to continue its execution. We have defined two types of events that trigger *MainScript*: periodic and sporadic. Periodic applications have a period greater than zero and they wait the timer expiration before to interpret *Main-Script*. This setting is useful to implement applications changing the resource representation periodically. For sporadic applications the period is less than zero and *MainScript* is called when a sporadic event happens (e.g., message received).

This type of setting is useful to implement applications that perform activities when observed resources change. A particular application flow based on a period less than zero has been implemented, Fig. 2.c, to provide applications able to run *MainScript* once after resources representation are retrieved.

3.5   Application RESTful Interface

The goal of PyFUNS is to enable easy management (in terms of parameter reconfiguration and code deployment) of dynamic application installed in ubiquitous WSNs. To reach a seamless integration of the framework in motes it is necessary to abstract the application and its attributes. This can be done by using the REST paradigm in the context of IoT-based WSNs, or in other words by using the CoAP protocol, thus allowing sensor nodes to abstract resources and run embedded web services. Abstracting application and its attributes as CoAP resources enables the use of well known HTTP methods, GET, PUT, POST and DELETE, to administer code installed in a WSN. Moreover management of the application, (e.g., start or stop) can be performed by a user through a web site, or by another application through simple CoAP messages.

As described in Section 3.2, an application is defined by its components which are managed in PyFUNS as sub-resources of /apps. The resulting application structure is shown in Table 2. Resource /apps is created statically during the start up phase. This resource is the container of all applications installed on the node and it can be managed through CoAP methods to list currently installed applications and check their validity. The methods of /[app_name] provide the services to create/delete a specific application, retrieve the current state of the application, and start/stop its execution. The /[app_name] resource and its sub-resources are created by allocating the required memory only once, when the application is installed. The use of CoAP methods to manage the execution of a specific application (start/stop) enables the possibility to install on a node several applications related to each other in order to implement complex services.

Resource /period represents the current application period value, and must be set following the rules described in Section 3.4. A set of methods are provided

Table 2. The structure of an application resource

/apps			# list currently installed apps [GET]
			# check a specific app [POST]
	/[app_name]		# retrieve the application state [GET]
			# create/delete a specific app [PUT|DELETE]
			# start/stop a specific app [POST]
		/period	# retrieve/update the period [GET|PUT]
		/preScript	# retrieve/update/delete the *PreScript* [GET|PUT|DELETE]
			/version	# retrieve/update the *PreScript* version [GET|PUT]
		/mainScript	# retrieve/update/delete the *MainScript* [GET|PUT|DELETE]
			/version	# retrieve/update the *MainScript* version [GET|PUT]
		/postScript	# retrieve/update/delete the *PostScript* [GET|PUT|DELETE]
			/version	# retrieve/update the *PostScript* version [GET|PUT]
		/variables	# list currently variables [GET]
			/[var_name]	# retrieve/observe/update the value [GET|PUT]

to manage the scripts: for each script, *PreScript*, *MainScript* and *PostScript*, it is possible to retrieve/update/delete the byte code and retrieve/update the version of them. `/variables` resource is the container of the variables used by the application to accomplish its functionalities. By interacting with it, the list of current variables can be retrieved. For each variable a new resource is created and it is possible to retrieve/update the value. The purpose of this resource is to exchange data among different scripts of the same application, or among different applications. Each `/[var_name]` resource can be observed, even by other applications, enabling a smart functionality to be used in complex systems.

3.6   PyFUNS Implementation

Native code replacement and loadable modules on the one hand enable services updates, on the other hand imply a higher cost since downloaded modules are more coarse-grained compared to a virtual machine application. Moreover, these methods require to maintain information about the software version in each node, and the implementation is hardware dependent. To fully decouple applications from the sensing infrastructure we use a virtual machine to run the applications.

Most of the virtual machine based approaches enable highly efficient updates: low cost for transmitting new code and abstraction from the platform. The software updates sent from front-end-device to different nodes (based on different platform) are always the same. However, VMs introduce overhead in term of memory and computational overhead, which is overcome by more powerful devices present on the market. Python, Java and JavaScript are the most common interpreted languages used for virtual machine approaches with substantial libraries of pre-written code. The last two are object-oriented languages; whereas Python supports multiple programming paradigms, including object-oriented, imperative and functional programming styles. JavaScript script is too big to be installed in a WSN node and it cannot be compiled into byte code. Using byte code for reprogramming leads to an extremely powerful system in which microcontrollers can be programmed interactively without the typical compile/link/flash/run cycle. Both Python and Java allow for platform-independent processing functions that can be freely exchanged among nodes, but we preferred the former approach because, as discussed in Section 2.1, programming in Python is really simple and supports multiple programming styles.

We implemented PyFUNS on top of Contiki OS [DG1] that provides native support for 6LoWPAN and CoAP. A Python interpreter has been ported to the target operating system to enable script interpretation on constrained devices. We ported PyMite [PM1], a reduced Python interpreter that runs a significant subset of the Python language on microcontrollers with very few resources.

PyFUNS provides a set of APIs, summarized in Tab. 3, that can be used in Python scripts to implement applications. Such APIs allow: (i) to manage variables (create/delete/get/set); (ii) to send a generic CoAP message specifying the method (GET, POST, PUT, DELETE), the node address, the URI of target resource, the eventually payload and the eventually variable where store the result of the operation; (iii) to set/unset observation to a specific resource defined by its IPv6 address and URI; and finally (iv) to stop the execution of the application. The IPv6 address parameters are expressed without the prefix (e.g., [0,0,0,2]), as we have provided the messages exchanged among different applications that can be performed only inside the same network. Notice that sendMsg and obs functions have a parameter var to be associated with the request. In case of var is not present, it is automatically created inside the functions.

Table 3. PYFUNS APIs

Function	Description
newVar(name, value)	Create new variable
delVar(name)	Delete variable
getVar(name)	Get variable value
setVar(name)	Set variable value
sendMsg(met, addr, uri, payload, var)	Send CoAP message
obs(addr, uri, var)	Send CoAP observe
delObs(addr, uri)	Delete CoAP observe
exit()	Stop the application

A prerequisite of PYFUNS is that each node runs a web service to expose its resources, since the framework uses CoAP methods to interact with them. Instead, PYFUNS framework can be installed only on a subset of nodes.

3.7   Example of Usage

To evaluate PYFUNS performance, we implemented a Security service application which has the purpose to detect any motion in a room and trigger an alarm. In such example the network is composed of three PIR sensors, on nodes 2, 3 and 4 with the URI coap://[aaaa::2]/sen/pir, coap://[aaaa::3] /sen/pir and coap://[aaaa::4]/sen/pir respectively, and one alarm, on node 5 with URI coap://[aaaa::5]/act/alarm. The application implementing the service can be installed in any node inside the network using the RESTful interface defined in Section 3.5. The intent of Security service is to observe the PIR sensors, and trigger the alarm whenever a notification of motion detection is received. To implement such envisioned application we need to write and install the *PreScript*, *MainScript* and *PostScript*. *PreScript*, Listing 1.1, issues OBSERVE messages to all three PIR sensors and associates the requests to variables, p1, p2 and p3, used to maintain the representation of the sensors. Since the *MainScript* runs whenever a notification is received, the period of the application is set with a number less than zero: execute *MainScript* after a sporadic event happens (Fig. 2.c).

Listing 1.1. The *PreScript* of Security application

```
from pyfuns import *
obs([0,0,0,2], "sen/pir", "p1")
obs([0,0,0,3], "sen/pir", "p2")
obs([0,0,0,4], "sen/pir", "p3")
```

MainScript(Listing 1.2) is called whenever a notification from observed sensors is received. The operations carried out are very simple: retrieve the representation of the variable associated to each PIR sensors and issue a POST request to coap://[aaaa::5]/act/alarm to trigger the alarm, if one of the variables is equal to one, or to stop the alarm otherwise. Listing 1.3 shows the Python script related to *PostScript*. It sends messages to the PIR resources in order to delete the subscription when the application has stopped. The scrips byte code to be installed on nodes can be obtained by compiling the presented Python scripts.

Listing 1.2. The *MainScript* of Security application

```
from pyfuns import *
if getVar("p1") or getVar("p2") or getVar("p3"):
  sendMsg(2, [0,0,0,5], "act/alarm", "1")
else:
  sendMsg(2, [0,0,0,5], "act/alarm", "0")
```

Listing 1.3. The *PostScript* of Security application

```
from pyfuns import *
delObs([0,0,0,2], "sen/pir")
delObs([0,0,0,3], "sen/pir")
delObs([0,0,0,4], "sen/pir")
```

4   Performance Evaluation

To evaluate PYFUNS performance we implemented it on top of Contiki OS by integrating/porting PyMite on two constrained platforms: (i) WiSMote, equipped with a MSP430F5 microcontroller having 16 kB of RAM and 256 kB of flash, and (ii) CC2538dk, equipped with an ARM Cortex^{TM} M3 microcontroller having 32 kB of RAM and 512 kB of flash. In the rest of the section we first prove the feasibility of PYFUNS by checking that in both selected target platforms the performed implementation requires flash memory and RAM which are within the physical limits. Then we evaluate PYFUNS overhead in terms of run time and energy consumption. Finally we present an extensive evaluation of PYFUNS framework by implementing one real service: Security. To deploy the system bases on real platform, and test it in a real life scenario, we integrated: (i) sensors, such as PIRs, and (ii) actuators, such as alarms, on target platforms.

4.1   Flash and RAM Requirements

To assess the possibility of deplying PYFUNS on the selected devices we measured both the flash and RAM occupation. Table 4 shows the memory occupied by the software for both platforms, the WiSMote and the CC2538dk. The software installed on each WSN node includes the Contiki OS, the PyMite interpreter, PYFUNS, plus the possibly required memory to install two PYFUNS applications. In case of WiSMote platform the whole firmware occupies 93% of the available RAM and 38% of the available flash. In case of the CC2538dk platform the firmware requires the 62% of the available RAM and the 19% of

Table 4. Code size and RAM requirements for a WiSMote and CC2538dk devices

Nodetype	RAM[bytes]	Flash[bytes]
WiSMote	14 918 (93%)	98 077 (38%)
CC2538dk	19 904 (62%)	96 732 (19%)

the available flash. Such a notable occupation of memory, especially RAM, is mainly due to PyMite, which alone requires 45 kB of flash and 8 kB of RAM. In order to reduce the RAM occupation we are planning to implement a tool to store Python byte codes into the flash. The current version of PYFUNS stores the Python scripts in RAM, which is usually more constrained comparing to the flash memory.

4.2   Native Code versus Python Script

PYFUNS overhead in terms of run time and energy consumption has been evaluated with respect to a native code solution. Both performance figures have been measured by using two different set of benchmarks: (i) five test applications implementing algorithms showing a different complexity level; (ii) three applications implementing CoAP methods. Each benchmark has been executed by considering a C language based native code solution, and its Python version.

The first benchmark set is composed of five algorithms, characterized by different complexity levels, and chosen from *"dada's perl lab"*[1]. More specifically, we selected the following algorithms, listed in function of their complexity (from lower to higher): (i) ACK - Ackermann's Function(3, N) that is a classic recursive function with N=3; (ii) FIB - Fibonacci Numbers(N) that computes the Fibonacci sequence with N=17; (iii) MAT - Matrix Multiplication(N) that performs the multiplication between two matrices with size 5 and N=10; (iv) HEAP - Heapsort(N) that sorts a vector with a size N=100 of integer numbers, and initialized with strictly decreasing value; and (v) MET - Method Calls(N) that implements activation of class methods using object-oriented style. The second benchmark test, instead, includes: (i) an application that issues a POST request to a resource installed in a neighbor node (POST); (ii) an application that issues a POST request to a resource installed in a neighbor node and waits the acknowledgement message from the resource (POST2); and (iii) an application that issues a GET request to one resource installed in a neighbor node, waits the reply, processes it and sends a POST request to another resource installed in a neighbor node (GET). All performance results are reported in Table 5.

All results have been obtained by running each test 1000 times in Cooja, the Contiki network simulator. Cooja allows to run the same binary files to be used on real platforms while enabling a quick testing and debugging of the system. In the simulator all tests have been performed by using only the WiSMote platform

---

[1] A benchmark comparison of a number of programming languages:
http://dada.perl.it/shootout/craps.html

Table 5. Performance benchmarks in Cooja

	C		Python		Python/C	
	Time(ms)	Energy(μJ)	Time(ms)	Energy(μJ)	Timeratio	Energyratio
ACK	4.08	0.029	645.25	4.765	158.1	164.3
FIB	9.95	0.072	1344.84	9.932	135.2	137.9
MAT	5.06	0.037	687.31	5.076	135.8	137.1
HEAP	1.95	0.014	379.68	2.804	194.7	197.7
MET	1.16	0.009	207.28	1.531	178.8	177.2
POST	1.22	0.009	5.35	0.039	4.4	4.3
POST2	8.61	0.328	12.68	0.357	1.4	1.1
GET	17.26	0.604	26.19	0.671	1.5	1.1

(CC2538dk is not supported at time of writing), moreover to prove the Cooja accuracy we ran also two benchmark tests on a real WiSMote platform. In Table 5 the C and Python columns show the run times and the energy consumption for all benchmark applications, while the last column labeled as Python/C reports the ratio between PyFUNS and native code approaches. For the first benchmark set the time performance penalty of PyMite is between 135 and 195, while showing a performance gap between 137 and 198 in energy consumption. Such a difference between C and Python is mainly caused by the extensive use of the heap memory in PyMite when performing complex operations such as recursive calls. On the contrary, in CoAP methods tests the run time performance penalty is between 1.5 and 4.4 with an energy consumption performance gap between 1.1 and 4.3. This is the overhead introduced by PyMite to perform CoAP methods in WSNs, while enabling a powerful tool providing platform abstraction and reconfigurable in-network processing that can compensate the overhead. To prove the validity of the aforementioned results obtained with Cooja simulator, we also ran the Python version of Ackermann's Function and POST method on a real WiSMote platform. The obtained results are reported in Table 6, and they are very similar to those obtained by using the Cooja simulator.

Table 6. Performance benchmark on WiSMote

	Time(ms)	Energy(μJ)
ACK	649.79	4.799
POST	5.52	0.040

4.3 Real Case Evaluation

Performance of a distributed application depends on the network topology and in-network distribution of application components. We evaluated PyFUNS performance in terms of energy consumption, actuation delay and network traffic, to provide real services such as the one presented in Section 3.7. The application components were distributed among the nodes or centrally placed at the border router. For the energy consumption we considered the overall network consumption. The actuation delay represents the elapsed time between the detection of the event and the associated actuation, while network traffic measures the total amount of bytes exchanged in the network. As we want to evaluate the impact of PyFUNSonly, we take into account only CoAP messages without counting traffic generated by underlying layers (e.g. RPL messages).

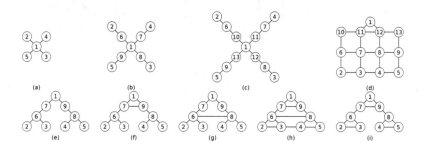

Fig. 3. Network topologies: star (a-b-c), mesh (d) and tree (e-f-g-h-i)

To avoid impact of the changing environment and measurement overhead of real world experiments we installed PyFUNS on Cooja simulator. The Security service was deployed on multi-hop, IoT-based WSN, configured with nine network topologies shown in Fig. 3: three star topologies with 5, 9, and 13 nodes; one mesh topology with 13 nodes; and 5 tree topologies each one of them with 9 nodes and different transmission links. The power transmission of nodes was fixed for all the topologies except for the topology from Fig. 3.a which was evaluated also with a higher transmission power. This was done to compare topology having multi-hop transmissions (Fig. 3.b) with a network having smaller number of nodes but covering similar geographical area.

For the security service scenario nodes 2, 3 and 4 in Fig. 3 were simulated with an attached PIR sensor and the node 5 with an attached buzzer. We tested different placements of security service components as depicted in Table 7.

Table 7. Security Control service deployment configurations

(a)	(b)	(c)(d)	(e)(f)(g)(h)(i)
BR (1)	BR (1)	BR (1)	BR (1)
PIR2 (2)	PIR2 (2)	PIR2 (2)	PIR2 (2)
Alarm (5)	Alarm (5)	Alarm (5)	PIR4 (4)
	Node 6	Node 6	Alarm (5)
	Node 9	Node 9	Node 6
		Node 10	Node 7
		Node 13	Node 8
			Node 9

Figure 4 shows the energy consumption measurement for all topologies. As we expected the minimum energy consumption for star topology is when PyFUNS application is installed on the Border Router. This is because the amount

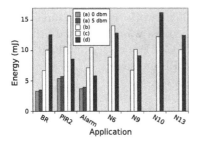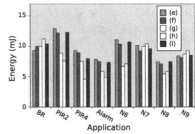

Fig. 4. Energy consumption in star (a-b-c), mesh (d) and in tree (e-f-g-h-i) topologies. The label on the x-axis indicates in which node the Security application is installed.

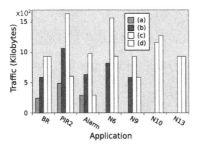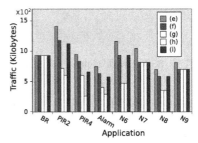

Fig. 5. Network traffic in star (a-b-c), mesh (d) and in tree (e-f-g-h-i) topologies. The label on the x-axis indicates in which node the Security application is installed.

of data exchanged in such configuration is minimum (Fig. 5). In fact, when the transmission is between nodes distant by more than one hop an additional 6LoW-PAN header overhead (due to the addressing and hop limit fields) is observed.

However, in case of mesh topology (Fig. 4 right side) the minimum energy consumption of the overall network is observed when the service is distributed among the nodes rather than placed on the Border Router. For all topologies it is the number of transmission hops that plays dominant role in the total amount of network traffic, and consequently in energy consumption. For instance, in topology (e) (purple columns) it is possible to see that the energy consumed when the application is installed in nodes PIR2 and 6 (which are closely located) is bigger than a centralized approach (application on BR). On the basis of energy consumption parameter the best choice for (e) (f) (g) is node 8, with a consumed energy equal to 7.47 mJ, 7.12 mJ and 5.43 mJ respectively, for (h) is node 4 with 5.36 mJ, and for (d) and (i) is node 5 with 5.85 mJ and 7.39 mJ respectively.

We also evaluated delay introduced by the framework in triggering the actuator node when a motion detection event happens. Figure 6 presents the delay for all topologies, it depends on the number of hops between sensor and actuator.

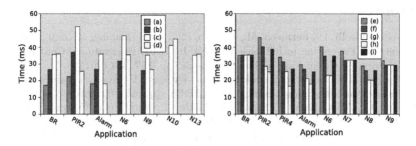

Fig. 6. Delay time (ms) in star (a-b-c), mesh (d) and in tree (e-f-g-h-i) topologies. The label on the x-axis indicates in which node the Security application is installed.

5   Conclusions

As WSNs moved from the academic world to the industrial scenario new challenges have been raised up to reach a wide adoption of the WSNs in several domains. Some of the main issues are: interoperability, ease of reprogramming and reliability. To address such issues we propose PYFUNS, a Python framework for ubiquitous sensor networks. By leveraging on IoT-based protocols (i.e., 6LoW-PAN and CoAP) PYFUNS guarantees a higher interoperability and reliability with respect to old-style WSNs. Moreover, thanks to its adopted virtual machine design based on Pymite, a reduced Python interpreter, PYFUNS enables ease of reprogramming in WSNs. In a real scenario PYFUNS can be used as complementary tool of a framework able to allow users to easily write Python-based IoT applications (e.g., through a graphical interface) to be remotely installed on WSN nodes hiding the whole installation process. This feature can be provided by PyoT, a system for macro-programming and managing IoT-based WSNs.

In the paper we first presented PYFUNS by detailing its design and implementation choices by carefully explaining its usage in building simple and complex services. Then we evaluated PYFUNS performance considering the WiSMote and CC2538dk platforms with the aim of proving its feasibility in real constrained devices, and its overhead in terms of run time and energy consumption with respect to native code solutions. Finally PYFUNS performance in star, mesh and tree network topologies were evaluated for a Security service by considering both centralized and distributed application logic solutions. Presented results, aside of proving PYFUNS feasibility and performance, highlight further possible optimization to be investigated: RAM memory requirement reduction, scripts execution time and energy consumption, communication failures handling. While RAM memory occupancy can be merely solved by saving Python scripts in flash and leaving the RAM for regular applications, other optimizations require a deeper analysis, and they will be addressed in future investigations.

References

[AP1]   Alessandrelli, D., Petracca, M., Pagano, P.: T-Res: Enabling Reconfigurable In-network Processing in IoT-based WSNs. In: IEEE International Conference on Distributed Computing in Sensor Systems, pp. 337–344 (2013)

[C1]   Carboni, D., Crs Parco Tecnologico Pula: PySense: Python Decorators for Wireless Sensor Macroprogramming. In: ICSOFT, pp.165–169 (2010)

[CA1]   Cao, Q., Abdelzaher, T., Stankovic, J., He, T.: The LiteOS Operating System: Towards Unix-Like Abstractions for Wireless Sensor Networks. In: International Conference on Information Processing in Sensor Networks, pp. 233–244 (2008)

[DG1]   Dunkels, A., Gronvall, B., Voigt, T.: Contiki - A Lightweight and Flexible Operating System for Tiny Networked Sensors. In: IEEE International Conference on Local Computer Networks, pp. 148–157 (2004)

[F1]   Fangohr, H.: A comparison of C, Matlab and Python as teaching languages in engineering. In: International Conference in Computational Science, pp. 1210–1217 (2004)

[HC1]   Hui, J.W., Culler, D.: The Dynamic Behavior of a Data Dissemination Protocol for Network Programming at Scale. In: International Conference on Embedded Networked Sensor Systems, pp. 81–84 (2004)

[HS1]   Hojung, C., Sukwon, C., Inuk, J., Hyoseung, K., Hyojeong, S., Jaehyun, Y., Chanmin, Y.: RETOS: Resilient, Expandable, and Threaded Operating System for Wireless Sensor Networks. In: International Symposium on Information Processing in Sensor Networks, pp. 148–157 (2007)

[JC1]   Jaein, J., Culler, D.: Incremental network programming for wireless sensors. In: IEEE Communications Society Conference on Sensor and Ad Hoc Communications and Networks, pp. 25–33 (2004)

[KP1]   Koshy, J., Pandey, R.: Remote incremental linking for energy-efficient reprogramming of sensor networks. In: European Workshop on Wireless Sensor Networks, pp. 354–365 (2005)

[LC1]   Levis, P., Culler, D.: Mate: a tiny virtual machine for sensor networks. In: International Conference on Architectural Support for Programming Languages and Operating System, pp. 85–95 (2002)

[MA1]   Munawar, W., Alizai, M.H., Landsiedel, O., Wehrle, K.: Dynamic TinyOS: Modular and Transparent Incremental Code-Updates for Sensor Networks. In: IEEE International Conference on Communications (ICC), pp. 1–6 (2010)

[MD1]   Miller, J.S., Dinda, P.A., Dick, R.P.: Evaluating a BASIC Approach to Sensor Network Node Programming. In: ACM Conference on Embedded Networked Sensor System, pp. 155–168 (2009)

[MP1]   Mottola, L., Picco, G.P.: Programming Wireless Sensor Networks: Fundamental Concepts and State of the Art. ACM Comput. Surv. 43, 19:1–19:51 (2011)

[P1]   Prechelt, L.: An empirical comparison of seven programming languages. Computer 33, 23–29 (2000)

[PM1]   PyMite (2013), http://code.google.com/p/python-on-a-chip/

[RL1]   Reijers, N., Langendoen, K.: Efficient Code Distribution in Wireless Sensor Networks. In: ACM International Conference on Wireless Sensor Networks and Applications, pp. 60–67 (2003)

[SC1]   Simon, D., Cifuentes, C., Cleal, D., Daniels, J., White, D.: Java on the Bare Metal of Wireless Sensor Devices: The Squawk Java Virtual Machine. In: International Conference on Virtual Execution Environments, pp. 78–88 (2006)

[TM1]   Tridgell, A., Mackeras, P.: The rsync algorithm (1998), http://rsync.samba.org/tech_report155-190

On Target Counting by Sequential Snapshots of Binary Proximity Sensors*

Tongyang Li[1], Yongcai Wang[1,**], Lei Song[1], and Haisheng Tan[2]

[1] IIIS, Tsinghua University, Beijing, China
[2] Jinan University, Guangzhou, China
wangyc@tsinghua.edu.cn

Abstract. Counting and tracking multiple targets by binary proximity sensors (BPS) is known difficult because a BPS in "on" state cannot distinguish how many targets are presenting in its sensing range. Existing approaches investigated target counting by utilizing joint readings of a network of BPSs, called a snapshot [2,11]. A recent work [14] presented a snapshot-based target counting lower bound. But counting by individual snapshot has not fully utilized the information between the sequential readings of BPSs. This paper exploits the spatial and temporal dependency introduced by a sequence of snapshots to improve the counting bounds and resolution. In particular, a dynamic counting scheme which considers the dependency among the snapshots were developed. It leads to a dynamic lower bound and a dynamic upper bound respectively. Based on them, an improved precisely counting condition was presented. Simulations were conducted to verify the improved counting limits, which showed the improvements than the snapshot-based methods.

1 Introduction

Binary proximity sensors (BPS) is an extracted model for a large category of sensors, such as infrared, ultrasound, microwave, and magnetic sensors. It has an extremely simple sensing model, which outputs a single bit "1" when one or more mobile targets are in its sensing range and "0" otherwise. A BPS sensor cannot distinguish the targets, decides how many distinct targets are presenting in its range, nor judges the targets' moving directions.

Despite of the very limited information provided by one BPS, prior works [11][9] showed the feasibility to track a single target using a collaborative network of BPSs. In [9], the authors showed that if only one target was presenting, the worst case location error is bounded by $\Omega(\frac{1}{\rho R^{d-1}})$, where ρ is the sensor density, R is the sensing range, and d is the dimension of the space. However, significant difficulties are

---

* This work was supported by in part by National Natural Science Foundation of China Grant 61202360, 61073174, 61033001, 61061130540, the Hi-Tech research and Development Program of China Grant 2006AA10Z216, and the National Basic Research Program of China Grant 2011CBA00300, 2011C-BA00302.
** Corresponding author.

T. Abdelzaher et al. (Eds.): EWSN 2015, LNCS 8965, pp. 19–34, 2015.

encountered for tracking multiple targets because each "on" sensor cannot distinguish how many targets are presenting in its sensing range. Therefore, a fundamental challenge is to count the number of targets precisely.

Existing approach investigated the target counting problem by exploiting individual snapshot captured from a network of BPS. We call such case *static counting*. In [11], Singh et al. presented that accurate target counting could be achieved by a snapshot if the targets are separated by at least $4R$, where R is a sensor's sensing radius. Recent work in [14] presented a lower bound of static counting, which stated that the number of presenting targets equals to the minimum clique partition of the UDG formed by the "on" sensors. However, *static counting* has not fully utilized the information provided by the sensors' reading sequences. In this paper, we show that the upper and lower bounds on target counting can be further improved by exploiting the temporal, spatial dependencies between the sequential snapshots.

Different from the existing approaches, we take the *sequential events reported from sensors during a period* as the problem's input. In this case, a *dynamic counting* technique to infer the lower bound of the target number was designed. We showed theoretically and numerically that the lower bound given by dynamically counting can effectively improve the existing lower bound in static counting. For estimating the upper bound of the number of targets, we firstly propose a packing-based upper bound for snapshot cases under an assumption of minimum pair-wise separation distance between targets. Later on, a dynamic counting algorithm is designed to improve the static upper bound, whose effectiveness is also verified by simulations.

Furthermore, the condition for precisely target counting is discussed in our work. In [12], J. Singh et al. proved that at least $4R$ pairwise separation among targets was required for precisely static counting. In this work, by the upper bound and lower bound obtained from dynamic counting, a new separation distance for precise counting was derived, which reduced the $4R$ separation requirement by approximately $\frac{R}{4}$. It shows that dynamic counting can relax the pair-wise separation condition for precisely target counting.

The rest of the paper is organized as follows. Section 2 presents the problem model and the most related works. Section 3 and Section 4 present the lower bound and the upper bound of the target number by dynamic counting, respectively. In Section 5, the condition for precise target counting is discussed. Section 6 provides simulation results which correspond to our algorithm proposed in Section 3 and Section 4. The paper is concluded in Section 7 with discussion of future directions.

2   Problem Model and Background

2.1   Preliminaries

We consider N binary sensors which are deployed in 2-D area of interest (AOI). Each sensor detects objects within its sensing radius R, and generates one bit of information: "1" for presence of targets and "0" for absence. We assume that the binary sensing is ideal, noiseless, and provides no other information about the location, speed, or direction information of the targets. All sensors are assumed timely synchronized and their locations are assumed calibrated in an initialization process [8]. We also assume that the AOI is fully covered by the sensing areas of BPSs. Sensors work collaboratively to track the targets. Since the targets move continuously in the AOI, the binary readings of a BPS are efficiently encoded by the time intervals between the BPS's "on" and "off" events. Each BPS reports "1" or "0" when a corresponding transition between 1 and 0 happens, which is enough for a centralized processor to interpolate the real-time states of all sensors at any snapshot. We assume that all "on", "off" events are successively collected via some supporting routing and MAC protocols. At the server side, it receives the sequential events reported from the BPS sensors and reconstructs the sensing snapshots at each event. Each snapshot is a length-M binary vector $\mathbf{S}_t \in [0,1]^M$ at time t. Although the presented techniques are applicable for sensors with non-ideal sensing models, such as non-regular sensible region, we focus our analysis on the disk-shape ideal sensing model.

Patch-based Location Description: Traditionally, the underlying locations of targets are described by "patches" formed by the sensing regions of BPSs. M BPSs can partition the AOI to at most $L \leq M^2 - M + 2$ patches [10,9]. Each patch indicates a region which is covered by the same set of sensors and each patch is coded by a length-M vector based on the coverage situations of M sensors. For example, in a network of four sensors, a patch with code "1100" means the patch is covered by the first two sensors, but is not covered by the other two sensors.

Arc-based Location Description: By taking the event time into consideration, targets' locations can be further narrowed down to *arcs*. When a sensor reports a state transition event, the target that triggers this event must be presenting on the edge of this sensor's sensing region. By jointly considering the states of surrounding sensors, we can infer the target's location to be on an *arc* between two patches whose state change. Each arc can be uniquely encoded by the codes of two neighboring patches. E.g., the arc between "100" and "110" can be coded by "100110". Fig.1 shows an example trace of a target represented by patch sequence and arc-time sequence respectively. The arc representation can specify the location of the target at a given time. We will show in following sections that

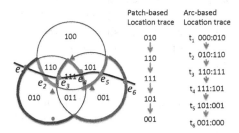

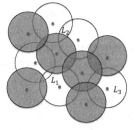

Fig. 1. Location traces of a target represented by patch index and time-arc index respectively

Fig. 2. A snapshot, where feasible areas are partitioned into three isolated islands

Table 1. Notation List

Notation	Meaning
R	Radius of each sensor
M	Number of sensors in the area of interest (AOI)
N	Number of snapshots given in input
v	Total number of isolated feasible islands
L_i	The ith isolated feasible island
$P(s)$	Coverage area of sensor s
f_a	Feasible Crossing Arc (at a certain time t_a)
$T = \{t_1, \cdots, t_k\}$	Set of time corresponding to given snapshots
U	All $t \in T$ whose snapshot triggers on a previous "off" sensor
D	All $t \in T$ whose snapshot triggers off a previous "on" sensor
S_{t_k}	Snapshot at time t_k
G_k	Patch graph at time t_k

this property of arc representation can help to improve the counting resolution by dynamic counting.

Problem specification: Under above system model, we consider multiple target counting problem by sequential snapshots. Each snapshot at t is the captured states of M BPSs when some sensor in the region reports a change. That is, a snapshot at time $t \in T := \{t|\mathbf{S}_t \neq \mathbf{S}_{t-\epsilon}$ for sufficiently small $\epsilon > 0\}$. *The problem input* is a sequence of N snapshots $\{\mathbf{S}_{t_1}, \mathbf{S}_{t_2}, \cdots, \mathbf{S}_{t_N}\}$. Without loss of generality, we assume $t_1 < t_2 < \cdots < t_N$. We also assume the number of targets participating in the AOI will not change during t_1 to t_N and each target's moving speed is upper bounded by V_{max}. *The problem output* is a lower bound and an upper bound of the number of targets.

Notation list: Notations used in our paper are listed in Table 1.

2.2   Background

Target counting problem by one snapshot has been investigated intensively in the literature. A notable concept presented in [11,14] is the *feasible area*. Given a snapshot, the feasible area where targets may present can be determined by $\mathbf{F} = P(\mathbf{A}) - P(\mathbf{A}) \cap P(\mathbf{E})$, where $P(\mathbf{A})$ is the coverage area of the "on" sensors and $P(\mathbf{E})$ is the coverage area of the "off" sensors. An example of the feasible area is shown in Fig.2, in which the sensing regions of "on" sensors are in white and sensing regions of "off" sensors are in grey. In the figure, the feasible area is partitioned into three feasible islands L_1, L_2, L_3, which are called *isolated feasible islands*.

Existing Lower Bounds. For point model of targets, the target number in the feasible area have no upper bound. Estimating the lower bound of target number is the foundation of target counting.

• In [11], a lower bound is given by Singh et al. for counting targets moving in one dimensional space, i.e., on a line. In their method, if "on" sensors can be partitioned into at most X *positively independent sets*, where the positively

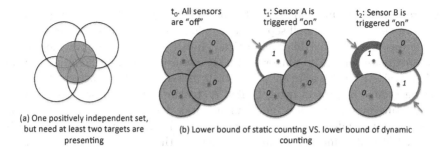

(a) One positively independent set, but need at least two targets are presenting

(b) Lower bound of static counting VS. lower bound of dynamic counting

Fig. 3. Examples to illustrate and compare different lower bounds for target counting

independent sensors are "on" sensors whose sensing regions do not overlap, or separated by at least one "off" sensors, Theorem 4 in [11] stated that the number of targets is not less than the cardinarity of X, i.e., $|X|$.

- A recent work in [14] investigated the target number lower bound in 2-D space. They showed that the lower bound given in [11] was conservative in 2-D space. A unit disc graph (UDG) model was proposed to model the structure of the feasible area, based on which an improved lower bound was given. It equals to $\sum_{i=1}^{v} c_i$, where c_i is the minimum number of cliques partitioning the UDG of the ith feasible isolated island.

- In this paper, we show that the lower bound in [14] can be further improved if the temporal and spatial dependences between snapshots are taken into consideration. The basic intuition is shown in Fig.3, which compares the lower bounds mentioned above. In Fig.3a), we can see the four "on" sensors are in one positively dependent set, so that the lower bound given by [11] will be *one*. But the lower bound given by [14] will be *two* because the UDG formed by the "on" sensors has at least two cliques. So the lower bound in [14] is more accurate in 2-D space than that in [11], but it can be further improved. As illustrated in Fig.3(b), at t_2, from the UDG structure, the lower bound given by [14] will be *one*. But by considering the event sequence from t_0 to t_2 and the limited moving speed of the target, we can judge that the target triggers the sensor A at t_1 cannot trigger the sensor B at t_2. Consequently, the lower bound of the target number should be *two* in dynamic counting.

Other Related Works. Most other related works focused on the multiple target tracking algorithms. To deal with the difficulty of multiple targets, Busnel et al. [2][1] investigated the trajectory identification properties. They converted the BPS network into a state graph and presented trajectory identifiable and unidentifiable properties on the state graph. In other works, the number of targets were either assumed known or online estimated by the trajectory disaggregation algorithms. FindingHuMo [4] proposed Hidden Markov Model (HMM) to track a known number of targets by a BPS network. MiningTraMo [17] proposed multiple pairs shortest path algorithm based on walking speed variance to infer the most possible trajectories or targets. In [19], compressive sensing based method was proposed to count and track the multiple targets, when the targets were known to be sparse, i.e., well separated. In [6], a hybrid multiple target tracking scheme was proposed by He et al., which conducted coarse-scale tracking by binary proximate sensors to narrow down search area, and used high-end sensors for fine-grained tracking. In [3], Cao et al. presented collaborative scheme for tracking groups of targets using BMSs. A distributed PIR-based people number counting system in office environment was developed in [16]. Algorithms and systems for indoor locating using ultrasound systems were investigated in [18][20]. Without going into details of target locating and tracking, we focus on the basic properties of multiple target counting by the sequential snapshots of a BPS network.

3   Lower Bound of Target Number by Dynamic Counting

3.1   Preliminary

We firstly investigate lower bound of target number by utilizing a sequence of snapshots captured by BPSs. For convenience, we divide the time set $T = \{t_1, t_2, \cdots, t_N\}$ corresponding to the given snapshots into two sets U and D, namely *up-set* and *down-set*. $t_k \in U, k \in \mathbb{N}$ if and only if an "off" sensor in $\mathbf{S}_{t_{k-1}}$ is triggered on in $\mathbf{S}_{t_k}$, and $t_k \in D, k \in \mathbb{N}$ if and only if an "on" sensor in $\mathbf{S}_{t_{k-1}}$ is triggered off in $\mathbf{S}_{t_k}$. Next, we define *feasible crossing arc* to indicate the possible locations of the targets that trigger a state transition event.

Definition 1 (Feasible Crossing Arc (FCA)). *When a sensor's state change is detected, the feasible crossing arc indicates the arc segments where the targets are traversing to trigger the event without violating the states of other sensors.*

Based on FCA, we propose Theorem 1 to specify the necessary time-space restriction for two events being triggered by the same target. The theorem is based on the fact that a target's moving speed is limited. Therefore, only if the distance between the FCAs of these two events are not beyond the moving scope of the target, can the two events be triggered by the same target.

Theorem 1 (Time-Space Restriction). *If a sensor A is triggered "on" by one target at time t_A and the FCA is f_A; another sensor B is triggered on by the same target at time $t_B \geq t_A$ with FCA f_B, then $\|f_A - f_B\|_2 \leq (t_B - t_A)V_{\max}$, where V_{max} is the maximum moving speed of the target.*

3.2   Dynamic Counting Using the Time-space Restriction

The time-space restriction could improve the lower bound of the number of targets. An example to show the basic idea is illustrated in Fig.4. It shows six snapshots captured from a BPS network. The ground truth happened during this period is that: three targets, in terms of "red", "green", and "orange" are presented as shown in Snapshot 1. At Snapshot 2, the red target moves outside a little bit, and then turns back quickly as shown in Snapshot 3. Then in a very

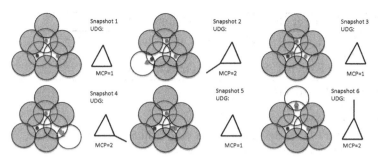

Fig. 4. Improvement by time-space restriction

close snapshot, the orange target moves outside a little bit as shown in Snapshot 4, and then turns back quickly as shown in Snapshot 5. Then in another close by snapshot, the green target moves outside.

By static counting method, the UDGs besides each scenario show the static counting result. The number of MCP for UDG from snapshot 1 to snapshot 6 are one, two, one, two, one, two respectively. Therefore, the estimated lower bound of the number of targets during this period, given by static counting is *two*.

However, since the procedure finishes in ephemeral time, by considering the spatial and temporal dependency between the snapshots we know that the sensors which are triggered on in Snapshot 2, 4 and 6 must be triggered by totally different targets due to the limited speed of the targets. Therefore, in Snapshot 6, we could deduce that a disparate target other than the two targets triggering events at Snapshot 2 and 4 must be presenting. Therefore, the lower bound of the target number is *three* by utilizing time-space restriction.

Based on the idea above, we develop a dynamic counting method to estimate the target lower bound more precisely. To initialize the algorithm, the *beginning patch graph* G_0 is built based on the UDG model in static counting. *Count* is defined as the estimated lower bound of the target number, which is set to $\mathrm{MCP}(G_0)$ initially. After that, a loop runs from the first snapshot to the last snapshot in order to construct patch graphs dynamically. More specifically, for a snapshot at time $t_k \in U$, assume the sensor l is triggered from "off" to "on". In this case, we will firstly construct all edges between sensor l and other intersected "on" sensors whose common intersection is not fully covered by the regions of the "off" sensors. After that, we examine all these edges: if an edge violates the time-space restriction, the edge will be deleted.

For a snapshot at time $t_k \in D$, we need to delete the vertex of the sensor from the UDG, which is just turned from "on" to "off" in the graph, and delete all its corresponding edges. In addition, it is a necessity to delete the edges whose corresponding intersection area is fully covered by this newly "off" sensor.

After finishing each loop, we calculate the MCP of the new patch graph. *count* would be updated if this MCP is larger than the previous *count*. The algorithm ends after looking at all snapshots in time sequential order. The whole procedure is named as dynamic counting of targets, and we develop Algorithm 1 for this method. The dynamic counting algorithm leads to Theorem 2.

Algorithm 1. Lower Bound Dynamic Counting Algorithm

Input: Set $T = \{t_1, t_2, \cdots, t_N\} = U \cup D$ (up-set and down-set);
$\mathbf{S}_{t_k}, \mathbf{A}_{t_k}, \mathbf{E}_{t_k}, \forall 0 \leq k \leq N$; Patch graph G_0 of time t_0;
Output: Lower bound of the number of targets: *count*;

---

1   Initialize *count* $\leftarrow \mathrm{MCP}(G_0)$;
2   **for** $k \leftarrow 1$ **to** N **do**
3   **if** $t_k \in U$ **then**
4   **Define** l to be the sensor which is "off" in $\mathbf{S}_{t_{k-1}}$ but "on" in $\mathbf{S}_{t_k}$; F_l to be the feasible crossing arc of sensor l;
5   **Define** $G_k = G_{k-1} \cup \{l\}$;
6   **for** $i \leftarrow 1$ **to** $M, i \neq l$ **do**
7   **Define** F_i to be the feasible crossing arc of sensor i;
8   **if** $D_{i,l} \leq 0$ *AND sensor i and sensor l have intersecting region and the intersected region is not fully convered by the regions of the "off" sensors* **then**
9   add an edge in G_k between i and l

    if $t_k \in D$ **then**
10   **Define** l to be the sensor which is "on" in $\mathbf{S}_{t_{k-1}}$ but "off" in $\mathbf{S}_{t_k}$;
11   **Define** $G_k = G_{k-1}/\{l\}$ by deleting vertex l and its corresponding edges;
12   **if** *sensor i, j, l have intersecting region pairwise and the intersected region of sensor i and j is fully convered sensor l* **then**
13   delete the edge in G_k between i and j

14   *count* $\leftarrow \max\{count, \mathrm{MCP}(G_k)\}$;
15 **return** *count*;

Theorem 2 (Lower Bound of the Target Number). *Let N_L be the real number of targets that matches the sequential snapshots of sensors. Then the return value 'count' of Algorithm 1 must not be larger than N_L, i.e., $N_L \geq count$.*

Proof. Based on the discussion of Algorithm 1, it is clear that G_k constitutes the snapshot at time t_k. In order to prove the theorem, we suffice to show that $N \geq \mathrm{MCP}(G_k)$ for each k since *count* is the maximum of all $\mathrm{MCP}(G_k)$.

Let us assume the contrary that $N < \mathrm{MCP}(G_k)$ for a certain k. As a result, we could re-partition all "on" sensors of the UDG at time t_k into $\mathrm{MCP}(G_k) - 1$ groups such that each group of sensors has a common intersection while each pair of sensors does not violate the time-space restriction. This partition is equivalent to a clique partition of G_k with $\mathrm{MCP}(G_k) - 1$ cliques, but this contradicts with the fact that $\mathrm{MCP}(G_k)$ is a minimum clique partition of G_k.

Our algorithm also has a reasonable time complexity. By [5], MCP of a patch graph could be calculated by a polynomial time approximation scheme (PTAS) with $(1 + \epsilon)$-approximation and time complexity $O(M^{O(1/\epsilon^2)})$ where M is the number of sensors in the area of interest (AOI). In addition, line 2 to line 13 in the algorithm could be done in $O(M)$ time in each cycle. Therefore, Algorithm 1 is also a PTAS with $(1+\epsilon)$-approximation and has time complexity $O(N \cdot M^{O(1/\epsilon^2)})$ where N is the number of snapshots.

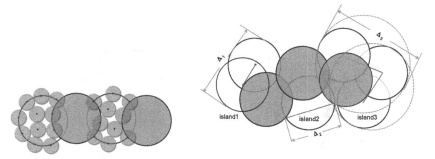

Fig. 5. Example of calculating the upper bound of target number

Fig. 6. Example of minimum separation distance

4   Upper Bound by Dynamic Counting

In real applications, the physical targets, such as humans, animals, vehicles, are generally not arbitrarily close to each other. In this section, we assume a *minimum separation distance* $r > 0$ between each pair of targets.

4.1   Static Counting

Based on the assumption of minimum separation distance, we can estimate the upper bound of target number by modeling it as a packing problem, which is a classical geometric optimization problem in mathematics that attempts to pack objects together into containers. The goal is to pack the containers as densely as possible using the objects. In 1910, Thue [15] established a theorem for the density of circle packing into a connected surface:

Theorem 3. *Assume a set of at least two circles with radius r are packed into a connected surface. Denote the sum of area of all small circles with radius r to be S' and denote the area of the surface to be S, respectively. Then $\frac{S'}{S} \leq \frac{\pi}{\sqrt{12}}$.*

In our problem, we treat the areas of each feasible island as containers, and objects are circles with radius r. Then the upper bound of the number of targets equals to the number of circles that can be packed into the feasible area. In our problem, we only restrict the centers of objects, i.e., the positions of targets cannot exceed the boundary of the container. Therefore, we allow the objects to cover at most distance r beyond the boundary of containers, as an example shown in Fig.5. Given a snapshot as the input, the most number of targets in the feasible area of the snapshot can be estimated.

Theorem 4 (Upper Bound of the Target Number). *Let A_i and C_i be the area and circumference of the ith feasible island respectively. Suppose the minimum separation distance between targets is r, then the number of targets in the feasible area must be smaller than $\sum_{i=1}^{v} \frac{A_i + rC_i}{\sqrt{12}r^2}$, where $\frac{A_i + rC_i}{\sqrt{12}r^2}$ is the upper bound of target number in the ith feasible island.*

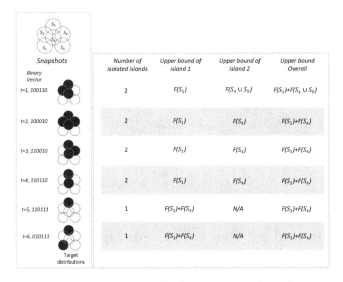

Fig. 7. Illustration for dynamic upper bound

Using the similar idea of improving lower bound, we introduce a dynamic counting method to utilize snapshot dependences to improve the upper bound of the target number.

4.2   Improvement by Dynamic Counting

For a feasible region S, we define $f(S) := \frac{A+rC}{\sqrt{12}r^2}$ where A is the area of S and C is the circumference of S. By Theorem 4, $f(S)$ is an upper bound of the number of targets in S. Denote the set of feasible islands of the initial snapshot at time t_0 to be $S_{island} = \{S_1, \cdots, S_K\}$.

The basic idea of dynamic counting to improve the upper bound is based on the fixed number of targets in a feasible island which is not connected to other feasible islands during the concerned time. See Fig. 7 as an illustration. This is an instance of six snapshots, in which the first four snapshots are composed of two feasible islands and the last two snapshots are composed of a single feasible island. From snapshot 1 and 2, we know that the number of targets in the first and second feasible island is at most $f(S_1)$ and $f(S_5)$, respectively. Therefore, the best upper bound of the number of targets in this instance is $f(S_1) + f(S_5)$. However, if we only consider the last snapshot, the upper bound obtained is $f(S_2 \cup S_4 \cup S_5 \cup S_6)$, which could be much worse than the bound given from the dynamic view. Using this inspiration, we develop Algorithm 2 to improve the upper bound of the number of targets. Basically, when the number of feasible islands is not changed in an interval of snapshots, the number of targets in each feasible island is bounded by its smallest region in this interval. When a feasible island breaks up into several islands or some feasible islands are combined into a single feasible island, the set of feasible islands and the upper bound of the number of targets in each feasible island are both reassigned.

Algorithm 2. Dynamic Upper Bound Counting Algorithm

Input: Set $T = \{t_1, t_2, \cdots, t_N\} = U \cup D$ (up-set and down-set);
$\mathbf{S}_{t_k}, \mathbf{A}_{t_k}, \mathbf{E}_{t_k}, \forall 0 \leq k \leq N$; Feasible islands $S_{island} = \{S_1, \cdots, S_K\}$ at time t_0;
Output: Upper bound of the number of targets: $count_{upper}$;

---

1 **for** $i \leftarrow 1$ **to** K **do**
2 $\quad \lfloor \; u_i \leftarrow f(S_i)$

3 Initialize $count_{upper} \leftarrow \sum_{i=1}^{k} u_i$;
4 **for** $k \leftarrow 1$ **to** N **do**
5 $\quad$ **if** $t_k \in U$ **then**
6 $\quad\quad$ Define l to be the sensor which is "off" in $\mathbf{S}_{t_{k-1}}$ but "on" in $\mathbf{S}_{t_k}$;
7 $\quad\quad$ **if** $P(l) \cap S_{island} = \emptyset$ **then**
8 $\quad\quad\quad \mid$ Update $S_{island} \leftarrow S_{island} \cup P(l)$; $u_l \leftarrow f(P(l))$;
9 $\quad\quad$ **else if** $P(l)$ *intersects with at least two islands in* S_{island} **then**
10 $\quad\quad\quad$ Define $S' \subseteq S_{island}$ to be islands intersect with $P(l)$;
11 $\quad\quad\quad$ Define $S_l := S' \cup P(l)$;
12 $\quad\quad\quad$ Update $S_{island} \leftarrow (S_{island}/S') \cup S_l$;
13 $\quad\quad\quad$ Update $u_l \leftarrow \sum_{S_i \in S'} f(S_i) + f(P(l))$;
14 $\quad\quad$ **else**

$\quad$ **if** $t_k \in D$ **then**
15 $\quad\quad$ Define l to be the sensor which is "on" in $\mathbf{S}_{t_{k-1}}$ but "off" in $\mathbf{S}_{t_k}$;
16 $\quad\quad$ Define l to be in feasible island S_i;
17 $\quad\quad$ **if** $S_i/P(l)$ *is not connective* **then**
18 $\quad\quad\quad$ Define $S_i/P(l)$ to be $m \geq 2$ feasible islands $S_{i1}, \cdots, S_{im}$;
19 $\quad\quad\quad$ Update $S_{island} \leftarrow (S_{island}/S_i) \cup \{S_{i1}, \cdots, S_{im}\}$;
20 $\quad\quad\quad$ $u_{ij} \leftarrow f(S_{ij})$ for $\forall 1 \leq j \leq m$;
$\quad\quad$ **else**
21 $\quad\quad\quad \lfloor \; u_i \leftarrow \min\{u_i, f(S_i/P(l))\}$;

22 $\quad \lfloor \; count_{upper} \leftarrow \min\{count_{upper}, \sum_i u_i\}$

23 **return** $count_{upper}$;

In the algorithm, we also divide the time of snapshots into up-set and down-set. For both cases, the isolation and combination of islands are carefully constructed to make the connectivity of all "on" sensors following the truth. In addition, we update each island's upper bound of the number of targets every round. In particular, when an "on" sensor is turned off in a snapshot, we catch up the possibility of decreasing the upper bound of the target number in line 21.

In Algorithm 2, $O(M)$ time suffices from line 1 to line 3 where M is the number of sensors in the AOI. In either $t_k \in U$ or $t_k \in D$, the cycle could be finished in $O(M)$ time. In total, the time complexity of Algorithm 2 is $O(MN)$ where N is the number of snapshots in total.

Based on the lower bound and the upper bound of target number, we can investigate a more interesting property of the binary target counting problem, i.e., the minimum separation distance for precisely target counting.

5   Condition for Precisely Target Counting

A more interesting problem we may ask is: under what condition can we always precisely count the number of targets without error. This problem was previously studied by [12], which showed that when the separation distance r between each pair of targets is larger than $4R$, the number of targets can be precisely counted. This traditional requirement of $4R$ separation distance is rather large. What we are interested is that: whether can we find a smaller separation distance $r < 4R$ such that the number of targets can be precisely counted.

Consider the relationship between the upper bound and lower bound of the target number in a feasible island. For the ith feasible island, suppose that the lower bound of the target number is l_i. When the separation distance between each pair of targets is r_i, the following relationship must hold:

$$\frac{A_i + r_i C_i}{\sqrt{12 r_i^2}} > N_i \geq l_i$$

The minimally required separation distance for precisely target counting in island i is the minimum value of r_i which restricts the upper bound of target number not larger than one plus the lower bound of the target number, i.e., the minimum value of r_i to keep $l_i + 1 > \frac{A_i + r_i C_i}{\sqrt{12 r_i^2}} \geq l_i$. Therefore:

Theorem 5. *The minimum required separation distance between each pair of targets for precisely counting targets is* $\gamma = \max\{\gamma_1, \gamma_2, \cdots, \gamma_v\}$, *where* $\gamma_i = \frac{C_i + \sqrt{C_i^2 + 8\sqrt{3} A_i (l_i + 1)}}{2\sqrt{3}(l_i + 1)}$ *for all i.*

Here γ_i is the solution of the equation $\sqrt{12}(l_i + 1)\frac{\gamma_i}{2}^2 - C_i \frac{\gamma_i}{2} - A_i = 0$, which is the minimum separation distance to make the upper bound of target number equal to the lower bound in island i. Moreover, γ_i could be even smaller if use the upper bound of the target number by dynamic counting.

Theorem 5 reveals that the separation distance required for precisely target counting is different in disparate snapshots and even varies at different locations in a snapshot. If the upper bound is unlimited, the minimum separation distance is the largest diameter of the cliques formed by the positive sensors. An example is shown in Fig.6, we can see the minimum separation distance $\min\{\Delta_1, \Delta_2, \Delta_3\} < 4R$, which shows a better potential of using BPS network for precisely target counting than the traditional results.

6   Evaluation

To verify the counting bound, agents based simulation was conducted based on *PSensorSimulator* platform[13]. Multiple agents, which simulated the mobile targets were programmed to move independently along random paths in the area of interest. The area of interest was a $L \times L$ rectangle area. In the area, M BPS sensors were deployed. We investigated two kinds of sensor deployment. 1) *regular deployment*, as shown in Fig. 8, in which the sensors were deployed in

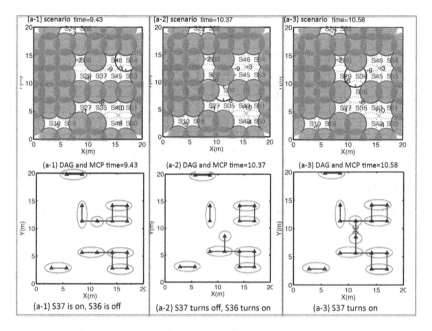

Fig. 8. Dynamic counting can fix boundary-pacing error

a grid topology, which fully covered the AOI. 2)*random deployment*, in which, enough sensors were deployed randomly in a region and a subregion was selected as the AOI, as shown in Fig.9(a).

For rendering the target tracking scenario, a graphical interface was developed. As shown in Fig.8, the feasible area of targets were rendered by the internal region surrounded by the red arcs. The sensors in the "off" state were in grey with blue dashed lines. The feasible crossing arcs were colored in black if one target was entering the sensor region, and was colored green if the sensor was turned off because of target leaving. The UDG corresponding to the sensor's readings was illustrated in Fig.8, in which the vertex denoted the sensors in the "on" state. The construction of UDG could be referred to [14]. We implemented Algorithm 1 and 2 on the simulation platform to contrast the upper and lower bound with the ground-truth number of targets.

6.1 Evaluation on Lower-bound

As a core unit of Algorithm 1, MCP-calculation routine is called every time the state of a sensor changes. Since MCP-calculation is proved to be NP-Complete problem, we use a PTAS approximation to implement MCP [7] calculation.

Regular deployment: At first, a particular example is shown in Fig.8 to illustrate the effectiveness of the dynamic counting algorithm on improving the counting lower bound. The scenario contains 64 sensors. Only the labels of the "on" sensors are shown, and ten targets are moving in the area. As shown in Fig.8, at 9.43 second in this scenario, the sensor 36 was "off" and sensor 37 was

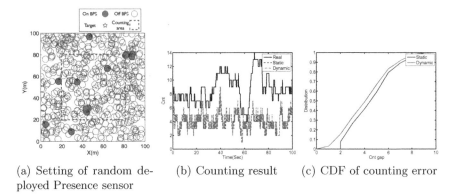

(a) Setting of random de-   (b) Counting result   (c) CDF of counting error
ployed Presence sensor

Fig. 9. Dynamic counting vs statistic counting on random deployment

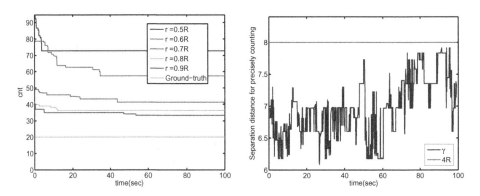

Fig. 10. UpperBound of differen r **Fig. 11.** Separation versus $4R$

"on". The MCP of the UDG of this scenario indicates the lower bound of the target number is 9. At the 10.37 second, sensor 36 turned "on" and sensor 37 turned "off" simultaneously. In this case, the target which left sensor 37 could only enter sensor 29 or sensor 45. After a short duration of 0.21 seconds, at the 10.58 second, the sensor 37 was turned "on" again. Since 0.21 seconds was not enough for the target which triggered sensor 36 to reach the edge of sensor 37 due to time-space restriction, it must be the return of the previous target in sensor 37, and this target is different from the target in sensor 36. Therefore, in the DAG of (a-3), the edge between S36 and S37 was deleted. Deletion of this edge improved the lower bound from 9 to 10, which verified the effectiveness of the dynamic counting for lower bound improvement.

Random Deployment: To further investigate the performance of dynamic counting method, we evaluated the target counting performances when the sensors are randomly deployed. The setting is shown in Fig.9(a), in which sensors are deployed with density of 0.2 per square meter in an 100m*100m area. A subregion in the centric part of the area is selected as the AOI. So that in this evaluation, the number of targets within the AOI may change overtime, therefore, we delete line 14 in algorithm 3 in simulation. The number of targets in AOI given by both dynamic and static counting algorithm were evaluated. The result in a 100 seconds experiment is shown in Fig.9(b). We can see that the lower bound given by dynamic counting is slightly better than that given by static counting. The CDF curve in Fig.9(c) summarized the performance difference, in which the counting gap indicates the gap to the real number of targets. In conclusion, dynamic counting showed better performance than the static counting.

6.2 Evaluation on Upper-bound

To verify the upper bound of counting, Algorithm 2 was implemented in *PSensorSimulator*. For each isolated island formed by "on" sensors, circumference and area were calculated with numeric method. According to Theorem 4, ratio between predefined separation radius and sensing radius matters. Therefore, we calculated the upper bound with different ratio. As shown in Fig.10, the upper bound could be twice to 4 times to the ground-truth according to different ratios.

6.3 Evaluation on Separation Distance

Theorem 5 gives a non-trivial minimum separation distance γ for precise counting. We compared this γ with classical separation distance $4R$ by simulation. As shown in Fig.11, during 100 seconds experiment, the γ is always below $4R$. This results told us that, introducing dynamic information can improve the separation for precisely counting by about $\frac{R}{4}$.

7 Conclusion

This paper investigated target counting problem by a network of binary proximity sensors. For the lower bound of the target number, we considered the time-space restriction between a sequence of snapshots and proposed a dynamic counting technique which improved the lower bound given by individual snapshot. As for the upper bound of the target number, we showed that if a minimum separation distance between targets was considered, an upper bound could be given by packing theorem. Moreover, a dynamic counting algorithm was proposed to improve this upper bound. At last, by matching the upper bound and lower bound, we investigated the condition for precisely target counting and showed that the minimum separation distance for precisely counting could be $\frac{R}{4}$ smaller than the previously known limit $4R$. In the future work, the dynamic counting method can be exploited to enhance existing multiple target tracking algorithms. Apart from theoretical works, dynamic counting technique can be applied in occupying sensing or enemy detection and tracking.

References

1. Busnel, Y., Querzoni, L., Baldoni, R., Bertier, M., Kermarrec, A.-M.: On the deterministic tracking of moving objects with a binary sensor network. In: Nikoletseas, S.E., Chlebus, B.S., Johnson, D.B., Krishnamachari, B. (eds.) DCOSS 2008. LNCS, vol. 5067, pp. 46–59. Springer, Heidelberg (2008), http://link.springer.com/chapter/10.1007/978-3-540-69170-9_4

2. Busnel, Y., Querzoni, L., Baldoni, R., Bertier, M., Kermarrec, A.-M.: Analysis of deterministic tracking of multiple objects using a binary sensor network. ACM Trans. Sen. Netw. 8(1), 8:1–8:27 (2011)
3. Cao, D., Jin, B., Das, S.K., Cao, J.: On collaborative tracking of a target group using binary proximity sensors. Journal of Parallel and Distributed Computing 70(8), 825–838 (2010)
4. De, D., Song, W.-Z., Xu, M., Wang, C.-L., Cook, D., Huo, X.: FindingHuMo: real-time tracking of motion trajectories from anonymous binary sensing in smart environments. In: ICDCS, pp. 163–172 (2012)
5. Dumitrescu, A., Pach, J.: Minimum clique partition in unit disk graphs. Graphs and Combinatorics 27(3), 399–411 (2011)
6. He, T., Bisdikian, C., Kaplan, L., Wei, W., Towsley, D.: Multi-target tracking using proximity sensors. In: MILCOM, pp. 1777–1782 (2010)
7. Humyn, A.: Maximal Clique (May 2008)
8. Liu, H., Darabi, H., Banerjee, P., Liu, J.: Survey of wireless indoor positioning techniques and systems. Trans. Sys. Man Cyber Part C 37(6), 1067–1080 (2007)
9. Shrivastava, N., Madhow, R.M.U., Suri, S.: Target tracking with binary proximity sensors: fundamental limits, minimal descriptions, and algorithms. In: SenSys 2006, pp. 251–264. ACM, New York (2006)
10. Shrivastava, N., Mudumbai, R., Madhow, U., Suri, S.: Target tracking with binary proximity sensors. ACM Trans. Sen. Netw. 5(4), 30:1–30:33 (2009)
11. Singh, J., Madhow, U., Kumar, R., Suri, S., Cagley, R.: Tracking multiple targets using binary proximity sensors. In: IPSN 2007, pp. 529–538. ACM, New York (2007)
12. Singh, J., Madhow, U., Kumar, R., Suri, S., Cagley, R.: Tracking multiple targets using binary proximity sensors. In: IPSN 2007. ACM (April 2007)
13. Song, L.: PSensorSimulator, https://bitbucket.org/leisong03/PSensorSimulator
14. Song, L., Wang, Y.: Multiple target counting and tracking using binary proximity sensors: Bounds, coloring, and filter. In: Proceedings of the 15th ACM International Symposium on Mobile Ad Hoc Networking and Computing, MobiHoc 2014, pp. 397–406. ACM, New York (2014)
15. Thue, A.: Über die dichteste Zusammenstellung von kongruenten Kreisen in einer Ebene. na (1910)
16. Wahl, F., Milenkovic, M., Amft, O.: A distributed PIR-based approach for estimating people count in office environments. In: CSE 2012, pp. 640–647 (2012)
17. Wang, C., De, D., Song, W.-Z.: Trajectory mining from anonymous binary motion sensors in smart environment. Knowledge-Based Systems 37, 346–356 (2013)
18. Wang, Y., Song, L.: An algorithmic and systematic approach for improving robustness of TOA-based localization. In: 2013 IEEE 10th International Conference on High Performance Computing and Communications 2013 IEEE International Conference on Embedded and Ubiquitous Computing (HPCC_EUC), pp. 2066–2073 (November 2013)
19. Zhang, B., Cheng, X., Zhang, N., Cui, Y., Li, Y., Liang, Q.: Sparse target counting and localization in sensor networks based on compressive sensing. In: 2011 Proceedings IEEE INFOCOM, pp. 2255–2263 (April 2011)
20. Zhao, J., Wang, Y.: Autonomous ultrasonic indoor tracking system. In: International Symposium on Parallel and Distributed Processing with Applications, ISPA 2008, pp. 532–539 (December 2008)

Detecting and Avoiding Multiple Sources of Interference in the 2.4 GHz Spectrum

Venkatraman Iyer[1], Frederik Hermans[2], and Thiemo Voigt[1,2]

[1] Uppsala University, Sweden
{venkatraman.iyer,frederik.hermans}@it.uu.se
[2] SICS Swedish ICT, Sweden
thiemo@sics.se

Abstract. Sensor networks operating in the 2.4 GHz band often face cross-technology interference from co-located WiFi and Bluetooth devices. To enable effective interference mitigation, a sensor network needs to know the type of interference it is exposed to. However, existing approaches to interference detection are not able to handle multiple concurrent sources of interference. In this paper, we address the problem of identifying multiple channel activities impairing a sensor network's communication, such as simultaneous WiFi traffic and Bluetooth data transfers. We present Speck-Sense, an interference detector that distinguishes between different types of interference using a unsupervised learning technique. Additionally, SpeckSense features a classifier that distinguishes between moderate and heavy channel traffic, and also identifies WiFi beacons. In doing so, it facilitates interference avoidance through channel blacklisting. We evaluate Speck-Sense on common mote hardware and show how it classifies concurrent interference under real-world settings. We also show how SpeckSense improves the performance of an existing multichannel data collection protocol by 30%.

1 Introduction

Low-power wireless sensor networks (WSN) operating in the 2.4 GHz spectrum often face interference from other wireless technologies that share the same frequency band. Typically, IEEE 802.15.4-compliant sensor nodes compete for channel access with an increasing number of WiFi and Bluetooth devices such as laptops, smartphones, and tablet PCs. This results in long contention delays and collisions that degrade sensor network performance [1, 2].

Several mitigation approaches [3, 1, 4, 2] have been proposed to tackle the problem of external interference in sensor networks. Knowing the type of interference enables a sensor node to choose a suitable mitigation strategy [5, 6, 1]. In this regard, interference classification is prerequisite towards mitigation. Recent work on interference classification [6, 7] addresses the problem by mapping RSSI observations or patterns of corrupted packets to a known class of interference such as WiFi, Bluetooth or microwave ovens. Such designs are intrinsically constrained by a direct mapping of channel observations to a fixed number of interference classes.

T. Abdelzaher et al. (Eds.): EWSN 2015, LNCS 8965, pp. 35–51, 2015.

In particular, they do not address the predominant case of *multi-source* interference, i. e., multiple device types and instances that transmit on a channel. For example, a combination of WiFi and Bluetooth interference on a channel is likely to be reported as either WiFi or Bluetooth, depending on the dominant interferer. In this regard, the detection of multiple interfering sources offers interesting insights on channel utilization. The number of distinct interfering sources on a channel has a marked influence on its utilization – for example, concurrent traffic over WiFi and Bluetooth traffic has a greater interference impact than either in isolation. Moreover, interfering channel traffic from multiple sources can be independently inspected for temporal patterns such as periodicity. This enables a wireless device to identify periodic control signals on an active WiFi channel, and blacklist it for sensor network operation. Lastly, multiple interference detection enables wireless devices to disambiguate external interference from in-network channel traffic. This provides a clearer context for motivating interference mitigation mechanisms as in [1, 2].

We present *SpeckSense* , a service that enables nodes to detect and classify multiple sources of interference in the 2.4 GHz band. In doing so, SpeckSense provides explicit recommendations on which channels are good for use. In contrast to earlier work [6,8], SpeckSense performs an explicit interference detection step prior to classification. The detection step uses RSSI values to account for channel observations, and clusters them based on pre-determined RSSI intervals in which they belong and also the time duration for which a sequence of similar RSSI values persist. Each cluster thus represents a distinct interference pattern, which is handed to a classification algorithm.

SpeckSense is primarily designed for avoiding WiFi and other forms of severe interference in indoor WSN deployments. To this end, SpeckSense performs two main operations — distinguishing between different forms of data traffic (WiFi beacons, periodic and non-periodic channel traffic) and identifying the number of sources transmitting periodic signals – for example, WiFi access points. SpeckSense uses the average time interval between recurring RSSI patterns to distinguish between conditions of moderate (web browsing) and intense (bulk data transfer) channel traffic. In doing so, SpeckSense provides a channel utilization measure that determines whether the channel is suitable for reliable communication. Furthermore, identifying beacons enables a sensor node to effectively blacklist channels affected by WiFi interference.

We evaluate SpeckSense in an office corridor characterized by many interference sources that include several WiFi and Bluetooth-enabled devices. We show that SpeckSense distinguishes between the predominant sources of interference, and in particular, identifies multiple WiFi access points in the presence of data traffic. We demonstrate the usefulness of SpeckSense by adding it to a multi-channel data collection protocol [2]. We evaluate the combined solution on a large-scale indoor testbed and observe a significant improvement in data yield facilitated by avoiding interfered channels.

In this paper we make the following contributions:

- We design and develop SpeckSense, a new approach for detecting and classifying *multiple concurrent sources of interference* in the 2.4 GHz spectrum.
- We facilitate interference avoidance by distinguishing between different extremes of channel traffic (web browsing vs. file transfers), and identifying periodic WiFi beacons.
- We show how an existing data collection protocol can benefit from using SpeckSense to recommend WiFi-free channels. Our experimental evaluation on a large testbed comprising 85 nodes shows a 30% improvement in data yield when using SpeckSense.

2 SpeckSense Design

Indoor environments such as offices or residential areas are witness to concurrent wireless activity across multiple standards such as WiFi, Bluetooth and IEEE 802.15.4 devices that operate in the 2.4 GHz spectrum. The resulting channel interference is therefore a combination of multiple transmissions that differ from each other in radio bit rate, message size, transmit power, channel attenuation and timing constraints [8]. As a result, their respective emissions exhibit characteristic patterns in intensity, duration, and timing. For example, emissions from a WiFi access point are distinctly different from a Bluetooth device's emissions. The central idea of SpeckSense is to disambiguate the concurrent emissions from the interferers so that the present interferers can be identified. To do so, SpeckSense accounts for collective emissions from the interferers by sampling the received signal strength (RSSI), i.e., the energy in the channel.

SpeckSense comprises two components, that perform *interference detection* and *classification* in sequence. The *interference detection* uses an *RSSI sampler* that captures the emissions from all interferers as a series of RSSI bursts. *Interference detection* involves an unsupervised learning approach, i. e., clustering, to distinguish the bursts from the different interferers. The output of the *interference detection* component is passed to a *classification* component that inspects each cluster for periodicity. Doing so enables SpeckSense to identify WiFi beacons on a given channel, as well as periodic traffic from other sources besides WiFi routers. Additionally, the classification component quantifies channel occupancy, which enables blacklisting of channels that are severely interfered.

Unlike earlier work [6, 8], SpeckSense decouples interference detection from explicit classification. This decoupling allows distinguishing the emissions from multiple interferers, and also classifying them in isolation. We now describe SpeckSense's components in more detail.

3 Interference Detection

SpeckSense's interference detection consists of an *RSSI sampler* and a *clustering process*, which are described in the following subsections.

3.1   RSSI Sampler

The RSSI sampler captures the energy in the channel due to the interferers' emissions, e.g., WiFi beacons or Bluetooth data packets. It continuously reads the RSSI register of the sensor nodes' radio chip. The readings are quantized, run-length encoded, and so-called bursts, i. e., contiguous sequence of high RSSI samples, are identified. The detected bursts are then processed by the clustering component.

Quantization is motivated by two observations. First, the emissions from a given interferer may vary slightly over time in their strength. These minor variations are not relevant to detecting the interferer, and hence they can be abstracted away by quantizing the RSSI reading. Second, storing raw RSSI readings is prohibitively memory-intense on a constrained sensor node. Storing quantized readings in memory is a simple means to reduce the memory requirement.

The number of quantization intervals represents a trade-off between the number of distinctly observable RSSI patterns and memory overhead. Using a higher number of intervals allows to capture more distinct channel activities, but requires more memory to store the observations. We establish power level 1 for RSSI values below -90 dBm, and divide the RSSI range above > -90 dBm evenly over the remaining number of levels. For example, using four quantization intervals would require defining the following power levels: power level 1 (RSSI ≤ -90 dBm), power level 2 (-90 dBm $<$ RSSI ≤ -60 dBm), power level 3 (-60 dBm $<$ RSSI ≤ -30 dBm), and power level 4 (-30 dBm $<$ RSSI).

The quantized RSSI readings are then run-length encoded to further reduce the memory overhead. Run-length encoding works by simply counting the number of subsequent occurrences of a power level. For example, consider the following RSSI sequence: -92, -91, -57, -58, -57, -29, -28, -59, -59, -59, -94. Quantization and run-length encoding produces the following sequence of 2D vectors: $(1, 2), (3, 3), (4, 2), (3, 3), (1, 1)$. The first component of each vector denotes the power level, and the second component denotes the duration of the observation.

Finally, the RSSI sampler extracts *bursts* of activity from the quantized, run-length encoded vector sequence. A burst is defined by a contiguous subsequence where the channel is not idle, i.e., the power level is greater than 1. The RSSI sampler represents the burst by the weighted mean power level and the total duration of the subsequence. The previous example contains the non-idle subsequence $(3, 3), (4, 2), (3, 3)$, which corresponds to the RSSI burst: $(\frac{3 \times 3 + 4 \times 2 + 3 \times 3}{3 + 2 + 3}, 3 + 2 + 3) = (3.25, 8)$.

SpeckSense's interference classification relies on the temporal patterns of an interferer's emissions, so it is important that processing a sample on a sensor node takes a constant amount of time. Otherwise, the duration value in an RSSI burst would be misleading. In our implementation, processing an RSSI sample (reading it, quantizing it, and performing run-length encoding) takes 47 µs on average, giving a sampling rate of 21 KHz. This allows the detection of energy levels from WiFi beacons and Bluetooth data packets that have transmission times several magnitudes higher than 47 µs [9, 8]. More crucially, the variance in the processing delay is 0.04 µs, which is low enough to assume practically constant sampling speed. As per the suggestions by Boano et al., the RSSI sampler is implemented to avoid saturation in the radio transceiver's automatic gain control [10].

3.2 Clustering Algorithm

The clustering component groups together RSSI bursts that are likely to come from the same interferer. In a later step, the clusters can then be analyzed independently from each other to classify the interferer.

Prior to clustering, the RSSI bursts are normalized. Note that the mean power level of a burst can be at most 4, whereas the duration of a burst can take much larger values. Thus, normalization is required to avoid burst duration having a dominating influence on the clustering. Considering that the emissions could take 10 ms (microwave oven emissions), we scale up the average power level for all bursts by a factor of 16.

SpeckSense uses the k-means algorithm to group a set of normalized RSSI bursts B into clusters. k-means clustering is a general algorithm to group a set of observations into clusters such that similar observations belong to the same cluster [11]. We briefly describe the algorithm's operation.

Assume the bursts in B are to be grouped into k clusters. The cluster i is represented by a 2D vector μ_i called its cluster center. The vector's first component represents the average power level of bursts in the cluster, and the second component represents the average duration. Initially, the k cluster centers are chosen at random from the RSSI bursts in B. Then, the algorithm repeatedly assigns RSSI bursts to clusters and updates cluster centers until a termination condition is met.

Cluster assignment. Each RSSI burst is assigned to the cluster that has the closest center. More specifically, an RSSI burst $b_i \in B$ is assigned to the cluster j whose center has the minimal Euclidean distance to b_i. We denote the cluster center to which b_i is assigned by $m(b_i)$, defined as $m(b_i) = \text{argmin}_{\mu_j} \|b_i - \mu_j\|$.

Cluster center update. After the cluster assignment, the cluster centers are recomputed. Let M_j be the set of bursts that were assigned to the jth cluster in the preceding step. Then, the cluster center μ_j is updated to be the average of all bursts in M_j. Specifically, $\mu_j = \frac{1}{|M_j|} \sum_{b \in M_j} b$.

Termination. The preceding two steps are repeated until a cost function (which is evaluated after each update step) converges, i. e., decreases by less than a fixed threshold. The cost function C describes how close the bursts are to the centers of their assigned clusters, and thus intuitively reflects the quality of the clustering: $C = \frac{1}{|B|} \sum_{b_i \in B} \|b_i - m(b_i)\|^2$. We have empirically found that a threshold of 0.001 gives good clustering performance.

The described algorithm groups the RSSI bursts into k clusters. However, the number of clusters k, which is related to the number of interferers, is not known a priori. Therefore, SpeckSense iteratively executes the algorithm for different

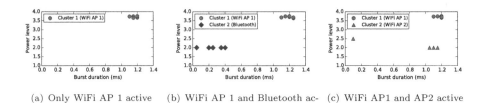

(a) Only WiFi AP 1 active   (b) WiFi AP 1 and Bluetooth ac- (c) WiFi AP1 and AP2 active
                              tive

Fig. 1. Clusters detected by SpeckSense in the anechoic chamber for different interference scenarios. Each marker represents an RSSI burst, and the marker's shape indicates which cluster the burst was assigned to. The number of clusters found by SpeckSense corresponds to the number of interferers.

values of k. Starting from $k = 1$, the cost function at termination is noted and k is increased by one. When the difference in cost at termination for k and $k + 1$ is less than 0.001, the algorithm terminates.

In summary, the clustering component arranges the RSSI bursts into groups such that bursts that are similar in duration and power level are assigned to the same group. The underlying intuition is that similar bursts are likely to come from the same interferer. The clustering component outputs the number of clusters k that yielded the best clustering, the center clusters $\mu_1, \ldots, \mu_k$, and which burst was assigned to which cluster. To validate SpeckSense's ability to cluster different interference patterns, controlled experiments were performed in an anechoic chamber. Figures 1(a), 1(b) and 1(c) show the different clusters detected by SpeckSense in a set of artificially induced interference scenarios. The specific cases comprise beacons from a WiFi Access Point AP1, a combination of WiFi beacons from AP1 and Bluetooth traffic between a pair of devices, and beacons from two WiFi access points AP1 and AP2. Each point in the figures represents a RSSI burst, and bursts belonging to a cluster have the same marker. The figures show that it is possible to disambiguate between different emissions based on average burst size (Figure 1(b)), as well as power level (Figure 1(c)).

Note that emissions from different sources may overlap in time, for example, microwave emissions overlapping with Bluetooth bursts. In such cases, the clustering algorithm detects only the *dominant* interferer (i. e., the microwave). SpeckSense addresses this concern by observing RSSI values over a longer duration (i. e., one second), thereby increasing the likelihood of detecting multiple interference sources.

4   Interference Classification

SpeckSense classifies interference by inspecting each detected cluster for temporal patterns in RSSI bursts. In doing so, SpeckSense informs link-layer protocols whether the observed channel activity is periodic, bursty or a combination of both. This facilitates a meaningful assessment of channel quality and enables

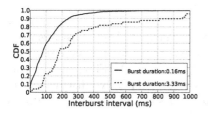

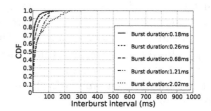

(a) Bluetooth file transfer, Avg. Interburst interval = 253 ms

(b) WiFi-enabled file download, Avg. Interburst interval = 23 ms

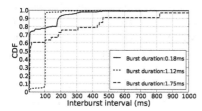

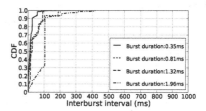

(c) Web browsing over WiFi, Avg. Interburst interval = 146 ms

(d) WiFi repeater traffic, Avg. Interburst interval = 50 ms

Fig. 2. Empirical CDFs of the inter-burst separations per detected cluster, for different interference scenarios. SpeckSense distinguishes between different extremes of channel traffic, using a 100 ms threshold on the observed average inter-burst separation.

nodes to make informed decisions on channel selection. In this regard, Speck-Sense deviates from earlier classification work such as SoNIC [6] that maps channel observations to specific labels such as WiFi, Bluetooth and microwave. This section elaborates on two aspects of interference classification, namely distinguishing different extremes of prevalent 2.4 GHz data traffic and identifying periodic signals such as WiFi beacons.

4.1 Distinguishing Channel Traffic

Interference in the 2.4 GHz spectrum is largely attributed to concurrent traffic over WiFi and Bluetooth, as well as electromagnetic emissions from microwave ovens. The impact from channel interference on a wireless network application is determined by several factors such as device usage patterns, application data requests as well as underlying communication protocols in use. Therefore, it is reasonable to expect that certain applications contribute to a greater degree towards channel interference than others – for example, a file download over WiFi causes more channel interference than web browsing. SpeckSense distinguishes between diverse applications at the physical layer based on their characteristic contribution to channel traffic. Specifically, SpeckSense computes the average inter-burst separation for each interference cluster, and checks whether it is below a predetermined threshold. If so, the channel is said to be severely interfered and hence blacklisted for sensor network operation.

To empirically determine the threshold inter-burst separation, we conduct experiments involving controlled interference, in which SpeckSense gathers RSSI samples for different scenarios that included a Bluetooth file transfer, WiFi file download, WiFi web browsing, video streaming over WiFi, WiFi repeater traffic, and microwave oven emissions. Figure 2 shows the cumulative distribution of the inter-burst separation for different clusters for some of the aforementioned cases (for additional details, refer to [12]). We observe that for cases where bursty traffic is involved, such as in Figures 2(b), and 2(d), 80% of the inter-burst separations are below 100 ms. Note that channel activity bursts owing to Bluetooth transfers and WiFi-enabled web browsing are not as frequent as WiFi file download and repeater traffic. This is attributed to factors such as Bluetooth frequency hopping that effectively schedules packet transmissions over non-overlapping channels, as well as temporally sparse patterns in web browsing. Further, a reduced average inter-burst separation is correlated to an increase in the number of detected clusters.

Based on these observations, SpeckSense uses an average inter-burst separation threshold of 100 ms, which has shown good results in distinguishing conditions of light channel traffic (cf. Figures 2(a), and 2(c)) from severe interference (cf. Figures 2(b) and 2(d)).

4.2   Identifying Periodic Beacons

Concurrent traffic over WiFi constitutes a major part of cross-technology interference in the 2.4 GHz ISM band [1]. Therefore it is necessary that a sensor node avoids operating on channels that overlap with WiFi activity. While usage patterns of WiFi may vary over time depending on varying user needs, there is a stable pattern in control signaling on the WiFi channels. Predominant IEEE 802.11 management frames include WiFi beacons, probe responses from access points, and probe requests from WiFi clients. Particularly, beacon messages are sent at a default periodic interval of 100 ms. Identifying them can thus be regarded as an indication of WiFi presence. Towards this end, SpeckSense uses the results from its multi-source interference detector, and classifies a clustered sequence of periodically recurring RSSI bursts as WiFi beacons. This is, however, a non-trivial problem and entails addressing the following challenges. WiFi management frames such as probe requests and probe responses may have similar on-air transmission times as beacons, and are also transmitted over non-periodic intervals (see Figure 3(a)). Moreover, beacons from multiple WiFi access points within interference range may have similar on-air transmission times and RSSI values (see Figure 3(b)), and get clustered together. The random occurrences of WiFi probes and beacons from multiple APs collectively represent a challenge in identifying periodic patterns.

Accounting for these challenges, SpeckSense employs an algorithm (see Algorithm 1) that is run once for each cluster obtained from the interference detection outlined in Section 3.2. In every run, the input to the algorithm is a temporal

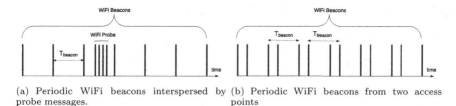

(a) Periodic WiFi beacons interspersed by (b) Periodic WiFi beacons from two access
probe messages.   points

Fig. 3. WiFi beacons may be interspersed by probe messages or beacons from other
access points, making their identification non-trivial

Algorithm 1. Algorithm to detect periodic bursts

1: **Inputs**
2: ▷ n is the number of RSSI bursts over
   time T
3: ▷ $d_T = (d_t^1, d_t^2 \ldots d_t^{n-1})$ is the sequence
   of inter-burst separations
4: **Outputs**
5: ▷ $P(d_\tau)$ is the confidence value for every
   $d_\tau \in L$
6: ▷ t_p is the detected periodicity of the
   sequence
7:
8: $L \leftarrow \emptyset$
9: **for** $d_t^i \in d_T$ ADDTOSET(L, d_t^i) **end for**

10: **for** $d_t^i \in (d_t^1, d_t^2 \ldots d_t^{n-1})$ **do**
11:    $s \leftarrow d_t^i$
12:    **for** $d_t^j \in (d_t^{i+1}, d_t^{i+2} \ldots d_t^{n-1})$ **do**
13:        $s \leftarrow s + d_t^j$
14:        UPDATESET(L, s)
15:    **end for**
16: **end for**
17: **for each** $d_\tau \in L$ **do**
18:    $n_\tau \leftarrow \lfloor \frac{T}{d_\tau} \rfloor$
19:    $P(d_\tau) = 2C(d_\tau)/(n_\tau(n_\tau + 1))$
20: **end for**
21: $t_p = \text{argmax}_{d_\tau} P(d_\tau)$

---

sequence of RSSI bursts from a cluster. Let t_i denote the time at which the ith
burst in the cluster was recorded by the node, where $1 \leq i \leq n$. The inter-burst
separation is denoted by the sequence $d_T = (t_1 - t_0, t_2 - t_1, \ldots, t_n - t_{n-1})$.

The algorithm populates a set L with values denoting time periods at which
RSSI bursts are captured. This is performed by inspecting every inter-burst
separation value in the sequence d_T, and checking to see whether they are already
included in the set L (Procedures 1, line 2 in *AddToSet*). Specifically, the check
takes the form of a modulus operation, such that an inter-burst separation of
kd_τ is not added to L, if d_τ has already been included. The modulo operation
allows a certain variance ϵ_δ to account for factors such as clock speed variations
of the node recording RSSI, as well as channel backoffs by the interfering source.
Setting ϵ_δ to 7 RSSI sampling intervals allows a jitter of $2\epsilon_\delta \approx 0.65$ ms, which
we have found to empirically give good results.

After populating L, the algorithm maps every $d_\tau \in L$ to a counter value $C(d_\tau)$.
$C(d_\tau)$ is a measure of how periodic the RSSI sequence is in d_τ. Intuitively, the
algorithm checks over a time window T, whether there are RSSI bursts at times
$d_\tau, 2d_\tau, 3d_\tau \ldots kd_\tau$, where $k = \lfloor \frac{T}{d_\tau} \rfloor$. Since the entries in L are determined from
d_T, this step is performed by scanning every value $d_t^i \in d_T$ in sequence. For every
d_t^i, the algorithm adds the inter-burst separations from d_t^{i+1} to d_t^{n-1}, and checks
at each step, whether the partial sum is periodic in any $d_\tau \in L$ (Procedures 1,

---

Procedures 1. Updating entries in candidate set L

1: **procedure** ADDTOSET(L, d_t)	1: **procedure** UPDATESET(L, d_t)
2: **if** $\forall d_\tau \in L, d_t \pmod{d_\tau} \in$ $(\epsilon_\delta, d_\tau - \epsilon_\delta)$ **then**	2: **if** $\exists d_\tau \in L \mid d_t \pmod{d_\tau} \notin$ $(\epsilon_\Delta, d_\tau - \epsilon_\Delta)$ **then**
3: $L \leftarrow L \cup d_t$	3: $C(d_\tau) \leftarrow C(d_\tau) + 1$
4: $C(d_t) \leftarrow 0$	4: **else**
5: **end if**	5: $L \leftarrow L \cup d_t$
6: **end procedure**	6: $C(d_t) \leftarrow 1$
	7: **end if**
	8: **end procedure**

---

line 2 in *UpdateSet*). If not, the sum is added to the list, and its count is set to 1 (Procedures 1, lines 5–6 in *UpdateSet*). In general, if n_τ denotes the number of RSSI bursts that are periodic in d_τ over time T, then $n_\tau = \lfloor \frac{T}{d_\tau} \rfloor$. This results in a maximum of $\frac{1}{2} n_\tau (n_\tau + 1)$ summations that are periodic in d_τ, or equivalently, $C(d_\tau) \le \frac{1}{2} n_\tau (n_\tau + 1)$. Therefore, the fraction $P(d_\tau) = 2C(d_\tau)/(n_\tau(n_\tau + 1))$ represents a normalized confidence measure for periodicity in d_τ. Possible values for $P(d_\tau)$ range from 0 and can also exceed 1, especially when multiple RSSI bursts occur with the same periodicity, as in Figure 3(b). The periodicity check in *UpdateSet* is allowed a greater threshold, i.e., $\epsilon_\Delta > \epsilon_\delta$, in order to to account for accumulated variance over summing up inter-burst separations. We find that setting ϵ_Δ to 30 RSSI sampling intervals, or approximately 1.4 ms, gives good results. SpeckSense uses round($P(d_\tau)$) as a measure for the number of distinct RSSI subsequences that are periodic in d_τ.

The period t_p of the RSSI sequence is determined to be $\text{argmax}_{d_\tau} P(d_\tau)$, with the additional constraint, round($P(d_\tau)$) ≥ 1. The value of t_p is approximately 100 ms for WiFi beacons, which is the default beaconing interval on most WiFi access points. Algorithm 1, however, is also generally applicable to detect RSSI bursts of any period, in contrast to other approaches [9, 13] that explicitly check for predetermined values. This makes it a viable option to detect and classify other forms of interference that include periodic transmissions in 802.15.4 networks [14] as well as microwave bursts [12].

5   Evaluation

We implement SpeckSense on the Tmote Sky hardware featuring a CC2420 radio transceiver. There are, however, no special features that prevent porting Speck-Sense to other sensor node hardware platforms that allow fast RSSI sampling. The code for SpeckSense is implemented using the Contiki operating system and fits within 21 KB of program memory. The overall RAM usage is contained within 6 KB, of which the clustering algorithm takes only about 4 KB of program memory and a total of less than 800 bytes of RAM.

We evaluate SpeckSense's ability to distinguish between multiple sources of interfering traffic, and its ability to identify the presence of WiFi access points in the 2.4 GHz band. We conduct our experiments in two indoor environments: an

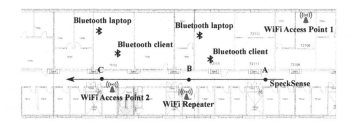

Fig. 4. Experimental setup in the office corridor. We evaluate SpeckSense at locations A, B and C in the presence of WiFi and Bluetooth interference.

office corridor and a 85-node indoor testbed that spans three floors. These environments represent challenging conditions for SpeckSense because they induce strong multipath fading. We present our results in the following order. First, we showcase the multi-source interference detection results of SpeckSense from the office corridor. Then, we show how SpeckSense improves the data gathering performance of a multichannel protocol [2] on a 85-node testbed.

5.1 Detecting Concurrent Interferers

Indoor environments represent challenging conditions for SpeckSense due to non-line of sight between nodes that causes multipath fading effects. The extent of these effects may also vary over time, e.g., due to people moving, thereby increasing the variance in received signal strength on a sensor node. SpeckSense relies on RSSI observations to detect interference, so it is important to characterize its performance in such an environment.

Experimental Setup. The setup in the office corridor is shown in Fig. 4. There are two WiFi access points (operating on WiFi channel 1 and 11, respectively) a WiFi repeater (operating on channel 1), as well as four Bluetooth devices. Sensor nodes run SpeckSense at locations A, B and C. Nodes at location A face interference from WiFi AP 1 and the WiFi repeater, as well as sporadic Bluetooth interference. Nodes at location B operate on a different channel and are exposed to Bluetooth interference as well as beacons from WiFi AP 2. Nodes at location C face interference from Bluetooth and WiFi data transfers.

We perform over 100 experimental runs in sequence. In each run, nodes perform RSSI sampling for 1 second, followed by interference detection and classification. The RSSI sampler uses four power levels to quantize signal strength information, as described in Sec. 3.1. Each detected interference cluster is classified as follows: *(i)* WiFi beacons that have a period of 100 ms, *(ii)* periodic traffic and *(iii)* non-periodic traffic. To quantify SpeckSense's performance, we define a *detection rate* for every interference class. The *detection rate* for an interference class is measured as the percentage number of runs in which SpeckSense identifies it.

Data traffic from IEEE 802.15.4 compliant sensor nodes also contributes to co-channel interference in the 2.4 GHz spectrum. To validate that SpeckSense

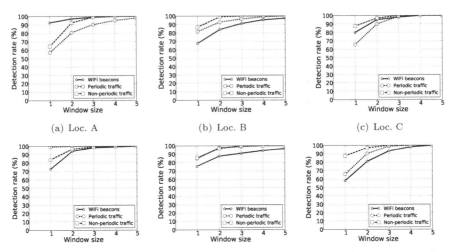

(a) Loc. A   (b) Loc. B   (c) Loc. C

(d) Loc. A, with 802.15.4 traffic (e) Loc. B, with 802.15.4 traffic (f) Loc. C, with 802.15.4 traffic

Fig. 5. Detection rates for the three locations in the office corridor. For window sizes of three and larger, SpeckSense's detection rate exceeds 90%.

can classify multiple interferers even in the presence of WSN activity, we perform our experiments under two scenarios, namely with and without 802.15.4 traffic. To generate the channel traffic, we add two sensor nodes to the setup – one node sends packets every 125 ms, while the other receives them. In every setup, the sender node is co-located with the node running SpeckSense, and the receiver node is placed 6 m away from the sender. We refer to these nodes as the 802.15.4 sender and the 802.15.4 receiver.

Results. Figure 5 shows the detection rates for SpeckSense at different locations, both in the presence and absence of 802.15.4 traffic. Accounting for multipath fading effects that inhibit a seamless classification, we aggregate the detection rates over a window representing a sequence of runs. An interference class is detected when it is observed at least once over the window. The plots show the detection rate of SpeckSense for different window sizes. SpeckSense achieves a detection rate of over 90% in all cases when using a window size of 3 or greater. Depending upon the specific interference context described in the experimental setup, *non-periodic* and *periodic* traffic relate to different sources of channel activity. For example, *periodic traffic* in Figures 5(a), 5(b), and 5(c) represents periodic TCP bursts in WiFi data transfers. In contrast, *periodic traffic* in Figures 5(d), 5(e), and 5(f) also comprises additional 802.15.4 traffic, which has a period of 125 ms. *Non-periodic traffic* at location A relates to WiFi data transfers, and at locations B and C, relates to a combination of WiFi and Bluetooth data traffic.

Channel activity in the office corridor also includes beacons from additional WiFi APs outside of our control, such as the university's WiFi. Table 1 shows the 50th and 90th percentile of WiFi access points that SpeckSense identifies at different locations. In general, SpeckSense identifies fewer access points in

Table 1. SpeckSense can detect multiple WiFi access points deployed over different locations on the office corridor. The values (50th and 90th percentile) indicate that SpeckSense can detect WiFi activity even in the presence of ambient 802.15.4 traffic.

	Number of detected WiFi access points (percentile)					
802.15.4	Location A		Location B		Location C	
traffic	50th	90th	50th	90th	50th	90th
No	3	4	1.5	4	1	3
Yes	1	3	2	4	1	2

the presence of 802.15.4 traffic. We attribute this to an artifact of our experimental setup – the periodic 802.15.4 acknowledgement frames from the 802.15.4 receiver have burst durations similar to WiFi beacons. SpeckSense therefore detects a cluster that has multiple, yet distinct periods, which our approach (see algorithm 1) does not handle at present. We plan to address this issue in future work. Nonetheless, the results show that SpeckSense identifies multiple access points, even in the presence of Bluetooth and 802.15.4 traffic.

5.2 Improving Data Collection Performance

Data collection applications for indoor WSN deployments suffer from degraded performance on account of WiFi interference. To mitigate the effects of external interference, multichannel protocols [2] coordinate node communication on different radio channels. These approaches achieve resilience against interference by either hopping through a fixed sequence of channels [15, 16], or by switching channels when interfered [2]. However, they do not address the problem of finding a relatively interference-free channel.

As a solution, we run SpeckSense independently on every node to perform a deployment-time assessment of WiFi-free radio channels. We evaluate SpeckSense as a link-layer service for Chrysso [2], a multichannel protocol that adaptively switches radio channels on interfered nodes. Sensor nodes independently run SpeckSense at network bootstrap and blacklist channels in which SpeckSense detects WiFi beacons or interfering channel activity with an average inter-burst separation less than 100 ms.

We compare SpeckSense's results against three other strategies that differ on channel selection policy, namely Chrysso *default*, Chrysso *best channels*, and Chrysso *threshold*. Chrysso *default* employs a random channel selection scheme over all 16 channels, whereas Chrysso *best channels* performs a random selection over a restricted set of channels, namely 15, 20, 25 and 26. The channels are chosen such that they empirically exhibit the best packet reception rates among all other channels on the testbed [16], and do not overlap with commonly used WiFi channels 1, 6 and 11. Chrysso *threshold* is closest in design and objective to SpeckSense on interference avoidance, and ranks channels based on their quality. The channel quality is computed as a ratio of the number of channel *idle* RSSI

Table 2. Data collection performance (averaged over six runs) on a 85-node testbed, highlighting the advantages derived from interference avoidance. SpeckSense with Chrysso performs best compared to other alternatives on avoiding interfered channels.

	Data collection performance		
Protocol	Data yield	Duty cycle	Energy per delivered packet
Chrysso *default*	73.3 %	2.9 %	4.22 mJ
Chrysso *best channels*	95.3 %	2.3 %	2.6 mJ
Chrysso + *threshold*	91.4 %	2.4 %	3.1 mJ
Chrysso + SpeckSense	**94.8 %**	**2.3 %**	**2.9 mJ**

samples (RSSI ≤ -90 dBm) over the total number of RSSI samples, as suggested by Musăloiu-E. et al. [17]. In our implementation, Chrysso *threshold* uses the best four channels in decreasing order of channel quality.

We experimentally evaluate the aforestated strategies on the Indriya WSN testbed [18], using a network of 85 nodes including the sink. Every node generates one packet per minute over a two-hour duration, and duty cycles its radio wakeup over an interval of 125 ms, using the X-MAC protocol [19]. We perform six experimental runs for each variant of Chrysso described above.

Table 2 contrasts data collection performance of the revised Chrysso variants against its original implementation, Chrysso *default*. In general, avoiding interfered channels improves both the average data yield and the energy per transmitted packet for Chrysso. Specifically, running SpeckSense with Chrysso increases the average data yield (packets received by the sink) by approximately 30% over Chrysso *default*. This improvement is mainly attributed to avoidance of WiFi-interfered channels by SpeckSense. To validate our claim, we find that SpeckSense blacklists 802.15.4 radio channels that overlap with commonly used WiFi channels 1, 6 and 11, in more than 80% of the nodes. For the same reason, Chrysso SpeckSense performs comparably with Chrysso *best channels* that explicitly avoids the aforesaid WiFi channels. The 95% confidence intervals for both Chrysso SpeckSense and Chrysso *best channels* overlap on all three performance metrics. The overlap indicates that neither variant outperforms the other, in accordance with rules of analysis in [20]. However, SpeckSense presents a more general solution that applies to indoor environments wherein co-located WiFi networks may operate on channels other than 1, 6 and 11. Lastly, SpeckSense outperforms *rssi threshold* on average data yield and duty cycle. This suggests that for the same energy cost in RSSI sampling (334.6 mJ on average per node), SpeckSense is more effective at avoiding WiFi-interfered channels than a simple approach that computes channel utilization using a threshold. In conclusion, the results show that an existing multichannel protocol such as Chrysso benefits from the interference classification output provided by SpeckSense.

6   Related Work

As the number of wireless devices operating in the license-free frequency bands is steadily increasing, the problem of interference is receiving more attention. A few other approaches are similar to ours in that they sample the RSSI. Zacharias et al. [8] classify interference based on a fixed set of simple conditions. In contrast to SpeckSense, their classification includes processing of computationally expensive tasks such as FFTs and execution on a PC rather than on motes. Also Boers et al. [21] sample the spectrum for interferer classification but they only target interference occurring at regular intervals. Likewise, Zhou et al. [9, 13] propose an algorithm that is restricted to detecting WiFi beacons from RSSI traces. Another approach based on spectrum sampling is by Bloessl et al. [22]. In contrast to SpeckSense, their approach is limited to the detection of single interference sources. Ansari et al. [23] propose an approach to detect WiFi networks by using a synchronized pair of nodes to scan adjacent channels. In contrast, SpeckSense bases its observations of multiple interferers on a single node. Rayanchu et al. [24] detect WiFi access points and other non-WiFi devices using commodity WiFi hardware. However, their approach relies on device-specific WiFi features and involves computationally intensive processing, making it infeasible for resource-constrained sensor nodes. Hermans et al. [6] present SoNIC interference classification without spectrum sampling relying only on the information provided by corrupted packets. As their approach does not rely on spectrum sampling it is less energy-consuming than SpeckSense but it does not provide higher level information such as the number of WiFi access points. There are efforts for channel selection that use the average energy in a channel [25, 17, 26], or packet reception counts [27] as selection criteria. In contrast to these approaches, we take the source of interference into account.

7   Conclusion

In this paper we have presented SpeckSense, a detection and classification scheme for concurrent multi-source interference affecting wireless sensor networks. Experiments in a real setting have shown that SpeckSense detects multiple interferers in over 90% of the cases. We have also evaluated SpeckSense as a low-layer service to recommend interference-free channels for WSN data collection. Experiments combining the results of SpeckSense with a multichannel protocol have shown a significant improvement in data yield at lower duty cycle.

Acknowledgement. This work has been partially supported by the European Commission with contract INFSO-ICT-317826 (RELYonIT) and SSF.

References

1. Liang, C.M., Priyantha, N.B., Liu, J., Terzis, A.: Surviving Wi-Fi interference in low power ZigBee networks. In: ACM SenSys (2010)
2. Iyer, V., Woehrle, M., Langendoen, K.: Chrysso – a multi-channel approach to mitigate external interference. In: IEEE SECON (2011)
3. Hauer, J., Willig, A., Wolisz, A.: Mitigating the effects of RF interference through RSSI-based error recovery. In: Silva, J.S., Krishnamachari, B., Boavida, F. (eds.) EWSN 2010. LNCS, vol. 5970, pp. 224–239. Springer, Heidelberg (2010)
4. Boano, C.A., Voigt, T., Tsiftes, N., Mottola, L., Römer, K., Zúñiga, M.A.: Making sensornet MAC protocols robust against interference. In: Silva, J.S., Krishnamachari, B., Boavida, F. (eds.) EWSN 2010. LNCS, vol. 5970, pp. 272–288. Springer, Heidelberg (2010)
5. Chowdhury, K.R., Akyildiz, I.F.: Interferer classification, channel selection and transmission adaptation for wireless sensor networks. In: ICC (2009)
6. Hermans, F., Rensfelt, O., Voigt, T., Ngai, E., Nordén, L.-Å., Gunningberg, P.: SoNIC: classifying interference in 802.15.4 sensor networks. In: IPSN (2013)
7. Zacharias, S., Newe, T., O'Keeffe, S., Lewis, E.: A lightweight classification algorithm for external sources of interference in IEEE 802.15.4-based wireless sensor networks operating at the 2.4 GHz. IJDSN (2014)
8. Zacharias, S., Newe, T., O'Keeffe, S., Lewis, E.: Identifying sources of interference in RSSI traces of a single IEEE 802.15. 4 channel. In: ICWMC (2012)
9. Zhou, R., Xiong, Y., Xing, G., Sun, L., Ma, J.: ZiFi: wireless LAN discovery via ZigBee interference signatures. In: ACM MobiCom, pp. 49–60 (2010)
10. Boano, C.A., Voigt, T., Noda, C., Romer, K., Zuniga, M.: JamLab: Augmenting sensornet testbeds with realistic and controlled interference generation. In: ACM IPSN (2011)
11. MacQueen, J., et al.: Some methods for classification and analysis of multivariate observations. In: Proceedings of the Fifth Berkeley Symposium on Mathematical Statistics and Probability, California, USA, vol. 1(281-297), p. 14 (1967)
12. Iyer, V.G., Hermans, F., Voigt, T.: Detecting and avoiding multiple sources of interference in the 2.4 GHZ spectrum. Department of Information Technology, Uppsala University, Tech. Rep. 2014-023 (December 2014)
13. Gao, Y., Niu, J., Zhou, R., Xing, G.: Zifind: Exploiting cross-technology interference signatures for energy-efficient indoor localization. In: IEEE Infocom 2013, pp. 2940–2948 (2013)
14. Ferrari, F., Zimmerling, M., Thiele, L., Saukh, O.: Efficient network flooding and time synchronization with Glossy. In: IPSN, pp. 73–84 (2011)
15. Tang, L., Sun, Y., Gurewitz, O., Johnson, D.B.: EM-MAC: a dynamic multichannel energy-efficient MAC protocol for wireless sensor networks. In: ACM MobiHoc 2011, p. 23 (2011)
16. Al Nahas, B., Duquennoy, S., Iyer, V., Voigt, T.: Low-Power Listening Goes Multi-Channel. In: IEEE DCOSS, Marina Del Rey, CA, USA (2014)
17. Musaloiu-E, R., Terzis, A.: Minimising the effect of WiFi interference in 802.15. 4 wireless sensor networks. IJSN 3(1), 43–54 (2008)
18. Doddavenkatappa, M., Chan, M.C., Ananda, A.L.: Indriya: A low-cost, 3D wireless sensor network testbed. In: Korakis, T., Li, H., Tran-Gia, P., Park, H.-S. (eds.) TridentCom 2011. LNICST, vol. 90, pp. 302–316. Springer, Heidelberg (2012)
19. Buettner, M., Yee, G.V., Anderson, E., Han, R.: X-MAC: a short preamble MAC protocol for duty-cycled wireless sensor networks. In: ACM SenSys 2006, pp. 307–320 (2006)

20. Jain, R.: The art of computer systems performance analysis. John Wiley & Sons (2008)
21. Boers, N.M., Nikolaidis, I., Gburzynski, P.: Sampling and classifying interference patterns in a wireless sensor network. ACM TOSN 2012 9(1), 2 (2012)
22. Bloessl, B., Joerer, S., Mauroner, F., Dressler, F.: Low-Cost Interferer Detection and Classification using TelosB Sensor Motes. In: ACM MobiCom, pp. 403–406 (2012)
23. Ansari, J., Ang, T., Mähönen, P.: WiSpot: fast and reliable detection of Wi-Fi networks using IEEE 802.15.4 radios. In: ACM MobiWac 2011, pp. 35–44 (2011)
24. Rayanchu, S., Patro, A., Banerjee, S.: Catching whales and minnows using WiFiNet: deconstructing non-WiFi interference using WiFi hardware. In: Proc. of USENIX NSDI (2012)
25. Ansari, J., Mähönen, P.: Channel selection in spectrum agile and cognitive MAC protocols for wireless sensor networks. In: ACM MobiWac (2010)
26. Noda, C., Prabh, S., Alves, M., Boano, C., Voigt, T.: Quantifying the channel quality for interference-aware wireless sensor networks. ACM SIGBED Review 8(4), 43–48 (2011)
27. Doddavenkatappa, M., Chan, M.C., Leong, B.: Improving link quality by exploiting channel diversity in wireless sensor networks. In: IEEE RTSS 2011, pp. 159–169 (2011)

Extracting Human Behavior Patterns
from Appliance-level Power Consumption Data

Alaa Alhamoud[1], Pei Xu[1], Frank Englert[1], Andreas Reinhardt[2],
Philipp Scholl[3,*], Doreen Boehnstedt[1], and Ralf Steinmetz[1]

[1] Multimedia Communications Lab, Technische Universität Darmstadt,
Darmstadt, Germany
{firstname.lastname}@kom.tu-darmstadt.de
[2] Institute of Informatics, Technische Universtität Clausthal,
Clausthal-Zellerfeld, Germany
reinhardt@ieee.org
[3] SAP AG, Walldorf, Germany
pscholl@gmail.com

Abstract. In order to provide useful energy saving recommendations,
energy management systems need a deep insight in the context of energy
consumption. Getting those insights is rather difficult. Either exhaustive user questionnaires or the installation of hundreds of sensors are
required in order to acquire this data. Measuring the energy consumption of a household is however required in order to find and realize saving
potentials. Thus, we show how to gain insights in the context of energy
consumption directly from the energy consumption profile. Our proposed
methods are capable of determining the user's current activity with an
accuracy up to 98% as well as the user's current place in a house with
an accuracy up to 97%. Furthermore, our solution is capable of detecting anomalies in the energy consumption behavior. All this is mainly
achieved with the energy consumption profile.

1 Introduction

The realization of energy efficiency in buildings has become an important research topic in industrial as well as research community. The main motivation
for this increasing importance is the conservation of energy in a world where
energy prices are always fluctuating and very sensitive to political as well as
natural crises. This is also driven by the wide spread of wireless sensor networks
which made it possible to collect fine-grained data about the building context
as well as the context of its inhabitants. In this paper, we develop three novel
experiments which exploit the huge information provided by the smart home
to achieve the main goal of our research efforts which is to conserve energy in
smart homes while maintaining user comfort. The main focus of our work in
this paper is the analysis of our smart home dataset which we call from now

---

* Co-author is employed by SAP AG; however, the opinions and results expressed in
this paper are his own and do not denote the point of view of SAP AG.

T. Abdelzaher et al. (Eds.): EWSN 2015, LNCS 8965, pp. 52–67, 2015.

on SMARTENERGY.KOM dataset[1]. SMARTENERGY.KOM dataset is a large dataset which contains about 42 million data points of sensor readings and user feedback which we have collected from two smart home environments for the primary purpose of detecting human activities based on wireless sensor networks [2], thus to save unnecessary consumed energy. In the first deployment, a wireless sensor network was deployed for about 82 days. More than 22 million activity related sensor events were generated by corresponding sensors. The duration of deployment 2 was about two months, during which about 20 million sensor readings were recorded. We have used two types of wireless sensor nodes in both deployments. On one hand we deployed Plugwise[2] sensors for sensing the appliance-level power consumption of the household. Each device in the house was connected to a Plugwise sensor which measures the load of the device. On the other hand we deployed Pikkerton[3] sensors for sensing the temperature, brightness as well as the motion in the environment. In both deployments, nine daily user activities were monitored:

Deployment 1: Sleeping, Watching TV, Not at Home, Reading, Eating, Cooking, Working at PC, Making Coffee and Cleaning Dishes.

Deployment 2: Sleeping, Watching TV, Not at Home, Reading, Eating, Making Tea, Listening Radio, Slicing Bread and Ironing.

These activities have been chosen based on the available electrical appliances which can be monitored at home. Some of these activities like "Watching TV" can be directly related to the power consumption. Other activities such as "Sleeping" and "Not at Home" can be indirectly inferred from the power consumption. This list of activities does not necessarily contain all the activities performed by the user at home. Therefore, we have provided the user with the option "Ignore" which implies as a feedback that the user's current activity does not belong to the list of activities provided by us. This option helps preserving the privacy of the user as well by giving her/him the choice whether to report her/his current activity or not. All sensor readings which are related to the option "Ignore" have been excluded from the dataset before conducting our experiments. Based on these two deployments, we have built an activity detection framework which uses the feedback provided by the user to learn his current activity and relate it to the collected sensor readings. The remainder of this paper is structured as follows. Section 2 surveys related research projects whose main focus is the analysis of datasets collected by wireless sensor networks in the context of smart home. In Section 3, we present our novel concept for user localization in indoor environments based on real-time appliance-level power consumption. In Section 4, we analyze the temporal relations between the user activities and examine whether the discovered relations could increase the accuracy of our activity detection framework. In Section 5, we analyze the user's daily power consumption behavior. We conclude the paper in Section 6.

---

[1] The dataset is available for download under: http://www.kom.tu-darmstadt.de/
research-results/software-downloads/software/smartenergykom
[2] http://www.plugwise.com/
[3] http://www.pikkerton.com/

2   Related Work

In recent years, analyzing datasets collected from wireless sensor networks in smart homes has become of great interest to computer science researchers. This is mainly driven by the great potential offered by these datasets for developing IT services which can improve the life quality as well as the energy efficiency of the smart homes. Data mining techniques have been utilized in order to extract all the possible useful hidden patterns contained in such datasets. In the work of Chen et al. [4], they analyzed a dataset which contains more than 100,000 sensor events collected from two apartments. The primary purpose of their work was to recognize human activities performed in these two apartments and understand the related energy usage. They applied clustering techniques for identifying the normal power consumption patterns, thus to detect abnormal energy usage. Using classification techniques, they trained a model for predicting the energy usage of an inhabitant based on her/his currently performed activities. Another example is given by Hoque et al. [8], where 26 days of activity related sensor events collected from a single resident home is analyzed. Based on the hypothesis that each activity will trigger a set of specific sensors, they applied pattern mining to find all simultaneously fired sensors. In the next step, different to [4], clustering is used for discovering events based on previously extracted patterns. Besides, they utilized clustering for labeling the instances. Finally, they build a classification model for recognizing the activities. Fogarty et al. [6] analyzed 3.4 million sensor readings from a home shared by two adults. Their goal was to detect water usage related activities by configuring microphone based sensors that listen for the water flow into and out of a home. They applied the classification algorithm support vector machine to train a model for recognizing different types of water usage. Fluctuations of sound waves returned by the sensors are considered as features for training the classification model. Activated sensors together with their temporal characteristics are then combined to form patterns for identifying the activities. Different from the aforementioned research projects, our analysis is conducted on a much larger dataset. Moreover, the three experiments conducted in our work have not been covered by any of these research works although similar data mining techniques are utilized.

3   Sensing Power Consumption for User Localization

User localization has always been one of the central challenges in the design of smart home environments. A wide variety of sensors such as Passive Infrared sensors can be used in order to achieve this goal. Currently, the usage of electricity consumption data for occupancy detection started to gain attention among the research community as we see in [11] where the authors used the data collected from smart meters for the purpose of occupancy detection. This leads us to the idea of utilizing new kind of sensors for user localization in smart home, namely the appliance-level power sensors which sense the power consumption of individual household appliances. Therefore, in this paper we examine the usage of these sensors for the purpose of user localization in smart home where we aim at localizing users with a better resolution than shown in [11]. Usually, users perform specific activities in specific places, such as cooking in the kitchen, sleeping in the sleeping room and so on. Therefore, each activity is associated with certain appliances which consume energy during this activity. In other words, by knowing the devices which are consuming energy, we can infer the location of the user in the smart home. In order to verify this theory, we use supervised learning techniques where the input of the classification model will be the user's real-time appliance-level power consumption and the output is the location of the user. In the following sections, we explain the construction of the training set for the supervised learning model and we evaluate the accuracy of this model.

3.1   Construction of the Training Set

The first step in supervised learning is to construct a training set for building the classification model. As mentioned before, each user's location in the smart home is accompanied with a set of sensor readings representing the real-time appliance-level power consumption. These sensor readings represent the input for the supervised learning model along with the labels which represent the user's location. Sensor readings were recorded every ten seconds during the deployment. However, activities normally last for several minutes or even hours e.g. sleeping. In other words, if we directly construct a training set from these sensor readings, the size of the training set will be extremely large leading to an inefficient model construction. Therefore, we need to reduce the size of the training set without affecting the accuracy of the trained classification model. To this end, we divide the whole time series of sensor readings into timeslots of two minutes. We chose the period of two minutes as it helps achieving a good accuracy while minimizing the overlapping between activities in one timeslot. Then, for each sensor, we extracted its maximum value in each timeslot as one feature for constructing the feature vector. This means, every two minutes will represent a training instance in which the features are the maximum values of sensor readings during this timeslot. In order to provide the labels of the training instances, we relied on the user feedback which informs us about the user current activity. By knowing the current user activity, we can infer the current location of the user, because each activity is performed in one and only one location. The labeling process mainly relies on the time interval between one activity and the next activity, namely the duration of each activity. Therefore, by examining in which time interval the timestamp of an instance is falling into, we can assign the location of the corresponding activity in that time interval to the instance. The final generated form of the instances is shown in Eq. 1, where $S_{n\_max}(slot_i)$ means the maximum sensor value of sensor n in ith timeslot, and m is the total number of timeslots. Therefore, the training set is composed by a set of such instances $< I_1, I_2, ..., I_m >$.

$$Ii = < S_{1\_max}(slot_i), S_{2\_max}(slot_i), ..., S_{n\_max}(slot_i),$$
$$Class(slot_i) > \qquad i \in [1, m]$$

(1)

3.2   Building and Evaluation of the Classification Model

After obtaining the training instances, we built the prediction model for both deployments by applying the random forest classifier provided by Weka [7]. We have chosen the random forest algorithm as it proved to be the most suitable algorithm for our dataset as well as other datasets similar to it as shown in [5][16]. In order to find a good balance between accuracy and size of model e.g. to prevent overfitting the model, we first build the model with training instances of one week and then accumulate the training set by one week data points each testing. This is necessary as in real-life deployments, the learning phase should be as short as possible. Both deployments have the following four locations to be predicted, by "Outside", we refer to the instances where the user was not at home:

Deployment 1: Kitchen, Living room, Work area, Outside.

Deployment 2: Kitchen, Living room, Sleeping room, Outside.

To evaluate the built model, we apply10-folds cross validation [12] which partitions the training set into 10 subsets and always uses one subset to test the model built upon the remaining 9 subsets. This process is repeated 10 times and produces a mean accuracy over all rounds. Figure 1(a) demonstrates the accuracy of

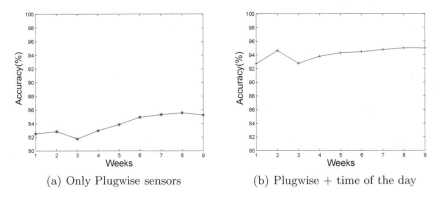

(a) Only Plugwise sensors   (b) Plugwise + time of the day

Fig. 1. Accuracy of location recognition model built for deployment 2

the model built for deployment 2. As we can see in the figure, the random forest algorithm reaches its highest accuracy, namely 85.5% with a training set of 8 weeks. However, we can conclude from the figure that a training set of 2 weeks is already sufficient for acquiring a high accuracy. This conclusion is based on the fact that the accuracy only rises about 2.5% when the number of weeks included in the training set increases from 2 weeks to 8 weeks. This conclusion allows us to shorten the duration of the data collection process in the deployments to come which lessens the burden on the user in providing feedback and therefore leads to a more acceptance of the system. In order to obtain a better understanding of the classification accuracy, we list the precision, recall, and F-measure values

Table 1. Accuracy by classes for deployment 2 by using two weeks dataset

Classes	Precision	Recall	F-Measure
(K)itchen	87.40%	49.30%	64.10%
(S)leeping room	76.70%	99.80%	86.80%
(L)iving room	97.70%	94.10%	95.90%
(O)utside	0.00%	0.00%	0.00%

Table 2. Confusion matrix for deployment 2 by using two weeks dataset

	(K)	(S)	(L)	(O)
(K)	**49.33%**	44.91%	5.76%	0.00%
(S)	0.10%	**99.83%**	0.07%	0.00%
(L)	2.11%	3.82%	**94.08%**	0.00%
(O)	0.34%	99.49%	0.17%	**0.00%**

for each location in Table 1. Moreover, we show the associated confusion matrix in Table 2. The result represents the model built for deployment 2 with a training set of 2 weeks. Although the overall accuracy reached by this model is 83% (cf. Figure 1(a)), the recall values of the classes "Kitchen" and "Outside" are very low with 49.3% and 0% respectively as shown in Table 1. In order to understand the reasons for this phenomenon, we have to look on the confusion matrix in Table 2. From the confusion matrix, we can see that 44.91% of the instances of the class "Kitchen" have been falsely classified as "Sleeping room" instances. Besides, almost all the instances of the class "Outside" have also been falsely classified as "Sleeping room" instances. This can be explained based on the following facts. First of all, the confusion between the classes "Outside" and "Sleeping room" can be returned to the fact that when the user is outside or sleeping, all Plugwise sensors were almost keeping in silence as no appliances are required to perform these activities. Although, there are some values of Plugwise sensors (e.g. lamp sensor) related to the "Sleeping room" class stored in the dataset, the lamp was in most cases not turned on while sleeping. Furthermore, the instance of the class "Outside" were classified as "Sleeping room" and not the other way around because "Sleeping room" is a dominant class. This is due to the fact that the duration of sleeping is much longer than that of being outside in this deployment which leads to more training instances for the class "Sleeping room" than for the class "Outside". The activity of "Eating" was the major reason of falsely classifying instances of "Kitchen" into "Sleeping room". This activity is supposed to be identified through the Plugwise sensor connected to the radio in the kitchen. However, the radio was not always turned on or only turned on for a part of time during the activity of "Eating". To solve this problem, we need a strong discriminator which can help distinguishing the classes "Outside" and "Sleeping room". We thought about a feature which can be used in the learning process in order to achieve this task. One feature which can fully perform this role is the time of the day. By using the time of the day as a feature for building the machine learning model, we add a strong discriminator especially between

Table 3. Accuracy by classes for deployment 2 by using two weeks dataset (with time)

Classes	Precision	Recall	F-Measure
(K)itchen	81.80%	73.30%	73.30%
(S)leeping room	98.20%	99%	98.60%
(L)iving room	96.10%	96.80%	96.50%
(O)utside	83.50%	86.30%	84.90%

Table 4. Confusion matrix for deployment 2 by using two weeks dataset (with time)

	(K)	(S)	(L)	(O)
(K)	**73.32%**	9.59%	4.99%	12.09%
(S)	0.99%	**98.97%**	0.03%	0.0%
(L)	0.65%	0.0%	**96.84%**	2.50%
(O)	7.77%	0.33%	5.57%	**86.31%**

the classes "Outside" and "Sleeping room". We use the "hh:mm:ss" time format as Weka can deal with this time format automatically. After using the time as a feature in addition to the previous features, the overall accuracy of the model has increased as shown in Figure 1(b). To better understand the effect of adding the time to the feature set, we present the precision, recall, and F-measure values for each location in Table 3. Furthermore, we present the associated confusion matrix in Table 4. The results in these two tables have been achieved for deployment 2 with a training set of 2 weeks. As we can see from Table 3 and Table 4, the time has functioned as a strong discriminator between the class "Sleeping room" and the classes "Outside" and "Kitchen" respectively. The use of the time as a feature makes it easy to solve the confusion between the class "Sleeping room" and the class "Outside" as the user in deployment 2 always goes outside during the day and not during the night. The location "Kitchen" can also benefit from the usage of time as a feature, because the user performs most of his activities in the kitchen during the day.

4   Mining Human Behavioral Patterns

As humans tend to follow a regular routine in their daily life, their everyday activities tend to happen in a certain order which mostly repeats itself everyday. Discovering temporal relations between these daily activities may assist in enhancing the accuracy of our activity detection framework. Hence, in this section, we first try to detect any behavioral patterns which might exist in the data collected in both deployments and then we examine whether these detected patterns can help increasing the accuracy of the activity detection framework we have previously developed.

4.1   Extraction of Temporal Activity Patterns

As mentioned in [3], temporal relations between two activities (A, B) can be represented as A happens after B, before B, overlaps with B and so on. According to the user feedback in both deployments, activities were performed consecutively one after another which was a precondition for our dataset. Hence, we only examine the "before" and "after" relations between two activities. In the following section, we introduce four terms related to the analysis before explaining the operations of the pattern mining process.

Episode: According to [15], an episode is characterized by a pair of begin and end timestamps, during which one or more activities can happen. As the user's daily activities are the major interest of our analysis, we specify the duration of an episode as a single day. Hence, an episode is composed of all activities performed during the day, namely all the activities between timestamps [00:00:00, 23:59:59]. This concept is expressed in Eq. 2, where A represents one activity, T is the associated timestamp, n is the number of activities of the day, while d refers to the number of days in that deployment. After that, we construct an episode dataset by collecting all episodes during the whole deployment. By examining the dataset, we obtained 64 valid days for deployment 1 and 61 valid days for deployment 2. Days of deployment 1 are much less than the actual duration of the deployment (about 82 days). This is due to the fact that the feedback was not provided by the user in the last 18 days.

$$Episode_i =< A_1(T_1), A_2(T_2), ..., A_n(T_n) > \qquad i \in [1, d] \qquad (2)$$

Sequence: A sequence is formed by at least two successively performed activities. For instance, <Eating, WatchingTV> means the activity "Watching TV" happens directly after "Eating".

4.2   Apriori Algorithm

For the extraction of the temporal relations between activities, we apply the Apriori algorithm [1] which aims to discover frequent activity sequences based on what is called their support and confidence:

Support: In our case, support measures the frequency of an activity sequence appearing in the episodes dataset. It is computed as the number of episodes that contain this sequence, divided by the total number of episodes (Eq. 3). A frequent sequence can be defined as a sequence whose support is larger than a predefined threshold (minSupp).

$$Support(< A, B >) = \frac{\#episodesContaining < A, B >}{\#episodes} \qquad (3)$$

Confidence: It represents the dependency between two activities i.e. the probability that one activity occurs given that a certain previous activity has occurred.

Table 5. Examples of temporal activity patterns

A	Cooking	Eating	Making Coffee
B	Eating	WorkingAtPC	Eating
Supp. (%)	25.0	51.6	28.2
Conf. (%)	84.2	67.4	53.1

Hence, confidence for the sequence <A, B> is computed as the support of <A, B> divided by the support of A. The main principle of the Apriori algorithm is to scan the whole episodes dataset in order to find all frequent items (activities) and exclude those which are rarely performed. However, a rarely performed activity does not necessarily imply the nonexistence of a regular temporal activity pattern which involves this activity. An example from our dataset is the "Reading" activity. This activity has a support of 4.7% in deployment 1. However, if the user always sleeps after reading, then the sequence <Reading, Sleeping> can also be considered as a meaningful pattern due to its high confidence. As shown above, a threshold has to be specified which determines the minimum value the support of a sequence should have in order to be considered by the Apriori algorithm as a regular sequence. This threshold is called the minSupp. On one hand, a high minSupp value might cause the exclusion of meaningful patterns because it involves activities with low support value. On the other hand, a small minSupp value might cause the generation of a numerous number of meaningless patterns by the Apriori algorithm. In order to overcome this problem, we utilize the multiple minimum supports mechanism [14]. This mechanism assigns a $miniSupp_i$ to each item (A_i) by multiplying a user defined global miniSupp by the item's own support as shown in Eq. 4. By doing this, useful patterns regarding to the rarely performed activities will not be neglected during the process. Meanwhile, patterns regarding to one activity with support lower than the assigned minSupp will be filtered out. Therefore, we define the global_minsupp as 18%.

$$minSupp_i = global\_minsupp \times support(A_i) \qquad (4)$$

By applying Apriori algorithm, we obtained a list of temporal activity patterns for each deployment. Table 5 lists some of the extracted patterns from the first deployment where A denotes the previous activity and B denotes the current activity. As we can see from the table, the user usually starts with the eating activity directly after cooking with a confidence of 84.2%. After eating he often works at PC with a confidence of 67.4%. The activity after making coffee is also eating with a confidence of 53.1%. These examples show the existence of a certain routine in our daily life. In the following section, we use the extracted patterns in the activity detection process in order to see if it can help improving the accuracy of this process.

4.3 Utilizing Patterns in Activity Detection

In this step, we integrate the patterns extracted by Apriori algorithm as extra features in building the activity prediction model. The features we used for

Table 6. Activity detection accuracy with and without patterns (random forest)

	Deployment 1		Deployment 2	
	Accuracy	F-Measure	Accuracy	F-Measure
without	92.8%	92.7%	97.3%	97.3%
with	96.1%	96.1%	98.3%	98.3%

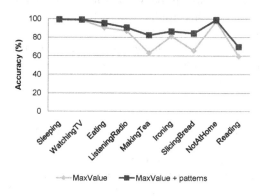

Fig. 2. Activity detection accuracy by classes, results of with and without patterns are compared

the activity detection process were the maximum sensor values (Plugwise and Pikkerton) in timeslots of two minutes. As extra features, we added the previous activity combined with the most likely current activity as it appears in the sequences extracted by Apriori algorithm. Hence, the new feature vector is a combination of all these features as shown in Eq. 5, where A_{n-1} and A_n represent the previous and the most probable current activity respectively. For labeling the instances, we use the user feedback denoted as $Class(slot_i)$.

$$
Instance_i = < S_{1\_max}(slot_i), S_{2\_max}(slot_i), ..., S_{n\_max}(slot_i),
$$
$$
A_{n-1}, A_n, Class(slot_i) > \qquad i \in [1, m] \tag{5}
$$

Table 6 shows the accuracy of the activity detection process for both deployments before and after adding the patterns extracted by Apriori algorithm. The used classification algorithm is random forest. The overall accuracy explicitly increases after adding the patterns. Furthermore and in order to obtain a more comprehensive representation of the classification accuracy for each individual activity, Figure 2 shows the results coming from deployment 2 using random forest. As we can see in Figure 2, the detection accuracy of each activity has also explicitly increased after adding the patterns. The reason for this improvement is that, besides the intrinsic features of the activities, namely the sensor readings, the machine learner will also learn the temporal relations between the activities from the patterns, thus recognize activities that occur in certain patterns more accurately.

5   Analysis of the Daily Power Consumption Traces

In this section we focus on the analysis of daily power consumption traces in our two deployments. The main goal is to understand the daily power consumption of individuals in smart homes and to find out based on time series analysis if the people follow a regular power consumption pattern which repeats itself over the days. The result of this analysis can be of great importance in many application scenarios: it can help developing applications which allow individuals living in smart homes to inspect their energy usage over the time leading to a more energy-aware power consumption behavior. Besides, it can be of great benefit to utility companies which by knowing the power consumption behavior of their customers can recommend a more suitable tariff and direct the smart grid to work more efficiently, thus to save energy.

5.1   Obtaining Hourly Power Consumption of Each Day

For the analysis to be conducted, we first need to compute the hourly power consumption of each day. We calculate the power consumption for each hour by summing up the power consumption within all timeslots of two minutes in that hour. However, since Plugwise values are stored in unit "Watt", we need to convert them into "Wh" (Watt hour) for acquiring the power consumption. To do this, we first compute the associated power consumption of each Plugwise sensor in each timeslot. This is achieved by averaging the readings of each sensor in that timeslot and dividing the average value by 30. We divided the average by 30 as we only need the power consumption in timeslots of two minutes. Then, for obtaining the total power consumption in each timeslot we sum all the converted values of the Plugwise sensors in that timeslot. The computation is indicated in Eq. 6, where j denotes the sensorId, i denotes the ith timeslot, $S_j(Slot_i)$ denotes the average value of sensor j during timeslot i, and n denotes the number of sensors. To compute the total power consumption in an hour, we sum up the power consumption in all timeslots within that hour as indicated in Eq. 7 where m denotes the number of timeslots, and h denotes the hour of the day.

$$P_{slot_i} = \frac{\sum_{j=1}^{n} S_j(Slot_i)}{30} \tag{6}$$

$$P_h = \sum_{i=1}^{m} P_{slot_i} \qquad h \in [1, 24] \tag{7}$$

To make the results more comprehensive, we plot the obtained hourly power consumption for each day. Figure 3 shows an example in which we see that the user consumes more energy from 01:00 pm to midnight than from 3:00 am to noon. When comparing this distribution to another one obtained from the same deployment as shown in Figure 4, we can easily observe the similarity between these two distributions. In both days, the user followed a similar power

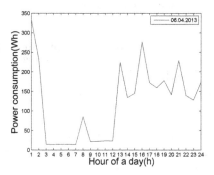

Fig. 3. Power consumption with regard to the hours of the day on 2013-04-06 from deployment 1

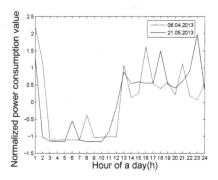

Fig. 4. Hourly power consumption distributions on 2013-04-06 and 2013-05-21 from deployment 1, consumption values are normalized

consumption pattern only shifted in time. The values in the figure are all normalized so that they have a mean of zero and a standard deviation of one for the purpose of comparison. Based on our observation from Figure 4, we conduct a similarity comparison process on all the distributions which belong to the same deployment. By verifying that all the distributions from the same deployment follow some level of similarity, we can prove the user to have a regular power consumption behavior which is the goal of this experiment as stated before. In the following section, we introduce the process of similarity comparison, the used algorithm, as well as the obtained results.

$$Similarity = \frac{1}{1 + warping\_score} \quad (8)$$

5.2 Similarity Comparison

Similarity comparison between two time series can be conducted using several algorithms. One of the these popular algorithms is the approach of symbolic

Table 7. Results of similarity comparison of power consumption distributions in each deployment

	Deployment 1	Deployment 2
Min_similarity	81.72%	88.13%
Max_similarity	97.13%	97.68%
Avg_similarity	90.32%	93.50%

representation [13] in which we convert each time series into a sequence of symbols and calculate the distance of these resulting sequences of symbols. The main disadvantage of this approach is that it does not take time shifting into consideration. Thus, it will not recognize two series like the ones shown in Figure 4 similar to each other only because they are shifted in time. In order to address this problem, we apply the Dynamic Time Warping (DTW) algorithm [10] which aims to find the best alignment between two time series. The result is represented by a warping path that indicates how each point of one distribution is aligned to the point of another distribution. Besides, it also produces a warping score to indicate the distance between two distributions after the alignment. In order to verify the similarity between each pair of distributions, we converted the warping score into a similarity measure based on Eq. 8 as clarified in [9]. The result after applying the DTW algorithm is a set of similarity values coming from the warping scores after comparing all the distributions. Table 7 summarizes the minimum, maximum as well as the average similarity obtained from both deployments. As shown in the table, the power consumption distributions in deployment 1 are at least 81.72% similar to each other while the minimum value in deployment 2 reaches a similarity value of 88.13%. The maximum values in both deployments exceed 97%. Moreover, daily power consumptions in deployment 1 are 90.32% similar to each other on average. The average value reaches 93.50% in deployment 2. As a result of this analysis we can conclude that the daily power consumption in both deployment follows a regular pattern which confirms the fact that the inhabitants in both deployments tend to consume power in a regular pattern which repeats itself everyday. Additionally, as similarity values from deployment 2 are higher than those from deployment 1, we can say that the user in deployment 2 tends to have a more regular power consumption behavior. In order to verify these results, we conducted a further analysis in the following section in which we examine abnormal power consumption values which occur very rarely in both deployments but might contradict with our conclusion in this section. By examining these values and showing that they are rare and untypical, we make our conclusion in this section more reliable.

5.3   Further Analysis

In order to filter out abnormal power consumption behavior, we extracted the minimum and maximum power consumption of each hour over the whole deployment. Using these values we formed an area as shown in Figure 5(a) where the

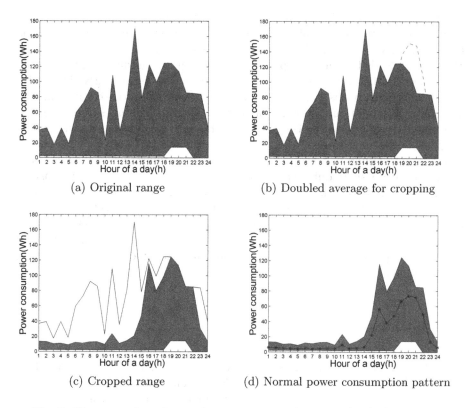

(a) Original range

(b) Doubled average for cropping

(c) Cropped range

(d) Normal power consumption pattern

Fig. 5. The generation of normal power consumption range for deployment 2

x axis represents the hour of the day, and the y axis represents the associated power consumption. By doing this, all power consumption values are ensured to be contained in this area. Figure 5(a) is generated from the values of deployment 2. As we can see from the figure, although the daily energy distributions were verified to follow similar trend, they fluctuate in a certain range. At some point in time, the fluctuation is especially large. For instance, value at 14:00 varies from 0 to 160Wh. In order to verify whether the peaks in Figure 5(a) are only outliers and do not represent the regular power consumption behavior, we defined an empirical threshold which is equal to the double of the average hourly power consumption. If the power consumption at a certain hour exceeds this threshold, this consumption is considered to be an outlier and thus should be excluded from the dataset. The threshold for cropping the area is indicated in the dashed line in Figure 5(b). Figure 5(c) is the cropped area which covers the majority of the power consumption values. As we can see from the figure, a part of the area was cropped out, especially the peaks. This verifies that the peaks are actually the abnormal power consumption values and do not reflect the regular consumption pattern. Figure 5(d) depicts the remaining area after cropping. The dotted line with the asterisks indicates the average value after removing the outliers. As shown in the figure, the power consumption keeps low from the beginning of the day to the midday. There are several reasons for this phenomenon. First of all, the user normally sleeps during some hours of this range which leads to almost no power consumption. Furthermore and according to the user feedback, the user in deployment 2 used to get up early. The activity after getting up was either eating or going out with both activities having low power consumption. Although the radio was used sometimes during eating, only small amount of energy is required for this activity. Another activity which happens in the morning is "Making Tea". Although this activity consumes a high amount of energy, it was only performed three times during the whole deployment with a short duration. This also explains why some outliers existing during this period. The higher power consumption in later hours is mainly due to the activity of "Watching TV". The extracted power consumption range can be of great benefit and importance in many application scenarios. One application scenario is security combined with energy conservation in which the user can be alerted if her/his real-time power consumption exceeds the normal power consumption area.

6   Conclusions

In this work we presented three experiments conducted on our SMARTEN-ERGY.KOM dataset. In the first task, we successfully built a classification model that is able to predict a user's current location based on his real-time power consumption. In the second experiment, we extracted the temporal relations between the activities performed in each deployment. Furthermore, we showed that these temporal patterns can be treated as features for improving the accuracy of our activity detection platform. In the third experiment, we studied the distributions of daily power consumption with regard to the hours of the day. By comparing the similarity of these distributions we showed that the user in each deployment has a regular power consumption behavior. Moreover, we extracted the normal power consumption pattern for each user which can be of great benefit in many application scenarios. Our solution is capable of determining the user's location, activity as well as common patterns. All this information is mainly mined from electricity consumption of common home appliances. Thus, our work is a strong foundation for energy consumption feedback systems and represents the next important step towards energy management systems without a human in the loop.

Acknowledgments. This work has been financially supported by the German Research Foundation (DFG) in the framework of the Excellence Initiative, Darmstadt Graduate School of Excellence Energy Science and Engineering (GSC 1070) and has been co-funded by the Social Link Project within the Loewe Program of Excellence in Research, Hessen, Germany.

References

1. Agrawal, R., Srikant, R., et al.: Fast algorithms for mining association rules (1994)
2. Alhamoud, A., Ruettiger, F., Reinhardt, A., Englert, F., Burgstahler, D., Bohnstedt, D., Gottron, C., Steinmetz, R.: Smartenergy.kom: An intelligent system for energy saving in smart home. In: 2014 IEEE 39th Conference on Local Computer Networks Workshops (LCN Workshops), pp. 685–692 (September 2014)
3. Allen, J.F., Ferguson, G.: Actions and events in interval temporal logic. Journal of Logic and Computation 4(5), 531–579 (1994)
4. Chen, C., Cook, D.J., Crandall, A.S.: The user side of sustainability: Modeling behavior and energy usage in the home. Pervasive and Mobile Computing 9(1), 161–175 (2013)
5. Englert, F., Schmitt, T., Koessler, S., Reinhardt, A., Steinmetz, R.: How to auto-configure your smart home?: High-resolution power measurements to the rescue. In: Proceedings of the Fourth International Conference on Future Energy Systems, e-Energy 2013, pp. 215–224. ACM, New York (2013)
6. Fogarty, J., Au, C., Hudson, S.E.: Sensing from the basement: a feasibility study of unobtrusive and low-cost home activity recognition. In: Proceedings of the 19th Annual ACM Symposium on User Interface Software and Technology, pp. 91–100. ACM (2006)
7. Hall, M., Frank, E., Holmes, G., Pfahringer, B., Reutemann, P., Witten, I.H.: The WEKA data mining software: an update. SIGKDD Explor. Newsl. 11(1), 10–18 (2009)
8. Hoque, E., Stankovic, J.: AALO: Activity recognition in smart homes using active learning in the presence of overlapped activities. In: 6th International Conference on Pervasive Computing Technologies for Healthcare (PervasiveHealth), pp. 139–146. IEEE (2012)
9. Johanyák, Z.C., Kovács, S.: Distance based similarity measures of fuzzy sets. In: Proceedings of SAMI (2005)
10. Keogh, E., Ratanamahatana, C.A.: Exact indexing of dynamic time warping. Knowledge and Information Systems 7(3), 358–386 (2005)
11. Kleiminger, W., Beckel, C., Staake, T., Santini, S.: Occupancy detection from electricity consumption data. In: Proceedings of the 5th ACM Workshop on Embedded Systems for Energy-Efficient Buildings, BuildSys 2013, pp. 10:1–10:8. ACM, New York (2013)
12. Kohavi, R., et al.: A study of cross-validation and bootstrap for accuracy estimation and model selection. IJCAI 14, 1137–1145 (1995)
13. Lin, J., Keogh, E., Lonardi, S., Chiu, B.: A symbolic representation of time series, with implications for streaming algorithms. In: Proceedings of the 8th ACM SIGMOD Workshop on Research Issues in Data Mining and Knowledge Discovery, pp. 2–11. ACM (2003)
14. Liu, B., Ma, Y., Wong, C.-K.: Classification using association rules: weaknesses and enhancements. In: Data Mining for Scientific and Engineering Applications, pp. 591–605. Springer, Heidelberg (2001)
15. Lymberopoulos, D., Bamis, A., Savvides, A.: Extracting spatiotemporal human activity patterns in assisted living using a home sensor network. Universal Access in the Information Society 10(2), 125–138 (2011)
16. Reinhardt, A., Baumann, P., Burgstahler, D., Hollick, M., Chonov, H., Werner, M., Steinmetz, R.: On the accuracy of appliance identification based on distributed load metering data. In: Sustainable Internet and ICT for Sustainability, pp. 1–9 (October 2012)

SocialSense: A Collaborative Mobile Platform for Speaker and Mood Identification

Mohsin Y. Ahmed, Sean Kenkeremath, and John Stankovic

University of Virginia, Computer Science Department
Charlottesville, Virginia, USA
{mya5dm,stk4zn,stankovic}@virginia.edu

Abstract. We present *SocialSense*, a collaborative smartphone based speaker and mood identification and reporting system that uses a user's voice to detect and log his/her speaking and mood episodes. SocialSense collaboratively works with other phones that are running the app present in the vicinity to periodically send/receive speaking and mood vectors to/from other users present in a social interaction setting, thus keeping track of the global speaking episodes of all users with their mood. In addition, it utilizes a novel event-adaptive dynamic classification scheme for speaker identification which updates the speaker classification model every time one or more users enter or leave the scenario, ensuring a most updated classifier based on user presence. Evaluation of using dynamic classifiers shows that SocialSense improves speaker identification accuracy by 30% compared to traditional static speaker identification systems, and a 10% to 43% performance boost under various noisy environments. SocialSense also improves the mood classification accuracy by 4% to 20% compared to the baseline approaches. Energy consumption experiments show that its device daily lifetime is between 10-14 hours.

Keywords: social interaction, assisted living, depression, smartphone.

1 Introduction

Speaker identification systems based on in-home/on-body/smartphone microphones are used for various applications such as voice based authentication, home health care, security, and daily activity monitoring. With the pervasive usage of smartphones in everyday life, it is an exceptionally suitable unobtrusive platform for speaker identification reducing the overhead of on-body or contextual sensors. Besides speaker identification, speaker mood detection is another important problem in human interaction studies and social psychology research. The challenges of smartphone based speaker identification and mood detection include preserving user privacy, maintaining identification accuracy, accurate operation of the system irrespective of smartphone location, resilience against ambient noise and operating under energy constraints.

Both speaker and mood identification are part of a bigger and important health sensing problem, detection of human social interaction, which is an important indicator of mental and physical health in people of all ages. Regular good social interaction

T. Abdelzaher et al. (Eds.): EWSN 2015, LNCS 8965, pp. 68–83, 2015.
© Springer International Publishing Switzerland 2015

brings many health benefits including reduced risk for cardiovascular and Alzheimer's disease, some cancers, osteoporosis and rheumatoid arthritis, steady blood pressure and reduced risk of depression and other mental disorders. On the other hand, social isolation culminates to loneliness and depression, physical inactivity and overall having a greater risk of death for older people. Therefore, a system able to detect people's social interactions and mood would be greatly beneficial for caregivers to more accurately diagnose and treat patients suffering from psychological disorders.

We present SocialSense, a collaborative smartphone based speaker and mood identification and reporting system which logs user speaking and mood episodes from his/her voice. A person can be uniquely identified by his smartphone Bluetooth ID. After SocialSense detects its user's speaking episode and mood, it broadcasts a message containing the user ID, the speaking episode timestamp, and corresponding mood to all neighboring phones via Bluetooth broadcasting. Thus every phone logs a global scenario of the social interaction environment. In a nutshell, SocialSense can answer the following questions:

- When is the phone user speaking?
- What is the mood of the user during speaking?
- With whom is the user speaking to? Who else are present around?
- When are the other persons in the environment speaking?
- What are the moods of other persons while they speak?

Besides detecting the smartphone user's mood, understanding the moods of other persons present in a social interaction is an important indicator of the global mood, hence the quality of the social interaction. Having this feature, SocialSense can potentially be used to demonstrate and verify the effect of mood contagion, i.e. how multiple individuals in a social interaction reach a mood convergence [1]. Using the idea of mood contagion, SocialSense can be used as a recommender system where it can recommend happy persons as potential conversation partners of sad persons to cheer them up. The actual use of SocialSense for mood contagion is outside the scope of this work.

Our prime target for the usage of SocialSense is in assisted living facilities for the elderly where the prevalence and magnitude of depression is of major concern. More than 1 million Americans reside in assisted livings presently. Studies found that, 20% to 24% of assisted living residents have symptoms of major or minor depression which is likely to cause physical, cognitive, and social impairment and delayed recovery from medical illness and surgery to these elderly. The scary fact is that, many depressive older adults end up committing suicide. Among men of age 75 and over, rate of suicide is 37.4 per 100,000 population. Several diagnostic barriers exist for the screening and treatment of depression in assisted livings which includes lack of regulatory requirements, privacy concerns, cost, and misinterpretation of depression. It is suggested that assisted living staff (nurse, therapist, medical director) should proactively assess for depressive syndromes instead of self-reporting of mood changes by the residents. SocialSense can be used as an automated diagnostic tool to monitor the mood and social interactions of the assisted living residents where each of the residents is provided with a smartphone with our system. [16]

Since SocialSense can capture the global scenario of a social interaction setting, it can be used as a data collection system for various social psychology and human interaction research. In addition, SocialSense incorporates a dynamic event-driven classification scheme for speaker identification. New people can enter into a social interaction while some people may leave at any time. SocialSense periodically refreshes its Bluetooth neighbor set and whenever it detects a change in the set, i.e., some people entered or left, it recreates the classification model based on the new neighbor set. For this purpose, it imports the user training feature files from the newly arrived phones to re-compute the classification model.

The main contributions of SocialSense are:

- An unobtrusive voice based speaker identification and mood detection system using user's smartphone. It does not use any on-body or contextual sensors thus contributing to mobility and user-friendliness.
- A practical, easy, and short training scheme to train a phone to detect a person's own speaking episodes. One key novelty of SocialSense is that it avoids the need of exhaustive training by all users in a social interaction setting and still accurately detects all speakers by collaboration among the phones.
- SocialSense has privacy support for users. No audio samples are recorded or stored in the phone and features are extracted in real time and after classification they are removed from the system. There is no way to reconstruct the original audio signal at a later time from SocialSense.
- SocialSense's voice based mood detection module in every phone is conventional, however by collaboration among the phones, it can detect the mood of the members of a conversation group and the change of one's mood when he/she switches between conversation groups, i.e., demonstrate mood contagion. This novel idea hasn't been explored before and such a system would be invaluable for further experiments on social mood dynamics. Also, using a random forest classifier for mood detection compared to GMM and SVM classifiers used in baseline systems [7, 8], our system has a 4% to 20% increase in accuracy compared to the baselines.
- SocialSense supports real life environments where new people enter and existing people leave the social interaction environment. SocialSense periodically refreshes its Bluetooth neighbor set to detect such changes in the environment.
- Another novel feature of SocialSense is its dynamic event-driven classification scheme where it performs speaker identification using an up-to-moment classifier based on the current users present in the scenario. This yields an average 30% increase in classification accuracy compared to static classification.
- Evaluation with respect to noisy environments has been performed by injecting various artificial noise to simulate real life noisy environments and results demonstrates that SocialSense improves speaker identification accuracy in noise by 10%-43% based on different types of noise and mood detection accuracy in noise by 33% compared to the state-of-the-art systems. SocialSense has been evaluated by training with noise to yield these performance boosts, which hasn't been done in baseline approaches.

2 Related Work

Many of the existing speaker identification systems require the total number of speakers to be static, and they employ static classification schemes so that each speaker needs to train the system beforehand, which makes them less realistic [2, 3]. Social-Weaver [4] uses a multi-level classification for speaker identification. The first level uses energy histogram classifiers while the second level uses a GMM based classifier. Neary [5] uses similarity of sound environment to detect conversational fields. These energy and loudness based approaches have greater error in noisy conditions and they fail if there is a person present in the scenario without his phone. SpeakerSense [6] is a speaker identification platform built on a heterogeneous multi-processor architecture. It attempts to reduce training overhead by training from real life events as phone calls and one-to-one conversations, but does not evaluate the system in noisy environments. Also, it requires the total number of speakers to be static and does not support realistic dynamic environments where speakers enter and leave on the fly.

There are a number of existing systems which detect user's mood from voice. EmotionSense [7] provides dual systems for speaker identification and emotion detection from user's voice using Gaussian mixture methods. [8] provides SVM based classifiers that recognize human emotional states from their utterances. However, these systems can only capture mood of a single person or entity and, therefore, are not suitable for social psychology experiments where a system would need to know moods of everyone in a social interaction. Also, there is no evidence that these systems would operate well under real life noisy environments.

Besides speaker identification and mood detection, there have been systems which detect other aspects of social interaction using different modalities. Some of the existing work on social interactions uses only on-body sensors such as accelerometers, gyroscopes, GPS, microphones, and cameras. Pierluigi et al. [9] built a badge having a triaxial accelerometer and a JPEG camera which is used to detect the presence of other people. Crowd++ [18] estimates the number of people talking in a certain place by unsupervised machine learning technique from smartphone audio inference. CenceMe [10] can automatically detect activities of individuals and share the sensing results through social networks.

Another type of work uses ambient sensors. [11] uses a sociometric badge equipped with infrared transmitter/receiver and microphone which senses and models human networks. In [12] four video cameras and audio collectors are placed in public areas such as the dining room, living room and hallway which can detect high-level social interactions among people such as greeting, standing conversation, and walking together.

We compare SocialSense with some state-of-the-art smartphone based sensing systems in table 1.

Table 1. Comparison of State-of-the-art

System	Operations	Classifiers used	Results
Emotion-Sense [7]	Speaker identification, mood detection	GMM	90% speaker ID accuracy, 70% mood detection accuracy
Speaker-Sense [6]	Speaker identification	GMM	95% speaker identification accuracy
Social Weaver [4]	Speaker identification, conversation group clustering	Loudness histogram, GMM	90% speaker ID accuracy, 70-90% accuracy for conversation clustering
Neary [5]	Detect conversational fields i.e detecting multiple persons who are in a conversation	No classifier	96.6% precision and 67.9% recall achieved in a controlled experiment
Qiang et al [13]	User activity, speaker ID, proximity, location	Naive Bayes, Discriminant, Boosted tree, Bagged tree	92% accurate speech detection
Social Sense	Speaker identification, mood detection, mood contagion sensing	Logistic regression, Random forest	94% speaker ID accuracy, 90% speaker ID accuracy in noise, 80% mood detection accuracy, 76% mood detection accuracy in noise

3   SocialSense System Design and Operation

The assumption behind SocialSense is that every user in a social interaction setting carries his/her own phone with the SocialSense app running in it. However, if one or more persons is present without his phone, only his speaking and mood episodes will remain undetected and unreported, while all other users' speaking and mood episodes will be detected and broadcasted without any error.

Figure 1 shows the system diagram. The SocialSense app runs continuously in each phone listening to audio streams. Silent frames are detected by comparing each frame's energy to a threshold, and filtered from further processing to save energy. Each phone periodically updates its phone-set within its Bluetooth proximity range (~10 m). It is required that the system meets the energy constrains of mobile devices in order to make it usable in realistic scenarios. SocialSense is capable of running for 10 to 14 hours continuously in smartphones and tablets which is good enough for its usage as a healthcare, research and data collection tool in assisted living. SocialSense is made up of a number of modules described in the following sections.

3.1   Phone-set Formation

A phone's phone-set is defined as the set of phones running the SocialSense app situated within the Bluetooth proximity range from that phone. This module running in every phone refreshes its phone-set periodically (generally every 30s) to keep the most recent neighboring phones in its phone-set. The periodic interval is set so that it is neither too short to trigger redundant phone-set discovery process nor too long to miss significant changes in the phone-set, considering realities of human social interaction. All members of a phone-set are assumed to be close enough to participate in a conversation. Conversely, phones not belonging to the phone set are assumed to be not participating in a conversation.

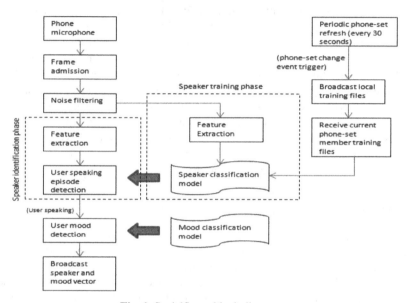

Fig. 1. SocialSense block diagram

3.2   Speaking Episode Detection Module

This module determines whether a voice segment belongs to the phone user or not. The speaker identification is a binary classification problem where every non-silent audio segment must be classified into one of two classes: "phone user's voice" or "anything else" (e.g. others' voice or ambient noise). It uses a dynamic logistic regression based classifier, which can be easily trained by the user (or support personnel in assisted living). The user trains the speaker classification system by speaking for 60 seconds in front of the phone in normal tone and loudness. This simple, easy-to-use and short self- training scheme allows the classifier being updated with the latest voice samples of the user. In assisted living facilities, this training will be done by the staff.

Some existing smartphone based speaker identification systems classify speakers based on the loudness of the perceived audio signal [4], [13]. The hypothesis behind those works is that, a user's voice is loudest in his own phone in a particular time instant compared to any other neighboring phones at the same time (as the user is supposed to be the closest person to his phone). However, this scheme doesn't work well in noisy environments, and also in the situation where a person without any phone is talking with people having their phones. In the latter case, when the person not having his phone is talking, his voice will be loudest to the person's phone who is closest to him, so that phone will incorrectly assume that the person without his phone is its user and classify positively, which is incorrect. Other systems like SpeakerSense [6] require training a speaker model for each individual who needs to be recognized, thus incurring large training overhead and resulting in complex, power-hungry classifiers.

SocialSense, on the other hand, uses a simple logistic regression based binary classifier with very little training overhead using 39 MFCC (mel-frequency cepstral coefficient) features. The phone-user (or staff) can train the system easily by speaking for 60 seconds in front of the phone in normal tone and volume to create a speaker classification model. As human voice may occasionally change depending on his physiological state, using this easy-to-use training scheme, the system can detect when its user is speaking irrespective of his voice quality, in the presence of noise and even when a person without his phone is present in the scenario as well. Unlike volume based systems, SocialSense does not fail when a user is present without his phone. Only his speaking and mood episodes remain undetected, but the systems in other users' phones work fine. The presence of a user without his phone does not incur any error or failure in the overall system operation.

3.3   Mood Detection Module

Detecting speaker mood in a mobile platform is a major challenge in this work. If a voice segment has been classified as a user's voice by the speaking episode detection module, this module further determines the user's mood (happy, sad, angry, neutral) from his voice. Then it generates a speaking and mood vector consisting of the starting and stopping timestamp of the user's speaking episode and mood during that speaking episode. This module extracts 39 MFCC coefficients from each user utterance window and calculates 9 different statistics on each MFCC coefficient culminating to 351 audio features. These statistics are: geometric mean, harmonic mean, arithmetic mean, range, skewness, standard deviation, z-scored average, moment and kurtosis. The MFCC coefficients combined with these statistics carry a large amount of prosodic and energy based information correlated to emotion. It then uses these features to train a random forest classifier from the EMA emotional utterance dataset [15] for detecting mood.

3.4   Message-Exchange Module

SocialSense forms a Bluetooth network among all members of a phone-set. When a phone has a speaking and mood vector to send, it broadcasts the vector using flooding over the network. It has an incoming thread and an outgoing thread to handle incoming and outgoing messages, respectively. It maintains a message queue, new vectors to be broadcasted are enqueued in the queue and the outgoing thread sends vectors one by one from the queue.

3.5 Dynamic Event-Driven Classification Module

For speaker identification, the logistic regression classifier uses a positive training file to keep training samples from the phone's user, and uses another negative training file to keep training samples from all other users. During startup of a conversation, SocialSense broadcasts its local positive training file to all neighbors which they use for their negative training. If there are 4 phones in the scenario, each phone uses its local file for positive training and 3 other files received from others for negative training. The phone-set discovery process triggers every 30 seconds to refresh the phone-set. If there is a change in the phone-set during a periodic phone-set refresh (an old user leaves or a new user enters), an event is triggered. When the event triggers, each phones broadcasts its positive training file over the network and updates its negative training using only the files received from phones present in the current scenario, and then rebuilds an updated classifier for speaker identification. This improves classification accuracy by 33% on average compared to static training and makes the training process for each user simple, which is shown in the evaluation section.

4 Evaluation

The evaluation consists of multiple parts. First, we evaluate how accurate SocialSense is in identifying speakers. Then we evaluate the effectiveness of mood identification. We have done these evaluations in quiet and noisy (artificially injected) environments, showing that training with noise in noisy environments yields good increase in performance. We have demonstrated the impact of window size, amount of training data, and dynamic classification for speaker identification. We also compare our results with some state-of-the-art solutions.

4.1 Speaker Identification Evaluation

We have evaluated the performance of SocialSense's speaker classification module in terms of the classification accuracy, which is the overall correctness of the model. The data for these evaluations are taken from voice segments collected from 7 persons. There were 4 females and 3 males among them. A 1.5 hour long conversation on various random topics between two of these females was recorded by us. Another 6 conversations, each around 5 minutes in length, between a male and a female, were collected from the internet. We collected 3 solo speech recordings from the remaining 3 persons for 10 minutes each. We extracted individual voice recordings from each of these 7 speakers separately from these recorded conversations and simulated 2, 3, 4 and 5 person conversations from these. We performed all the speaker identification experiments from these simulated conversations. For example, for simulating 3 person conversations, we trained the logistic regression classifier with one person as positively trained, and the other two persons as negatively trained, with all 3 combinations of three persons, and all 35 possible selections of 3 persons from a set of 7 persons.

Training Size. Intuitively speaker identification accuracy increases with the increase of training data, as the classifier can encode more information with a longer training. This phenomenon is shown in figure 2. The training and testing data were taken from voice samples collected from 7 persons, with 2, 3, 4 and 5 person simulated conversations. The accuracy for 3 separate window sizes is shown for training up to 180 seconds.

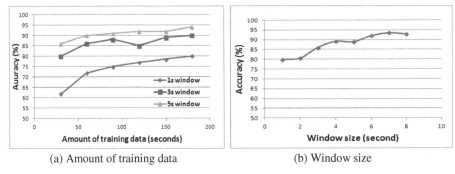

(a) Amount of training data   (b) Window size

Fig. 2. Speaker identification accuracy vs. (a) Amount of training data; (b) Window size

As we can see from figure 2(a), there is a sharp increase in accuracy between 30s and 60s of training, and beyond that the accuracy increases slowly. Also the accuracy is highest for a 5s window size. These values are the lower bounds on the training data needed to accurately identify the speaker on the phones, i.e. a minimum of 60 seconds of training is required with a minimum of a 5 second window size.

Window Size. This test was conducted on 2 person conversations. One person was trained as positive while the other was trained as negative for 60 seconds. The window size was varied from 1 to 8 seconds and each window was classified using the logistic regression classifier.

Results from figure 2(a) and 2(b) suggest that, a window size between 5 to 7 seconds is optimal for speaker identification. 3-4 second long window sizes yield accuracy of 86-89% which is acceptable. 5-7 second long window sizes can be used for warm conversations where each speaker talks for a long time before switching turns, while a 3-4 second window can be used for cold conversations with frequent turn-takings with short speaking duration in each turn.

Effect of Noise. Noise is a very important and realistic issue to consider to evaluate a smartphone based speaker identification system. It is very likely that users will move with their phones to different places (both indoor and outdoor) engaging in social interactions. Therefore, the system must be able to correctly identify its speaker under various types of noise.

Evaluation has been done to test the effect of artificial noise on speaker recognition accuracy. These tests were also done using 2 person conversations collected from 7 speakers. We used Audacity [14], an open-source sound editing software to inject artificial white and Brown noise into voice samples, and observed classification accuracy under different levels of noise. White noise is quite similar to television static or the humming of an air conditioner and Brown noise is similar to gusty wind. Therefore, these artificial noises can simulate real indoor and outdoor noisy environments.

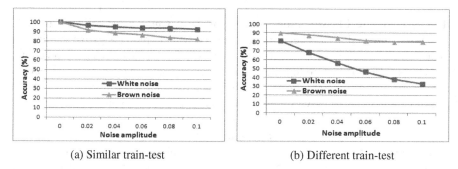

| (a) Similar train-test | (b) Different train-test |

Fig. 3. Effect of noise on speaker recognition accuracy, (a) With similar train-test set; (b) With different train-test

Figure 3(a) shows the effect of white and Brown noise on SocialSense speaker recognition accuracy with similar train test set. During no noise, the accuracy is best at 100%, while during maximum noise, the accuracy degrades to 82%, which is an 18% drop. However, because the train and test sets are similar in this case, this is not a realistic scenario. Figure 3(b) shows the effect of noise under different train-test sets. Here, the best accuracy during no noise is 90.2% and the worst accuracy is only 33%, which is a shocking 57% drop, and demonstrates how the system will fail in presence of noise, if no measure is taken.

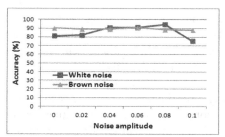

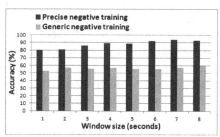

Fig. 4. Effect of noise on speaker recognition accuracy, with training in noise

Fig. 5. Effect of dynamic training vs. generic training

It is a design characteristic of SocialSense that a phone user can have his own phone trained for detecting his speaking episodes. This adds a lot of flexibility to the system. In noisy environments, the user can have his phone trained in noise to enhance speaker identification accuracy. Because of the short training session and each user needing to train only himself (as opposed to other systems where all user need to train every phone), the training overhead is low.

Figure 4 shows the effect of noise when the training is done in noise as well. It shows that even in worst noisy conditions the accuracy drops to 76% for white noise and 89% for Brown noise, which is a 43% performance boost for white noise and 10% boost for Brown noise. We have limited the noise amplitude to 0.1 in these experiments as this level is commensurate to real life extremely noisy environments.

Effect of Dynamic Classification. Because of the dynamic event-driven classification scheme in SocialSense, every phone is trained with a precise negative training set comprised of the voices of all other persons present in the social interaction setting. The phones update their training files by message exchange whenever a new person enters or leaves the Bluetooth range. Without the dynamic classification, every phone had to use a generic negative training comprising of generic voices from arbitrary persons, since no apriori knowledge of the users is available.

We used voice samples from 5 persons for precise training, with 1 trained as positive and other 4 trained as negative. The testing samples had voices from all 5 persons. For generic training, we used a separate voice collection from 3 people (The EMA dataset [15]) for negative training, and used the same test set as precise training.

The performance comparison of precise and generic training is shown in figure 5, which shows a significant classification improvement (30% on average) due to dynamic training. Consequently, this novel aspect of our solution results in a major performance improvement.

Worst Case Analysis of Dynamic Speaker Classification. The phone-set refresh process triggers once in every 30 seconds. If there is a change in the phone-set immediately after a refresh process, all the phones will stay with outdated classifiers for 30 seconds in the worst case. There are 2 cases to consider: i) some new phones arriving, ii) some existing phones leaving. In the first case, if some new phones arrive right after the refresh process, they will remain unknown to the existing phones for 30 seconds until the next refresh process. In this time, the newly arrived phones cannot send or receive any vectors, so their social interactions will not be logged. Also, during this time, the newly arrived phones will have a blank negative set, so all persons' speaking episodes will be considered as positive in these phones. To avoid classification errors due to the initialization in the newly arrived phones, voice segments during this initialization window are ignored. The second case, where some existing phones leave right after the refresh process, is less complicated than the first case. In this case, all the remaining phones will stay with redundant negative sets, containing trainings from people who doesn't exist anymore. But, there will be no classification error in these phones unlike the first case. For both cases, situation comes back to normal in at most 30 seconds, after the immediate next phone-set refresh.

4.2   Mood Detection Evaluation

Because of the difficulty associated to get real life data for mood evaluation, we performed both training and testing from the Electromagnetic Articulography dataset [15], which contains 680 acted utterances of a number of sentences in 4 different emotions (anger, happiness, sadness and neutrality) by 3 speakers. We used 3 different classifiers to model each mood using MFCC features with 9 statistics (total 351 features), naive Bayes, random forest, and decision tree. We also varied the acoustic window size from 1 to 10 seconds.

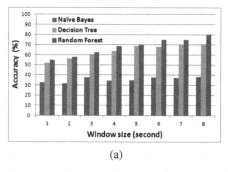

| Real | Classified as | | | |
mood	Angry	Happy	Neutral	Sad
Angry	144	19	1	2
Happy	32	110	4	18
Neutral	4	11	125	16
Sad	1	4	23	154

(a)   (b)

Fig. 6. (a) Effect of audio sample length on emotion recognition accuracy with various classifiers; (b) Confusion matrix for emotion recognition with random forest classifier

The random forest classifier yielded best cross classification results for 10 folds, as shown in figure 6(a). This classifier resulted in a 4% to 10% increase in accuracy compared to the baseline EmotionSense [7] with varying window size, and a 20% increase for speaker independent model compared to [8]. The results for the baselines are taken from corresponding existing works. The figure demonstrates that mood classification accuracy increases with increasing window sizes, however beyond 6s window size it becomes stable and doesn't change much. The confusion matrix for the random forest classifier is shown in figure 6(b).

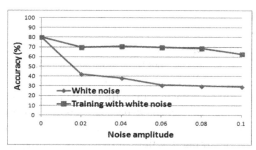

Fig. 7. Effect of noise and improvement with training with noise for mood classification

Similar to the speaker identification module, we evaluated the performance of mood detection module under noise. The effect of white noise has been noticed as to be more detrimental than brown noise, so we have done this experiment for white noise only. We injected white noise with amplitudes varying from 0.02 up to 0.1 into the mood dataset. We trained with mood utterances without noise and tested with utterances in noise.

As expected, the performance dropped drastically, as shown in figure 7. However, similar to the speaker identification module, we trained the mood dataset in noise and performed a 10 fold cross validation, which yielded a 33% performance boost in the worst 0.1 noise amplitude, as shown in figure 7. The existing mood detection systems hasn't evaluated the possibility of training with noise, which in our case, yielded a significant increase in performance.

4.3   Energy

SocialSense consumes energy in two ways: (i) idle listening, and (ii) once a speech episode is identified, it runs various modules and classifiers. Experiments were run to determine the lifetime of tablets and smartphones running SocialSense. The least energy cost for SocialSense is if it is idle listening and there are no speech episodes to process. Our experiments showed that Nexus 7 tablet ran for 14 hours and the HTC one smartphone ran for 12 hours for this *best* situation. When SocialSense is actively processing speech episodes there are 5 modules in the system which consume the majority of energy: i) acoustic processing and feature extraction, ii) logistic regression speaker identification classifier, iii) random forest mood detection classifier, iv) speech and mood vector transmit/receive, and v) periodic phone-set refresh, training file exchange and classification model file recreation. In a second set of experiments we modified the system to run all these modules continuously as if there was continuous speech. This is the worst case in regards to energy costs. In these experiments the Nexus 7 tablet ran for 12 hours (down from 14 hours) and HTC one smartphone ran for 10 hours (down from 12 hours). Consequently, SocialSense can operate between 12-14 hours on a tablet, and between 10-12 hours on a smartphone. This demonstrates that SocialSense can indeed be used as a healthcare device in assisted living since such devices can be charged over night.

5   Discussion

SocialSense detects speaking episodes and the mood of a user, and by collaboration it imports the speaking episodes and moods of the neighboring users as well. A user interface can be built upon this fine grained information showing the social interaction history of a user within a particular time-frame. Such a user interface will be able to display a user's common conversation partners, his amount of participation and engagement during a conversation with a particular partner, his mood during a conversation and hence mood during that time of that particular day, change of his mood with time or change of conversation partner and so on. Many of these quantities are of interest to psychologists when they treat a potentially depressive patient, and hence ask him relevant questions. The patients' answers are often vague, confusing and erroneous because most of the time they do not remember their social interaction history and mood for a very long time. SocialSense can eliminate the need for these oral questionnaires and hence avoid all the errors as it logs the social interaction data of a user with his moods. Therefore, this system can be used in places like an assisted living facility where depression and related psychological disorders are common among the occupants.

Robustness. As we argue that SocialSense is usable among the elderly in assisted living facilities, we are aware of the fact that the elderly are prone to forgetfulness, and it is very likely that they may sometimes forget to carry their phones during a social interaction. Though SocialSense is most accurate if every person carries his smartphone in order to detect everybody's speaking episodes and moods, the system does not break down if such assumption is violated. If a person does not carry his phone during a social interaction, his own speaking and mood episodes will remain undetected and unreported and others will not have his information for complete mood contagion. All the other persons' speaking and mood episodes will be detected and reported correctly. This is a major system design enhancement compared to volume based systems [4, 13] which fail when one or more persons forget to carry their phones. It is also important to note that overall diagnosis involves many conversations over multiple days and some missing information when smartphones are forgotten or turned off does not necessarily cause problems.

Training in Assisted Livings. SocialSense's easy to use individual training scheme and adaptability to noisy environments is very suitable for its usage in assisted living. We have shown in the evaluation section that it only takes 60 seconds of training for the system to work in any particular environment. Assisted living residents generally pass specific time of their days in specific locations (e.g., mornings in the hall room, noon at lunch room, afternoon in the garden). The assisted living support person can train the smartphone for each of these common environments. If a resident moves to a new location where the system needs to be retrained because of different noise levels, the support person can do the training very easily with 60 seconds of data.

Mood Contagion. Using SocialSense it is possible to detect not only the mood of an individual user, but also the moods of others present in the social interaction setting. According to the best of our knowledge, no such system has been built yet which can detect such a global mood. Thus, SocialSense can be used as a platform to verify and conduct experiments on *mood contagion* which is a psychological process by which a group of people engaged in a social interaction reaches emotional convergence, i.e. they all have similar feelings after a certain time though their initial feelings may be different. It is hypothesized that interventions based on knowledge of mood contagion can be used to help treat depression in the elderly.

"In-Phone" vs. "In-Cloud" Scheme. We adopted an "in-phone" processing scheme as opposed to "in-cloud" processing as in [17]. The term "in-phone" means that all data acquisition, feature extraction, and classification are performed in the phone itself. A reasonable alternative to or solution is an "in-cloud" solution, where unprocessed raw data (conversation recordings) or semi-processed data (features) are sent to a central server where a web service performs further processing and classification. However, the "in-cloud" approach requires connectivity to the internet by wi-fi or 3G which is not always available or is sometimes unreliable. To handle the unreliability of connections various buffering and upload schemes have to be developed. A high-speed 3G/4G connection also imposes additional operating cost for each phone. The "in-phone" approach is cheaper and better supports mobility and could be used even when residents are away from the assisted living facilities.

Concurrent Speaking Episodes. In our experiments described above, we assumed that users did not speak concurrently. In reality, speakers do speak concurrently on some occasions. So we also evaluated our system to test how it performs when users speak concurrently. Ideally, when two or more users are speaking concurrently, each of their systems should detect their own speaking episodes and log them as "speaking" in their individual phones. We performed experiments with 4 speakers (2 male, 2 female), with two concurrent speakers at a time for all 6 possible pairs of conversations. As expected, the system performance degraded. On average, SocialSense was 55% accurate in detecting a particular user's speaking episode when 2 concurrent users were speaking. While this sounds low, this result only applies to the portion of the speaking episode when there is actual concurrency, e.g., when two people first both start speaking (but then one usually backs off) or when someone interrupts a speaker.

6   Conclusion

This paper presents the design, implementation, and evaluation of SocialSense which is a collaborative mobile platform for speaker identification and mood and mood contagion detection from users' voice. Aside from its ability to recognize speaker and mood with significant accuracy, we have demonstrated its performance relative to the amount of training data and length of window size, culminating in an optimal benchmarking of these parameters. We provide empirical evidence that SocialSense performs well under various noisy environments when trained with noise, with an easy-to-use training scheme. Also, with a dynamic classification scheme, SocialSense is 30% more accurate in speaker identification compared to generic training with static classification. SocialSense is 4%-20% more accurate in speaker independent mood sensing compared to the baseline state-of-the-art mood sensing systems. It was also shown that SocialSense lifetime on various devices is between 10 to 14 hours.

Acknowledgments. This work was supported, in part, by NSF Grants CNS-1319302 and CNS-1239483, and a gift from PARC, Palo Alto. We cordially thank the reviewers for their insightful comments and suggestions.

References

1. Neumann, R., Strack, F.: Mood Contagion: The automatic transfer of mood between persons. Journal of Personality and Social Psychology 79(2), 211–223 (2000)
2. Reynolds, D.A.: Speaker identification and verification using gaussian mixture speaker models. Speech Communication 17(1-2), 91–108 (1995)
3. Reynolds, D.A., Rose, R.C.: Robust text-independent speaker identification using gaussian mixture speaker models. Transactions on Speech and Audio Processing 3(1), 72–83 (1995)
4. Luo, C., Chan, M.C.: SocialWeaver: collaborative inference of human conversation networks using smartphones. In: 11th ACM Conference on Embedded Networked Sensor Systems (SenSys), Roma, Italy (2013)
5. Nakakura, T., Sumi, Y., Nishida, T.: Neary: conversation field detection based on similarity of auditory situation. In: 10th Workshop on Mobile Computing Systems and Applications (HotMobile), Santa Cruz, California, USA (2009)
6. Lu, H., Brush, B., Priyantha, B., Karlson, A.K., Liu, J.: SpeakerSense: Energy efficient unobtrusive speaker identification on mobile phones. In: IEEE Pervasive Computing and Communication (PerCom), Seattle, Washington, USA (2011)
7. Rachuri, K., Musolesi, M., Mascolo, C., Rentfrow, P.J., Longworth, C., Aucinas, A.: EmotionSense: A mobile phone based adaptive platform for experimental social psychology research. In: ACM International Joint Conference on Pervasive and Ubiquitous Computing (UbiComp), Copenhagen, Denmark (2010)
8. Yu, C., Aoki, P.M., Woodruff, A.: Detecting user engagement in everyday conversations. In: 8th International Conference on Spoken Language Processing, South Korea (2004)
9. Casale, P., Pujol, O., Radeva, P.: Face-to-face social activity detection using data collected with a wearable device. In: 4th Iberian Conference on Pattern Recognition, Portugal (2009)
10. Miluzzo, E., Lane, N.D., Fodor, K., Peterson, R., Lu, H., Musolesi, M., Eisenman, S.B., Zheng, X., Campbell, A.T.: Sensing meets mobile social networks: the design, implementation and evaluation of the CenceMe application. In: 6th ACM Conference on Embedded Networked Sensor Systems (SenSys), Raleigh, North Carolina, USA (2008)
11. Choudhury, T.: Sensing and modeling human networks. Ph.D. Thesis, Program in Media Arts and Sciences, Massachusetts Institute of Technology (2004)
12. Chen, D., Yang, J., Malkin, R., Wactlar, H.D.: Detecting social interactions of the elderly in a nursing home environment. ACM Transactions on Multimedia Computing, Communications and Applications 3(1), 1–22 (2007)
13. Li, Q., Chen, S., Stankovic, J.A.: Multi-modal in-person interaction monitoring using smartphone and on-body sensors. In: IEEE International Conference on Body Sensor Networks, Cambridge, MA, USA (2013)
14. Audacity, http://audacity.sourceforge.net/
15. Kim, J., Lee, S., Narayan, S.S.: An exploratory study of manifolds of emotional speech. In: Acoustics Speech and Signal Processing, Dallas, TX, USA (2010)
16. Stefanacci, R.G.: How big an issue is depression in assisted living? Assisted Living Consult 4(4), 30–35 (2008)
17. Miluzzo, E., Cornelius, C.T., Ramaswamy, A., Choudhury, T., Liu, Z., Campbell, A.T.: Darwin phones: the evolution of sensing and inference on mobile phones. In: 8th International Conference on Mobile Systems, Applications, and Services (MobiSys), San Francisco, California, USA (2010)
18. Xu, C., et al.: Crowd++: unsupervised speaker count with smartphones. In: ACM International Joint Conference on Pervasive and Ubiquitous Computing, Zurich, Switzerland (2013)

Discovering Latent Semantic Structure
in Human Mobility Traces

Budhaditya Deb[1] and Prithwish Basu[2],[*]

[1] Microsoft New England R&D Center, Cambridge, MA
budeb@microsoft.com
[2] Raytheon-BBN Technologies, Cambridge, MA
pbasu@bbn.com

Abstract. Human mobility is a complex pattern of movements and activities that are based on some underlying semantics of human behavior. In order to construct accurate models of human mobility, this semantic behavior needs to be unearthed from the data sensed as a human being moves around and visits certain classes of locations such as *home, work, mall, theater, restaurant* etc. The ideal data for understanding the semantics of mobility would constitute timestamped mobility traces with detailed geographic locations with annotations about the type of each location. One way of achieving this is by following a hybrid strategy of participatory sensing (with each person carrying a wireless sensor device) and deploying static sensors at each location of interest – the contacts between the mobile and (annotated) static sensors can be logged at each location, and then collated to form an appropriate mobility traces. For example, a person can connect with his mobile phone over Bluetooth or WiFi to a local hotspot while checking into FourSquare at a restaurant. In the absence of static sensors, a person may manually annotate the places he visits on his device over time. However, most mobility traces consist of network connectivity data from cell phones (e.g., contact with towers) which lack detailed geographic locations and are ambiguous, noisy and unlabeled. Thus, it is important to extract the semantics of mobility that is *latent* in the available contact traces. To this end, we propose in this paper the concept of Probabilistic Latent Semantic Trajectories (PLST), an unsupervised approach to extract semantically different locations and sequential patterns of mobility from such traces. PLST extracts semantic locations as contextually co-occurring network elements (cell towers and Bluetooth devices) and models the behavior of their sequence. PLST extracts distinct locations with spatial, temporal and semantic coherency and can be used for accurate prediction of the next place a user visits. PLST also analyzes the complexity of mobility traces using information theoretic metrics to study the underlying structure and semantic content in mobility traces. This semantic content can be extracted allowing us to investigate mobility patterns in a completely unsupervised manner.

[*] Research was sponsored by the Army Research Laboratory and was accomplished under Cooperative Agreement Number W911NF-09-2-0053. The views and conclusions in this document are those of the authors and should not be interpreted as representing the official policies, either expressed or implied, of the Army Research Laboratory or the U.S. Government. The U.S. Government is authorized to reproduce and distribute reprints for Government purposes notwithstanding any copyright notation here on. Deb was at BBN when this research was done.

T. Abdelzaher et al. (Eds.): EWSN 2015, LNCS 8965, pp. 84–103, 2015.
© Springer International Publishing Switzerland 2015

1 Introduction

Knowledge of human mobility patterns is crucial for geographic and social surveys of populations, urban planning, commercial aspects of targeted recommendations, content based opportunistic networking and tracking of people under surveillance for security purposes. A person's mobility consists of complex patterns of locations, situations and activities. This can mean visitation to different geographic locations but may also be different activities characterized by the presence of other people and environmental context, sometimes all in the same geographical location. Thus, to model human mobility, we need not only to extract the spatio-temporal patterns but also to understand the deeper semantic behavior within these patterns. Proliferation of smart phones, hand held GPS devices, sociometric badges and ever increasing use of location based social networking (LBSN) services can potentially provide the multi-modal data needed for such modeling. However, most mobility traces lack detailed information due resource limitations and privacy concerns. GPS tracking is frequently turned off in many applications and users may not enrich the traces with semantic annotations. Geo-tagged LBSN check-ins contain rich semantic information about location and activity but are usually too sparse for fine-grained analysis.

In the absence of the above, network connectivity data of cell towers, bluetooth encounters, and WiFi access points are frequently used as approximate sensors of location to understand spatiotemporal behavior and social interactions within a community [20,23,24,30]. Since these features are typically needed for normal operation of mobile devices, they can be recorded with little additional resources. In this paper, we make a realistic assumption of the availability of anonymized cell tower and bluetooth connectivity data as mobility traces, with geographic information removed. Cell towers are inherently ambiguous indicators of geographic locations due to their long range. Bluetooth devices have a short range but cannot be used as geographical landmarks since most bluetooth devices are mobile. They are better viewed as contextual information of environment or social interactions of a user. The data is also noisy since the indices exhibit frequent fluctuations due to load balancing of cell towers or temporal fading of signal, the user is out of range of cell towers, or the bluetooth devices are absent. In spite of these disadvantages we show that co-appearing indices contain sufficient geographical and contextual information to extract rich semantic structure of user mobility.

Our intuition is based on the following hypotheses. First, while individually the indices are ambiguous, collectively they are more informative about the location. Second, different sets of indices signify semantically different activities and situations, i.e., indices are contextual markers rather than geographical features. For example, an office and a conference room inside a building may be in the range of the same set of cell towers but have different sets of bluetooth devices. A large number of cell towers may signify a transit situation while a temporary absence can indicate an underground tunnel, i.e., even the absence of indices is informative. Third, by considering long sequences and enforcing a syntactic structure we can further reduce the effects of noise and ambiguity associated with the indices.

To this end, we introduce the notion of *Probabilistic Latent Semantic Trajectories*. PLST is an unsupervised approach to extract semantically different locations and sequential patterns of mobility while accounting for the ambiguity and noise in observations.

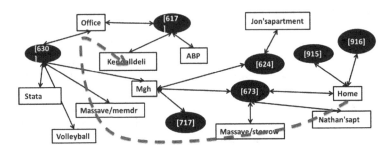

Fig. 1. PLST from ambiguous observations. Cell indices (circles) and semantic locations (rectangles) exhibit many-to-many relationship. Each cell covers multiple locations (Polysemy), e.g. [630] to Office, Mgh, Volleyball etc. Multiple cells can be associated with a single location (Synonymy) e.g. [673],[915] and [916] to 'Home'. Dotted line shows a potential semantic trajectory (home, transit, office, deli) which we intend to extract for a user from the ambiguous observations.

Figure 1 illustrates the concept of PLST. PLST models the semantic locations a user visits as a mixture density of latent variables (or abstract states). We find these *Latent Semantic Locations* (i.e., assign labels to observations) using a statistical Model Based Clustering (MBC) approach. To extract the *Latent Semantic Trajectory*, we extend the MBC to a Hidden Markov Model (HMM) and propose Maximum Likelihood and Bayesian approaches to predict the next observations. Finally we characterize the *Predictability* of user mobility through information theoretic measures of the latent structure.

We evaluate the PLST concept through the popular Reality Mining data set (RM, [8]). The semantic locations and index associations extracted using PLST show surprising levels of temporal, spatial and semantic coherency. PLST's structured approach to next place prediction shows superior performance when compared to two state-of-the-art prediction algorithms for unstructured sequences. The high degree of correlation between predictability and prediction rates validates our hypothesis that mobility sequences (even with ambiguous geographical information) not only contain rich semantic information but also that PLST is able to capture this deeper semantic behavior in user mobility.

2   Related Work

Comparison to Text Analysis: The PLST concept is similar to latent topic analysis for unlabeled text [1,15,16]. The indices define the vocabulary of a mobility document while location ambiguity is similar to the notions of *Polysemy* and *Synonymy* of word meanings. However, mobility data is characteristically different from text documents which makes this study novel. For text, terms in a *large* documents are assumed to be generated from a mixture of latent topics (or a *bag-of-words*). In contrast, PLST models mobility as a sequence of *short* documents, each generated from a single latent state to correspond to unique locations and driven by the sequence structure of states. Another distinction is that the Bernoulli distribution is shown to be more suited for mobility compared to the multinomial model typically used in text. Models with syntactic structure for text [14] are not directly applicable for next place prediction.

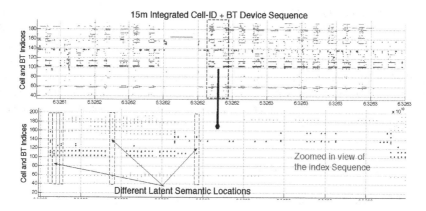

Fig. 2. (Top): Part of an observation sequence $I_{n,m}$ of Cell (blue) and Bluetooth (red) indices. (Bottom): Sequence is zoomed in to show the columns of the observation matrix. Each column indicates the cells and bluetooth indices appearing in a 15 min interval denoting a single semantic location.

Topic Models for Mobility: Topic models motivated from text analysis are mostly used for characterizing ensemble behavior of mobility rather than fine grained location extraction and prediction. Examples include clustering similar users or typical days (using RealityMining data) [7,10,25], and semantic enrichment of mobility flows (using Bike Sharing data) [5]. We note that while it is trivial to do ensemble analysis in PLST (by aggregating the topic distributions) fine-grained location extraction and prediction is not possible with topic based models.

Sequential Models: Sequential models have been used on GPS traces for example, order-2 Markov Models in [11,29], n-gram Markov model in [3], HMM in [12] and Dynamic Bayesian Network (DBN) in [31] (anonymized GPS traces) The original RM paper [8] also used an HMM to annotate the mobility sequences but considered only four broad categories of places namely home, office, no-signal and elsewhere as latent states. These approaches are insufficient for extracting fine-grained latent structure or rely on detailed GPS traces.

Semantic Trajectories: Semantic trajectories can be extracted if GPS traces have rich annotations to infer user activities [21], [33]. When annotations are absent traces can be enriched semantically using GPS locations and services such as google places [32]. A slightly different approach has been to segment GPS traces as a sequence of atomic actions (e.g. stops, move, begin, end, stay-points) to describe a higher level user behavior as events or episodes. This has been surveyed quite extensively in [26]. These approaches are applicable only in supervised settings with detailed annotations.

Next Place Prediction: A number of prediction approaches involving DBN [31], Decision Trees [19],[33], Support Vector Machines [17], Conditional Random Fields [21] etc. have been studied in supervised settings with labeled data sets. We compare PLST to two high performing approaches [11,17] from the Nokia Data Challenge [18].

Entropy and Predictability: [2,13,28] consider the entropy of unstructured sequences to characterize predictability of sequences. In this paper we look at predictability through the latent semantic structure which provides a better understanding of the true complexity of the sequences.

To the best of our knowledge PLST is the first framework for latent semantic analysis of unlabeled mobility traces which allows the extraction of individual locations visited by users and and their sequence patterns at a level of detail adequate for accurate next place prediction and investigation of the user trajectories.

3   Overview and Preliminaries

The PLST concept is illustrated on the Reality Mining data set (RM, [8]). The RM data set consists of Nokia 6600 smartphone traces of 106 students, staff and faculty in the MIT Media Labs, and Sloan School of Business. The traces record cell tower IDs, MAC addresses of Bluetooth encounters, call records and a variety of data specified by users. In this paper we only consider the cell towers and bluetooth encounters to model mobility. User traces also contain semantic names of cell towers (e.g. home, office, road location) and time stamps which are not used for modeling the user mobility. However they provide useful information to qualitatively evaluate the relevancy of models.

We first define the observation matrix from the user trace which will be the input for modeling the user trajectory as follows:

User Observation Matrix: We first convert the physical addresses of cells and bluetooth devices to unique indices. Next, we divide the raw sequence of indices into 15 minute patches. 15 minutes was a reasonable segmentation period for unique locations and long enough to smooth out the large number of aperiodic short lived entries in the traces. Each unit of observation, X_n is defined by an $M \times 1$ binary indicator vector $I_{n,m}$ and a frequency vector $f_{n,m}$ where M is the total number indices. The vectors contain the list of indices appearing in the 15 min segment. For N 15-minute periods we have an $M \times N$ observation matrix where each column denotes a semantic location. Figure 2 shows a section of the observation sequence for a certain user.

Next we define PLST based on the following concepts:

Semantic Location: User location defined according to higher level semantic activity or situation, for example *home*, *office*, *restaurant*, *gym* etc., each of which is distinguished not only by their geographic location but also by some underlying activity.

Latent Semantic Location: Since we assume that user traces do not contain semantic annotations, we assign each observation to some *latent class* or abstract state which are semantically distinct. Although we cannot retrieve the actual semantic activity (hence it is a latent or a hidden class), we can infer the semantic differences in the latent classes by observing the temporal distributions and index labels associated with different classes.

Latent Semantic Trajectory: A sequence of latent semantic classes assigned to a user trace. While two users may visit the same set of semantic locations (such as home, office, gym), they may do it in a different order. Thus the semantic trajectory defines the syntactic differences in user mobility.

PLST is a probabilistic model that aims to model the above from indices which are not only ambiguous (many-to-many relationship as illustrated in Figure 1) but also noisy. More specifically, it associates observations to latent classes by solving the following problems:

1. *Index disambiguation*: associate indices (cells and bluetooth devices) to latent classes and cluster/distinguish semantically related/different indices.
2. *Location disambiguation*: associate observations (co-occuring indices in a 15-minute period) to latent classes.
3. *Latent syntactic structure*: learn the sequential patterns of mobility through transitions among latent classes.
4. *Next place prediction*: given the history of observations, predict the next observation in the sequence.

In Section 4, we tackle the PLST problems 1 and 2. In Section 5, we tackle the PLST problems 3 and 4.

4   Latent Semantic Locations

Using the observation matrix our aim is to 1) assign a class label to each column and 2) learn the association of indices to latent classes (the PLST problems 1 and 2). Since a location is defined by the co-occurrence of indices in a 15 minute period, one approach would be to use an index adjacency matrix and cluster indices into closely associated groups. However the adjacency matrix does not model the ambiguity and noise in the observations. We propose a model based probabilistic clustering solution.

Model Based Clustering (MBC). We consider a probabilistic approach where instead of a hard cluster assignment, we find the distribution of indices and observation vectors over the latent classes. We model the observations as a generative process involving a mixture density of latent states which is depicted as a Bayesian Network in plate notation in Figure 3. To generate an observation (each column of observation matrix) from the model $\Theta = \{\mu, \pi\}$, we sample a location $z_n = k$ according to mixing distribution π_k and then sample L_n indices in the observations according to μ_{mk}.

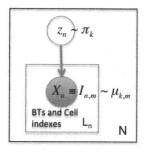

Fig. 3. Bayesian Network for MBC to extract Semantic Locations

N: Total number of 15min intervals in user trace
X_n: set of L_n indices appearing in the nth observation
$m \in 1, .., M$: vocabulary of observation indices
$I_{n,m} = 1 \iff m \in X_n$: observation indicator vector
$f_{n,m}$: observation index frequency
$\Theta = \{\mu, \pi\}$: parameters of the mixture model
$\mu_{mk} = p(m|k)$: probability of m appearing in location k
$\pi_k = p(k)$: mixing distribution for visiting the location k
$z_n = k \in [1, K]$: latent location class of observation n

Above, we have implicitly assumed that each observation is generated from a single component k which makes sense as each observations represents a single semantic location. Longer observation durations (for example an entire day) can be generated from a mixture of components. We also assume that a latent location z_n is sampled independently and each index in the observation is conditionally independent given z_n. The likelihood of observations is given by the mixture model in equation 1. Our aim is to find the parameters Θ which maximizes the joint likelihood of N observations in equation 2.

$$L(X_n|\Theta) = \sum_{z_n} p(X_n|z_n; \Theta)p(z_n|\Theta) = \sum_k \pi_k p(X_n|z_n = k) \qquad (1)$$

$$L(X_1 \ldots X_N|\Theta) = \prod_{n=1}^{N} \left\{ \sum_k \pi_k p(X_n|z_n) \right\} \qquad (2)$$

Above, $p(X_n|z_n)$ is the probability of an observation and is also known as emission probability in mixture modeling. The emission probability is meant to incorporate the specific characteristics of the data. We employ three different multi-variate emission probability distributions in our analysis.

$$p_{bin}(X_n|z_n) = \prod_{m \in X_n} \mu_{mk}^{I_{n,m}} \qquad (3)$$

$$p_{bern}(X_n|z_n) = \prod_{m \in X_n} \mu_{mk}^{I_{n,m}} \prod_{m \notin X_n} (1 - \mu_{mk})^{1-I_{n,m}} \qquad (4)$$

$$p_{mult}(X_n|z_n) = \prod_{m \in X_n} \mu_{mk}^{f_{n,m}} \qquad (5)$$

The choice of emission probability is central to the idea of model based clustering paradigm. The Bernoulli distribution models a latent location not only with the indices which occur but also the indices which are missing. Thus it is more informative than the binomial model which might prove crucial in differentiating context. Both these distributions are multiple trial models but have a different observation space from the multinomial distribution. The index frequencies in the multinomial model may provide some subtle information about the locations and activity. For example a person in transit, an indoor location with variable cell connectivity, or an outdoor location would have different frequencies of observed cells. However, owing to its Polya urn model, the multinomial favors strong clustering (akin to a hard clustering solution) which might be counter-productive for prediction task. Since our observations consist of few indices, some analogy may be drawn with sentence classification and retrieval (short documents) in text analysis where the Bernoulli mode has proved more effective [22]. In our evaluations we quantitatively compare the three distributions for modeling and prediction.

To find the optimal parameters $\Theta = \{\mu, \pi\}$, we maximize the likelihood $L(X|\Theta)$. Since the assignments z_n are not observed we need to maximize over all possible assignments of z_n. Note that equation 2 contains inner sums which makes this intractable. We use the Expectation Maximization (EM) algorithm to solve the problem. We start with some initial assumption about the parameters Θ. In the E-step, we compute the posterior distribution of the latent variables $p(Z|X, \Theta^{old})$, using the current estimate of

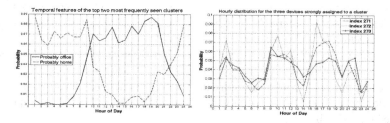

Fig. 4. (a) top 2 frequently occurring states; (b) 3 cell towers appearing in a latent state

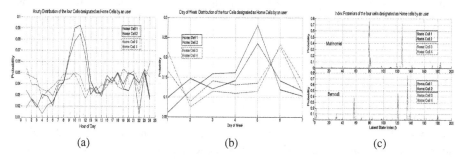

(a)   (b)   (c)

Fig. 5. Semantic Disambiguation of 2 pairs of cells designated as Home.(a) Hourly Distribution (b) Day of Week Distribution (c) Posterior probability of cells shows distinct peaks for the two pairs.

the parameters. In the M-Step we find the expectation of the complete likelihood function $Q(\Theta|\Theta^{old}) = \sum_Z p(Z|X, \Theta^{old}) \ln p(X, Z|\Theta)$ and maximize it with respect to the parameters Θ.

For emission probabilities in the exponential family (as the three distributions in equations 3, 4, 5) the E and M step assumes a simple form given by equations 6 and 7. We iterate between the steps and monitor the likelihood score given by equation 2 to test for convergence.

$$\text{Expectation}: \quad \gamma_{nk} = \frac{\pi_k P(X_n|z_n) + \epsilon}{\sum_k P(X_n|z_n) + \epsilon} \tag{6}$$

$$\text{Maximization}: \quad \mu_{mk} = \frac{\sum_{n=1}^N \gamma_{nk} I_{nm}}{\sum_{n=1}^N \gamma_{nk}}, \ \pi_k = \frac{1}{N}\sum_{n=1}^N \gamma_{nk} \tag{7}$$

Above, $\gamma_{nk} = p(z_n = k|X_n; \Theta)$ is the posterior probability (or a soft cluster assignment) that $X_n \equiv I_n$ is assigned to the location k and is the MBC solution. For a data set involving a large number of indices, there can be a severe problem of sparsity such that a test sequence is likely to contain indices and their combinations not seen previously in learning. Problems such as these can be handled using Laplace smoothing by adding ϵ in the $\gamma_{m,k}$. This assigns a non-zero probability to all members of μ and is equivalent to a non-informative uniform prior used in Bayesian models such as LDA[1].

Location and Index Disambiguation. The two problems using the MBC are to infer the latent state labels for both indices and observations. The Bayesian network graph for MBC in Figure 3 models the sampling process to generate observations going from root to leaf nodes. For inference we compute the posterior distributions going in the opposite direction (i.e. leaf to root).

In equation 6, γ_{nk} is the posterior probability of an observation to a latent state. Since it is assumed that observations are generated from a single latent component (corresponding to a unique semantic location), the label assignment can be approximated to the Maximum A-posteriori Probability (MAP) estimate of $\gamma_{n,k}$, i.e., the component k with the highest probability.

For a similar label assignment for indices, we compute the posterior probability of indices, $p(k|m) = \mu_{km}^p$ using the Bayes' theorem in equation 8 and assign the label k for the component in μ_{km}^p with the maximum value. The denominator in the R.H.S. is simply the normalizing coefficient since $p(k|m)$ is a probability distribution and must sum to 1.

$$\mu_{km}^p = p(m|k)p(k)/p(m) = \pi_k \mu_{mk} / \sum_k \pi_k \mu_{mk} \tag{8}$$

The above label assignment to indices only provides the most-likely (MAP) location for an index. To find a more general association, we can consider measures such as Cosine Similarity or Shannon-Jensen Divergence between the index-posterior distributions μ_{km}^p.

Qualitative Interpretation of the Latent Clusters. The MBC model is essentially a statistical representation which can perhaps improve some quantifiable task such as predicting the next observations. However it would be more significant if the latent states also have some real, semantic interpretation.

We first consider the temporal coherence of the latent states. Figure 4(a) shows that the hourly distribution of top two frequently visited states for a user. It has two distinct patterns which can be interpreted as home and office which is what we expected from a typical participant of RM. Locations labeled to less frequent states were seen to have more complicated (yet coherent) patterns. For example, Figure 4(b) shows the hourly distribution for three indices appearing in a latent state have a complex but a characteristic profile.

The MBC approach can also semantically differentiate indices which may be co-located geographically. Consider Figure 5 where we have plotted the profiles of four cell towers labeled as "home" by an user. The temporal profiles are quite similar within the two pairs [Cell 1, Cell 2] and [Cell 3, Cell 4] but quite distinct across the pairs. The *day of week* distribution shows that the first pair (blue) appears mostly during the week while the second pair (red) appears more in the weekend. Further, we see that the second pair has a uniform hourly distribution which may indicate that the person was at home during the weekends. The index posteriors μ_{km}^p for the four cells are plotted for the multinomial and Bernoulli distributions in Figure 5c. The distinct peaks in the distribution illustrates that the two pairs are differentiated as distinct semantic locations even though the temporal features were not used. We also see that while the multinomial has a single high peak for each pair, the Bernoulli has some ambiguity (two peaks for the first pair) indicating that an index can belong to different latent locations.

Next, we investigate index disambiguation in more detail. We use the cosine similarity to cluster indices and then sort the indices according to their assigned classes for the plots in Figure 6. Figure 6(top row) shows the posterior distribution of indices μ_{km}^p with different number of latent states. This is shown for the Bernoulli distribution but we get similar figures with the other two. It is clear that as the number of latent states is increased, the index to latent state associations become more well defined. Figure 6(second row) plots the pairwise similarity of clustered indices for the three distributions. The multinomial produces a similarity matrix with the least ambiguity. It is well known that multinomials can *overfit* a clustering solution which leads to saturated distributions equivalent to a hard clustering (e.g. see figure 5c). Bernoulli has more ambiguity but also has more balanced groups which are neither too small or too large. A quantitative comparison presented later shows that ambiguity is beneficial for next place prediction as

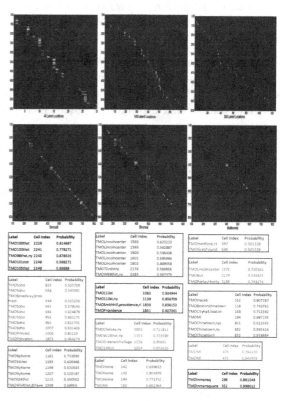

Fig. 6. (Top row) Posterior distribution of indices sorted according to assigned classes for 40, 100 and 200 Latent classes (uses the Bernoulli Distribution); **(Second row)** Cosine similarities of clustered indices for the Bernoulli (left), Binomial (centre) and Multinomial (right) distributions; **(Bottom)** Cell indexes grouped using cosine similarity. Associated user defined labels show semantic coherency.

it correctly models the inherent nature of the data set. Finally, to get a better sense of the index associations, Figure 6(bottom) illustrates groups of semantically similar indices along with their semantic labels provided by a user. The label groups show surprising levels of semantic and geographic coherency which emerge purely based on the models used.

5 Latent Syntactic Structure of Mobility

While the MBC approach can extract semantically coherent latent states, it assumes that these states appear independently. Mobility usually has a sequential and causal behavior: next place a person visits may depend on the previous steps taken. In this section we model the *latent syntactic structure* of mobility to investigate the transition behavior between latent states. We also consider the problem of predicting the next state and observations.

Syntactic Structure with MBC. We first impose a sequential structure on the latent states extracted by MBC. We assume that the state sequence is Markovian (next state is dependent only on the previous state). We calculate the state transition matrix $A_{i,j}$ using the posterior state distributions γ_n (equation 6) as follows.

$$A_{jk} = p(z_{n,k}|z_{n-1,j}) = \frac{\sum_{n=2}^{N} \gamma_{n-1,j}\gamma_{n,k}}{\sum_{k=1}^{K}\sum_{n=2}^{N} \gamma_{n-1,j}\gamma_{n,k}} \tag{9}$$

Above, $A_{i,j}$ is the probability to go from state j in the $n-1^{th}$ step to state k in the nth step. To predict the $n+1^{th}$ observation given the observations up to X_n, we calculate the posterior γ_n for observation X_n and then calculate the transition probability to go to the location k at the $n+1^{th}$ step using equation 10.

$$Tran_k^{n+1} = p(z_{n+1} = k|X_n) = \sum_{j=1}^{K} \gamma_{n,j} A_{j,k} \tag{10}$$

To estimate the next observation indices, we use two slightly different notions. In the first, the notion of Maximum Likelihood (ML)is used for estimation: we find the most likely transition given by $\hat{k} = Argmax_k(Trans)$ and assume $\hat{k}$ as the the next state. Then, for this state the predictive probability of indices is given as:

$$Pr^{ML}(m \in X_{n+1}|\hat{k}) = \mu_{m\hat{k}} \tag{11}$$

In the second notion, we compute the Bayesian Estimate (BE) of the index probabilities by marginalizing over all transitions to get the posterior probabilities of the observation indices.

$$Pr^{BE}(m \in X_{n+1}) = \sum_{k}\sum_{j} \gamma_{n,j} A_{j,k} \mu_{m,k} \tag{12}$$

We note that the model itself is not a full Bayesian generative model: we only estimate the index probabilities as the posterior mean.

Syntactic Structure with HMM. In MBC, we imposed a simple pairwise sequence structure on the extracted latent states. Such a model inherently lacks the informative power of a long observation sequence. However, we need to enforce the history dependence on the predictive probability of the observations while keeping the parameter space small. This can be achieved by extending the MBC in Figure 3 to a DBN. We impose Markovian transitions (on the latent

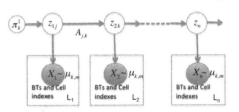

Fig. 7. Dynamic Bayesian Network of the MBC as an HMM to extract Syntactic Structure

states rather than the observations) to create a particular type of DBN, namely the Hidden Markov Model (HMM). Here, the emissions are sets of indices, rather than a single element as shown in Figure 7. It can be shown that while the latent states are Markovian (z_{n+1} is conditionally independent of z_{n-1} given z_n) the distribution of interest, the predictive probability, $p(X_{n+1}|X_1, ..., X_n)$ does not have this conditional independence and hence it depends on all the previous observations. HMM is specified by the parameters $\Theta : \{\pi^1, A, \mu\}$, the initial, transition, and emission probabilities. HMM has is exactly the same number of parameters, $O(K^2)$ as MBC-sequence and thus we have not increased the complexity of the model. We also use the same emission probability functions (equations 3-5) thus preserving the ability to extract similar latent semantic locations. The difference with HMM is that we learn the parameters, label the states and predict the observations jointly over the entire sequence. Thus HMM allows us to model complex sequences while keeping the parameter complexity under control.

We use the EM algorithm to learn the HMM parameters. While the M-step is similar to that in the MBC, the sequential dependencies complicates the E-step. We use the scaled version of the forward-backward (or the Baum-Welch) algorithm [27], which uses dynamic programming and sum-product rules of probability to calculate the expectation terms over all possible latent paths in the sequence.

Expectation

$$c_n \alpha(z_n) = p(X_n|z_n) \sum_{z_{n-1}=1}^{K} \alpha(z_{n-1})p(z_n|z_{n-1}) \tag{13}$$

$$c_{n+1}\beta(z_n) = \sum_{z_{n+1}=1}^{K} \beta(z_{n+1})p(X_{n+1}|z_{n+1})p(z_{n+1}|z_n) \tag{14}$$

$$\gamma(z_n) = \alpha(z_n)\beta(z_n) + \epsilon \tag{15}$$

$$\xi(z_{n-1}, z_n) = \alpha(z_{n-1})p(X_n|z_n)p(z_n|z_{n-1})\beta(z_n)/c_n \tag{16}$$

Maximization

$$\pi_k^1 = p(z_1 = k) = \gamma_{1,k}/\sum_{k=1}^{K}\gamma_{1,k} \tag{17}$$

$$A_{j,k} = p(z_{n+1,k}|z_{n,j}) = \frac{\sum_{n=2}^{N}\xi(z_{n-1,j}, z_{n,k})}{\sum_{k=1}^{K}\sum_{n=2}^{N}\xi(z_{n-1,j}, z_{n,k})} \tag{18}$$

$$\mu_{m,k} = p(X_n|z_n) = \sum_{n=1}\gamma_{n,k}I_{n,m}/\sum_{n=1}\gamma_{n,k} \tag{19}$$

In the E-step, we compute $\gamma_n = p(z_n|X, \Theta^{old})$, the posterior distribution of the latent states, and $\xi(z_{n-1}, z_n) = p(z_{n-1}, z_n|X, \Theta^{old})$, the joint probability of two successive latent states with the current parameter estimate Θ^{old}. We recursively compute $\alpha(z_n) = p(X_1, ..., X_n, z_n)$,the joint *forward* probabilities and $\beta(z_n) = p(X_{n+1}, ..., X_N|z_n)$, the conditional *backward* probabilities for the nth latent state. After a complete forward and backward sweep, we get γ_n using the chain rule for joint probabilities by multiplying α and β. Similar computation gives us $\xi(z_{n-1}, z_n)$.

In the M step, the expected values of γ and ξ are maximized to update the parameters of HMM. For emission distributions in the exponential family, this maximization again assumes the simple form as given in equations 17, 18 and 19. The initial probability π^1 is computed by normalizing γ_1, the marginal distribution of the first state, while the emission probabilities are computed by taking the expectation of the observation matrix for each of the k latent components with the posterior state distributions γ as the weights. Note that to compute the transition probability matrix $A_{i,j}$ we need $n - 2$ matrices of ξ (each of size $K \times K$). These are not stored but simply accumulated in $A_{i,j}$ during the backward sweep in the E-step.

Above, c_n is the scaling factor term which is used to keep the probabilities under machine precision for a long sequence. It can be computed as the normalization constant on the right hand side of equation 13. We again use ϵ for Laplace smoothing on γ similar to the EM steps in MBC.

We start the $\alpha - \beta$ recursions by setting $\alpha_1(z_n) = \pi^1 p(X_1|z_n)$ and $\beta_N = 1$. To initialize the EM iterations, we use the learnt parameters from MBC as initial values and use Laplace smoothing on the parameters before using them to remove model over-fitting. Initialization from MBC speeded up the EM convergence of HMM parameter learning. The learnt parameters for MBC were found to be relatively stable and thus proved a good initialization for the EM algorithm in HMM.

Labeling the States in the HMM. Similar to the MBC, the HMM can be used for labeling each observation to a latent state. HMM gives better sequences than MBC as evident from the prediction performance. The qualitative analysis is omitted due to lack of space. Figure 8 illustrates a typical observation sequence and their states using two approaches which are described next.

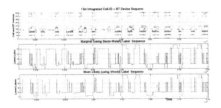

Fig. 8. Latent Label Sequences using the SumProduct (Marginal) and MaxSum (Most Likely) states depict the extracted latent semantic trajectory

Marginal State Sequence: To infer the labels, we compute the marginal distributions of the latent states conditioned on the observations over the entire sequence. For Bayesian networks which are trees (as HMMs are), this can be computed using the forward-backward sweeps in the EM algorithm to arrive at $\gamma_n = p(z_n|X)$ as the marginal distribution of the latent states. We then label the observations as $\widehat{k}_n = Argmax_k(\gamma_{n,k})$ to get maximum a posteriori allocations with individually most probable states. Since the marginals were calculated using the sum-product algorithm, we term these as $\widehat{k}_n^{SumProd}$.

Most Likely State Sequence: We can further constrain the sequence by considering only the *most likely sequence* of states. We use the max-sum recursions or the Viterbi algorithm for this purpose. While the max-sum algorithm can be implemented in the logarithmic domain, we implement a scaled version of the algorithm since we intend to use the forward probabilities for computing the predictive distribution. We introduce the scaling factors d_n in max-sum recursions as follows.

$$\omega(z_{n+1}) = \max_{z_1...z_n} p(X_1...X_n, z_1...z_n) = \ln p(x_{n+1}|z_{n+1}) + \max_{z_n}\{\ln p(z_{n+1}|z_n) + \omega(z_n) - \ln d_n\} \tag{20}$$

At the end of the final maximization at the Nth step, we get $\omega(z_N) = p(X, Z)$, the joint probability of the most-likely path. To label the most-likely path we keep track of jth component of $\omega(z_n)$ which contributes to the max value of $\omega(z_{n+1})$ in $\psi(k_{n+1}^{max}) = j_n$. Once the forward recursion is completed, we maximize $\omega(z_N)$ at the end state and backtrack recursively to get $\widehat{k}_n^{MaxSum} = \psi(k_{n+1}^{max})$ as the labels for the entire sequence.

In Figure 8 the label sequences using the two methods are practically identical, with the Viterbi sequence appearing a bit smoother with fewer transitions.

Prediction with HMM. As in the MBC approach, we have the ML and the BE notions for the predictive index probabilities. To predict the indices for the $n + 1^{th}$ step, we first infer the state sequence up to observation n, and then compute the predictive probabilities. Since we have two estimates of the state sequences, the Sum-Product and Max-Sum, we have four different predictive distributions.

$$Trans_{n+1}^{SumProd}(k) = p(z_{n+1} = k|X_n) = \sum_{j=1}^{K} \alpha_{n,j} A_{j,k} \tag{21}$$

$$Trans_{n+1}^{MaxSum}(k) = \sum_{j=1}^{K} e^{\omega(z_{n,j})} A_{j,k} \tag{22}$$

For the Sum-Product transitions, we use the $\alpha_{n,k}$ the normalized forward probabilities instead of $\gamma_{n,k}$ since the β indices are not available during predictions. For the Max-Sum transitions we use the $exp(\omega_{n,k})$ as the normalized forward probabilities. Then for ML, the next location is given by $\hat{k}_{n+1} = Argmax_k(Trans_{n+1})$ and the ML predictive index probabilities for the two state sequences is given by $Pr^{ML}(m \in X_{n+1}|\hat{k}) = p(m|\hat{k}) = \mu_{m,\hat{k}}$. Finally, the BE predictive distributions for are given by:

$$Pr_{SumProd}^{BE}(m \in X_{n+1}) = \sum_{k} \sum_{j} \alpha_{n-1,j} A_{j,k} \mu_{m,k} \tag{23}$$

$$Pr_{MaxSum}^{BE}(m \in X_{n+1}) = \sum_{k} \mu_{m,k} \sum_{j} e^{\omega(z_{n,j})} A_{j,k} \tag{24}$$

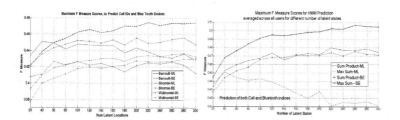

Fig. 9. F1 Scores (averaged across users): (a) MBC: for the three distributions using ML and BE prediction approaches. Bernoulli with BE has the best performance; (b) HMM: for the Bernoulli distribution using ML and BE prediction approaches. Prediction using Max-Sum state sequence and BE has the best performance.

Entropy and Predictability of the Sequences. We analyze the complexity of sequences using information theoretic measures. Since PLST (i.e. MBC and HMM) extracts some semantic patterns in the data and projects it onto a lower dimensional latent space, we expect the models to represent the inherent uncertainty and predictability sequences.

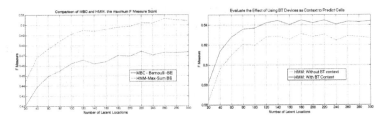

Fig. 10. Average F1 score comparisons: (a) MBC vs. HMM; (b) predict cell towers with and without Bluetooth devices in the observations. Bluetooths improve prediction by providing location context.

We analyze the complexity using cross entropy[1] as an upper bound on the entropy of a sequence [2]. Let $P(X_1, ..., X_N)$ denote the true probability distribution of the sequence. Since $P(X)$ is unknown, we learn a representative model $Q(X)$ on a training sequence and compute the entropy using Q on a test sequence. A lower cross-entropy provides a tighter estimate and indicates that a particular model is a better descriptor of the data. Thus, it may be used as a model selection criteria. The cross entropy is given as follows.

$$H_N(P(X)) \leq H_N(Q_K(X)) = \lim_{N \to \infty} \frac{1}{N} E[\log_K Q(X_1, ..., X_N)]$$

$$H_N(Q_K) \simeq \frac{1}{N} \sum_{n=1}^{N} \sum_{k=1}^{K} p(Q_{nk}) \frac{\ln p(Q_{nk})}{\ln(K)} \tag{25}$$

We use MBC and HMM as the representative models for P and use $p(Q_{n,k}) = \gamma_{nk}$ from equation 6 and 15. These represent the uncertainty of the observations as a distribution over K latent states. While the MBC draws the latent state space independently, the HMM further constrains the state space through dependencies in state transitions. The cross entropy may be interpreted as the *information transfer* rate or the minimum number of K-ary bits required to encode the mobility sequence. Thus, the cross entropy in equation 25 is computed in $\ln(K)$ units.

We are also interested in the *Predictability* of a sequence which is related to the *information flow* rate [9] or the reduction in uncertainty of a future state given the previous observations. This is estimated using the conditional entropy $HC_n^K(X_{n+1}, z_{n+1}|X_1, ..., X_n)$ given by:

$$HC_N^K \simeq \frac{1}{N} \sum_{n=1}^{N} \sum_{k=1}^{K} p(z_{n+1} = k|X) \frac{\ln p(z_{n+1} = k|X_1, ..., X_n)}{\ln(K)} \tag{26}$$

To compute the above, we use $p(z_n = k|X_1, ..., X_n) = \alpha_{nk}$, the forward transition probabilities. We can further reduce the uncertainty of the sequence by considering the distribution over the most likely sequence of states using the MaxSum forward probabilities ω_{nk} from equation 26. Finally, *Predictability* is defined as:

$$Predictability_n^K = 1 - HC_n^K \tag{27}$$

---

[1] Cross entropy is closely related to Perplexity (cross-entropy normalized per word) which is frequently in text analysis.

6   Evaluation of Next Place Prediction Algorithms

We consider users with more than 10,000 entries in their sequence (87 users out of the 106). For each user, we use 80% of the sequences for training and rest 20% for testing. The prediction is sequential: the nth observation is predicted using the previous $n - 1$ observations, after which we update the nth state using the observation X_n.

With predictive distribution $Pr(m \in X_{n+1})$ for the next observation we denote the predicted indices as the *Retrieved* set given by $Ret_{n+1}(m) = 1 : Pr(m \in X_{n+1}) > Threshold$. The actual observation provides the *Relevant* set or the ground truth given by $Rel_{n+1}(m) = 1 : m \in X_{n+1}$. We compute the prediction scores using information retrieval metrics of Precision: $P_n = |Rel_n \cap Ret_n|/|Ret_n|$, Recall: $R_n = |Rel_n \cap Ret_n|/|Rel_n|$ and F1-Measure: $F_n^1 = 2P_nR_n/(P_n + R_n)$. F1 is the harmonic mean of precision and recall and most closely identified with the accuracy of predictions since it provides the degree of overlap between the two sets. For the 87 users, the scores are computed for the three distributions with different number of latent states ($20 \leq K \leq 300$) and different thresholds ($0 \leq Threshold \leq 1$).

Prediction Performance with Model Based Clustering. Figure 9(a) illustrates the F-Measure scores for the Bernoulli, binomial and multinomial distributions using the MBC approach. We have already looked at the qualitative merits of the Bernoulli distribution for mobility modeling. Quantitatively, the Bernoulli distribution has the best prediction performance among the three distributions. Among the two prediction methods, BE is better than the ML for all the three distributions. The quantitative prediction scores also concur with evaluations based on cross entropy, discussed later in the section.

Prediction Performance with HMM. For HMM, we only show the results with the Bernoulli distribution. Our tests with the other two distributions reveal that Bernoulli has the best performance even in HMM. Figure 9(b) plots the the average F1 scores (across thresholds and users) for the four different prediction schemes. The BE predictive distribution with the Max-Sum state sequence (using the Viterbi algorithm) has the the best performance. Figure 10(a) compares the performance of HMM with the MBC and shows the advantages of modeling the sequence as an HMM. In Figure 9(b), we predicted both the cell and bluetooth indices. In general the bluetooth encounters provide context, but are less indicative of geographical location. Figure 10(b) compares the cell index prediction with and without bluetooth indices in the observation matrix. A higher prediction rate with bluetooth confirms our intuition that bluetooth provide informative location context.

Comparison with Baseline Prediction Algorithms. We evaluate two algorithms which involve the prediction with the unstructured sequence of observations to illustrate the benefits of using the latent structure of sequences.

Order-2 Markov Model (MM-2): We consider the sequence of cells as an order-k Markov Chain. We first compute the order-k cell transition probabilities in the training sequence. In the test sequence the next cell is predicted as the most likely cell given the previous k observations in the chain. In particular we consider MM-2 as it has been shown to outperform other predictive approaches in [11] and [29].

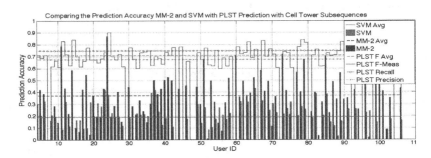

Fig. 11. Comparison of accuracy with different approaches: SVM (0.2), MM-2 (0.4) and PLST(0.7)

Prediction as a Multi-class Classification: We posed the prediction task as a multi-class classification problem and used SVM [4,6] to find the next place based on the features of the current state. We used previous 10 cell ids, hour of day, day of week, weekday, time of day (morning, noon etc.) and stay times at the current location as the features describing the current state. These features are similar to those used in [17] which was ranked 2nd in the next place prediction task of the Nokia Data Challenge [18].

Since the baseline approaches do not use the bluetooth devices, we compared them to the prediction of cell indices. Figure 11 shows the prediction rates for different users using the PLST (HMM with BE and MaxSum), SVM and MM-2. For each, we used the best user prediction scores across different algorithm parameters. For SVM and MM2 the rate is calculated as the fraction of correctly predicted cell indices in the test sequence. The performance of PLST is significantly better than the two baseline cases. Since the SVM and MM-2 shows the accuracy rates rather than F1, we also include the precision and recall rates to illustrate that the PLST is significantly better. For SVM and MM we expect to correctly predict 20% and 40% of the next cell indices. In contrast PLST accurately predicts close to 70% of the indices when measured as groups inside latent semantic locations.

Discriminative models (such as SVM) trained for multi-class prediction perform poorly when the class space (the indices) is large and essentially equivalent to the size of feature space used to discriminate the classes. Markov models are better at modeling short range dependencies since the effects of previous states drop exponentially with Markov distance. This is the reason why their performance saturates beyond the 2nd order. In addition SVM and MM-2 penalize prediction of synonyms (or multiple cells that belong to the same location). PLST achieves the best performance by extracting structure in the sequence, and incorporating longer dependencies through the transitions in latent space.

Entropy and Predictability of the Sequences. We plot the sequence cross entropies (eq. 25) and the conditional entropies (eq. 26) in Figure 12(a) in $\log(K)$ units. The raw entropy uses the normalized index frequencies as the probability distribution. The cross entropies for MBC are significantly lower than the raw index entropy. Among the three distributions, Bernoulli has the lowest entropy. In the conditional entropy plots,

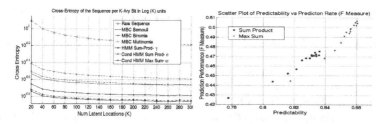

Fig. 12. (a) Cross Entropy depicting the complexity of modeled sequences. Lower cross-entropy denotes better model fit; (b) Scatter plot of Predictability vs. Prediction rates for different user sequences. Prediction rates show correlation to the derived Predictability measure.

the predictive Sum-Product (α) probabilities is slightly higher than the marginal Sum-Product (γ) which is expected. What is surprising is that the Max-Sum conditional entropy (ω) is even lower than the γ-rate and suggests why its prediction performance was far superior to the other approaches.

Finally, in Figure 12(b) the scatter-plot for the Sum-Product and Max-Sum predictive distributions shows that Predictability (equation 27) is highly correlated to the prediction rate. An important observation from all the plots is that a larger number of states provides better prediction for BE based predictions. A large number of states can potentially model complex behavior but can also overfit the training data. This affects the ML predictions but not the BE predictions due to marginalization and model averaging in BE across the state space. While the optimal number of states in latent variable models is highly debated, for prediction, the results show that we can choose the largest number of states under the limit that is computationally feasible.

7   Conclusions and Future Work

PLST provides an unsupervised approach for semantic modeling and analysis of user mobility in the absence of accurate geographic signals and semantic annotations. The evaluations and results validate our intuition that location sequences of users have an underlying structure and that structure can be extracted using the models described in this paper. While the approach is illustrated through the particulars of the RM data, we intend to generalize it to other types of data sets. PLST can prove important for anonymous tracking and profiling of users and the latent semantic structure can be used to identify uncommon behavior.

Several extensions to this work are ongoing. First, modeling and predictions may be further improved by accommodating temporal features or periodicity of users. Also, the methods can be potentially extended to incorporate knowledge of social network information and interactions (albeit incomplete and noisy) alongside the noisy physical connectivity traces to discover latent semantic aspects of *group mobility*.

References

1. Blei, D.M., Ng, A.Y., Jordan, M.I.: Latent dirichlet allocation. J. Mach. Learn. Res. 3, 993–1022 (2003)
2. Brown, P.F., Pietra, V.J.D., Mercer, R.L., Pietra, S.A.D., Lai, J.C.: An estimate of an upper bound for the entropy of english. Comput. Linguist. 18(1), 31–40 (1992)
3. Buthpitiya, S., Zhang, Y., Dey, A.K., Griss, M.: *n*-gram geo-trace modeling. In: Lyons, K., Hightower, J., Huang, E.M. (eds.) Pervasive 2011. LNCS, vol. 6696, pp. 97–114. Springer, Heidelberg (2011)
4. Chang, C.-C., Lin, C.-J.: Libsvm: A library for support vector machines. ACM Transactions on Intelligent Systems and Technology 2, 1–27 (2011), http://www.csie.ntu.edu.tw/~cjlin/libsvm
5. Coffey, C., Pozdnoukhov, A.: Temporal decomposition and semantic enrichment of mobility flows. In: Proceedings of the 6th ACM SIGSPATIAL International Workshop on Location-Based Social Networks, LBSN 2013, pp. 34–43. ACM, New York (2013)
6. Cortes, C., Vapnik, V.: Support-vector networks. In: Machine Learning, pp. 273–297 (1995)
7. Eagle, N., Pentland, A.: Eigenbehaviors: Identifying structure in routine. In: Joint Conference on Pervasive and Ubiquitous Computing (2006)
8. Eagle, N., Pentland, A.(S.): Reality mining: sensing complex social systems. Personal Ubiquitous Comput. 10(4), 255–268 (2006)
9. Ebeling, W., Frommel, C.: Entropy and predictability of information carriers. Biosystems 46(1), 47–55 (1998)
10. Farrahi, K., Gatica-Perez, D.: Discovering routines from large-scale human locations using probabilistic topic models. ACM Trans. Intell. Syst. Technol. 2(1), 3:1–3:27 (2011)
11. Gambs, S., Killijian, M.-O., del Prado Cortez, M.N.N.: Next place prediction using mobility markov chains. In: First Workshop on Measurement, Privacy, and Mobility, MPM 2012, pp. 3:1–3:6. ACM, New York (2012)
12. Gao, W., Cao, G.: Fine-grained mobility characterization: Steady and transient state behaviors. In: in Proceedings of Mobihoc (2010)
13. Gonzalez, M.C., Hidalgo, C.A., Barabasi, A.-L.: Understanding individual human mobility patterns. Nature 453(7196), 779–782 (2008)
14. Griffiths, T.L., Steyvers, M., Blei, D.M., Tenenbaum, J.B.: Integrating topics and syntax. In: In Advances in Neural Information Processing Systems 17, pp. 537–544. MIT Press (2005)
15. Griffiths, T.L., Tenenbaum, J.B., Steyvers, M.: Topics in semantic representation. Psychological Review 114 (2007)
16. Hofmann, T.: Probabilistic latent semantic analysis. In: Uncertainty in Artificial Intelligence, UAI, pp. 289–296 (1999)
17. Wang, B.P.J.: Periodicity based next place prediction. In: Procedings of Mobile Data Challenge by Nokia Workshop at the Tenth International Conference on Pervasive Computing (2012)
18. Laurila, J.K., Gatica-Perez, D., Aad, I., Blom, J., Bornet, O., Do, T., Dousse, O., Eberle, J., Miettinen, M.: The mobile data challenge: Big data for mobile computing research. In: Mobile Data Challenge by Nokia Workshop, Newcastle, UK (2012)
19. Nguyen, L.T., Heng-Tze, C., Pang, W., Senaka, B., Jiang, Z., Ying, Z.: Pnlum: System for prediction of next location for users with mobility. In: Mobile Data Challenge by Nokia Workshop at the Tenth International Conference on Pervasive Computing (2012)
20. Leguay, J., Lindgren, A., Scott, J., Friedman, T., Crowcroft, J., Hui, P.: CRAWDAD trace set upmc/content/imote (v. 2006-11-17) (November 2006), http://crawdad.cs.dartmouth.edu/upmc/content/imote

21. Liao, L., Fox, D., Kautz, H.: Extracting places and activities from gps traces using hierarchical conditional random fields. Int. J. Rob. Res. 26(1), 119–134 (2007)
22. Losada, D., Azzopardi, L.: Assessing multi-variate bernoulli models for information retrieval. ACM Transactions on Information Systems 26(3) (2008)
23. McDiarmid, A., Irvine, J., Bell, S., Banford, J.: CRAWDAD data set strath/nodobo (v. 2011-03-23) (March 2011), http://crawdad.cs.dartmouth.edu/strath/nodobo
24. Nahrstedt, K., Vu, L.: CRAWDAD data set uiuc/uim (v. 2012-01-24) (January 2012), http://crawdad.cs.dartmouth.edu/uiuc/uim
25. Nguyen, T., Phung, D., Gupta, S., Venkatesh, S.: Extraction of latent patterns and contexts from social honest signals using hierarchical dirichlet processes. In: IEEE International Conference on Pervasive Computing and Communications (PerCom), pp. 47–55 (2013)
26. Parent, C., Spaccapietra, S., Renso, C., Andrienko, G., Andrienko, N., Bogorny, V., Damiani, M.L., Gkoulalas-divanis, A., Macedo, J., Pelekis, N., Theodoridis, Y., Yan, Z.: Semantic trajectories modeling and analysis. ACM Computing Surveys (2012)
27. Rabiner, L.R.: A tutorial on hidden markov models and selected applications in speech recognition. Proceedings of the IEEE, 257–286 (1989)
28. Song, C., Qu, Z., Blumm, N., Barabasi, A.: Limits of predictability in human mobility. Science 327(5968), 1018–1021 (2010)
29. Song, L., Kotz, D., Jain, R., He, X.: Evaluating location predictors with extensive wi-fi mobility data. SIGMOBILE Mob. Comput. Commun. Rev. 7(4), 64–65 (2003)
30. Srinivasan, V., Natarajan, A., Motani, M.: CRAWDAD data set nus/bluetooth (v. 2007-09-03) (September 2007), http://crawdad.cs.dartmouth.edu/nus/bluetooth
31. Vincent Etter, E.K., Kafsi, M.: Been there, done that: What your mobility traces reveal about your behavior. In: Mobile Data Challenge by Nokia: Workshop at 10th International Conference on Pervasive Computing (2012)
32. Ying, J.J.-C., Lee, W.-C., Weng, T.-C., Tseng, V.S.: Semantic trajectory mining for location prediction. In: 19th ACM SIGSPATIAL International Conference on Advances in Geographic Information Systems, GIS 2011, pp. 34–43. ACM, New York (2011)
33. Zheng, Y., Li, Q., Chen, Y., Xie, X., Ma, W.-Y.: Understanding mobility based on gps data. In: 10th International Conference on Ubiquitous Computing, UbiComp 2008, pp. 312–321. ACM, New York (2008)

Mind the SmartGap: A Buffer Management Algorithm for Delay Tolerant Wireless Sensor Networks

Pehr Söderman[1], Karl-Johan Grinnemo[2], Markus Hidell[1], and Peter Sjödin[1]

[1] NSLab, School of ICT
KTH Royal Institute of Technology, Stockholm, Sweden
{pehrs,mahidell,psj}@kth.se
[2] Department of Computer Science
Karlstad University, Karlstad, Sweden
karlgrin@kau.se

Abstract. Limited memory capacity is one of the major constraints in Delay Tolerant Wireless Sensor Networks. Efficient management of the memory is critical to the performance of the network. This paper proposes a novel buffer management algorithm, SmartGap, a Quality of Information (QoI) targeted buffer management algorithm. That is, in a wireless sensor network that continuously measures a parameter which changes over time, such as temperature, the value of a single packet is governed by an estimation of its contribution to the recreation of the original signal. Attractive features of SmartGap include a low computational complexity and a simplified reconstruction of the original signal. An analysis and simulations in which the performance of SmartGap is compared with the performance of several commonly used buffer management algorithms in wireless sensor networks are provided in the paper. The simulations suggest that SmartGap indeed provides significantly improved QoI compared the other evaluated algorithms.

1 Introduction

Delay Tolerant Wireless Sensor Networks (DT-WSNs) are networks that combine concepts from delay-tolerant networking (DTN) and wireless sensor networks (WSN). In this work, we consider networks of constrained devices which sense their environment, and communicate sensor data (such as temperature and humidity) through wireless links. Sensor data is forwarded, possibly via multiple hops, to a sink node which gathers and stores the data for further processing.

Nodes in a DT-WSN can be stationary or moving; they can be location-aware or not; and, they can be homogeneous or heterogeneous. Connectivity between the nodes may be scheduled, intermittent or opportunistic. As an example, consider a WSN deployed in a rural area where there is no communication infrastructure. With the help of DTN data mules, sensor data is transported from the WSN to a central location where the data is stored and made available for further analysis. Figure 1 shows an example of such a network.

T. Abdelzaher et al. (Eds.): EWSN 2015, LNCS 8965, pp. 104–119, 2015.
© Springer International Publishing Switzerland 2015

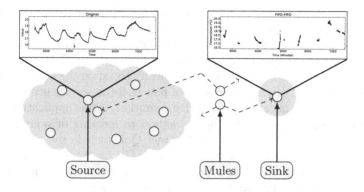

Fig. 1. An example of a DT-WSN comprising a number of spatially isolated wireless sensors. The source sensor nodes measure the environment by collecting measurement samples, which are transported by mobile data mules to a sink node. The sink attempts to reproduce the measurement from the samples. As the capacity of the network is limited, some samples are lost in transit, and the quality of the reproduced measurement is affected.

Although, there is a significant amount of work on both WSNs and DTNs, there is less work on the combination of the two network types. Previous work exists on DT-WSN systems in laboratory settings, such as the Wind Tunnel Monitoring system by Lou et al. [1] and the Data Elevator testbed by Pottner et al. [2]. Furthermore, Zennaro reports experiences from a field trial with a network to monitor water quality in the Blantyre district of Malawi [3].

In this work, we consider buffer management algorithms for DT-WSNs. The typically intermittent-delivery, long-latency and low-bandwidth characteristics of these networks, enforce a store-and-forward behaviour on the nodes, and make buffer management pivotal to uphold a high network performance. Yet, there is relatively little previous work on buffer management in DT-WSNs. To illustrate the importance of buffer management in DT-WSNs, consider a straightforward approach that uses a head-drop buffer policy. In this policy, when a buffer is full, the first packet in the buffer, i.e. the oldest one, is dropped. Assume that a node collects one sample per minute and stores the sample in the buffer. Further assume that, for some reason, the node is unable to communicate for a period of one hour. Then only the last 10 packets will remain in the buffer, and the remaining 50 packets will be dropped. In other words, newly arrived packets take priority over already queued packets. As a result, there could be long periods of measurements during which the sink node gets no measurement data at all.

Previous work on buffer management in DT-WSNs can be divided into two broad categories: work that considers packets to be *transparent* and work that considers packets *opaque*. If packets are considered transparent, buffer management has the capability to parse the data being transported and make decisions based on packet content. In contrast, if packets are opaque, buffer management decisions are only based on the information available in the header of the packets, and not on packet content.

There are some clear advantages with algorithms that treat packets as transparent. These algorithms can for example use compression of data or prioritise data based on content. This approach is typically based on the notion of *Quality of Information* (QoI) [4], i.e. a measure of how well the service provided by the network meets the applications' needs. By definition, QoI is application-specific, so there is no universally agreed upon method to measure or quantify it. Examples of such algorithms, all of which target QoI, include the work of Liu et al. [5], Humber and Ngai [6], and Alippi et al. [7]. In the algorithm proposed by Liu et al., the buffered data is replaced with a linear approximation when the buffer is full. Humber and Ngai estimates the importance of a packet when it is created based on how much the sampled value stored in the packet differs from previous values, and then assigns a priority class to the packet on the basis of this estimate. Lastly, Alippi et al. focus on energy saving, and dynamically adjust the sample rate based on the frequency of the property being sampled.

Algorithms that treat packets as opaque do not depend on code to parse the data being transported. Algorithms such as FIFO are easy to understand and implement, but their performance may not be optimal. One attempt to provide improved performance compared to FIFO while still considering packets opaque is the work by Nasser et al. [8] which proposes a Dynamic Multilevel Priority (DMP) packet scheduling scheme in which sensor nodes are organised into a hierarchical structure. Sensor nodes that have the same hop distance from the sink node are considered to be located at the same hierarchical level, and a Time Division Multiplexing Access (TDMA) scheme is used to prioritise packets from different levels. Another example is Lyu et al. [9] which suggests a multi-queue Last In First Out (LIFO) queueing policy. Their main argument is that LIFO works better than FIFO for real-time applications because it achieves a shorter delay in congested situations, especially when packets are limited by a deadline.

We see a clear need for algorithms which considers packets to be opaque: For one thing, we believe that transparent buffer management techniques in which sensor nodes parse the contents of packets are potentially expensive in terms of computational and energy resources. Also, they are not general purpose solutions and therefore inflexible – each sensor node must be equipped with code for parsing the data that flows through the network. In our scenario, the data mules would need to be aware of the format of the data they carry. At the same time, we see a need for buffer management algorithms that give priority to the data samples that are most important in the reconstruction of the original measurement at the sink node, i.e. QoI targeted buffer management algorithms.

In this work, we present *SmartGap* – a QoI-targeted buffer management algorithm which considers packets opaque. SmartGap is a novel buffer management algorithm that tries to maximise the combined value of the packets in the buffer. It accomplishes this by letting the priority of a packet be determined by the *gap* the packet would inflict – if dropped – on a complete series of measurement.

The remainder of the paper is organised as follows. Section 2 presents and explains the design of the SmartGap algorithm. An analysis of SmartGap's main characteristics is given in section 3. Section 4 provides a comprehensive evaluation of SmartGap and compares its performance with three commonly used buffer management algorithms in DT-WSNs. Section 5 discusses the benefits and limitations of SmartGap. The paper concludes in section 6 with a summary of the paper and some remarks on future work.

2   The SmartGap Algorithm

Buffer management schemes can typically be split up into two parts, a *queueing policy* and a *forwarding strategy* [10]. The queueing policy decides which packets in a buffer to discard when the buffer space is exhausted, while the forwarding strategy decides the order in which packets in the buffer should be forwarded.

An insight, which follows from the Nyquist-Shannon sampling theorem is that the quality of a reconstructed signal depends on the sampling frequency. So, to be able to reconstruct the signal as faithfully as possible, we wish to maximise the minimum number of samples in any given time period. In other words, the collected samples should be evenly distributed in time. As each sample is transported inside a packet, it follows that we want to minimise the maximum time gap between any two consecutive packets. Hence, the problem is to design a buffer management algorithm that during periods of congestion distributes packet losses evenly over time. The following section elaborates on the problem by demonstrating how common buffer management algorithms such as FIFO and Random distributes the packets. Next, we provide a detailed description of the SmartGap algorithm.

2.1   FIFO Buffer Management

Let us consider a DT-WSN that contains a source node, a sink node, and a data mule which moves in a random pattern between the source and sink nodes. The data mule collects data from the source node and uploads it to the sink node. Furthermore, assume that the the buffer space and transport capacity of the mule is insufficient to handle the load. Given that the source node employs FIFO (First In, First Out) as both queuing policy and forwarding strategy, the outcome could resemble that shown in Figure 2.

As follows from the figure, the delivered data is very unevenly distributed over time – during some periods, all sampled data is delivered, while there are also long periods with no or few data samples are delivered – something which makes it hard to reconstruct the original series of measurement. This is to be expected, as the FIFO strategy always picks the oldest packet in the buffer for forwarding or discarding.

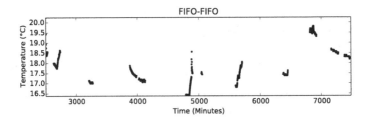

Fig. 2. Delivered data from a simulated DT-WSN (random-waypoint) which employs FIFO queueing policy and forwarding strategy. Note the long gaps in the delivered data.

2.2   Random Buffer Management

A naive attempt to spread out packets more evenly could be to use the Random algorithm, i.e. to randomly discard samples at times when the buffer is full, and to randomly pick the packet to forward next. Figure 3 shows the result of using such a buffer management policy for the same system as used in Figure 2. Compared to FIFO, the Random algorithm spreads out the data more. However, note that data is still clustered since the Random algorithm has a bias towards delivering recent packets. This can be explained by viewing the buffer management problem as an urn problem. Assume that data is constantly added to a buffer (urn), from which packets are randomly removed – either by forwarding or discarding. As this is an iterative process, a packet added early has higher probability to be chosen for removal than a packet added later. When we simulate the algorithm, we can clearly see this effect.

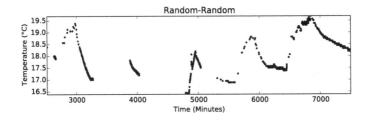

Fig. 3. Delivered data from a simulated DT-WSN (random-waypoint) which employs Random queueing policy and forwarding strategy. There are still gaps in the delivered data, but the gaps are reduced compared to the FIFO case.

2.3   SmartGap

The SmartGap algorithm attempts to further shorten the duration of periods with few delivered packets. SmartGap calculates the gap in time that would result from removing a specific packet from the buffer, and then gives priority to packets that cover large gaps. SmartGap is based on the notion of *creation time*: the time when a packet, P, was created at the source sensor node, $time(P)$.

Definition 1: Interpacket Gap. The interpacket gap represents the difference in creation time between two packets. For two packets P_i and P_j the interpacket gap is $|time(P_i) - time(P_j)|$.

Definition 2: The Gap Metric. The SmartGap algorithm is based on the *gap* metric. For a given packet buffer in a node, sort all packets in the buffer according to creation time. Then the gap metric for a packet P_n is the interpacket gap between the preceding packet, P_{n-1}, and the succeeding packet, P_{n+1}, packet in the buffer:

$$Gap(P_n) = |time(P_{n+1}) - time(P_{n-1})|$$

For example, consider a buffer with three packets, P_0, P_1, and P_2, with creation times 1, 3, and 4, respectively. Then we obtain:

$$Gap(P_1) = |time(P_2) - time(P_0)| = |4 - 1| = 3$$

The computations of the gap metric for the first and last packet in the buffer are slightly more complex, since these packets do not have both a preceding and a succeeding packet.

Depending on whether SmartGap is used as a forwarding strategy or a queuing policy, these two border cases are handled differently. When used as a queuing policy, SmartGap considers the first and last packets to have an infinite gap metric, and will therefore not discard them. When used as a forwarding strategy, SmartGap estimates the gap metric for the first and last packet as twice the interpacket gap between these packets and the closest packet in the buffer. This is based on an assumption that the packets are evenly distributed. Thus, if P_0 is the first packet and P_N the last packet, we have:

$$Gap(P_0) = 2 \cdot |time(P_1) - time(P_0)|$$
$$Gap(P_N) = 2 \cdot |time(P_N) - time(P_{N-1})|$$

2.4   SmartGap Queuing and Forwarding

SmartGap uses the gap metric to prioritise packets. As a queuing policy, Smart-Gap will discard the packet with the lowest gap metric. In other words, packets in bursts have higher probability of being discarded than single packets. When used as a forwarding strategy, SmartGap will forward the packet with the largest gap metric. This means that sparsly distributed packets are more likely to be forwarded than clustered ones.

Figure 4 illustrates how SmartGap is able to distribute the packets more evenly as compared to both the FIFO and Random buffer management schemes. The nodes still run out of buffer space when the path between the source and the sink node has insufficient capacity, but since SmartGap distributes packets more evenly, trends in the data are clearly visible.

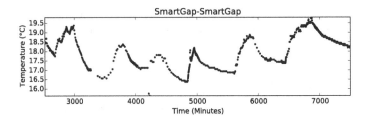

Fig. 4. Delivered data from a simulated DT-WSN (random-waypoint) which employs SmartGap. As follows, SmartGap gives even shorter periods with few or no delivered data as compared to a Random queuing policy.

3 Analysis

This section contains an analysis of the performance of SmartGap. First, an upper bound for the gap metric is established. Next, statistics for the variation of the gap in the examples in section 2 are presented. Finally, the computational complexity of SmartGap is discussed.

3.1 Upper Bound for the Gap

SmartGap determines which packets to discard and which to forward in the buffer. However, since the ultimate goal of SmartGap is to minimise the largest interpacket gap among all packets in the network, it is interesting to examine the effect on the largest gap of discarding a packet from the buffer. For this purpose, we use the term *maximum gap* of a set of packets to denote the largest interpacket gap between two consecutive packets in the sequence obtained by ordering the packets according to their creation time.

Theorem 1. Assume that $P_0 \ldots P_N$ are packets distributed among a number of nodes communicating reliably (i.e. without packet loss or with retransmissions on each hop). Each packet has an associated gap metric, calculated according to Definition 2. Discarding packet P_n, where $0 < n < N$, from a buffer will create an interpacket gap not larger than $Gap(P_n)$.

Proof. Assume without loss of generality that $P_0 \ldots P_N$ are ordered in a sequence according to creation time, so that P_0 is the youngest packet and P_N the oldest one, and that packet creation times are distinct – two different packets in the sequence do not have the same creation time. Let P_{n-1} denote the packet immediately before P_n in the sequence, and P_{n+1} the packet immediately after. Hence, discarding P_n will create an interpacket gap in the sequence of size $G = |time(P_{n+1}) - time(P_{n-1})|$. We want to show that $G \leq Gap(P_n)$.

Assume that the packets in the buffer where P_n is queued are ordered according to creation time (again, without loss of generality). If P_{n-1} and P_{n+1} are both in the same buffer as P_n, then P_{n-1} must be immediately before P_n, and P_{n+1} immediately after P_n. Hence, when discarding P_n, the size of the newly created interpacket gap (G) is equal to $Gap(P_n)$, the gap metric for P_n in the buffer (by Definition 2). Otherwise, if not both P_{n-1} and P_{n+1} are in the same buffer as P_n, it means that the packet immediately before P_n in the buffer is younger than P_{n-1}, and/or the packet immediately after P_n in the buffer is older than P_{n+1}. From this follows that $Gap(P_n)$, the gap metric for P_n in the buffer, is larger than G, the interpacket gap created by removing P_n. Hence, $G \leq Gap(P_n)$.   □

Theorem 2. The maximum gap created by discarding a packet in a buffer according to the SmartGap strategy is $2\frac{T}{N-1}$ where T is the interpacket gap between the oldest and the newest packet in the network, and $N \geq 3$ is the number of packets in the buffer.

Proof. Assume that the network has a single node, and the packets stored at a sensor node are evenly distributed in time between 0 and T. Also assume that packets are created at time 0 and at time T. Then the interpacket gap between any two consecutive packets is $\frac{T}{N-1}$, and the maximum interpacket gap in the buffer after discarding a packet is $2\frac{T}{N-1}$. If the packets are not evenly distributed between 0 and T there will be a packet P_n such that $Gap(P_n) \leq 2\frac{T}{N-1}$. If not, all consecutive pairs of interpacket gaps have to be larger than average, which is clearly impossible. If there are multiple nodes in the network, Theorem 1 tells us that the maximum gap will not grow larger due to the packets stored at the other nodes.   □

3.2   Variation of the Gap

The design goal of SmartGap is to minimise the maximum interpacket gap. In the simulation in section 2, three different algorithms are evaluated using a random waypoint mobility model and a buffer size of 110 packets. We repeat the simulation 30 times and calculate the confidence intervals for the mean, max and standard deviation of the interpacket gap. The result is presented in Table 1. As expected, there is no significant difference in the mean between the three algorithms. However, there is indeed a significant difference in both the maximum value and the variance: SmartGap provides a significant reduction of both maximum and standard deviation over FIFO as well as Random. The reason to this is the tendency of the FIFO and Random algorithms to discard consecutive packets.

Table 1. Interpacket gap in the three examples, 30 repetitions of the simulation, with 95% confidence intervalls presented. Note that SmartGap provides a lower maximum and standard deviation of the interpacket gap, as intended.

Algorithm	Mean	Max	Standard Deviation
FIFO	3.99 (3.64, 4.33)	800.43 (713.75, 887.11)	38.66 (34.98, 42.34)
Random	4.15 (3.79, 4.51)	388.16 (313.85, 462.47)	17.27 (14.66, 19.88)
SmartGap	4.17 (3.81, 4.53)	18.50 (15.94, 21.05)	3.86 (3.36, 4.35)

3.3 Computational Complexity

SmartGap has a low computational complexity. By memorising the gap metric for a packet, and keeping an ordered set of references to the packets in the buffer, the gap metric needs to be calculated at most three times for each packet received, and two times for each packet transmitted or discarded. So SmartGap has linear complexity, $\mathcal{O}(n)$, where n is the number of packets received by the node. Calculating the gap metric requires extracting the creation time from the header of the packets and performing basic arithmetic operations.

4   Evaluation

In the previous section, we established an upper bound for the size of the maximum interpacket gap. We also compared SmartGap with other buffer management algorithms and found that SmartGap provides a more even distribution of packets. This section provides a more comprehensive evaluation of SmartGap. Particularly, the QoI provided by SmartGap is compared with a select of other well-known buffer management algorithms, namely:

- First In First Out (FIFO),
- Random choice (Random),
- A priority queue based on Humber and Ngai [6] (Humber-Ngai).

All studied buffer management algorithms, including SmartGap, may be used both as queueing policy and forwarding strategy. FIFO and Random are straightforward algorithms that consider packets opaque. Humber-Ngai is a sliding-window algorithm which considers packets transparent. The algorithm calculates a sliding window over the packets as they are created, and if a new packet carries a value that differs more than a certain amount from the values in previous packets, the new packet is given a high priority. Humber-Ngai's algorithm also compresses data by removing samples when there are no significant changes.

Apart from the studied buffer management algorithms, we have also simulated Oldest First, Youngest First, and First In Last Out, however, since neither one of them differ much from FIFO in terms of performance, they are omitted from our evaluation. We have also considered the algorithms proposed by Liu et al. [5] and Alippi et al. [7], but found these algorithms to be less suited for DTN data mules. Instead, they are primarily intended for limiting the data rate on source nodes. We consider this approach complementary to the buffer management algorithms evaluated here.

In the following, to be able to differentiate between queuing policy and forwarding strategy, a particular buffer management scheme is denoted: *queuing policy-forwarding strategy*. For example, "FIFO-Random" denotes the buffering scheme that employs a FIFO queueing policy and a Random forwarding strategy.

4.1 Simulation Setup and Datasets

Therefore a custom-built simulation system has been developed, focusing on buffer management in DT-WSN. The simulation system has been built in Python, on top of the discrete event simulation package, SimPy [11]. In our simulation system, a DT-WSN is modelled as a set of nodes with pre-set buffer sizes connected with links. Packets emanate from source nodes that model wireless sensor devices. They are forwarded toward sink nodes, i.e. controllers, along network paths comprising links and intermediate nodes. The intermediate nodes model both fixed data aggregation nodes and mobile data mules. A separate mobility model is used to pre-calculate the meetings between data mules and their neighbouring nodes. Routing is done using the probabilistic routing protocol, PRoPHET [12], a routing protocol introduced by Lindgren et al. The rationale for using ProPHET is first and foremost that it is one of a few routing protocols for DT-WSNs that has been standardised and it is regularly used as a baseline when evaluating routing protocols, e.g. by Case et al. [13]. To allow the routing to stabilise, the simulation runs for 2500 simulated minutes, i.e. around 42 hours, before the actual experiment starts.

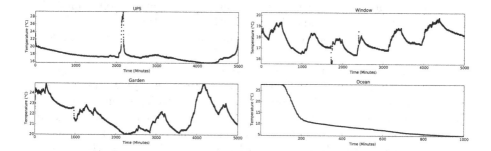

Fig. 5. The four temperature datasets used in the simulations. The data sets are available online [14,15,16,17]

Since the data being transported influences the outcome of the experiments, our simulation system is trace driven and runs from temperature data sets from real-world WSNs. Particularly, the evaluation is made against four different datasets, "Ocean", "UPS", "Windows", and "Garden", which are depicted in Figure 5. The datasets are selected to represent a spectrum of different types of WSN traffic. The "Ocean" dataset is based on a series of deep sea CDT (Conductivity, Temperature and Depth) measurements from the National Data Buoy Center (NDBC) [18], and is available online [17]. A reason for including this dataset in our evaluation is to enable comparisons between SmartGap and other buffer management algorithms beyond the three already included in the evaluation. Already, the "Ocean" dataset was used by Lou et al. [19] in a validation of their scheme for compressive sampling. The remaining three datasets, "UPS", "Windows" and "Garden", are all captured from a WSN deployed in and around a property in Uppsala, Sweden, and are available online [14,15,16].

4.2   Simulation Results

To evaluate the performance of SmartGap in terms of QoI, we simulate a DT-WSN of size 1000×1000 meters. The DT-WSN comprises ten nodes: one wireless temperature sensor node, one controller node and eight data mules. The mules move according to the widely used random-waypoint mobility model [20]. The speed of the mules is 5 metres/minute, and they have a range of 50 metres. We test multiple combinations of buffer sizes and buffer management algorithms. The QoI experienced in a simulation run is estimated using the mean absolute error or MAE between the original (f) dataset and the one being reconstructed at the controller node (g) using a cubic interpolation:

$$\text{MAE} = \frac{1}{N} \sum_{i=1}^{N} |f_i - g_i|$$

A low MAE reflects a high QoI. This method of estimating the QoI is based on the method used by Humber and Ngai [6]. We expect this measure of QoI to be correlated with the size and the distribution of the interpacket gaps. We repeat the simulation 30 times, re-seeding the random waypoint simulation each time. In this way, we vary the distribution of meetings, and this is what causes the differences in the outcome. We present mean results and confidence intervals.

Figure 6 shows the outcome of the simulations with a varying queueing policy and a fixed forwarding strategy, FIFO. In other words, the figure illustrates how the buffer algorithms perform as queueing policies with increasing buffer sizes. The smallest buffer we simulate is 10 packets. Buffers smaller than 10 packets leave little room for effective buffer management, and our experience is that for buffers of that size, the choice of algorithm has little impact on the outcome. The largest buffer we simulate is 1500 packets, which is a buffer large enough to acommodate all data without discarding any packets, and hence there is no difference between the buffer algorithms. We expect a smaller buffer to give a larger error, and thus a lower a QoI, and a larger buffer to give a smaller error, and thus a higher QoI.

Our first observation is that Humber and Ngai's algorithm [6] almost perform the same as FIFO. The MannWhitney U test (p=0.05) accepts the alternative hypothesis that the two algorithms performs differently for buffer sizes larger than 800 packets on the Window and Garden Data sets, but otherwise rejects it. It appears that the Humber and Ngai algorithm is sensitive to the parameterisation, which needs match the characteristics (primarily variance and autocovariance) of the data. We tried to find a reasonable configuration of the algorithm experimentally, but of the settings we tried significantly outperformed FIFO for all data sets and buffer sizes.

Next, we observe the scale of the MAE. The resolution of the temperature sensors is about 10^{-1}, and errors much smaller than this would for any practical application be dominated by the resolution of the sensors. In addition, we note that the confidence intervals in the outcome for the FIFO/Humber-Ngai

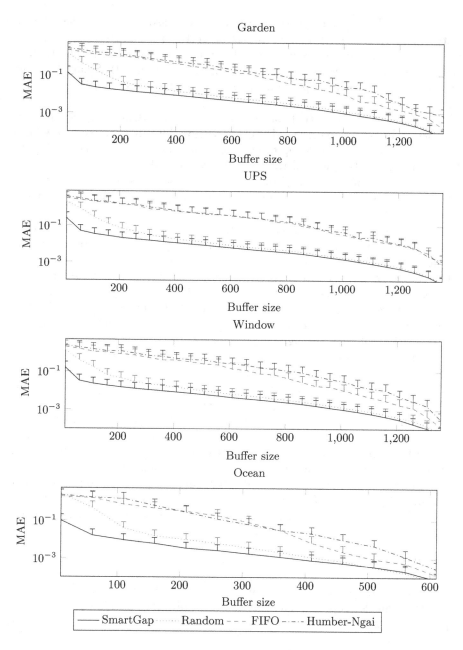

Fig. 6. Results from simulations using the FIFO forwarding strategy, with 95% upper confidence intervals presented. The lower confidence intervalls excluded for legibility. Humber-Ngai gives a small but significant reduction in MAE in the Ocean and Garden data sets, especially for larger buffer sizes. Random gives a significant reduction in MAE over both FIFO and Humber-Ngai, and SmartGap further reduces the MAE, especially for small buffer sizes.

strategies are large compared to SmartGap. The reason to this is that the selected mobility model has a larger impact on both FIFO and Humber-Ngai than
on SmartGap. Since we re-seed the mobility model for each run, the distribution of the meeting times will vary, and, in comparison with SmartCap, this
appears to have greater impact on the outcome of the FIFO and Humber-Ngai
simulations.

Another observation is that for all buffer sizes, SmartGap outperforms Random which in turn outperforms FIFO. In section 3.2 this trend is shown for a
single buffer size when studying the variance and maximum interpacket gap. In
the extended simulations reported here, we note that the observation holds true
across the range of buffer sizes simulated, regardless of which data set is used.
Thus, SmartGap fullfills the design goal of providing a significant improvement
in QoI.

It is interesting to note the scale of the buffer sizes. To obtain an MAE of
10^{-1}, SmartGap requires a buffer of about 10 - 15 packets. To obtain a similar
result with Random the buffer must be increased to 150 - 200 packets, while the
FIFO and Humber-Ngai discard policies require buffer sizes of 200 - 800 packets.
Hence, SmartGap creates the potential for a design choice. An application could
take advantage of this improved QoI, but could also maintain the QoI while
freeing up resources. This could for example be used to reduce device cost or
improve device lifetime through energy saving.

SmartGap can also be used as a forwarding strategy. As previously mentioned,
this will give priority to packets with a high gap metric when forwarding packets.
We expect the forwarding strategy to have a smaller impact on the experiment
outcome. The forwarding strategy decides the order in which packets are delivered towards the destination, and our QoI does not depend on delivery order.
Instead, it depends on whether a packet arrives to the destination or not. Repeating the experiment, using SmartGap as the forwarding strategy instead of
FIFO did not give a significant change in the experiment outcome.

To summarise, these results indicate that SmartGap could provide a significant improvement in QoI when used as a queuing policy, and that it provides
QoI at least on par with other algorithms when used as a forwarding strategy.

5   Discussion

After presenting the simulation results we follow with a short discussion of the
motivation for developing SmartGap and the limitations of this buffer management algorithm.

5.1   The Raison D'être of SmartGap

Although it might seem that SmartGap and similar buffer management solutions
are superfluous, and could be avoided through proper network provisioning, we
argue otherwise. For example, one seemingly straightforward way to provide a
high QoI would be to dimension buffers so that the likelihood of running out

of buffer space is minimal. However, predicting the required buffer space in a DT-WSN is extremely difficult, and the available hardware may not be capable of providing the required buffer space. In a survey by Hempstead et al. [21], the available storage space of the examined wireless sensors ranged from under 1 KB up to 138 KB. Moreover, even if the sampling is dimensioned for the lowest available bandwidth and buffer space, the sensor device will be unable to opportunistically take advantage of occasional extra available bandwidth, and buffer over-provisioning may in practice be a too costly alternative.

A seemingly attractive replacement to buffer management, would be to use compression or aggregation to reduce the amount of data being transferred between nodes in the wireless sensor network. For example, Vuran et al. [22] propose the use of temporal and spatial correlation in the data, and Al-Karaki et al. [23] present a number of suitable algorithms for data aggregation in WSNs. However, these and other approaches require data mules to be able to parse the data being collected, and perform potentially expensive operations, something which make them less suitable as general solutions. Still, it should be noted that compression and aggregation are indeed attractive solutions in specialised DT-WSNs, not least since they enable an explicit tradeoff between communication and computation resources, and thus could open up for significant energy savings.

5.2   Limitations of SmartGap

SmartGap relies on a few underlying assumptions, and if these do not hold true, SmartGap is unlikely to perform well. In particular, SmartGap assumes that the packets being transported in the DT-WSN are self-contained and correlated. In other words, the application must be able to interpret one packet alone, and there must be a correlation between packets to exploit. Normally, for environment sensing applications, sampling is done at a higher rate than the frequency of the underlying physical property being measured, as can be expected from Nyquist-Shannon. However, if the frequency of the underlying signal is too high, the correlation becomes weak. In that case, SmartGap would not provide any clear advantage. Consequently, in such scenarios it may be better to obtain a group of samples, collected very closely in time, and extrapolate the rest of the signal.

Self-containment is primarily a problem if samples do not fit into a single packet. This can for example happen if the sample is an image whose size is larger than the Maximum Transmission Unit, i.e. each sample will occupy multiple packets. If one packet is discarded, the rest of the packets that belong to the same sample become more or less worthless, and in this situation the strategy used by SmartGap is likely to cause more harm than good.

6   Conclusion

In this paper, we have proposed a novel buffer management algorithm, *SmartGap*, for Delay-Tolerant WSNs, i.e. WSNs with occasional connectivity between mobile and stationary wireless sensor nodes. SmartGap estimates the Quality of

Information, or QoI, of packets and gives priority to packets that contribute more to QoI. SmartGap determines the priority of a sample packet by the error or *gap* that a loss of this packet would impose on an overall series of measurements. An analysis and a simulation-based evaluation of SmartGap have been conducted, in which the algorithm is compared with a select of buffer management algorithms. According to the evaluation, SmartGap provides significant improvements in QoI compared to the alternative algorithms when used as a queueing policy, and performs at least as good as these algorithms when used as a forwarding strategy. The largest improvements are obtained in situations where the buffer space is small, and large amounts of data are discarded.

SmartGap is primarily intended for networks such as the water monitoring system in Malawi [3], where connectivity is opportunistic, memory space is limited, and the fidelity with which the the original signal can be recreated is crucial for the quality of the results.

The evaluation has been made using simulations with a random waypoint mobility model. A number of alternative mobility models have been developed [24], often in association with the development of routing protocols. One direction in which we wish to continue this work, is to test the performance under alternative mobility models, including replicating routing, and explore the interaction between the mobility model, the routing algorithm and the buffer management algorithm. As part of this work, we wish to study the fairness characteristics of SmartGap. Finally, encouraged by our promising simulation results, we would like to deploy SmartGap in a real world setting.

References

1. Luo, C.-J., Zhou, M.-T., Cao, Z.-Y.: Disruption-Tolerant Wireless Sensor Networks for Wind Tunnel Monitoring. In: International Conference on Apperceiving Computing and Intelligence Analysis, pp. 408–411 (2008)
2. Pöttner, W.-B., Büsching, F., von Zengen, G., Wolf, L.: Data elevators: Applying the bundle protocol in delay tolerant wireless sensor networks. In: Mobile Adhoc and Sensor Systems (MASS), pp. 218–226 (2012)
3. Zennaro, M.: Wireless Sensor Networks for Development: Potentials and Open Issues. Ph.D. dissertation, KTH Royal Institute of Technology (2010)
4. Sachidananda, V., Khelil, A., Suri, N.: Quality of Information in Wireless Sensor Networks: A Survey. ICIQ 1, 1–15 (2010)
5. Liu, C., Wu, K., Pei, J.: An energy-efficient data collection framework for wireless sensor networks by exploiting spatiotemporal correlation. IEEE Transactions on Parallel and Distributed Systems 18(7), 1010–1023 (2007)
6. Humber, G., Ngai, E.C.-H.: Quality-Of-Information Aware Data Delivery for Wireless Sensor Networks: Description and Experiments. In: IEEE Wireless Communication and Networking Conference, pp. 1–6 (April 2010)
7. Alippi, C., Anastasi, G., Di Francesco, M., Roveri, M.: An Adaptive Sampling Algorithm for Effective Energy Management in Wireless Sensor Networks With Energy-Hungry Sensors. IEEE Transactions on Instrumentation and Measurement 59(2), 335–344 (2010)

8. Nasser, N., Karim, L., Taleb, T.: Dynamic Multilevel Priority Packet Scheduling Scheme for Wireless Sensor Network. IEEE Transactions on Wireless Communications 12(4), 1448–1459 (2013)

9. Lyu, M.R.: Congestion performance improvement in wireless sensor networks. In: 2012 IEEE Aerospace Conference, pp. 1–9 (March 2012)

10. Lindgren, A., Phanse, K.K.: Evaluation of Queueing Policies and Forwarding Strategies for Routing in Intermittently Connected Networks. In: 1st International Conference on Communication Systems Software & Middleware, pp. 1–10. IEEE (2006)

11. Scherfke, S., Lünsdorf, O.: SimPy - Discrete Event Simulation for Python (2014), http://simpy.readthedocs.org/

12. Lindgren, A., Doria, A., Davies, E., Grasic, S.: Probabilistic Routing Protocol for Intermittently Connected Networks. RFC 6693 (Experimental), Internet Engineering Task Force (August 2012), http://www.ietf.org/rfc/rfc6693.txt

13. Spyropoulos, T., Member, S., Psounis, K.: Efficient Routing in Intermittently Connected Mobile Networks: The Multiple-Copy Case. EEE/ACM Transactions on Networking 16(1), 77–90 (2008)

14. Söderman, P.: UPS data set, figshare (May 2014), http://figshare.com/articles/UPS_data_set/1018702

15. Söderman, P.: Window data set, figshare (May 2014), http://figshare.com/articles/Window_data_set/1018703

16. Söderman, P.: Garden data set figshare (May 2014), http://figshare.com/articles/Garden_data_set/1018700

17. Söderman, P.: Ocean data set, figshare (May 2014), http://figshare.com/articles/Ocean_data_set/1018701

18. NOAA, National Data Buoy Center (2008), http://www.ndbc.noaa.gov/

19. Luo, C., Wu, F., Sun, J., Chen, C.: Compressive data gathering for large-scale wireless sensor networks. IEEE Transactions on Mobile Computing and Networking (800), 145–156 (2009)

20. Imielinski, T., Korth, H.F.: Dynamic Source Routing in Ad Hoc Wireless Networks. In: Mobile Computing, pp. 153–181 (1996)

21. Hempstead, M., Lyons, M.J., Brooks, D., Wei, G.-Y.: Survey of Hardware Systems for Wireless Sensor Networks. Journal of Low Power Electronics 4(1), 11–20 (2008)

22. Vuran, M.C., Akan, O.B., Akyildiz, I.F.: Spatio-temporal correlation: theory and applications for wireless sensor networks. Computer Networks 45(3), 245–259 (2004)

23. Al-Karaki, I., UI-Mustafa, R., Kamal, A.: Data aggregation in wireless sensor networks - exact and approximate algorithms. In: 2004 Workshop on High Performance Switching and Routing, HPSR, pp. 241–245 (2004)

24. Camp, T., Boleng, J., Davies, V.: A survey of mobility models for ad hoc network research. Wireless Communications and Mobile Computing 2(5), 483–502 (2002)

A Knapsack-Based Message Scheduling and Drop Strategy for Delay-Tolerant Networks

En Wang[1,2], Yongjian Yang[1], and Jie Wu[2]

[1] Department of Computer Science and Technology, Jilin University, China
wangen0310@126.com, yyj@jlu.edu.cn
[2] Department of Computer and Information Sciences, Temple University, USA
jiewu@temple.edu

Abstract. Because of the dramatic changes in topology and frequently interrupted connections between nodes, messages in delay-tolerant networks are forwarded in the store-carry-forward approach. Routing methods in such an environment tend to increase the number of messages to improve the delivery ratio. However, excessive message copies lead to buffer overflows because of limited storage space. Therefore, an efficient message-scheduling and drop strategy is vital to maximizing network resources, especially when bandwidth is limited and message sizes differ. We developed a theoretical framework called the knapsack-based message scheduling and drop strategy in theory (KMSDT) based on epidemic message dissemination. To improve the delivery ratio, this strategy sorts message copies by utility per unit and, if buffer overflows occur, it decides which messages to drop based on the solution to the knapsack problem. Furthermore, we developed a practical framework called the knapsack-based message scheduling and drop strategy in practice (KMSDP). Rather than collecting global statistics as done in the KMSDT, KMSDP estimates all parameters by using locally collected statistics. Simulations based on synthetic trace are done in ONE. Results show that, without affecting the average delay or overhead ratio, KMSDP and KMSDT achieve a better delivery ratio than other congestion-control strategies.

Keywords: Delay-tolerant networks, congestion, knapsack problem, sch-eduling strategy, drop strategy.

1 Introduction

Delay-tolerant networks (DTNs) [1], are a type of challenged network in which end-to-end transmission latency may be arbitrarily long due to occasionally connected links. Examples of such networks are those operating in mobile or extreme scenarios such as interplanetary networks [2], battlefields [3], rural areas [4], wildlife tracking [5], and pocket-switched networks [6, 7]. Fall first put forward this new network paradigm at SIGCOMM in 2003 [1].

Mobile ad hoc networks were treated, until recently, as connected graphs over which end-to-end paths had to be established. However, because of node

T. Abdelzaher et al. (Eds.): EWSN 2015, LNCS 8965, pp. 120–134, 2015.
© Springer International Publishing Switzerland 2015

mobility and intermittent-contact links, DTNs are occasionally connected. A bundle layer was proposed to solve this problem, which includes the store-carry-forward approach and the custody-transfer strategy that keeps a bundle while the next reliable hop is determined, unless the time to live (TTL) of the bundle expires. Thus, choosing the next nodes to which the messages could be forwarded is critical in such an approach. Many researchers have now begun to focus on developing efficient routing protocols in DTNs [8] to improve the delivery ratio. However, routing protocols in DTNs tend to increase the number of message copies, and store the message until it finds an available link to the next hop without considering the limited buffer space [9]. This is bound to bring storage and bandwidth overhead. In a real network environment, congestion results from stringent limitations on storage and bandwidth.

To address these congestion issues, this paper presents a study of a message scheduling and drop framework called the knapsack-based message scheduling and drop strategy in theory (KMSDT) and applies it to DTNs under epidemic routing. The strategy is the first to calculate the utility value of each message by evaluating the impact that either duplicating or dropping a message on the delivery ratio. Next, the messages are sorted according to their per-unit utility, and whether or not to drop the message is decided based on the knapsack problem. However, to derive the utility, KMSDT requires global information of the network, which makes its implementation difficult in practice, especially given the intermittently connected nature of the targeted networks. To amend this, we propose a second strategy called the knapsack-based message-scheduling and drop strategy in practice (KMSDP), which is a distributed algorithm that estimates the required network parameters by using locally collected statistics. Simulations based on synthetic trace are done in ONE, and results show that KMSDP and KMSDT achieve better delivery ratios than other congestion control strategies. The main contributions are summarized as follows:

(1) We propose a message scheduling and drop strategy KMSDT based on the improvement of GBSD [10], it calculates the probability of successful delivery for situations of limited bandwidth according to the contact-duration distribution, and maximizes the delivery ratio for different-size messages based on the knapsack problem.

(2) We improve the KMSDT into a knapsack-based message-scheduling and drop strategy in practice (KMSDP) through collecting the network parameters independently for messages of different sizes.

(3) We conduct extensive simulations on synthetic trace. The results show that KMSDP and KMSDT achieve a better delivery ratio than other congestion-control strategies.

The remainder of the paper is organized as follows. We introduce the related work in Section 2. The knapsack-based scheduling and drop strategies are presented in Sections 3, 4 and 5, respectively. In Section 6, we evaluate the performance of KMSDT and KMSDP through extensive simulations. We conclude the paper in Section 7.

2   Related Work

Several simple drop strategies under epidemic are (1) drop front (DF), in which the longest queued message in the buffer is dropped; (2) drop last (DL), in which the last message received in the buffer is dropped; (3) drop oldest (DO), in which the message in the buffer with the smallest remaining TTL is dropped; and (4) drop youngest (DY), in which the message in the buffer with the largest remaining TTL is dropped. In any case, researchers have proposed better buffer-management strategies: To reduce the impact on overall network performance, Dohyung et al. [11] drop messages with the largest expected number of message copies. Erramilli and Crovella [12] describe a strategy in which messages are scheduled according to priority, which is calculated based on the distance from the source node to the destination node.

All buffer-management strategies described above adopt a heuristic algorithm and cannot dynamically adapt to the changing topology in DTNs. Thus, solutions for certain performance metrics (such as delivery ratio) are suboptimal. Some groups have tried to develop a non-heuristic buffer-management strategy by dynamically collecting the network parameters and then deriving the optimal solutions for delivery ratio or average delay. For example, Elwhishi et al. [13] propose a scheduling scheme for epidemic routing and two-hop forwarding: they obtain the optimal solution for delivery ratio and average delay by solving the relevant ordinary differential equations. In the paper, they assume that all messages in the network are the same size and that the method used to collect the network parameters does not yield accurate parameter values. In addition, they do not consider the impact of bandwidth on delivery ratio. Krifa and Barakat have published three papers in this field: In [14], by optimizing delivery ratio and average delay, they obtain the utility value of a given message by calculating the impact of replicating or dropping the message, and then they drop the message with the smallest utility. Based on the result of [14], the work in [15] extends a scheduling strategy and, when forwarding, prioritizes messages with the highest utility. Considering that [14]'s proposed strategy results in over-loaded bandwidths due to excessive information storage and exchange, Krifa and Barakat [10] propose an idealized scheduling and drop strategy called the global knowledge-based scheduling and drop (GBSD) strategy. In this strategy signal overhead is reduced by optimizing the storage structure and the statistics-collection method.

The proposed KMSDT calculates the probability of successful delivery for situations of limited bandwidth according to the contact-duration distribution and, when buffer overflows occur, it maximizes the delivery ratio for different-size messages based on the knapsack problem. Furthermore, we improve the original GBSD utility model by accounting for the situation in which, more copies of a given message are created in the future. In addition, the network parameters are collected independently for messages of different sizes.

3 Model Description

In this section, we first describe the assumptions upon which our theoretical framework is founded and the issues that this framework can solve. Next, we identify which utility model to use for a given message by quantifying the influence of replicating or dropping the message.

3.1 Assumptions and Problem Formulation

In this paper, we make the following assumptions regarding the network environment: Each message has a given TTL, after which the message is no longer useful and should be dropped. Afterward, it chooses its source and destination nodes arbitrarily, and also chooses its size arbitrarily from a specified range, within which messages of different sizes can coexist. No node has an immunization strategy or a mechanism to send acknowledgments to confirm the receipt of packets. The bandwidth between each node pair is limited, and message transmission time cannot be ignored; when communicating with the destination node, we ignore the transmission time. If the transmission of a certain message is interrupted, the message must be retransmitted. Nodes move independently of each other, such as random walk and random waypoint; the intermeeting times and contact durations between nodes tail off exponentially [16, 17].

This paper primarily addresses the following two problems in buffer management: (1) when more than one message is in a node's local buffer and the node does not know if the contact will last sufficiently long to forward all messages, we maximize the delivery ratio by calculating which message to send first. (2) If a new message arrives at a node's buffer and the buffer is full, we maximize the delivery ratio by calculating which message the node should drop, considering those already in its local buffer and the newly arrived message.

To address these two problems, we propose the idealized scheduling and drop strategy KMSDT, which first expresses the delivery ratio as a function of dynamic network parameters. The per-message utility is derived from the marginal value of the delivery ratio. Message size and bandwidth limitations are considered in this process. (1) If the bandwidth is insufficient for the node to forward all messages in its local buffer, the node should replicate messages in decreasing order of their per-unit utility. (2) If buffer overflows occur, the node must decide which messages to drop based on its utility and the knapsack problem, as to maximize the total utility of all the local message copies.

3.2 Utility Model

In DTNs, the intermeeting time and contact duration will influence the message-delivery ratio. Here we define them as follows:

Definition 1. *Intermeeting time is time elapsed from the end of the previous contact to the start of the next contact.*

Definition 2. *Contact duration is the time during which a node pair is in contact.*

Table 1. Notation

Variable	Description
N	Total number of nodes in the network minus one
$K_{(t)}$	Number of distinct messages in the network at time t
TTL_i	Initial time to live (TTL) for message i
R_i	Remaining time to live (TTL) for message i
T_i	Elapsed time for message i since its generation $(T_i = TTL_i - R_i)$
$n_i(T_i)$	Number of copies of message i in the network
$m_i(T_i)$	Number of nodes (excluding source) that have seen message i
E_1	Average inter-meeting time between nodes
λ_1	Parameters in the exponential distribution of inter-meeting time $(\lambda_1 = \frac{1}{E_1})$
E_2	Average contact duration between nodes
λ_2	Parameters in the exponential distribution of contact duration $(\lambda_2 = \frac{1}{E_2})$
M_i	Size of message i
W	Bandwidth of contacts between two nodes
U_i	Utility of message i
P_{T_i}	Probability that message i has been successfully delivered now
P_{R_i}	Probability that undelivered message i will reach destination within R_i
ε_i	Probability that message i can be forwarded successfully during a contact
P_i	Probability that message i can be successfully delivered
P	Delivery ratio

As mentioned in the assumptions, the latest research shows that intermeeting times and contact durations are exponentially distributed under many popular mobility scenarios such as random walk, random waypoint, and random direction. Our simulation is based on the mobility scenarios: a synthetic one (the random-waypoint scenario).

Assume λ_1 and λ_2 are the parameters for the exponential distribution of intermeeting time and contact duration, and E_1 and E_2 denote the mathematical expectation values; then $\lambda_1 = \frac{1}{E_1}$ and $\lambda_2 = \frac{1}{E_2}$ (Table 1). Our goal is to express the probability P_i as a formal expression of n_i and to calculate the utility of message i by quantifying the effect of replicating or dropping a copy of i on P_i. To achieve this goal, some probability notations are defined in Table 1.

The probability for message i to be delivered is given by the probability that message i has been delivered and the probability that message i has not yet been delivered, but will be delivered during the remaining time R_i. Thus, P_i can be written as Eq. 1. Given that all nodes including the destination node have an equal chance of seeing message i, P_{T_i} can be written as Eq. 2.

$$P_i = (1 - P_{T_i})P_{R_i} + P_{T_i} \tag{1}$$

$$P_{T_i} = \frac{m_{T_i}}{N} \tag{2}$$

First, we consider the change of $n_i(t)$ over time. Based on the ordinary-differential-equation model used in [18], Eq. 3 is derived, where ε_i is the probability that message i can be forwarded successfully during contact, as indicated in

Table 1. $\lambda_1 = \frac{1}{E_1}$ is the reciprocal of the average intermeeting time. Furthermore, λ_1 is the average number of contacts between nodes per unit time.

$$\frac{dn_i(t)}{dt} = \varepsilon_i \lambda_1 n_i(t)[N - n_i(t)] \tag{3}$$

Assuming that the current time is T_i, the number of nodes that hold message i in buffers after time R_i can be expressed as Eq. 4. The parameter ε_i can be derived from the contact-duration distribution. Assuming bandwidth W and size M_i for message i, the contact duration should be greater than $\frac{M_i}{W}$ so that message i can be successfully forwarded. Because the contact durations follow an exponential distribution with parameter $-\lambda_2$, ε_i can be expressed as Eq. 5.

$$n_i(T_i + R_i) = \frac{N n_i(T_i)}{n_i(T_i) + [N - n_i(T_i)]e^{-\varepsilon_i \lambda N R_i}} \tag{4}$$

$$\varepsilon_i = e^{-\lambda_2 \frac{M_i}{W}} \tag{5}$$

With Eqs. 4 and 5 derived, we now consider the meaning of $1 - P_{R_i}$. The quantity $1 - P_{R_i}$ gives the probability that message i, which has not yet been delivered at T_i, will not be delivered in the remaining time $R_i(R_i = TTL - T_i)$. In other words, $1 - P_{R_i}$ gives the probability that the $n_i(T_i)$ nodes that have a message i in their buffers at T_i will not contact the destination node during R_i, and the new infected nodes will also not reach the destination node. Thus, P_{R_i} can be expressed as Eq. 6. By substituting Eqs. 2 and 6 into Eq. 1, we get the P_i expression as Eq. 7.

$$P_{R_i} = 1 - \frac{N^{\frac{1}{\varepsilon_i}}}{e^{\lambda N R_i}[n_i(T_i) - n_i(T_i)e^{-\varepsilon_i \lambda N R_i} + N e^{-\varepsilon_i \lambda N R_i}]^{\frac{1}{\varepsilon_i}}} \tag{6}$$

$$P_i = \frac{m_i(T_i) - N}{N} N^{\frac{1}{\varepsilon_i}} \frac{1}{e^{\lambda N R_i}[n_i(T_i) - n_i(T_i)e^{-\varepsilon_i \lambda N R_i} + N e^{-\varepsilon_i \lambda N R_i}]^{\frac{1}{\varepsilon_i}}} + 1 \tag{7}$$

Note that the delivery ratio P equals to the sum of P_i, which gives Eq. 8. Starting with Eq. 8, we can derive the effect of dropping or replicating a given message i, as follows:

$$P = \sum_{i=1}^{K_{(t)}} [\frac{m_i(T_i) - N}{N} N^{\frac{1}{\varepsilon}} \frac{1}{e^{\lambda N R_i}[n_i(T_i) - n_i(T_i)e^{-\varepsilon_i \lambda N R_i} + N e^{-\varepsilon_i \lambda N R_i}]^{\frac{1}{\varepsilon_i}}} + 1] \tag{8}$$

The scheduling and drop strategy described in our paper aims to maximize the delivery ratio within the network. Whenever a given message i is replicated during a contact, the number of message i copies increases by one $[\Delta n_i(T_i) = +1]$; if no operation is performed on message i, the number of message i copies remains unchanged $[\Delta n_i(T_i) = 0]$; when a copy of message i is dropped from the buffer, the number of message i copies decreases by one $[\Delta n_i(T_i) = -1]$. The utility of message i increases with the delivery ratio P. We obtain the following equation for calculating utility:

$$U_i = [N - m_i(T_i)]N^{\frac{1-\varepsilon_i}{\varepsilon_i}} e^{-\lambda N R_i} \frac{1}{\varepsilon_i}(1 - e^{-\varepsilon_i \lambda N R_i})$$

$$[n_i(T_i) - n_i(T_i)e^{-\varepsilon_i \lambda N R_i} + N e^{-\varepsilon_i \lambda N R_i}]^{\frac{-\varepsilon_i - 1}{\varepsilon_i}} \tag{9}$$

4   Idealized Knapsack-Based Scheduling and Drop Strategy

After calculating the message utility, the scheduling and drop strategy can be executed. A higher per-message utility indicates that replicating the message would lead to a more increase in the delivery ratio P. Thus, when two nodes are in contact, messages should be replicated in decreasing order of message utility to maximize P. In addition, a higher per-message utility also means that dropping the message would lead to a more decrease in the delivery ratio P. Thus, when buffer overflows occur, the message with the lowest per-message utility should be dropped. Previous studies [10, 14, 15] have proved that the above scheduling and drop strategy leads to a good delivery ratio. However, when message sizes differ, the strategy is no longer applicable.

In Fig. 1, the vertical rectangular boxes represent the local buffer of a node, and the smaller rounded rectangles represent the messages stored in the local buffer. The utilities per message satisfy $U_1 > U_2 > U_3$, and $U_2 + U_3 > U_1$. The message sizes satisfy $M_1 = 2M_2$ and $M_2 = M_3$. Fig. 1(a) shows two different scheduling methods. Assume that, because of the limited contact duration and bandwidth, only messages with no greater than M_1 bytes can be forwarded successfully. By leveraging the first scheduling method, only message 1 would be replicated, leading to a gain of U_1 in the delivery ratio. However, by leveraging the second scheduling method, messages 2 and 3 would be replicated leading to a gain of $U_2 + U_3$ in the delivery ratio. Thus, the second scheduling strategy obtains a better delivery ratio.

According to the above analysis, we see that the scheduling strategy that simply considers the per-message utility cannot be applied to networks where message sizes differ. Because bigger message sizes means that, for a given bandwidth, more buffer space is occupied and more transmission time is required, we schedule the messages according to the utility per unit $\frac{U_i}{M_i}$ and replicate messages in decreasing order of $\frac{U_i}{M_i}$.

In Fig. 1(b), the message utilities also satisfy $U_1 > U_2 > U_3$, and $U_2 + U_3 > U_1$. The message sizes satisfy $M_1 = 2M_2$ and $M_2 = M_3$. In addition, the local buffer is already full. Messages 2 and 3 are the smallest messages in size. When message 1 arrives and the buffer overflows, the message dropped should be chosen from among the message just received and all buffered messages. If we simply drop the message with the smallest utility, message 3 would be dropped first, followed by message 2. In this case, the delivery ratio would decrease by $U_2 + U_3$. If we adopt another strategy and only drop message 1, the delivery ratio would decrease by U_1. Thus, when message sizes differ, dropping the message with the smallest utility is not necessarily the best strategy.

Note that if the buffer sizes are fixed, the utilities of all the buffered messages and the newly arrived message can be obtained, and the aim of the drop strategy is to maximize the total utility of all messages in the local buffer. Thus, the drop problem takes the form of a typical $0-1$ knapsack problem. U_k is utility of the k_{th} message, and M is buffer size. M_k is size of the k_{th} message. n is the number

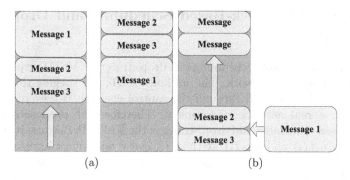

Fig. 1. Different schedule (a) and drop (b) strategies in a buffer

---

Algorithm 1. Dynamic programming to solve 0-1 knapsack problem

---

1: **for** $j = 0; j \leq totalWeight; j + +$ **do**
2:   **for** $i = 0; i \leq n; i + +$ **do**
3:     **if** $(i = 0 || j = 0)$ **then**
4:       $bestValues[i][j]=0;$
5:     **else**
6:       **if** $j < sizes[i - 1]$ **then**
7:         $bestValues[i][j]=bestValues[i - 1][j];$
8:       **else**
9:         $iweight=sizes[i - 1];$
10:        $ivalue=values[i - 1];$
11:        $bestValues[i][j]=MAX(bestValues[i - 1][j]);$
12:        $ivalue=ivalue+bestValues[i - 1][j - iWeight];$
13: **if** $bestSolution=null$ **then**
14:   $bestSolution=int[n];$
15: $tempWeight=totalWeight;$
16: **for** $i = n; i \geq 1; i - -$ **do**
17:   **if** $bestValues[i][tempWeight] > bestValues[i - 1][tempWeight]$ **then**
18:     $bestSolution[i - 1]=1;$
19:     $tempWeight=sizes[i - 1];$
20:   **if** $tempWeight=0$ **then**
21:     **break**;
22: $bestValue=bestValues[n][totalWeight];$

---

of all the buffered messages and the newly arrived message. x is a flag of whether the k_{th} message is buffered.

$$Max \sum_{k=1}^{n} U_k x_k$$

$$s.t. \quad \sum_{k=1}^{n} M_k x_k \leq M, \ x_k = \{0, 1\}, k = 1, 2, 3 \cdots n$$

To solve the $0-1$ knapsack problem as described above, we adopt the dynamic programming method (see Algorithm 1) to decide which messages should be buffered and which should be dropped (again, to maximize the delivery ratio).

5 Practical Knapsack-Based Scheduling and Drop Strategy

It is clear that the idealized scheduling and drop strategy KMSDT requires global information about the network. The authors of [16, 18] suggest that network parameters can be obtained through the control channel. However, this is not applicable in a real network environment. Therefore, we propose a practical knapsack-based scheduling and drop strategy: the KMSDP. Because it is difficult to determine $n_i(T_i)$ and $m_i(T_i)$ at time T_i, every node must approximate the current $n_i(T_i)$ and $m_i(T_i)$ for message i by using the history statistics of the once-stored messages. Each node maintains a list of messages for which it tracks the history in the network. For each message, it maintains a list of nodes that have already seen the message, and arrays in which it records whether or not the message is buffered. This history information is used to approximate $n(T)$ and $m(T)$, which allows the utility of each message to be calculated.

5.1 Collecting and Maintaining History Information

Each node selects a part of the once-stored messages for which history data must be collected, and puts them into its list of messages. Each item in the message list contains the message identification (ID) and the mature part of the message. The mature part of the message is a time field, which means that $n(T)$ and $m(T)$ before this time field are mature statistics (the meaning of mature statistics is explained in Section 5.2). Each node in the node lists maintains its node ID, stat_version, $n\_Bin[]$, and $m\_Bin[]$. The stat_version entry indicates the time unit (i.e., bin) in which the last update occurred. The $n\_Bin[]$ entry indicates whether or not the node buffers the message during a certain bin. Finally, the $m\_Bin[]$ entry indicates whether or not the node has already stored a copy of the message before the bin. Both $n\_Bin[]$ and $m\_Bin[]$ are Boolean arrays. For example, $n\_Bin[k]=1$ means that the node buffers a copy of the message during bin k, and $m\_Bin[k]=1$ means that the node saw a copy of the message before bin k (whether it still stores the copy of the message is not certain). The bin size (i.e., length of the time unit) for $n\_Bin[]$ and $m\_Bin[]$ is called Bin_Unit. Because the messages have a fixed TTL, a larger Bin_Unit translates into a smaller $n\_Bin[]$, so the node needs to maintain and exchange less data; however, with a larger Bin_Unit, some contact information would be omitted, leading to an inaccurate utility calculation. For a smaller Bin_Unit, the node needs to maintain more data, so the utility calculation is more accurate. However, because of the limited bandwidth, exchanging a large amount of data during a contact could easily make the strategy inoperable. Considering that the values stored in $n\_Bin[]$ and $m\_Bin[]$ can only be changed when the nodes contact each other, the size of Bin_Unit depends on the average intermeeting time E_1. For a good tradeoff between bandwidth overload and statistical accuracy, we argue that, based on [19], Bin_Unit should be $Bin\_Unit=\frac{E_1}{2}$.

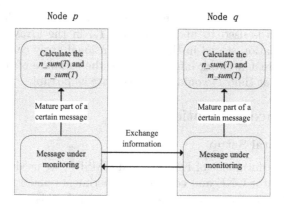

Fig. 2. Process to calculate $n\_sum(T)$ and $m\_sum(T)$

For example, the TTL of the message is $18000s$ and the average intermeeting time is $E_1 = 3000s$ (obtained by the intermeeting time statistics), then $Bin\_Unit = 1500s$ and the length of $n\_Bin[]$ and $m\_Bin[]$ is 12, and we may get the following bin arrays: $n\_Bin[] = (\,0\,0\,0\,0\,1\,1\,1\,0\,0\,0\,0\,0\,)$ and $m\_Bin[] = (\,0\,0\,0\,0\,1\,1\,1\,1\,1\,1\,1\,1\,)$. From the data in the bin arrays, we can learn that, during the first-four bins, the node had not stored or seen the message, that the message had reached the node during bin 5, and that it was dropped during bin 8. Given a message-generation interval t_m and n_m different message sizes, the average time that messages of a common size are generated is $t_m n_m$. This reasoning means that $\frac{TTL}{t_m n_m}$ messages should be monitored for each message type.

Each node in the data structure is supposed to maintain up-to-date statistics; the detailed update operation includes the following two parts: (1) At the beginning of each Bin_Unit, update $n\_Bin[]$ and $m\_Bin[]$ in the lists of nodes. If a certain field within $n\_Bin[]$ changes, update stat_version to the current time. Otherwise, keep stat_version unchanged. (2) When nodes encounter each other, they check whether or not they have monitored the same messages. If so, replace the old version with the new version.

5.2   Estimation of $n(T)$ and $m(T)$

For every message ever monitored, each node uses two one-dimensional arrays n_sum and m_sum, whose sizes equal to the sizes in their local buffer of $n(T)$ and $m(T)$ (e.g.,Bin_Number) to record the weighted average history statistics of $n(T)$ and $m(T)$, respectively. Note that the average time needed by the information to reach the current node is the average intermeeting time (i.e.,E_1) between nodes. In this paper, we assume that the current time is T, so history information prior to time T-E_1 is mature (i.e., complete) and can be used to update the mature data already stored.

Every time information regarding a certain message i becomes mature (as shown in Fig. 2), we first calculate $n_i(T_i)$ and $m_i(T_i)$ for this message. Next, we calculate the mean of the newly derived $n_i(T_i)$ and $n\_sum(T_i)$ that is already stored in the array n_sum. We then update $n\_sum(T_i)$ with the mean value. This same process is used to update $m\_sum(T_i)$ in the array m_sum. Thus, the history information stored in the one-dimensional array can be made more similar to the current network information, so the estimate of $n(T)$ and $m(T)$ for every message at time T would be as accurate as possible.

6 Performance Evaluation

6.1 Experimental Setup

To evaluate the performance of KMSDT and KMSDP, we used the opportunistic network simulator ONE and conducted experiments under scenarios implementing synthetic random-waypoint mobility model. In this scenario, each node repeats its own behavior: select a destination arbitrarily and walk along the shortest path to reach the destination.

To study the performance of KMSDT and KMSDP for different-sized messages, we first determine how messages are generated. We begin by generating messages with sizes selected arbitrarily from 0.5MB, 1MB, 1.5MB, and 2MB. The destination and source nodes are then selected arbitrarily from the entire network. Next, we allow a warm-up period collect and calculate the network parameters (without loss of generality, we set $TTL/2$ to make sure that the initial values of $n_i(T_i)$ and $m_i(T_i)$ may make KMSDP feasible). After the warm-up period, we use the epidemic routing protocol to forward messages. Seven buffer-management strategies (KMSDT, KMSDP, GBSD [10], DF, DL, DO, and DY) are implemented in order to compare their performances. The experimental parameters are given in Table 2. Three metrics are used to evaluate performance:

(1) Delivery ratio is the number of messages successfully delivered to the destination node divided by the total number of messages generated in the network.
(2) Average delay is the average time for the successful delivery of messages.
(3) Overhead ratio (load ratio) is the ratio of the difference between the number of messages successfully forwarded and the number of messages successfully delivered to the number of messages successfully delivered.

Table 2. Simulation parameters under random-waypoint scenario

Parameter	Value
Simulation Time	18000s
Simulation Area	4500m×3400m
Number of Nodes	100
Moving Speed	2m/s
Transmission Speed	250Kbps
Transmission Range	100m
Buffer Size	10MB,15MB,20MB,25MB,30MB
Interval of Message Generation	[5,15][15,25][25,35],[35,45]
TTL	300

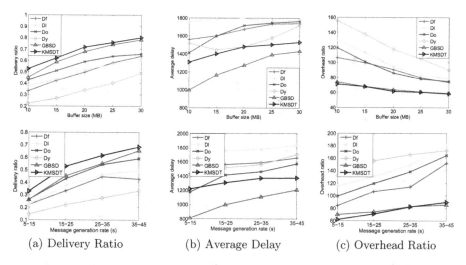

Fig. 3. Delivery Ratio, Average Delay, and Overhead Ratio as a function of buffer size and message generation rate under the random-waypoint scenario (same messagesize)

6.2 Performance Analysis with the Same Messagesize

First of all, to verify the accuracy of the message utility calculated by Eq. 9, we implement the six buffer-management strategies (KMSDT, GBSD , DF, DL, DO, and DY) with the same messagesize of 1MB under the synthetic random-waypoint mobility scenario. Results (as shown in Fig. 3) show that KMSDT obtains highest delivery ratio, lower average delay, and lowest overhead ratio regarding different buffer size, and message generation rate, compared with other buffer-management strategies.

6.3 Performance Analysis with Different Messagesizes

Performance Evaluation Under Random-Waypoint Scenario. We first discuss the experiments under the synthetic random-waypoint mobility scenario. One hundred nodes are placed by default on a 4500×3400 m^2 map. The buffer size is 10MB and the generation rate is 15−25 s per message. We vary buffer size and message generation rate to evaluate the performance of KMSDT, KMSDP, and the other buffer-management strategies.

Fig. 4-(a) shows that the delivery ratios of KMSDT and KMSDP are at 80% for a buffer size of 30MB, which is much higher than the delivery ratios of the five other buffer-management strategies.

Next, we study how the generation rate affects the buffer-management strategies. Note that, in Fig. 4-(a), the notation 5,15 for the message-generation rate means that a new message is generated every 5 to 15 s. Thus, the message generation rate decreases with increasing abscissa, resulting in a decrease in congestion. The results show that KMSDT and KMSDP outperform the other buffer-management strategies with respect to the delivery ratio.

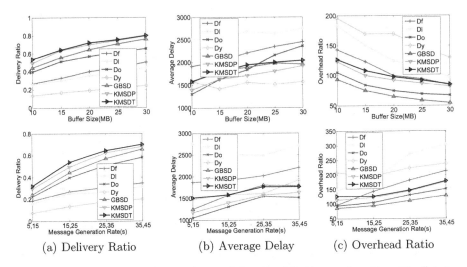

(a) Delivery Ratio   (b) Average Delay   (c) Overhead Ratio

Fig. 4. Delivery Ratio, Average Delay, and Overhead Ratio as a function of buffer size and message generation rate under the random-waypoint scenario

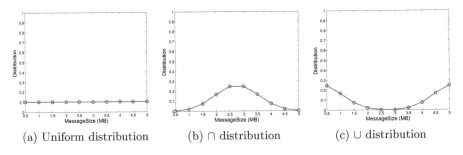

(a) Uniform distribution   (b) ∩ distribution   (c) ∪ distribution

Fig. 5. Different distributions of MessageSizes

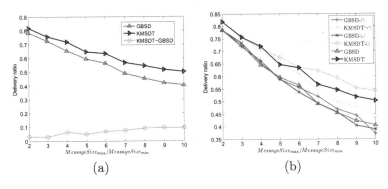

(a)   (b)

Fig. 6. Delivery ratio under different values of $Messagesize_{max}/Messagesize_{min}$

Messages in above experiments are all with sizes selected arbitrarily from 0.5MB, 1MB, 1.5MB, and 2MB. Aiming to show the applicability of KMSDT, we keep the minimal messagesize (0.5MB) unchanged, set the buffersize as 20MB and vary the ratio between maximal messagesize and minimal messagesize from 2 to 10. Results are shown in Fig. 6-(a), which indicates that the delivery ratios of both KMSDT and GBSD decrease along with increase of the ratio between maximal messagesize and minimal messagesize. However, KMSDT always performs better than GBSD. At the same time, the trend of difference between them changes to more obvious when the ratio between maximal messagesize and minimal messagesize is large enough.

Considering that the messagesizes of experiments in Fig. 6-(a) meet the uniform distribution. However, in order to verify that KMSDT still performs well under different distributions of messagesizes (as shown in Fig. 5), the binomial distribution ($p = 0.5$) and corresponding type U distribution are implemented. Results are shown in Fig. 6-(b), which indicates that KMSDT performs better than GBSD no matter in which distribution (∩ means binomial distribution and ∪ means corresponding type ∪ distribution). It is worth noticing that regarding to delivery ratio, KMSDT-∪ > KMSDT > KMSDT-∩, especially when the ratio between maximal messagesize and minimal messagesize is large enough. In other words, more disperse the distribution of messagesizes is , better performance KMSDT will get. More aggregate the distribution of messagesizes is, worse performance KMSDT will get. It is nature and reasonable, and can also proves that the knapsack-based solution has played a key role in KMSDT.

7 Conclusion

In delay-tolerant networks, the high mobility of nodes and their dramatically changing topologies lead to intermittent connectivity. The store-carry-forward principle is used by most routing protocols to efficiently forward messages. With limited storage space, excessive copies of messages can easily lead to buffer overflows, especially when the bandwidth is also limited and the message sizes differ. In this situation, the question of how to allocate network resources becomes important. In this paper, we present an idealized knapsack-based scheduling and drop strategy KMSDT, based on the epidemic routing protocol. This strategy, which aims to improve the delivery ratio, schedules messages according to their utility per unit and, when the buffer overflow occurs, it decides which messages to drop based on the solution to the knapsack problem. However, KMSDT cannot be applied in a real network environment because it requires global parameters. Therefore, we develop a practical scheduling and drop strategy KMSDP. KMSDT uses the distributed collected history information to approximate the global information, and uses these estimated parameters to calculate the utility. We conducted simulations in ONE under the synthetic random-waypoint mobility scenario. The simulation results show that, compared to other buffer-management strategies, KMSDT and KMSDP significantly improve the delivery ratio without affecting the average delay. Our buffer-management strategy aims to maximize the delivery ratio without compromising other performance metrics such as average delay. Future work will focus on developing a more efficient scheduling and drop strategy to optimize both the delivery ratio and the average delay.

References

1. Fall, K.: A delay-tolerant network architecture for challenged internets. In: Proc. of ACM SIGCOMM 2003, pp. 27–34 (2003)
2. Akyildiz, I., Akan, B., Chen, C.: Computer Networks. InterPlaNetary Internet: State-of-the-art and Research Challenges 43(2), 75–112 (2003)
3. Krishnan, R., Basu, P., Mikkelson, J.M.: The spindle disruption-tolerant networking system. In: Proc. of MILCOM 2007, pp. 1–7 (2007)
4. Pentland, A., Fletcher, R., Hasson, A.: Daknet: rethinking connectivity in developing nations. IEEE Computer 37(1), 78–83 (2004)
5. Juang, P., Oki, H., Wang, Y., Martonosi, M., Peh, L., Rubenstein, D.: Energy-efficient computing for wildlife tracking: design tradeoffs and early experiences with zebranet. In: Proc. of ASPLOS, pp. 96–107 (2002)
6. Xiao, M., Wu, J., Huang, L.: Community-Aware Opportunistic Routing in Mobile Social Networks. IEEE Transactions on Computers 63(7), 1682–1695 (2014)
7. Wu, J., Wang, Y.: Hypercube-based Multi-path Social Feature Routing in Human Contact Networks. IEEE Transactions on Computers 63(2), 383–396 (2014)
8. Zheng, H., Wang, Y., Wu, J.: Optimizing multi-copy two-hop routing in mobile social networks. In: Proc. of IEEE SECON (June 2014)
9. Wang, Y., Wu, J., Xiao, M.: Hierarchical cooperative caching in mobile opportunistic social networks. In: Proc. of IEEE GLOBECOM 2014 (December 2014)
10. Krifa, A., Barakat, C.: Message Drop and Scheduling in DTNs: Theory and Practice. IEEE Transactions on Mobile Computing 11(9), 1470–1483 (2012)
11. Dohyung, K., Hanjin, P., Ikjun, Y.: Minimizing the impact of buffer overflow in dtns. In: Proc. of CFI (2008)
12. Erramilli, V., Crovella, M.: Forwarding in opportunistic networks with resource constraints, in: Proceedings of the third acm workshop on challenged networks. In: Proc. of ACM CHANTS 2008, pp. 41–48 (2008)
13. Elwhishi, A., Ho, P., Naik, K., Shihada, B.: A Novel Message Scheduling Framework for Delay Tolerant Networks Routing. IEEE Transactions on Parallel and Distributed Systems 24(5), 871–880 (2013)
14. Krifa, A., Barakat, C.: Optimal buffer management policies for delay tolerant networks. In: Proc. of IEEE SECON 2008, pp. 260–268 (2008)
15. Krifa, A., Barakat, C.: An optimal joint scheduling and drop policy for delay tolerant networks. In: Proc. of IEEE WoWMoM 2008, pp. 1–6 (2008)
16. Yong, L., Meng, J.Q.: Adaptive optimal buffer management policies for realistic dtns. In: Proc. of IEEE GLOBECOM 2009, pp. 1–5 (2009)
17. Spyropoulos, T., Psounis, K., Raghavendra, C.S.: Performance analysis of mobility-assisted routing. In: Proc. of ACM Mobihoc 2006, pp. 49–60 (2006)
18. Aruna, B., Brian, L., Arun, V.: DTN routing as a resource allocation problem. In: Proc. of ACM SIGCOMM 2007, pp. 373–384 (2007)
19. http://en.wikipedia.org/wiki/Wiki/Nyquistrem

Integrating Mobility in RPL

Cosmin Cobârzan, Julien Montavont, and Thomas Noel

ICube laboratory (CNRS), University of Strasbourg, France
{cobarzan,montavont,noel}@unistra.fr

Abstract. In the last years the Low Power and Lossy Networks (LLNs), have become more and more popular. LLNs are inherently dynamic - nodes move, associate, disassociate or experience link perturbations. In order to meet the specific requirements for LLNs, the IETF has developed a new routing protocol - IPv6 Routing Protocol for Low-Power and Lossy Networks (RPL) that routes packets inside LLNs. RPL has to work in such dynamic environment and mechanisms that can mitigate such conditions are suggested in the standard such as Neighbor Unreachability Detection or Bidirectional Forwarding Detection. In this article, we show that such mechanisms fail to prevent serious node disconnection, which significantly increases the packet loss and leads to severe underachievements. To provide RPL the ability to mitigate network dynamics generated by node disconnection, we therefore propose a new cross-layer protocol operating at layers 2 and 3 known as Mobility-Triggered RPL (MT-RPL). MT-RPL benefits from the X-Machiavel MAC protocol that favors medium access to mobile devices. X-Machiavel has been extended to trigger RPL operations in order to maintain efficient connectivity with the network. MT-RPL is evaluated together with Neighbor Unreachability Detection and Bidirectional Forwarding Detection through an extensive simulation campaign. Results show that MT-RPL significantly reduces the disconnection time, which increases the packet delivery ratio and reduces energy consumption per data packet.

Keywords: Sensor networks, RPL, Network dynamics, Mobility.

1 Introduction

Smart objects, whether they are smart watches or intelligent home appliances, are surrounding us every day. What's "smart" is a sensor, which forms a network between it and others. Sensors can communicate wirelessly and form a class of networks called Low-Power and Lossy Networks (LLNs), where the routers and the devices they interconnect are constrained in terms of processing power, battery and communication range [5]. Interconnections between sensors are characterized by high loss rate, low data rates and instability [18].

Routing packets in LLN is done with a new protocol proposed by the IETF known as IPv6 routing protocol for Low-Power and Lossy Networks - RPL [18]. This protocol builds a Destination Orientated Directed Acyclic Graph (DODAG),

T. Abdelzaher et al. (Eds.): EWSN 2015, LNCS 8965, pp. 135–150, 2015.

which is shaped by a set of metrics/constraints. When a node connects to the graph, it chooses a parent (which will forward information to the root) and computes a rank (estimation of position in the graph). However, nodes can lose connectivity from the parent due to node actions (movement, association, disassociation or disappearance) or link perturbations (fading, shadowing or path loss). Such network dynamics have an impact on (re)organization, (re)configuration and routing protocol convergence that is likely to endanger network operations. RPL has been designed to cope with network dynamics and maintain network connectivity using external unreachability detection mechanisms.

There are three suggested unreachability detection mechanisms that help RPL to detect and repair communication problems: Neighbor Unreachability Detection (NUD) [17], Bidirectional Forwarding Detection [2] and hints from lower layers via Layer 2 (L2) triggers such as [6]. Those mechanisms act on different layers according to the needs of the application. In this article, we present a performance analysis of those three methods. To the best of our knowledge, they have not yet been evaluated side by side. Results presented in Sect. 5 show that those mechanisms fail to mitigate node mobility that make the network dynamic. As a result, nodes experience long disconnection time, increasing both packet loss and energy consumption. We therefore propose a new cross-layer protocol referred to as Mobility-Triggered RPL (MT-RPL). MT-RPL is a specific implementation of the generic L2 triggers with X-Machiavel [16] preamble sampling MAC protocol. X-Machiavel is part of our previous work and grants better access to transmission resources to mobile nodes. MT-RPL is further detailed in Sect. 4. The performance evaluation shows that MT-RPL shortens disconnection time and improves energy consumption and network usage. The main conclusion drawn from the work presented in this article is that LLNs require moving forward the layered protocol stack to achieve the best performance.

The rest of the paper is organized as follows. First, we present how RPL mitigates mobile nodes that make the network dynamic, without external unreachability detection mechanisms. Section 3 presents an overview of the mechanisms suggested by RPL to manage unreachability detection. Our proposal MT-RPL is described in Sect. 4. The simulation parameters and results of the performance evaluation are detailed in Sect. 5. The related work presented in Sect. 6 analyzes network dynamics in RPL. Finally, we give some concluding remarks along with future investigations in Sect. 7.

2   Problem Statement

RPL has been developed to enable IPv6 routing inside a LLN. It builds a Destination Orientated Directed Acyclic Graph (DODAG) toward the root, shaped by an objective function. The topology is built using new ICMPv6 messages: DODAG Information Object (DIO), DODAG Information Solicitation (DIS) and DODAG Destination Advertisement Object (DAO). The border router between the Internet and the LLN acts as the root for the graph. It starts building the graph by sending the first DIO. Nodes that receive DIO will build a parent set (potential next hops toward the root) and select their preferred parent. The preferred parent is a member of the parent set that is the preferred next hop toward the root. Such selection is based on the rank advertised in DIO. Once a preferred parent is chosen, nodes are considered attached to the graph and will advertise DIO further. Nodes that are not connected can either wait for a DIO or send a DIS requesting information about existing DODAG. Nodes in the neighborhood transmit a DIO in response to a DIS. Finally DAO advertises destination information upward to the root, enabling point-to-point and point-to-multipoint communication. Nodes in a RPL network use these messages when they connect to the DODAG as well as each time when, after a disconnection, communication needs to be resumed.

Network dynamics is an integral part of LLNs as the links are lossy and nodes have limited transmission and energy capabilities. Adding mobility in such scenarios enables building of new applications that are impossible to have with static nodes, such as target tracking or surveillance applications ([8], [9], [15]). This in turn makes communicating in this environment more challenging: in addition to link perturbations, ongoing communications can suffer from either node movement or disappearance, leading to network partitions as parents in the graph might be no longer reachable. RPL mitigates such problems by allowing nodes to reconnect to the graph by changing their preferred parent. Such operation occurs when a node receives a DIO, advertising a better rank than the one of the preferred parent. However, there is a situation where the preferred parent of a node is no longer reachable (due to mobility, failure, etc.) and all received DIO advertise a higher (worse) rank. In this situation, the node is disconnected from the graph because its preferred parent remains the best candidate in the parent set. Such disconnection is likely to increase packet loss, contention on the medium and energy consumption. This scenario is illustrated in Fig. 1.

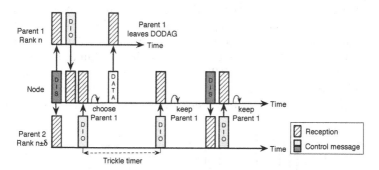

Fig. 1. RPL parent management

Furthermore, RPL does not specify how to manage the parent set, especially when and for what reason a node should be removed from a parent set. Nevertheless, RPL suggests the use of external mechanisms for unreachability detection such as Neighbor Unreachability Detection (NUD) [17], Bidirectional Forwarding Detection [2] and hints from lower layers via Layer 2 (L2) triggers [6]. When one of these mechanisms indicates that the preferred parent is unreachable, the node will search for a new parent. First it will search in the parent set and, if no parent is available, through a local repair. Local repair means announcing infinite rank in a DIO (disconnecting from the DODAG), removing all parents from the parent set (to be able to accept parents regardless of their rank) and sending DIS periodically until new DIO are received. RPL, together with one of these mechanisms should enable continuous communication on transient and lossy links. However, to the best of our knowledge, those methods have not yet been evaluated side by side in RPL. In the next section, we present how all three mechanisms signal node unreachability.

3   Unreachability Detection in RPL

3.1   Neighbor Unreachability Detection

Neighbor Unreachability Detection (NUD) is part of Neighbor Discovery for IP version 6 (IPv6) [17]. It tracks all paths between active neighboring nodes and specifies when a neighbor is unreachable. The state of connectivity between neighbors is stored locally on each node in a structure called neighbor cache. When a path to a neighbor appears to be failing, NUD signals the need for a new next hop, by deleting the neighbor cache entry. At RPL layer, this will trigger the node to remove the parent and start searching for a new one, either in the parent set (if it is not empty) or through a local repair.

NUD enables neighbors to exchange Neighbor Solicitation (NS) and Neighbor Advertisement (NA) messages to confirm reachability. Each neighbor has an entry in the neighbor cache for all connections it has with other nodes in the same network. Cached values for nodes can be: REACHABLE - communication is granted between nodes, STALE - the neighbor is no longer known to be reachable but no action is taken until traffic is sent to this neighbor, DELAY - optimized state that delays sending probe for $DELAY\_FIRST\_PROBE\_TIME$ seconds (node waits for reachability confirmation from upper layers) and PROBE - NS are sent until reachability is confirmed or the maximum allowed number of probes ($MAX\_UNICAST\_SOLICIT$) are sent. Timers, which are illustrated in Fig. 2, manage the exchange of control messages and trigger the removal of the cache entry. Default values for timers give a 30 sec reachable time window.

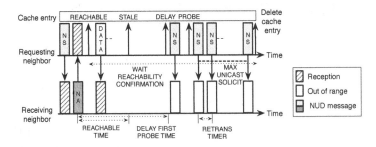

Fig. 2. NUD message exchange

After this time elapses, the first probe is sent with a default 5 sec delay (*DE-LAY_FIRST_PROBE_TIME*) and than each second until *MAX_UNICAST_SO-LICIT* probes are sent (3 retransmissions by default). In the worst case and considering the timer default values, it takes 38 sec for NUD to detect the unreachability of a neighbor. We doubt that such delay is short enough to allow RPL nodes to change parent seamlessly and without experiencing packet loss.

3.2 Bidirectional Forwarding Detection

Bidirectional Forwarding Detection [2] is a simple Hello protocol that detects failures in communication with a forwarding plane next hop. A pair of nodes exchanges BFD messages encapsulated in UDP packets to maintain reachability information. The path between two nodes is declared operational when two-way communication can be established. When no messages are received for long enough, BFD considers that the neighboring system has failed. At RPL layer, this will trigger the node to remove the parent and start searching for a new one, either in the parent set (if it is not empty) or through a local repair. RPL is paired with BFD asynchronous mode. In this mode, messages are sent periodically between systems. If a number of packets in a row are not received, the session is declared down, as connectivity is lost. Operation of BFD, along with the state of each system, is presented in Fig. 3. BFD packets are sent by default every 20 sec and if one packet is lost, the systems declare the state *DOWN*.

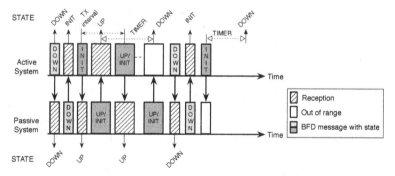

Fig. 3. BFD message exchange in asynchronous mode

3.3 Hints from Lower Layers via Layer 2 (L2) Triggers

Although specific to each MAC layer, the hints from lower layers via Layer 2 (L2) triggers [6] share common structure in the form of L2 Abstractions. Services between layers are provided in the form of primitives, which enable synchronous communication between layers. Two pairs of primitives are defined to be used when events occur: Request/Confirm and Indication/Response.

Primitives can be used in 3 different cases based on their types - *Type 1*: Provide information to upper layers; information is provided immediately to upper layer through a request-confirm message exchange; *Type 2*: Notify upper layer of L2 events asynchronously, indicating each occurrence of registered events to upper layers; *Type 3*: Control L2 actions from upper layers; Request primitive is used to interact with lower layer which will reply with Ack or Nack in a Confirmation primitive.

We are convinced that this solution will provide the best results. There are some MAC protocols like 802.14.5 in beacon mode that keep track of nodes associated to a PAN coordinator and detecting disconnection is already implemented in the protocol, but this is unavailable in most LLN MAC protocols. Using L2 triggers with any MAC layer allows events to be faster delivered to upper layer protocols. This is why we propose MT-RPL, a solution to communicate between MAC layer and RPL using *Type 2* primitives. In the next section, MT-RPL will be presented in more detail.

4 Mobility-Triggered RPL

The mechanisms presented in the previous section alongside local repair should manage mobile nodes that generate dynamics in the network. However, we are convinced that they are not adapted to LLN specifics, especially considering the number of exchanged messages (BFD) or the suggested timer values (NUD). Only L2 triggers seems to cope with LLN constraints but this is a generic solution that should be adapted regarding the MAC protocol in operation. In this section, we propose a new cross layer protocol that manages network dynamics in LLN. Mobility-Triggered RPL (MT-RPL) is a specific implementation of L2 triggers linking RPL and X-Machiavel [16] preamble sampling MAC protocol.

X-Machiavel is a variation of the well known X-MAC [12] preamble sampling MAC protocol. With X-MAC, a node starts to send preamble strobes in order to synchronize the destination for the pending transmission. Once the destination receives a strobe, it sends back an ACK to notify the sender to stop the preamble and proceed with the data. Upon data reception, the destination sends a new ACK to the sender. X-Machiavel slightly modifies this behavior to favor mobile node transmissions. X-Machiavel assumes that the network is composed of static and mobile nodes. On an idle channel, packets sent by mobile nodes can be opportunistically forwarded by static nodes. On a busy channel, mobile nodes can steal the medium of an ongoing transmission to send their packets first. For this, X-Machiavel introduces two new fields in the packet header. The type field defines whether the packet is a preamble frame (P0, P1 or P2), a data packet (DATA), an acknowledgement for a preamble (PK0 or PK1) or an acknowledgement for a data packet (ACK). P0 preamble strobes are used by mobile nodes to forbid channel stealing and allow opportunistic nodes to accept the pending data on behalf of the destination. P1 preamble strobes are used by static nodes and enable mobile nodes to steal the channel. Finally, P2 preamble strobes are also used by static nodes to forbid channel stealing. Preamble strobes are acknowledged with type PK0 acknowledgement sent by static nodes to acknowledge a P0 preamble that was not initially intended for them. This informs the mobile node that its data can be handled by another static node acting as an opportunistic forwarder. PK1 acknowledgement is sent in the other cases when nodes acknowledge preambles destined to them. In the flags field, a mobile node sets a M flag (on most significant bit - MSB) for data packets that is used to prioritize transmissions from mobile nodes. Fixed nodes that receive data with the M flag set forward it by using a P2 preamble so that other nodes cannot steal the medium and impair the transmission originating from the mobile node. For more information about how X-Machiavel works the reader can consult [16]. In the following, we present how X-Machiavel interacts with RPL to form MT-RPL.

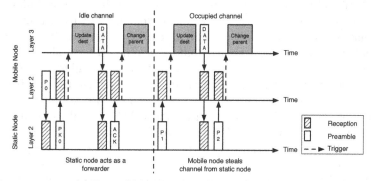

(a) Preamble is acknowledged or overheard

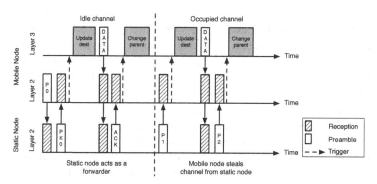

(b) Preamble is not acknowledged

Fig. 4. MT-RPL

X-Machiavel prioritizes the transmission from mobile nodes, elements that generate great dynamics in the network. To take advantage of this in MT-RPL, RPL registers a L2 trigger to be informed asynchronously every time the mechanism of X-Machiavel is triggered (e.g. channel stealing or using an opportunistic forwarder). For this, MT-RPL includes the rank computed at RPL layer in the layer 2 header. By this means, nodes can decide in a distributed way whenever it is worthwhile to act as an opportunistic forwarder or to steal the medium from an ongoing communication. MT-RPL operational modes are presented in the following. If the preamble is acknowledged (Fig. 4a) on an idle channel, a node sends a P0 type preamble including its rank computed at the RPL layer.

If the destination is in the neighborhood, X-MAC principles apply: the destination sends a PK1 acknowledgement and claims the data from the mobile node. On the other hand, if the destination is not in the neighborhood and another static node receives the P0 preamble, it can decide to act as an opportunistic forwarder for the pending data. This decision is based on the RPL rank announced in the preamble. If the rank of the sender is greater than the one of the potential forwarder (i.e. the sender is located further in the graph than the potential forwarder), the potential forwarder can send back a PK0 acknowledgement. Upon reception, the mobile node changes the destination to the forwarder and sends the data. This data may now be routed to the root using P2 preambles so that no other mobile nodes can steal the channel. Forwarders with a rank equal or greater that the one of the sender simply discard the overheard preamble.

Transmitting data on an occupied channel requires the mobile node to seize the opportunity to transmit its data between strobed preamble frames that are destined to another node. X-MAC principles require that the destination of preamble strobes send back an ACK between two strobes to notify the sender to stop the preamble and proceed with the data. MT-RPL allows mobile nodes to send their own data before such ACK from the original destination. However, MT-RPL enables this behavior only if the rank of the sender of the preamble is lower than the rank of the mobile node, i.e. the mobile node's data will progress forward toward the root of the graph. As a result, channel stealing operates as follows. First, a mobile node should overheard a P1 preamble destined to another node and announcing a RPL rank lower than its own RPL rank. Then, the mobile node changes the destination of its data to this sender and transmits the resulting packet between two preamble strobes. After receiving such packet, the forwarder still needs to send its own data and does that by using P2 preambles. Further along nodes operate as in X-MAC. Regardless of how the static nodes received data from mobile nodes, they will forward it using P2 preambles until the final destination is reached. If the preamble sent by a mobile node is not acknowledged (Fig. 4b), the mobile node is in an area where all surrounding nodes have a rank higher than its own, so the mobile node will change its rank to infinite. At the next retransmission, any neighbor can acknowledge the preamble and the mobile nodes data packet will be forwarded to the root using P2 preamble.

MT-RPL manages the parent set regarding the information received from layer 2 through L2 triggers. When the mobile nodes benefits from an opportunistic forwarder (by receiving a PK0 acknowledgment) or steals the medium from another node (sending a data between two preamble strobes from an ongoing communication), if the transmission is successful, the layer 2 provides the rank and the address of the effective next hop to the RPL layer. Upon reception, RPL set this node as the new preferred parent, computes the related rank and proceed with RPL operations whenever necessary (send new DAO and/or DIO). As a result, MT-RPL should smooth network dynamics by enabling nodes to promptly react to network change without generating extra control traffic.

5   Simulation Setup and Results

5.1   Simulation Scenario

In order to evaluate the mitigation of network dynamics by RPL, we used the WSNet software [4]. WSNet is a discrete event simulator dedicated to the study of wireless sensor networks. WSNet already provides a basic RPL module that we extended to operate as presented in both Sect. 3 and 4.

Table 1. Simulation parameters

Simulation parameter	Value
Topology	
Random topology	1 root, 60 static nodes, 5 mobile nodes
Grid topology	1 root, 36 static nodes, 5 mobile nodes
Data collection	Time driven
scheme	1 packet/30s static nodes → root
	1 packet/5s mobile nodes → root and root → mobile nodes
Data packet size	127 bytes
Mobility model	Billiard, 1m/s random trajectory
Routing model	RPL in non-storing mode using MinHop
RPL default values	DIO - given by trickle timer algorithm [14]
	DIS - 2s if empty parent set, until attached to DODAG
	DAO - 60s from every node, or when needed
Values for parameters of unreachability detection mechanisms	
NUD	Maximum number of NS transmission - 3, Delay first
(RFC 4861)	probe - 5s, Reachable time - 30s, Retransmission time - 1s
BFD	Desired TX interval - 30s, Missed BFD packets that bring
(RFC 5880)	session DOWN - 1
MAC model	X-MAC (for standard RPL, NUD and BFD)
	and X-Machiavel (for MT-RPL)
	Maximum number of retransmissions - 4
Radio model	Half-duplex, Channel 0, Sensibility level: -92dBm,
	15 kB/s bandwidth, 18m (60 feet) [10] unit disk range
Current consumption	TX: 31 mA, RX: 15.1 mA OFF: 400 nA (CC1100 chip)
Antenna model	Omnidirectional, modulation BPSK
Simulation setup	20 simulations/mechanism/topology,
	4 mechanisms, 2 topologies, 1 hour/simulation

All simulation parameters are presented in Table 1. We deployed a random topology of 60 nodes on a 100x100 m area with the root in the middle and a grid topology with 36 nodes and the root in the middle. To generate dynamism, 5 mobile nodes are distributed and move following a simplified version of random direction model, used also in [19]. Such nodes are pre-configured with the status of mobile node, as they have physical capabilities to move (e.g. node is on a platform with wheels). Standard RPL, NUD and BFD are coupled with X-MAC because X-Machiavel favors transmissions of data packets from mobile nodes, but the node which acknowledges the preamble, or from which the channel is stolen, may not be the parent at RPL layer and the packet even though it is sent, it is dropped by the receiving node. MT-RPL as it receives information from X-Machiavel takes advantage of this changes and adjusts accordingly the transmission of data packets. Only links between the mobile node and its parent are monitored using BFD, NUD or MT-RPL. On the rest of the path until the root, the packet is routed using standard RPL, as these links are not subject to network dynamics generated by the mobile node. With all methods, mobile nodes keep only the preferred parent in the parent list, which may change when DIO with a better rank is received or if the mobile node does a local repair. The path from the root to the mobile node is maintained up to date with DAO messages. Changes in topology are reported to the root in a timely fashion. Packets are delivered following source routing set by the root. In the analyzed scenarios, both mobile and static nodes send control messages as needed in order to maintain connectivity to the DODAG. The DODAG that RPL build needs a long time to stabilize [13]. Therefore, we started analyzing results only after 30 min from the start of the simulation, when the DODAG will be in a stable state and the mobile nodes start moving. After this time, the structure of the DODAG in the static part of the network will not change, in order to analyze only the changes induced by mobile nodes in the network. At the end of the simulation, packets were not sent for 15 min, so that all queues of packets from all nodes could be emptied.

5.2   Results

The results presented in this section were obtained after running 20 simulations of each scenario for each configuration for a total of 200 simulations. The presented results are the average of overall data collected from each set of simulations. The 95% confidence interval indicates the reliability of our measurements. We analyzed four parameters: disconnection time from the preferred parent, packet delivery ratio (PDR), overall number of control messages sent in the network and energy consumption.

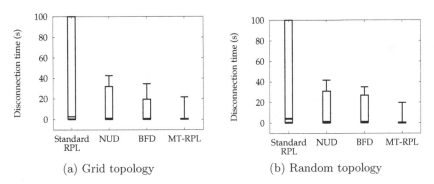

(a) Grid topology   (b) Random topology

Fig. 5. Average disconnection time from parent

Figure 5 illustrates the disconnection time for each scenario, i.e. the time between a mobile node going out of the radio range of its preferred parent and enforcing a new preferred parent at the RPL layer. As we can see, standard RPL shows the longest disconnection time (up to 700 sec. in the worst cases) as changing the preferred parent is only done by receiving a new DIO with a better rank. Therefore, it is likely that a mobile node remains disconnected for a long period because all received DIO present a higher (worse) rank. An unreachability detection mechanism is therefore mandatory in order to avoid such situation that could lead to severe underachievements. By contrast, the disconnection time is drastically reduced using RPL coupled with NUD or BFD. In those cases, when a mobile node does not receive reachability confirmation from its preferred parent, RPL removes the preferred parent, reset the rank to infinite and starts sending DIS. BFD lowers the maximum disconnection time because it reacts quicker than NUD thanks to its slightly lower reachable time (30s versus 38s for NUD). Variations occur, as mobile nodes need sometimes to send several DIS messages before they can reconnect to the DODAG. Finally, MT-RPL presents the lowest disconnection times. Thanks to the interaction between the layers 2 and 3, a mobile node always regains connectivity when an opportunistic node acknowledges its preamble and successfully receives the effective data. In addition, a mobile node regains connectivity whenever it successfully steals the medium from a neighbor node with a better rank. In those situations, the disconnection time is bound to the sending frequency of data packets and the number of preamble strobes sent before stealing the medium or opportunistic node acknowledgment. This explains the low disconnection time observed for MT-RPL in Fig. 5. However, a mobile node may be in a situation in which it cannot steal the medium or opportunistic node cannot acknowledge its preamble strobes. Such situation occurs when the mobile node moves in an area where the rank of all neighbors is lower (worse) than the rank of the mobile node. Nevertheless, MT-RPL allows a mobile node to reset its rank and remove its preferred parent after sending a whole preamble without receiving an acknowledgment, either from its preferred parent or from an opportunistic forwarder (as in Fig. 4b). As a result, in an unfavorable environment, the disconnection time is only increased by the transmission duration of a whole layer 2 preamble.

Lowering the disconnection time should increase the packet delivery ratio (PDR) on the paths from mobile nodes to the root and from root to mobile nodes. Note that we implemented the solutions so that mobile nodes only try to send data packets if a preferred parent is set. As a result, all solutions do not necessarily send the same number of data packets. Table 2 present the PDR together with the number of data packet sent by each solution in the both scenarios. Standard RPL, as it cannot ensure continuous connectivity of mobile nodes to their parents, has the lowest PDR from mobile nodes to the root. In addition, this scheme sent the largest number of data packets because mobile nodes have no means to remove an out of range preferred parent. Therefore, they keep trying to send data packets while their preferred parents are no longer reachable, increasing the packet loss together with the medium contention due to retransmissions. Results for the path from the root to mobile nodes are not meaningful because only few packets are actually sent. Most of the time, the

Table 2. Nb. of sent data packets and PDR with 95% confidence intervals

Grid topology			Standard RPL	NUD	BFD	MT-RPL
Mobile node to root	Packet delivery ratio	Avg. (%)	8.42	10.06	18.02	62.08
		± (%)	2.42	6.64	4.47	13.99
	Data packets sent	Avg.	666	184.61	501.84	410.15
		±	168.87	68.75	126.01	129.71

Root to mobile nodes	Packet delivery ratio	Avg. (%)	14.58	8.21	13.96	23.21
		± (%)	10.44	7.43	7.97	7.56
	Data packets sent	Avg.	23.95	22.46	47.42	64.60
		±	11.80	16.89	17.58	20.11

Random topology

Mobile node to root	Packet delivery ratio	Avg. (%)	9.32	12.99	18.93	66.56
		± (%)	1.40	4.00	2.94	4.69
	Data packets sent	Avg.	895.36	210.87	482.78	757.17
		±	23.76	67.72	43.74	46.67

Root to mobile nodes	Packet delivery ratio	Avg. (%)	33.59	37.01	36.53	36.14
		± (%)	15.34	22.20	14.83	12.03
	Data packets sent	Avg.	34.00	22.25	40.57	81.17
		±	13.89	9.75	13.12	18.12

root has no route to mobile nodes (DAO cannot be sent from mobile nodes when they are disconnected) and therefore buffers the packets. When an unreachability mechanism is present at the mobile nodes, values of PDR improve. Thanks to BFD or NUD, mobile nodes change their preferred parents more often, resulting in longer connections to the graph. This allows mobile nodes to send more data packets that successfully arrive at the root. However, values of PDR are still low, as the disconnection from the preferred parent may be reported after long period of time (up to 30s for BFD and 38s for NUD). During this time, preferred parents are still considered as reachable, but all transmitted data packets are lost.

By contrast, lower disconnection times for MT-RPL seen in Fig. 5 are translated into the highest PDR for both mobile nodes and the root. Channel stealing and opportunistic forwarding allow mobile nodes to connect to a parent with a better rank whenever possible. Such reconnection occurs without triggering a local repair, reducing the disconnection time together with the signaling overhead as neighbor nodes can keep a low transmission rate of DIO. However, data packets are still lost with MT-RPL as congestion can form on the path towards the root. The same observation is achieved on the path from the root to the mobile nodes.

Fig. 6 presents the signaling overhead of each solution. The low number of control packets sent in standard RPL further supports the assumption that the mobility of node are rarely reported with this solution. Furthermore, discovering and attaching to a new parent is done only with RPL control messages, which occur rarely. Adding unreachability mechanisms increases the signaling overhead in the network. Although BFD shows lower disconnection time and higher PDR than NUD, such results come with the expense of higher signaling overhead. BFD maintains sessions both ways between the mobile nodes and their parents by exchanging UDP packets every 30s (each entity manages its own timer). This explain the increased number of BFD control messages in both topologies. NUD on the other hand, relays more on messages sent by the mobile node, which has to check periodically (every 38s) the connectivity to its parent. Furthermore, both NUD and BFD trigger a local repair when the unreachability of the preferred parent is confirmed. Such procedure reset the trickle timer of all neighbor nodes. After a local repair, DIO are therefore sent at a high rate, increasing the signaling overhead reported at the RPL layer. By contrast, MT-RPL does not introduce new control messages. In addition, parent change is achieved without triggering local repair, thus reducing the overall signaling overhead. However, MT-RPL increases the number of reconnections, and therefore makes the use of a large number of DAO to report each parent change.

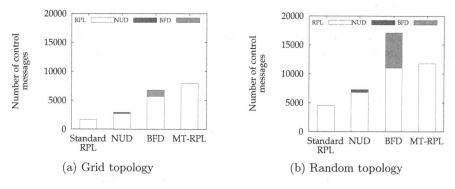

(a) Grid topology   (b) Random topology

Fig. 6. Average number of control messages sent

Energy consumption being one of the crucial point in LLN, we also evaluated the energy depletion of each node in the network. Results are reported in Fig. 7. The Y-axis represents the energy needed to send 100 data packets in order to have an uniform representation for all methods. As a general remark, mobile nodes consume more energy than fixed nodes because they send 1 data packet every 5s whereas fixed nodes only send 1 data packet every 30s. With standard RPL, nodes try to send packets even if the parent is not in the neighborhood. If the preamble is not acknowledged and the retransmission number is reached, the data packet is dropped whiteout being sent on the medium from the mobile node. This is why even with a large number of packets sent by standard RPL, energy consumption remains low, as only a few packets manage to actually be sent between nodes. Once mobile nodes are longer connected to their parent the energy consumption for them and the root rises. NUD and BFD send additional

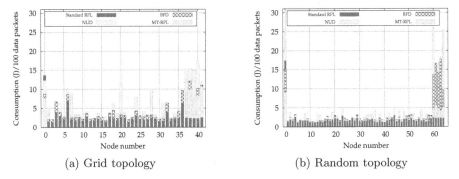

(a) Grid topology   (b) Random topology

Fig. 7. Average energy consumption of nodes
Node 0 - root. Last 5 nodes - mobile nodes. Intermediate nodes - static nodes

control messages in the network. Given the low number of data packets sent by
mobile nodes using NUD, the energy consumption to send 100 data packets is
the highest of all. BFD, although it sends control packets both ways between the
mobile node and parent, has lower consumption when we take into account the
energy consumed for 100 data packets. Using only RPL control messages sent
when changes occur in the network and are signaled by layer 2, MT-RPL achieves
the lowest energy consumption from all unreachability detection mechanism.

6   Related Work

In the literature authors have until now focused on analyzing path quality, packet
delivery ratio or route prevalence in a network with RPL. However, knowing
when a node should search for a new parent (as communication is no longer
possible with the current one) should improve network performance. Authors
in [3] analyze the quality of routes in RPL. Some routes are longer than the
optimal ones. In addition, dominant routes, the ones that are used primary by
nodes, are remarkably prevalent and long lived. Changes of routes degrade the
path in half route changes, so it is important to adapt to network dynamics in
order to preserve the best path. Their analysis also points out to the low PDR
offered by RPL. Loses occur especially when RPL chooses low quality links. We
can conclude that mitigating low quality links and maintaining routes close to
the optimal value by mitigating network dynamics will improve network performance. In [11], authors study the robustness of RPL. Their findings show that
RPL loses many packets and that congestion around the sink has an important
impact on performance, degrading the PDR when the sink's congestion increases.
Pointing out to the high dynamics observed even in a static network, changes in
the DODAG can occur even after the network stabilizes. A node that enters the
network or nodes that change parents, change the topology, introduce instability
and increase the number of control packets sent. According to the rank of these

nodes, their unreachability impacts RPL control message overhead greatly. Although the authors have drawn important conclusions, the mechanism to detect the node unreachability is not clearly presented. It is to our belief that knowing what mechanism is better suited to mitigate network dynamics improves performances. The article [7] makes an analysis of route change latency using RPL and 6LoWPAN Neighbor Discovery protocol. Their analysis is theoretical and does not take into account any network dynamics. On a perfect stable network, it would provide an insightful view of route change latency. But, as papers such as [11] show how unstable a network with RPL can be, we believe that the author's contribution to understanding the stability of routes using 6LoWPAN ND is limited.

All these papers address the problem of network dynamics in RPL, but until now, a clearer analysis of the core components that allow RPL to mitigate the dynamic situations has not been available. Our work makes a complete overview of the unreachability methods suggested by RPL and lifts the uncertainty on which one is better to use in LLNs with RPL.

7   Discussion and Perspectives

In this article, we analyzed how the IPv6 Routing Protocol for Low-power and Lossy Networks (RPL) manages network dynamics, especially the support of mobile nodes. From our simulation campaign, we showed that the mechanisms suggested in the standard to mitigate dynamicity fail to prevent serious node disconnection, which significantly increases the packet loss together with the energy consumption. To the best of our knowledge, this is the first time that such mechanisms have been evaluated side by side. Results presented here could therefore serve the research community to increase the efforts on novel proposals for supporting mobile nodes in RPL. Then, we proposed a new cross-layer protocol operating at layers 2 and 3 known as Mobility-Triggered RPL (MT-RPL) to support efficiently mobile nodes in RPL. MT-RPL favors medium access to mobile devices and triggers RPL operations in order to maintain efficient connectivity with the network. Results obtained from an extensive simulation campaign showed that MT-RPL significantly reduces the disconnection time, increases the packet delivery ratio while limiting the energy consumption. MT-RPL is therefore a serious solution.

Encouraged by the results here, our future work will focus on a more precise evaluation of our proposal through more realistic scenarios. Furthermore, MT-RPL suffers from a large number of parent changes, increasing the number of DAO sent to the root of the graph. We will first investigate methods to reduce the number of parent changes without affecting the overall performance of MT-RPL. Then, we will focus on extending MT-RPL to all nodes, being mobile or fixed. Currently, we are considering favoring neighbor nodes with a better rank to serve as an opportunistic forwarder by introducing a delay proportional to the rank before acknowledging preamble strobe on behalf of the preferred parent. Finally, we expect to benefit from the FIT IoT testbed [1] to extend our performance studies to large-scale experiments involving multiple mobile nodes. Many of the reasons why long disconnection time occurs are closely related to implementation, platform or operating system specifics that are quite delicate to do so properly with simulations.

References

[1] Future Internet (FIT) - Internet of Things testbed, http://fit-equipex.fr/
[2] Katz, D., et al.: Bidirectional Forwarding Detection (BFD). IETF RFC 5880 (2010)
[3] Ancillotti, E., et al.: RPL routing protocol in advanced metering infrastructures: An analysis of the unreliability problems. In: Sustainable Internet and ICT for Sustainability, SustainIT (2012)
[4] Ben Hamida, E., et al.: On the Complexity of an Accurate and Precise Performance Evaluation of Wireless Networks using Simulations. In: ACM International Conference on Modeling, Analysis and Simulation of Wireless and Mobile Systems, MSWiM (2008)
[5] Lewis, F.: Wireless sensor networks. Smart Environments: Technologies, Protocols, and Applications (2004)
[6] Teraoka, F., et al.: Unified Layer 2 (L2) Abstractions for Layer 3 (L3)-Driven Fast Handover. IETF RFC 5184 (2008)
[7] Kermajani, H., et al.: Route change latency in low-power and lossy wireless networks using RPL and 6LoWPAN Neighbor Discovery. In: IEEE Symposium on Computers and Communications, ISCC (2011)
[8] Allred, J., et al.: Sensorflock: an airborne wireless sensor network of micro-air vehicles. In: ACM SenSys (2007)
[9] Leguay, J., et al.: An efficient service oriented architecture for heterogeneous and dynamic wireless sensor networks. In: IEEE International Workshop in Practial Issues in Building Sensor Network Applications (SensApp) (2008)
[10] Polastre, J., et al.: Telos: enabling ultra-low power wireless research. In: International Symposium on Information Processing in Sensor Networks (2005)
[11] Heurtefeux, K., et al.: Experimental evaluation of a Routing Protocol for WSNs: RPL robustness under study. In: IEEE International Conference on Wireless and Mobile Computing, Networking and Communications (WiMob) (2013)
[12] M. Buettner et al.: X-MAC: A Short Preamble MAC Protocol for Duty-cycled Wireless Sensor Networks. In: ACM International Conference on Embedded Networked Sensor Systems (SenSys) (2006)
[13] Iova, O., et al.: Stability and efficiency of RPL under realistic conditions in WSN. In: IEEE International Symposium on Personal Indoor and Mobile Radio Communications (PIMRC) (2013)
[14] P. Levis et al.: The Trickle Algorithm. IETF RFC 6206 (2011)
[15] Sikka, P., et al.: Wireless ad hoc sensor and actuator networks on the farm. In: ACM International Conference on Information Processing in Sensor Networks (2006)
[16] Kuntz, R., et al.: Improving the medium access in highly mobile Wireless Sensor Networks. Telecommunication Systems (2013)
[17] Narten, T., et al.: Neighbor Discovery for IP version 6 (IPv6). IETF RFC 4861 (2007)
[18] Winter, T., et al.: RPL: IPv6 Routing Protocol for Low-Power and Lossy Networks. IETF RFC 6550
[19] Haas, Z.J., et al.: The performance of query control schemes for the zone routing protocol. IEEE/ACM Transactions on Networking (2001)

Limited-Memory Warping LCSS for Real-Time Low-Power Pattern Recognition in Wireless Nodes

Daniel Roggen[1], Luis Ponce Cuspinera[1], Guilherme Pombo[1], Falah Ali[1],
and Long-Van Nguyen-Dinh[2]

[1] Sensor Technology Research Centre, University of Sussex, United Kingdom
[2] Wearable Computing Laboratory, ETH Zurich, Switzerland
daniel.roggen@ieee.org

Abstract. We present and evaluate a microcontroller-optimized limited-memory implementation of a Warping Longest Common Subsequence algorithm (WarpingLCSS). It permits to spot patterns within noisy sensor data in real-time in resource constrained sensor nodes. It allows variability in the sensed system dynamics through warping; it uses only integer operations; it can be applied to various sensor modalities; and it is suitable for embedded training to recognize new patterns. We illustrate the method on 3 applications from wearable sensing and activity recognition using 3 sensor modalities: spotting the QRS complex in ECG, recognizing gestures in everyday life, and analyzing beach volleyball. We implemented the system on a low-power 8-bit AVR wireless node and a 32-bit ARM Cortex M4 microcontroller. Up to 67 or 140 10-second gestures can be recognized simultaneously in real-time from a 10Hz motion sensor on the AVR and M4 using 8mW and 10mW respectively. A single gesture spotter uses as few as 135μW on the AVR. The method allows low data rate distributed in-network recognition and we show a 100 fold data rate reduction in a complex activity recognition scenario. The versatility and low complexity of the method makes it well suited as a generic pattern recognition method and could be implemented as part of sensor front-ends.

Keywords: Activity Recognition, Wearable Sensing, Streaming pattern spotting, Distributed Recognition, Machine Learning, Event Processing.

1 Introduction

Spotting patterns in noisy signal streams is important in many sensor network applications [26], such as monitoring integrity of structures [12]; predicting crop needs [23]; or recognizing human activities from wearable or ambient sensors nodes [1], which is our motivation. Activity recognition is used in adaptive smart homes [18] and in wearable smart assistants [17]. In general, multiple networked nodes must be fused to increase accuracy [28] or resilience [20]. In order to minimize energy use and wireless bandwidth, processing should be distributed on the nodes so that only events are sent at low data rate for data fusion [25,9,14,2]. This requires efficient local pattern recognition on the nodes in the first place.

T. Abdelzaher et al. (Eds.): EWSN 2015, LNCS 8965, pp. 151–167, 2015.

In order to recognize complex patterns (hereafter *motifs*) in noisy sensor signals we present and evaluate a microcontroller-optimized *Limited-Memory* and *Warping* Longest Common Subsequence (LM-WLCSS) implementation of the WarpingLCSS algorithm analyzed offline in [16]. The resulting system allows a real-time streaming execution in memory constrained nodes. It has low computational complexity and uses only integer operations. It allows to dilate or contract the motif to accommodate for variations in the sensed system dynamics, such as human variability. LM-WLCSS has a high specificity to the target motif which allows to spot subtle activities. The sensitivity-specificity trade-off can be adjusted with a single parameter. Low-complexity training is possible on the node, which enables e.g. personalization of activity models at run-time. The method has a defined low latency, which allows use in critical applications. LM-WLCSS can process raw sensor signals or signal features which makes it applicable to scenarios beyond wearable sensing. The method can be used for distributed pattern recognition in sensor nodes by performing local recognition on individual nodes and combining these decisions in a central node, thus leading to significant reduction in network bandwidth.

2   Related Work

Spotting patterns in noisy signals has been extensively studied for activity and gesture recognition with wearable devices [3] and the principles generalize to other domains. A common approach combines *segmentation* (e.g. with a sliding window), *feature computation* on that segment, and *classification* of the features into pre-defined classes [1]. Features can be computationally complex and enough memory must be available to store the sensor data corresponding to the longest pattern to spot. This can be a constraint in sensor nodes[1]. With high sample rate, careful optimization is required to meet memory-performance tradeoffs [21], or powerful microcontrollers must be used, e.g. with hardware FPU for EMG analysis [4]. Code optimizations reduce CPU usage but are worthwhile only for general purpose algorithms, as this takes a lot of effort. For instance, hidden Markov models can be implemented in fixed-point arithmetic [27]. Template matching methods compare the sensor signal with a motif resulting in a matching score. Dynamic Time Warping (DTW) allows to dilate or contract the motif to accomodate for signal variability and was used in activity recognition [6,11]. Algorithms based on longest common subsequence were suggested in a sliding-window and a warping form (WarpingLCSS) for online activity recognition and outperformed DTW with noisy data [16,15]. WarpingLCSS computational cost is bound to linear order of the template size and and memory is bound to quadratic order of the template size. However, in previous works it was implemented in floating point and evaluated offline. DTW and WarpingLCSS approaches are both computationally light thanks to dynamic programming implementations and have a simple training process.

---

[1] The commonly used TMote Sky has 10KB RAM. With a 3D accelerometer and gyroscope sampled at 100Hz and 16 bit, the maximum activity length is 8 seconds.

In a sensor network bandwidth should be minimized. Complex higher-level patterns across multiple nodes can be inferred from lower level events broadcasted by the nodes using fuzzy logic [14], decision fusion [28], meta-classifier [2], sparsity classifier [25]. This can be supported by software frameworks [9]. Another approach is to rely on signal processing techniques such as compressed sensing to reduce bandwidth by exploiting signal statistics [8]. Sparse representations decompose the sensor signal along an optimized basis and also allow to reduce bandwidth as well as improve classification performance. The power usage of a recent implementation was 2W on a dual-core ARM A9 [24].

3   Limited-Memory Warping LCSS Recognition System

We introduce a microcontroller-friendly system to spot motifs in real-time within noisy streaming sensor signals. The system is based on a *Limited Memory* and *Warping* Longest Common Subsequence algorithm (LM-WLCSS), introduced and evaluated offline in [16] as WarpingLCSS[2].

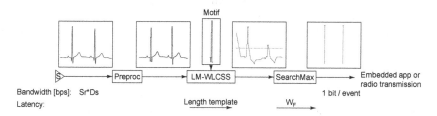

Fig. 1. The sensor data is acquired at Sr Hz and optionally pre-processed with downsampling, feature computation and quantization. LM-WLCSS computes the instantaneous matching score with the motif. Online local maximum search find scores above a detection threshold. This yields an event (1 bit) each time a motif is detected.

The overall pattern recognition system is illustrated in figure 1. The sensor is sampled with sample rate Sr and word length Ds and optionally pre-processed (e.g. by downsampling, computing signal features, or quantization). Afterwards, LM-WLCSS computes the instantaneous matching score between the pre-processed sensor data and the motif: the higher the score, the closer the pre-processed signal is to the motif. Finally, a local maxima search looks for matching scores above an acceptance threshold Thd, which indicates that the motif of interest has been spotted in the sensor signal. At this stage, a single bit or timestamp indicates that a pattern has been spotted. This can be used locally on the node or sent over radio for fusion with detectors on other nodes.

We refer to $\mathcal{S}(i)$ as the ith sample from the sensor (i.e. the input data stream), $\mathcal{T}(j)$ as the jth sample from the motif, and N_T the length of the the motif. The next two subsections describe LM-WLCSS and the local maximum search.

---

[2] The update equation is modified from the original work to address edge issues.

3.1 Limited-Memory Warping Longest Common Subsequence

LM-WLCSS can be efficiently implemented with dynamic programming by solving the problem of matching a shorter motif and a shorter stream and keeping intermediate results in memory (see [22] for the classical, non-warping, LCSS). We define $\mathcal{M}(j,i)$ the matching score between the first i samples of the stream and the first j samples of the motif. Thus, $\mathcal{M}(j,i)$ can be computed as follows:

$$\mathcal{M}(j,i) = \begin{cases} 0 & \text{if } i \leq 0 \text{ or } j \leq 0 \\ \mathcal{M}(j-1,i-1) + R & \text{if } |\mathcal{S}(i) - \mathcal{T}(j)| \leq \epsilon \\ max \begin{cases} \mathcal{M}(j-1,i-1) - P \cdot (\mathcal{S}(i) - \mathcal{T}(j)) \\ \mathcal{M}(j-1,i) - P \cdot (\mathcal{S}(i) - \mathcal{T}(j)) \\ \mathcal{M}(j,i-1) - P \cdot (\mathcal{S}(i) - \mathcal{T}(j)) \end{cases} & \text{if } |\mathcal{S}(i) - \mathcal{T}(j)| > \epsilon \end{cases}$$

$$(1)$$

R is a reward added to the matching score when two samples match. In case of mismatch a penalty proportional to the mismatch between samples scaled by P is applied. A tolerance ϵ allows approximate matches. Warping occurs in case of mismatch with the max operation selecting one of three options: accepting a mismatch between one sample from the data stream and the motif (line 1);

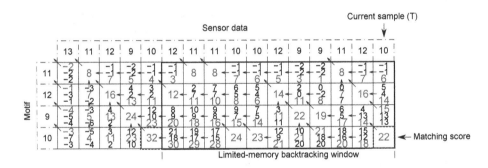

Fig. 2. LM-WLCSS computes the matching score between a motif of length 4 and data coming from a sensor. $R = 8$, $p = 1$, $\epsilon = 0$. The red bold value in the cells is $\mathcal{M}(j,i)$: a single value indicates a match between motif and sensor data; 3 values indicate a mismatch and the 3 possible scores before the max operation in equation 1. The last line $\mathcal{M}(N_T, i)$ is the matching score between the motif and the sensor data at time i. A local search of score maxima shows two maxima with score 32 (a perfect match) and 22 at the current sample. The backtracking variable $\mathcal{B}$ is represented by the arrow between cells. Backtracking from the perfect match shows that the motif is aligned with the sensor data without warping. Warping is illustrated when backtracking from the current sample: the motif is dilated and aligned against 9 sensor samples. As a new sample is acquired, a column would be added on the right to compute the updated matching score and backtracking. The limited-memory implementation stores only the last column to update the matching score, and the backtracking is limited in time. Thus, LM-WLCSS is a constant memory algorithm.

repeating one element of the data stream (i.e. contracting the motif on line 2); or repeating one element of the motif (i.e. dilating the motif on line 3).

$\mathcal{M}(N_T, i)$ indicates the matching score between the entire motif and the sensor data at time i. We consider that the motif has been found in the sensor data when a local maxima in $\mathcal{M}(N_T, i)$ is found above a trained acceptance threshold. This indicates the end-time of the match. As the algorithm allows for motif warping, the start-time of the match is found by *backtracking* from the end-time, using a backtrack variable $\mathcal{B}(j, i)$ that indicates which option was selected in the assignment of $\mathcal{M}(j, i)$ in equation 1. Figure 2 illustrates how LM-LCSS matches a motif against the sensor data in a matrix representation of $\mathcal{M}$ and $\mathcal{B}$, and how to find the start and end times of the match.

```
Input: sample: the current sensor data
Output: score: the resulting matching score
/* Limited-memory backtracking window                              */
B(1...N_T, 1...W_B - 1) ← B(1...N_T, 2...W_B);
/* Initialization                                                  */
mu ← 0; /* Score in the upper cell                                 */
mul ← 0; /* Score in the upper-left cell                           */
for j ← 1 to N_T do /* Update the matching score                   */
    ml ← M(j); /* Score in the left cell                           */
    if |sample − T(j)| < ε then /* sample matches the motif        */
        score ← mul + R;
        B(j, W_B) ← 0;
    else /* mismatch                                               */
        t = p · |sample − T(j)|;
        score, midx = max(mul − t, mu − t, ml − t); /* Returns the maximum of the
        arguments and its 0-based index                            */
        B(j, W_B) ← midx
    end
    mul ← ml;
    mu ← score;
    M(j) ← score;
end
```

Fig. 3. This function updates the matching score whenever a new sample is acquired. M is a vector of size N_T, B is the backtracking window of size $N_T \times W_B$, and T is a the motif of size N_T; these state variables are kept in-between calls to this function.

Implementation memory can be minimized by realizing that it is not necessary to store the entirety of $\mathcal{M}(j, i)$; instead, only the last column of $\mathcal{M}(j, i)$ is required to compute $\mathcal{M}(j, i + 1)$ when the next sample is acquired. Finding the start point of the match requires the backtracking variable $\mathcal{B}(j, i)$. However, application knowledge can be used to provide an upper bound on the amount of warping allowed. Therefore, instead of storing the entirety of $\mathcal{B}(j, i)$, a backtracking window of size W_B can be defined to keep only the most recent (closest to current time T) entries of $\mathcal{B}(j, i)$. The resulting algorithm (figure 3) is called each time a new sensor sample is received to update the matching score.

3.2   SearchMax

Each time the score is updated the function represented in figure 4 is called to find whether the score is a local maxima above above a threshold. This algorithm keeps data storage to a minimum and deals with the issue that signals carrying noise produce many local extrema. The algorithm looks for a local maxima in a sliding window without the need to store that window. The algorithm compares current score (S) with the last score (P) in order to determine whether there is a positive slope. When this is true a flag is set and the maximum value is stored (Max); a counter (K) is used to determine whether the stored value is the maximum within a window (W_F). The the maxima is above a detection threshold Thd the function returns indicating that a motif may have been spotted.

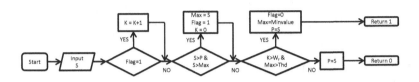

Fig. 4. Algorithm returning whether the current matching score is a local maxima above a threshold within a sliding window of size W_F.

3.3 Embedded Training

Training consists of defining the motif and the threshold Thd. Embedded training is possible, for instance for activity recognition. In training mode, the node indicates when it is ready for the user to demonstrate a gesture, e.g. by emitting a sound. The user demonstrates the gesture and the node continuously records the motion sensor data until the user stops moving. The recorded data is the gesture motif. This process can be repeated to evaluate the variability between the gestures and define an optimal detection threshold. One motif (e.g. the first recording) is selected, and the matching score between that motif and the subsequent recordings is computed. In order to spot all the gestures in that dataset, Thd should be equal to the lowest obtained matching score. However to be robust to outliers setting $Thd = \mu_{score} - n \cdot \sigma_{score}$ allows to adjust the sensitivity-specificity tradeoff of the algorithm in a with n^3. Training with cross-validation can be done offline for better multiparametric optimization [16,15].

3.4 Embedded Implementation

We implemented the system in C. A timer interrupt is used to sample the sensor data at regular intervals. The entire pattern spotting process can be executed in the timer interrupt as the processing time is predictable. Alternatively, the timer interrupt can store the data in a buffer, which is processed from the main program code later.

---

[3] This expression allows to approximate a suitable threshold in an online implementation; with n=2-4 our experiments showed good sensitivity-specificity tradeoffs. A better training uses cross-validation but may require too much memory to hold all patterns to be suitable for the sensor node.

The indexing variables looping through the motif and backtracking window are 16-bit on the AVR and 32-bit on the M4. The entries in the backtracking window are 8-bit. For benchmarking, we used different word size for the samples, matching scores, penalty and reward: 8-bit, 16-bit and 32-bit integers and single precision (32-bit) float. While smaller bit-width may be preferred, there is a lower limit defined by the matching score range. The maximum matching score is equal to $N_T \cdot R$. The minimum matching score is a negative value that depends on the incoming sensor data, N_T and P. As the data distribution can only be statistically characterized, there must be enough room to hold a "large" negative value, otherwise the scores may wrap around. In our implementation we scaled the sensor readings and parameters to ensure no wrap around ever occurred. Alternatively saturation arithmetic could be used, but it is much slower.

When using integer arithmetic the ratio of R to P can be selected to approximate a floating point implementation (such as the offline version presented in [16] which fixes $R = 1$ and assumes $0 < P < 1$). We implemented the backtracking array as a circular buffer, thus avoiding memory moves in algorithm 3. Thus the algorithm speed is independent of the size of the backtracking window. The backtracking window is an optional feature: when deactivated, the start point of the match cannot be found but the memory used is significantly reduced. We show in section 5 that backtracking may not be needed for many spotting applications. We stored the templates in RAM. However if the motif is static or trained infrequently, it could be stored in Flash to free up more RAM.

4   Technical Evaluation

We characterize the system on two platforms. The first is a custom 8-bit Atmel AVR motion sensor node [19]. It is 44mm×25mm×17mm node with Bluetooth (BlueNiceCom III), a 3D ADXL330 accelerometer, a 2D IDG650 gyroscope and an ATmega1284P microcontroller at 8MHz (see fig 7 left). The AVR has hardware supports for 8-bit multiplications, 128KB of program Flash, and 16KB of RAM. GCC 4.8.1 with O2 optimization is used to compile the system. The second platform is a STM32F4DISCOVERY board with a 32-bit STM32F407 ARM Cortex M4 microcontroller with 1MB of program Flash, 192KB of RAM and a hardware single-precision floating point unit. The microcontroller uses the external crystal with the PLL set to generate an 8MHz CPU frequency. GCC 4.8.4 with O2 optimization is used to compile the system using the thumb2 instruction set. Benchmarking was done using internal timers. The timer resolution was 128μS on the AVR node and 1ms on the M4 board. All benchmarks ran at least one second to minimize measurement error. A serial link (over UART and USB for the AVR node, SWO on the M4 board) is used to report the timings.

We benchmark individually LM-WLCSS, SearchMax and their combination. The reward and penalty parameters or the range of the motif and sensor data have no influence on speed. Benchmark results are presented in figure 5. Note that the algorithm is linear in $O(N_T)$ in time *for each sample*. Smaller templates allow faster execution, however for very small templates the function call overhead appears in the benchmark. The AVR is faster with smaller word sizes;

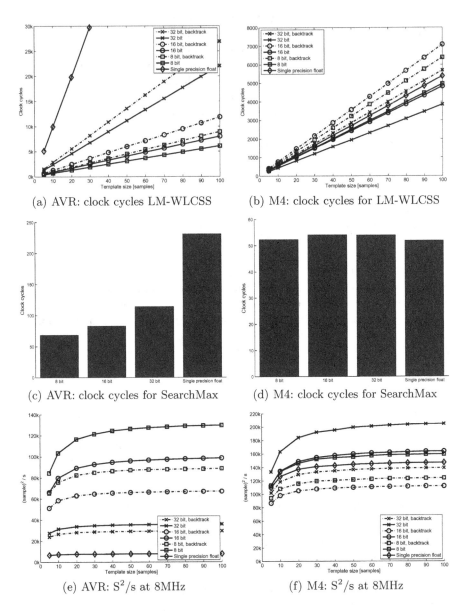

(a) AVR: clock cycles LM-WLCSS   (b) M4: clock cycles for LM-WLCSS

(c) AVR: clock cycles for SearchMax   (d) M4: clock cycles for SearchMax

(e) AVR: S^2/s at 8MHz   (f) M4: S^2/s at 8MHz

Fig. 5. (a,b) show the number of clock cycles for the execution of the LM-WLCSS algorithm only; (c,d) show the number of clock cycles for SearchMax only; (e,f) show the overall system performance when LM-WLCSS and SearchMax are combined in samples^2/second at 8MHz. This unit is the product of the motif length by the maximum sample rate. It is asymptotically a constant. The AVR does 130K sample^2/second at 8MHz. This means it can sustain a sample rate of 1300Hz with a motif of length 100, or 130Hz with a motif of length 1000. The benchmark was performed with different motif sizes; with small motifs the performance decreases due to function call overheads.

however 16-bit is an ideal operating point as shown in section 5. The ARM is faster with 32-bit word size, as smaller arithmetic operations must be emulated.

The RAM usage can be derived from the algorithm description. The *state variables* can be statically allocated. LM-WLCSS requires memory to store the limited-memory backtracking window $\mathcal{B}$ and the latest column of $\mathcal{M}$. The RAM used of for state data is thus: $N_T \cdot ws + N_T \cdot W_B$ with ws the word size in bytes. If backtracking is disabled, the RAM used for state data is only: $N_T \cdot ws$ SearchMax requires only 5 state variables, regardless of the size of the SearchMax window W_F. A few additonal *working variables* are needed (e.g. mu, mul, ml in algorithm 3), but this is constant and small in contrast to the memory used for the state variables. The compiler may even optimize them out with registers. Consider a 32-bit implementation with a motif of length 30 (i.e. allowing to spot a pattern of 1 second with 30Hz sensor sample rate, which is typical in activity recognition) allowing to find the starting point of the pattern in the data stream even if the pattern is twice slower than the original. Then $W_B = 60$, $N_T = 30$, and the memory needed is: $30 \cdot 4 + 60 \cdot 30 = 1920$ bytes. Note that in section 5 we demonstrate successful spotting without relying on backtracking. If backtracking is disabled, the memory used is only $N_T \cdot ws = 120$ bytes.

In table 1 we report the program size for LM-WLCSS and SearchMax in bytes computed based on the disasembly of the executable. In the float implementation, an additional library for floating point operations is required. Its size is estimated by adding all the functions dealing with floats in the executable. The M4 float implementation is significantly more compact due to the hardware FPU. As few as 434 (16-bit on AVR) and 284 (32-bit on M4) bytes of code are required for the full system with backtracking.

Table 1. Program memory (Flash) usage in bytes for LM-WLCSS (top) and Search-Max (bottom). The floating point implementation requires in addition a floating point library, whose estimated size is indicated in parenthesis.

	Platform	8 bit	8 bit, bt	16 bit	16 bit, bt	32 bit	32 bit, bt	float
LM-WLCSS	AVR	186	246	234	310	468	534	578 (+860)
	M4	176	200	184	222	140	180	192 (+3622)
SearchMax	AVR	92		124		194		222 (+860)
	M4	106		110		104		118 (+3622)

The latency of the system is defined by the length of the motif and the size of the SearchMax window W_F. The maximum matching score is reached once the *end* of the motif is identified in the data stream (see fig. 2). Thus, shorter templates reduce the latency of the system, but may decrease its specificity. The SearchMax window avoids detecting multiple events when in reality only one occured (e.g. with noisy data). The ideal W_F is selected experimentally, but it can be much smaller than the motif size (e.g. 5-10 samples in section 5).

5   Pattern Spotting Examples

We illustrate the versatility of the algorithm on 3 examples of pattern recognition typical of wearable sensing and activity recognition. The system parameters have been selected to illustrate the algorithm behavior, not necessarily to achieve the optimal performance. We purposely show a variey of sample rate and motif lengths. In all the examples, we use a 16-bit implementation of the system.

Physiological Signal Analysis. We first illustrate spotting physiological patterns. The top plot in figure 6(a) illustrates the ECG (v2) of a healthy subject sampled at 200Hz. A motif of 20 samples (100ms) is defined around the QRS complex. The system parameters are: $R = 16$, $P = 8$, $\epsilon = 2$, $W_F = 30$, $W_B = 100$, $Thd = -200$. The middle plot shows the matching score which increases above the detection threshold (horizontal line) when the QRS complex is observed and decays as unrelated data is observed. The second last heart beat appears slightly different and only just passes above the threshold. This shows how the threshold can control the sensitivity-specificity tradeoff of the algorithm. A lower threshold would guarantee to spot all the heart beats, but a higher threshold may be desired to spot anomalies in the QRS complex. The lower plot shows the overall latency of the system and indicates the effective time at which the QRS complex is detected. The motif is found some time after the peak in the matching score (controlled by W_F), and the peak occurs when the *end* of the motif is matched against the signal.

The Pan-Tompkins algorithm [10] is the de-facto method to spot the QRS complex. It is based on filtering, derivation, squaring, integration and thresholding, with numerous optimized embedded implementations of the initial algorithm. In comparison LM-WLCSS is very competitive: it offers very low complexity (N_T multiplications per sample), and provides more flexibility than Pan-Tompkins-based methods, as the motif can be adjusted. For instance, it could be used to biometrically identify the user of a device by the ECG shape.

The AVR achieves $65KS^2/s$ at 8MHz for a motif of 20 samples (fig. 5). A dedicated system could run the CPU at only 490KHz to spot the QRS complex. This would allow operation at 1.8V, using 360uW of power (extrapolated from the datasheet) for the signal processing.

Recognition of Everyday Activities. We show the recognition of everyday activities from an arm-worn accelerometer based on the "Drill run" of the OPPORTUNITY dataset, which is a recognized highly challenging benchmarking dataset as reported in [7]. A person performs 20 repetitions of a scripted but realistic sequence of everyday activities in a home environment, including opening/closing doors/windows/drawers, cleaning a table, drinking, etc. We evaluated LM-WLCSS on the detection of very similar gestures: drinking from a cup while seated, and drinking from a cup while standing or walking. Only one axis of an acceleration sensor node on the dominant lower arm is used. It is quantized in the range -64 to 63 and downsampled from 30 Hz to 10Hz. The WM-LCSS parameters are: $R = 16$, $P = 1$, $\epsilon = 5$, $W_F = 10$, $W_B = 100$. The drink sitting and standing motifs are 61 and 48 samples respectively. The detection threshold were optimized by cross-validation.

Figure 6(b) shows a closeup of 3 of the 20 repetitions of the activity sequence. The sensor data appears very noisy, and there are only very subtle differences between the two motifs. Drinking seated can be recognized more robustly than

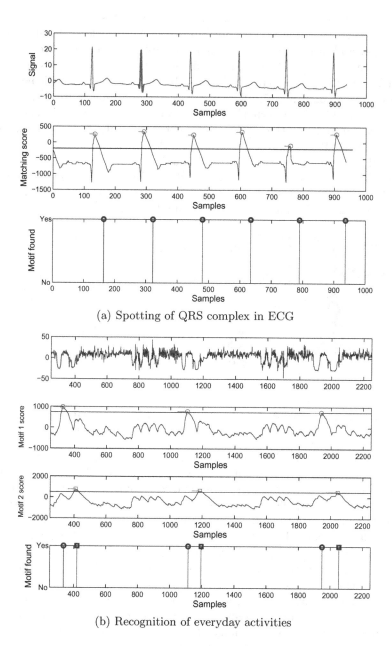

(a) Spotting of QRS complex in ECG

(b) Recognition of everyday activities

Fig. 6. (a) Detection of the QRS complex in ECG recordings with LM-WLCSS. Top: original signal and highlighted motif. Middle: matching score, threshold, and identified local maxima. Bottom: effective detection of the QRS complex, with the additional latency of SearchMax. **(b)** Detection of "drinking seated" (2nd plot) and "drinking standing" (3rd plot) gestures from a 1 axis acceleration channel on the lower arm.

drinking standing, as the peak in matching score in the first case is more marked, which allows to set a higher detection threshold. Nevertheless, the algorithm is able to spot and distinguish the two kinds of subtly different gestures.

Assuming a motif length of 100 and 10Hz sample rate (i.e. gestures of up to 10 seconds), the AVR can do $67KS^2/s$ with the 16-bit backtracking implementation. This allows to recognizing 67 different gestures in real-time at 10Hz using 8mW (3.3mA at 2.4V with the internal 8MHz RC oscillator). Alternatively, one gesture could be recognized with the CPU running at 120KHz only. At 1.8V and with the internal 128KHz RC oscillator this gives 135uW for a single gesture spotter. On the M4, the fastest backtracking implementation does $140KS^2/s$. This allows to recognize 140 gestures at 10Hz with the CPU at 8MHz with power consumption of 10mW (3.3V, 3mA at 8MHz according to the datasheet). Power decreases by more than 50% by disabling backtracking in all cases.

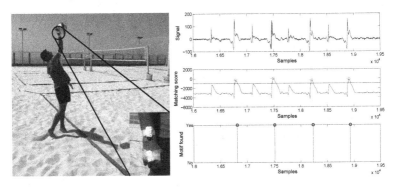

Fig. 7. Sensors placement for beach volleyball serve analysis (left) and detection of selected Beach Volleyball serves from a forearm gyroscope sensor (right)

Beach Volleyball. We show the recognition of beach volleball serves from one gyroscope placed on the forearm as shown in Figure 7. The player was asked to serve several times from different parts of the court and varying power, and data was collected from 64 serves using the AVR-based sensor node described in section 4. We observed that the player's routine before serving included a smack on the ball to remove the sand on it, therefore the LM-WLCSS algorithm was used to analyze the data and evaluate the discrimination of both events. Selected data is shown in Figure 7, showing the serve template (of size 50 samples) and the smack before serving. The LM-WLCSS parameters are $R = 1$, $P = 1$, $\epsilon = 10$, $Thd = -1000$, $W_F = 25$. Using a single axis of the gyroscope, we recognized the servers with only 1 false positive and 20 false negatives. These results are promising considering the variability of serves [5] and that there has not been any particular optimization for this application.

6   Extensions and Discussion

When using LM-WLCSS on raw acceleration readings the system is sensitive to sensor displacement and rotation. Other template matching methods suffer from

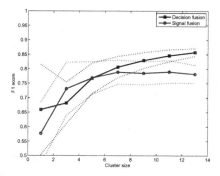

Fig. 8. Average performance (standard deviation in dashed lines) from an exhaustive evaluation of clusters of size 1 to 13 nodes on the upper limbs in an everyday activity recognition task (17 activity classes). In signal fusion, the nodes stream raw data to a central node that runs LM-LWCSS. In decision fusion, nodes run locally LM-LWCSS; when recognizing a pattern they send an event to a central node that fuses the individual decisions with majority voting. Decision fusion requires much lower datarate.

the same issue. One solution is to apply the method on features derived from the acceleration, such as the acceleration magnitude which is rotation independent. Displacement can be handled by first detecting on-body sensor placement in order to select adequate motifs for recognition [13].

The main behavioral difference between this implementation and the Warp-ingLCSS work in [16] results from the use of integer arithmetic. We found out that an 8-bit implementation is generally inadequate for acceleration data, however 16-bit (or more) are adequate for the scenarios presented here.

Memory is reduced by decreasing the size of the backtracking window. This limits the maximum dilation (but not the contraction) of the motif if the start point of the match is desired. If the start point of the match is not desired the backtracking window can be eliminated altogether.

We showed the recognition of at most 2 simultaneous patterns in the drink example. This can be extended to more motifs[4]. One challenge is that several motifs may be simultaneously spotted if the data is very noisy. This can be addressed by a conflict resolution as presented in [16], or by ranking the activity likelihood using the matching score which can be used with decision fusion.

Results were obtained from a single sensor channel. Multiple sensor channels (e.g. 3D acceleration) can be combined before being processed by LM-WLCSS with K-means clustering [16,15], or by modifying the sample matching to a vector Euclidian distance (e.g. to handle 3D acceleration). This *signal fusion* can be used to fuse multiple channels on a single node, or across multiple nodes when they stream their raw signals to a central node doing K-means clustering and running LM-WLCSS. Alternatively, nodes can perform individual local pattern recognition with LM-LWCSS and send events to central node which performs

---

[4] Memory usage with multiple motifs is the sum of the memory needed to recognize each motif individually.

decision fusion, for example using majority voting [28] or meta-classifiers [2]. This leads to very low data rates, as radio transmission only occurs when a pattern is recognized by a node and needs as few as $log_2(C)$ bits, with C the number of classes.

In figure 8 we compare signal fusion and decision fusion performance on the recognition of 17 distinct activities (340 gestures in total) from the OPPOR-TUNITY "Drill run" for clusters of nodes of various size [7]. We consider 13 nodes on the upper limbs. Each node is a 1 axis acceleration or rate of turn sensor. We assess all combinations of clusters of size N out of the 13 nodes and report averages and standard deviation. In signal fusion, all nodes in the cluster stream raw data (16-bit per sample) to a central node at 10 Hz which performs a k-means clustering (k=20) before applying LM-LCSS with 17 motifs. The total bandwidth is $10 \cdot 16 \cdot N$ bps. In decision fusion, each node of the cluster performs local classification and send 5 bit each time an event is recognized. We consider a worst case setup for decision fusion, which assumes no null-class. The total bandwidth is $5 \cdot N$ bit per gesture; given the average duration of a gesture is 3.8 seconds, the bandwidth for decision fusion is $1.3 \cdot N$ bps. This leads to a reduction of bandwidth by 2 orders of magnitude (from $160 \cdot N$ bps to $1.3 \cdot N$ bps), while keeping similar recognition performance in this scenario. As expected, performance increases with the size of the cluster as more information is available to recognize the user's activities. Although it appears that decision fusion outperforms signal fusion we cannot make such a general statement from the limited amount of data used.

The simplicity of the LM-WLCSS codepath makes it is suitable for silicon-level implementation, for instance based on a multiply-and-accumulate unit to to execute in n clock cycles the algorithm 3 for a motif of length n. A silicon implementation would allow ultra-low power pattern spotting, and could be included in sensor frontends of microcontrollers.

LM-WLCSS allows a training by demonstration that is important as ever more assisted living and smart assistant applications require *personalization* to handle human variability. It also allows a simple control of the sensitivity and specificity tradeoff with Thd, which can be adapted depending on the application need (e.g. to spot any drink even v.s. only specific drink events). An increase in Thd increases the specificity of the method and decreases its sensitivity. The system parameters can be optimized by cross-validation [16,15].

7   Conclusion

We have shown a motif matching method to spot patterns in noisy signal streams suitable for real-time execution with low-latency on sensor nodes. We presented two variants of the algorithms: one that simply spots the moment that a motif is observed in the sensor data, the other is capable of *backtracking* to find the start time of the match, which indicates how much the motif has been "warped". The first implementation uses only as much RAM as the length of the motif and is sufficient to spot patterns in a wide range of applications, as demonstrated in this paper with 3 scenarios involving 3 different kinds of sensors.

With backtracking, we reach a performance of $67KS^2/s$ for a 16-bit implementation on an 8-bit AVR microcontroller, and $140KS^2/s$ on a 32-bit Cortex M4 microcontroller. For a motif of length 100 (e.g. a gesture of maximum 10 seconds at 10Hz) the AVR and M4 at 8MHz can recognize respectively 67 and 140 motifs in real-time from a 10Hz sensor, consuming respectively 8mW and 10mW and using as few as 434 or 284 bytes of code for the full system. The AVR can realize a single gesture spotter using only 135uW. In a distributed activity recognition scenario, LM-WLCSS allows a bandwidth reduction by 2 orders of magnitude with identical performance to a signal fusion approach. This is especially interesting to support context awareness in opportunistic sensing scenarios.

LM-WLCSS is a generic algorithm which we demonstrated to be useful in a wide range of pattern recognition scenarios. This makes LM-WLCSS well suited for distributed in-network pattern recognition, which could be implemented in next generation smart accessories (smart-watches, smart-bracelets), smart environments, and more generally in the Internet of Things. Future work may include silicon implementation to further reduce power in smart nodes.

References

1. Avci, A., Bosch, S., Marin-Perianu, M., Marin-Perianu, R., Havinga, P.: Activity recognition using inertial sensing for healthcare, wellbeing and sports applications: A survey. In: Proc Int. Conf. on Architecture of Computing Systems, pp. 1–10 (2010)
2. Bahrepour, M., Meratnia, N., Havinga, P.: Sensor fusion-based event detection in wireless sensor networks. In: Mobile and Ubiquitous Systems, pp. 1–8 (2009)
3. Bao, L., Intille, S.S.: Activity recognition from user-annotated acceleration data. In: Ferscha, A., Mattern, F. (eds.) PERVASIVE 2004. LNCS, vol. 3001, pp. 1–17. Springer, Heidelberg (2004)
4. Benatti, S., Farella, E., Benini, L.: EMG embedded HMI for smart garments. In: Atelier of Smart Garments and Accessories Workshop at Ubicomp (2014)
5. Buscà, B., Moras, G., Peña, J., Rodríguez-Jiménez, S.: The influence of serve characteristics on performance in men's and women's high-standard beach volleyball. Journal of Sports Sciences 30(3), 269–276 (2012)
6. Pham, C., Plötz, T., Olivier, P.: A dynamic time warping approach to real-time activity recognition for food preparation. In: de Ruyter, B., Wichert, R., Keyson, D.V., Markopoulos, P., Streitz, N., Divitini, M., Georgantas, N., Mana Gomez, A. (eds.) AmI 2010. LNCS, vol. 6439, pp. 21–30. Springer, Heidelberg (2010)
7. Chavarriaga, R., Sagha, H., Calatroni, A., Digumarti, S., Millán, J., Roggen, D., Tröster, G.: The opportunity challenge: A benchmark database for on-body sensor-based activity recognition. Pattern Recognition Letters 34, 2033–2042 (2013)
8. Chen, Z., Ranieri, J., Zhang, R., Vetterli, M.: DASS: Distributed adaptive sparse sensing. arXiv:1401.1191 (1013)
9. Fortino, G., Guerrieri, A., Bellifemine, F.L., Giannantonio, R.: SPINE2: Developing BSN applications on heterogeneous sensor nodes. In: Proc. IEEE Symposium on Industrial Embedded Systems (2009)
10. Pan, J., Tompkins, W.J.: A real-time QRS detection algorithm. IEEE Transactions on Biomedical Engineering 32(3) (1985)

11. Kale, N., Lee, J., Lotfian, R., Jafari, R.: Impact of sensor misplacement on dynamic time warping based human activity recognition using wearable computers. In: Proc Wireless Health (2012)

12. Kim, S., Pakzad, S., Culler, D., Demmel, J., Fenves, G., Glaser, S., Turon, M.: Health monitoring of civil infrastructures using wireless sensor networks. In: 6th Int. Symp. on Information Processing in Sensor Networks, pp. 254–263 (2007)

13. Kunze, K., Lukowicz, P.: Dealing with sensor displacement in motion-based onbody activity recognition systems. In: Proc. 10th Int. Conf. on Ubiquitous Computing (2008)

14. Marin-Perianu, M., Lombriser, C., Amft, O., Havinga, P., Tröster, G.: Distributed activity recognition with fuzzy-enabled wireless sensor networks. In: Nikoletseas, S.E., Chlebus, B.S., Johnson, D.B., Krishnamachari, B. (eds.) DCOSS 2008. LNCS, vol. 5067, pp. 296–313. Springer, Heidelberg (2008)

15. Nguyen-Dinh, L.V., Calatroni, A., Tröster, G.: Robust online gesture recognition with crowdsourced annotations. Journal of Machine Learning Research 15, 3187–3220 (2014)

16. Nguyen-Dinh, L.V., Roggen, D., Calatroni, A., Tröster, G.: Improving online gesture recognition with template matching methods in accelerometer data. In: Proc 12th Int Conf. on Intelligent Systems Design and Applications, pp. 831–836 (2012)

17. Patel, S., Park, H., Bonato, P., Chan, L., Rodgers, M.: A review of wearable sensors and systems with application in rehabilitation. Journal of NeuroEngineering and Rehabilitation 9(21) (2012)

18. Rashidi, P., Cook, D.J.: The resident in the loop: Adapting the smart home to the user. IEEE Transactions on Systems, Man, and Cybernetics Journal, Part A 39(5), 949–959 (2009)

19. Roggen, D., Bächlin, M., Schumm, J., Holleczek, T., Lombriser, C., Tröster, G., Widmer, L., Majoe, D., Gutknecht, J.: An educational and research kit for activity and context recognition from on-body sensors. In: Proc. IEEE Int. Conf. on Body Sensor Networks (BSN), pp. 277–282 (2010)

20. Sagha, H., Bayati, H., del R. Millán, J.: On-line anomaly detection and resilience in classifier ensembles. Pattern Recognition Letters 34(15), 1916–1927 (2013)

21. Stäger, M., Lukowicz, P., Perera, N., von Büren, T., Tröster, G., Starner, T.: Sound-Button: Design of a Low Power Wearable Audio Classification System. In: Proc of the 7th International Symposium on Wearable Computers, pp. 12–17. IEEE Computer Society Press, Los Alamitos (2003)

22. Vlachos, M., Hadjieleftheriou, M., Gunopulos, D., Keogh, E.: Indexing multi-dimensional time-series with support for multiple distance measures. In: Proc 9th ACM SIGKDD Int. Conf. on Knowledge Discovery and Data Mining, pp. 216–225. ACM, New York (2003)

23. Wark, T., Corke, P., Sikka, P., Klingbeil, L., Guo, Y., Crossman, C., Valencia, P., Swain, D., Bishop-Hurley, G.: Transforming agriculture through pervasive wireless sensor networks. IEEE Pervasive Computing Magazine 6(2), 50–57 (2007)

24. Wei, B., Yang, M., Shen, Y., Rana, R., Chou, C.T., Hu, W.: Real-time classification via sparse representation in acoustic sensor networks. In: Proc 11th ACM Conf. on Embedded Networked Sensor Systems, vol. (21) (2013)

25. Yang, A.Y., Jafari, R., Sastry, S.S., Bajcsy, R.: Distributed recognition of human actions using wearable motion sensor networks. Journal of Ambient Intelligence and Smart Environments 1, 1–13 (2009)

26. Yick, J., Mukherjee, B., Ghosal, D.: Wireless sensor network survey. Computer Networks 52(12), 2292–2330 (2008)
27. Zappi, P., Farella, E., Benini, L.: Hidden markov models implementation for tangible interfaces. In: Nijholt, A., Reidsma, D., Hondorp, H. (eds.) INTETAIN 2009. LNICST, vol. 9, pp. 258–263. Springer, Heidelberg (2009)
28. Zappi, P., Roggen, D., Farella, E., Tröster, G., Benini, L.: Network-level power-performance trade-off in wearable activity recognition: a dynamic sensor selection approach. ACM Transactions on Embedded Computing Systems 11(3) (2012)

Sensor-Based User Authentication

He Wang[1], Dimitrios Lymberopoulos[2], and Jie Liu[2]

[1] University of Illinois at Urbana-Champaign, Champaign, IL, USA
hewang5@illinois.edu
[2] Microsoft Research, Redmond, WA, USA
{dlymper,liuj}@microsoft.com

Abstract. We study the feasibility of leveraging the sensors embedded on mobile devices to enable a user authentication mechanism that is easy for users to perform, but hard for attackers to bypass. The proposed approach lies on the fact that users perform gestures in a unique way that depends on how they hold the phone, and on their hand's geometry, size, and flexibility. Based on this observation, we introduce two new unlock gestures that have been designed to enable the phone's embedded sensors to properly capture the geometry and biokinetics of the user's hand during the gesture. The touch sensor extracts the geometry and timing of the user hand, while the accelerometer and gyro sensors record the displacement and rotation of the mobile device during the gesture. When combined, a sensor fingerprint for the user is generated. In this approach, potential attackers need to simultaneously reproduce the touch, accelerometer, and gyro sensor signatures to falsely authenticate. Using 5000 gestures recorded over two user studies involving a total of 70 subjects, our results indicate that sensor fingerprints can accurately differentiate users while achieving less than 2.5% false accept and false reject rates. Attackers that directly observe the true user authenticating on a device, can successfully bypass authentication only 3% of the time.

1 Introduction

As sensitive information, in the form of messages, photos, bank accounts, and more, finds its place on mobile devices, the need to properly secure them becomes a necessity. Traditional user authentication mechanisms, such as lengthy passwords that include combinations of letters, numbers and symbols, are not suited for mobile devices due to the small on-screen keyboards. Given that users need to authenticate on their mobile devices tens or even hundreds of times throughout the day, the traditional password authentication technique becomes a real bottleneck.

To simplify the authentication process, users tend to leave their mobile devices completely unprotected, or they leverage simple authentication techniques such as 4-digit pins, picture passwords (Windows 8), or unlock gestures (Android). Even though these techniques allow easy and intuitive user authentication, they compromise the security of the device, as they are susceptible to simple shoulder-surfing attacks [14]. Pins, picture passwords, and unlock gestures can be easily retrieved by simply observing a user authenticating on his/her device once.

Ideally, the user authentication process should be easy and fast for users to perform, and at the same time difficult for an attacker to accurately reproduce even by directly observing the user authenticating on the device.

T. Abdelzaher et al. (Eds.): EWSN 2015, LNCS 8965, pp. 168–185, 2015.

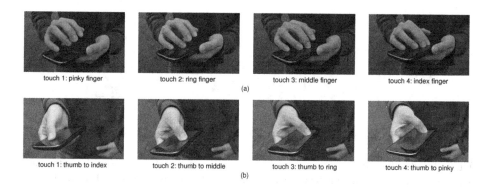

Fig. 1. Proposed unlock gestures for capturing the biokinetics of the user's hand. Users can perform the gesture anywhere on the screen, and at the speed they feel comfortable with. (a) 2-hand gesture: the user sequentially taps his four fingers on the touch screen starting from the pinky finger, and ending with the index finger. (b) 1-hand gesture: the user uses his/her thumb to touch each of the rest four fingertips through the touch screen starting with the index finger, and ending with the pinky finger. The 1-hand gesture was designed to avoid the need to use both hands at the expense of more noisy sensor data. **A video demonstrating both gestures can be seen in [1,2]**

Towards this goal, Android devices recently brought face recognition to the masses by enabling user authentication through the front-facing camera. Even though intuitive and fast, this type of authentication suffers from typical computer vision limitations. The face recognition performance degrades under poor or different lighting conditions than the ones used during training. Given that mobile devices constantly follow their users, such fluctuations on the environmental conditions are common.

More recently, iPhone enabled users to easily and securely unlock their devices by embedding a fingerprint sensor in the home button. Even though this approach addresses both the usability and security requirements of the authentication process, it is fundamentally limited to devices with large physical buttons on the front, such as the home button on iPhone, where such a sensor can be fitted. However, as phone manufacturers push for devices with large edge-to-edge displays, physical buttons are quickly replaced by capacitive buttons that can be easily embedded into the touch screen, eliminating the real-estate required by a fingerprint sensor. Embedding fingerprint sensors into touch screens behind gorilla glass is challenging, and has not been demonstrated.

In this paper, we study the feasibility of enabling user authentication based solely on generic sensor data. The main idea behind our approach is that different users perform the same gesture differently depending on the way they hold the phone, and on their hand's geometry, size, and flexibility. These subtle differences can be picked up by the device's embedded sensors (i.e., touch, accelerometer, and gyro), enabling user authentication based on sensor fingerprints. With this in mind, we introduce two new unlock gestures, shown in Figure 1, that have been designed to maximize the unique user information we can extract through the device's embedded sensors.

While the user performs the gesture, we leverage the touch screen sensor to extract rich information about the geometry and the size of the user's hand (size, pressure, timing and distance of finger taps). We also leverage the embedded accelerometer and

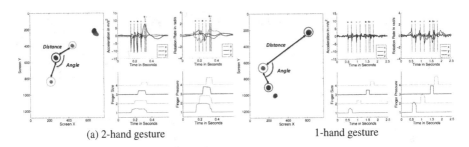

(a) 2-hand gesture   1-hand gesture

Fig. 2. Raw data from the touch, accelerometer, and gyro sensors. Dots and asterisks on the sensor plots correspond to the moments of pressing and releasing.Touch screen data enables the extraction of: distances between every pair of fingertips, angles defined by any combination of 3 fingertips, and the exact timing of each fingertip. Acceleration and gyro data capture the displacement of the device in user's hand during the gesture.

gyro sensors to record the phone's displacement and rotation during the gesture. To avoid the impact of gravity, we use linear acceleration provided by Android API.

When combined, the information from touch, accelerometer, and gyro sensors provides a detailed view into *how* the individual user performs the gesture, and, as we show in this work, it can be used as a sensor fingerprint to authenticate the user. Attackers willing to bypass this authentication mechanism, face a much harder task as they have to *simultaneously* reproduce the timing, placement, size, and pressure of each finger tap, as well as the accelerometer and gyro sensor signatures. Even though faking each of this information individually might be easy, *simultaneously* reproducing all this information is quite challenging even when the attacker has the opportunity to closely observe the actual user performing the unlock gesture.

In summary, this work makes three contributions. First, we propose two new unlock gestures that were designed to enable a device's sensors to extract as much information as possible about the user's hand biokinetics. Second, we collect 3000 sensor fingerprints across 50 users, and show that different users indeed perform the same gestures differently, and in a way that embedded sensor's can accurately capture and differentiate. In particular, we demonstrate false accept and false reject rates lower than 2.5%, when only a small number of training gestures per user is used. Third, we simulate realistic attack scenarios, by showing videos of real users authenticating on their devices to attackers, and then asking the attackers to reproduce the unlock gestures. Experimental results from 2000 attacks from 20 different attackers show that the proposed approach can achieve success attack rates that are lower than 3%.

2   Motivation and Challenges

To better illustrate how the biokinetics of the user's hand are captured by the proposed gestures shown in Figure 1, Figure 2 shows the raw data recorded by the touch, accelerometer, and gyro sensors when a user performs each of the gestures.

In both cases, four finger taps are recorded through the touch screen in the form of pixel coordinates. Since each of the recorded touch points directly (2-hand gesture) or indirectly (1-hand gesture) corresponds to a fingertip, the touch screen captures the geometry of the user's hand. In particular, the distance between every pair of fingertips, and the angles defined by any combination of 3 fingertips, can be used to characterize the size and geometry of the user's hand. At the same time, the timestamps of the finger taps highlight the speed at which the user is able to flex his fingers to perform the required gesture. The duration of each finger tap, as well as the timing between pairs of finger taps varies across users depending on the size and flexibility of the user's hand.

The touch screen on most smartphones is also able to record the pressure and size of each finger tap. Both of these values depend on the size and weight of the user's hand, on how much pressure the user applies on the display, as well as on the angle at which the user holds the device while performing the gesture.

The accelerometer and gyro sensors complement the touch sensor by *indirectly* capturing additional information about user's hand biokinetics. Every time a user performs one of the unlock gestures, the device is slightly displaced and rotated. As shown in Figure 2, the displacement and rotation of the device is clearly reflected in the accelerometer and gyro sensor data.

When combined, the information from touch, accelerometer, and gyro sensors forms a sensor fingerprint that captures the geometry and biokinetics of the user's hand.

2.1   Challenges and Contributions

The use of sensor data for user authentication poses several challenges. First, the recorded sensor data can vary across different gesture instances depending on how the actual user performs the gesture or holds the device. Even worse, this variability can be user-specific. For instance, some users can be very accurate in reproducing the exact timing or distance between the finger taps, but fail to accurately reproduce other parts of the sensor data, such as the pressure or angle signatures, and vice versa. An authentication mechanism should be automatically tailored to the capabilities of each user.

To enable direct comparison of the sensor fingerprints across users and gesture instances, we introduce personalized dissimilarity metrics for quantifying the difference of any pair of sensor fingerprints in both the touch and sensor domain. The personalized dissimilarity metrics are designed to emphasize more on those features of the sensor data that exhibit the least variability across gesture instances, and thus are the most descriptive of user's gesture input behavior.

Second, mobile devices support high sensor sampling rates (up to $200Hz$). At this sampling rate large amounts of data is generated creating a processing bottleneck that can slow down the device unlock process, and render the proposed technique unusable. To address this problem, we exploit the tradeoff between sensor downsampling and overall accuracy, and show that by properly downsampling sensor data, we can achieve device unlock times of $200ms$ without sacrificing recognition accuracy.

3   Architecture

Figure 3 provides an overview of the sensor-based authentication system. During the user enrollment phase, the true user repeatedly performs the unlock gesture on the

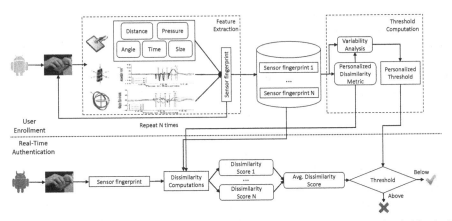

Fig. 3. Overview of the sensor-based authentication process. The processing pipeline is identical for the 2-hand and 1-hand gestures: 4 finger taps are recorded and processed in the same way.

touch-enabled device. For each gesture, the touch sensor is used to record finger taps and extract information about the timing, distance, angle, pressure, and size of finger taps. At the same time, the accelerometer and gyro sensors are continuously sampled to capture the displacement and rotation of the device during the unlock gesture. The data extracted from the finger taps, along with the raw accelerometer, and gyro data becomes the actual sensor fingerprint for the user. In that way, multiple sensor fingerprints across different gesture instances are collected. This collection of fingerprints represents the identity of the user in the sensor domain.

To determine if a random sensor fingerprint belongs to the true user or not, a way to quantify the difference of two sensor fingerprints is required. We introduce a dissimilarity metric that takes into account the unique gestural behavior of the user to quantify how close two sensor fingerprints are. Given this dissimilarity metric, we analyze the variability of the recorded sensor fingerprints for a given user, and based on this variability we derive a threshold for admitting or rejecting an unknown sensor fingerprint. For those users with low variability, a stricter threshold should be enforced, while for users with high variability, a more lenient threshold should be adopted to properly balance false positives and false negatives.

At run time, when a user performs the unlock gesture, a new sensor fingerprint is recorded. The distance of this fingerprint to the true user is computed as the average dissimilarity between the recorded fingerprint and every single fingerprint recorded in the user enrollment phase. If the average dissimilarity is below the personalization threshold, the user is successfully authenticated, otherwise the device remains locked.

The next sections describe in detail the composition of sensor fingerprints, the dissimilarity metric, and the personalized threshold computation.

3.1   Sensor Fingerprints

Touch, accelerometer, and gyro sensor data are combined to form the sensor fingerprint. In the case of accelerometer and gyro sensors, the process is straightforward as the raw sensor data is directly used as part of the sensor fingerprint.

Table 1. Features extracted from the 4 finger taps' touch information. All features depend on the relative, and not absolute, locations of the finger taps. This enables users to perform the gesture anywhere on the screen. Indices 1, 2, 3, and 4 correspond to each finger tap as shown in Figure 1.

Feature Type	Features	Num. of Features
Distance	$D_{1,2}, D_{1,3}, D_{1,4}, D_{2,3}, D_{2,4}, D_{3,4}$	6
Angle	$A_{1,2,3}, A_{1,2,4}, A_{1,3,4}, A_{2,3,4}$	4
Size	S_1, S_2, S_3, S_4	4
Pressure	P_1, P_2, P_3, P_4	4
Duration	$Dur_1, Dur_2, Dur_3, Dur_4$	4
Start Time Difference	$STD_{1,2}, STD_{1,3}, STD_{1,4}, STD_{2,3}, STD_{2,4}, STD_{3,4}$	6
End Time Difference	$ETD_{1,2}, ETD_{1,3}, ETD_{1,4}, ETD_{2,3}, ETD_{2,4}, ETD_{3,4}$	6
Distance Ratio	$\frac{D_{1,2}}{D_{2,3}}, \frac{D_{1,2}}{D_{3,4}}, \frac{D_{2,3}}{D_{3,4}}$	3
Size Ratio	$\frac{S_1}{S_2}, \frac{S_1}{S_3}, \frac{S_1}{S_4}, \frac{S_2}{S_3}, \frac{S_2}{S_4}, \frac{S_3}{S_4}$	6
Pressure Ratio	$\frac{P_1}{P_2}, \frac{P_1}{P_3}, \frac{P_1}{P_4}, \frac{P_2}{P_3}, \frac{P_2}{P_4}, \frac{P_3}{P_4}$	6
Duration Ratio	$\frac{Dur_1}{Dur_2}, \frac{Dur_1}{Dur_3}, \frac{Dur_1}{Dur_4}, \frac{Dur_2}{Dur_3}, \frac{Dur_2}{Dur_4}, \frac{Dur_3}{Dur_4}$	6
Total number of touch features		55

The touch sensor reports three distinct types of information for each finger tap: pixel location, pressure, and size. As shown in Figure 2, both pressure and size are continuously reported for as long as the finger touches the screen. Given that the variation of pressure and size is quite small for each finger tap, we average all the reported pressure and size values, and use them as two distinct features. Given the four finger taps, 4 pressure and 4 size values are generated (Table 1).

The majority of the touch-based features are extracted directly from the pixel locations of the 4 finger taps. First, the distances in the pixel location space are computed for every pair of finger taps. In that way, 6 feature values are computed (Table 1). At the same time, every combination of 3 finger taps uniquely defines an angle (Figure 2). We consider all possible angles defined by a set of three finger taps, and generate an additional 4 features (Table 1).

The touch sensor also reports a start and end timestamp for every finger tap, indicating the time the finger initially touched the screen and the time it lost contact. Using these timestamps, we compute the total duration of each finger tap, as well as as the time that elapses between the start and end time between every pair of fingerprints. In that way, the timing of each finger tap, as well as the timing across finger taps is captured. As shown in Table 1, 16 temporal features are computed.

To better capture the spatial and temporal signature of the user's hand during the gesture, we compute an additional set of meta-features that focus on capturing the dynamics across the individual features described above. In particular, we compute the ratio of every pair of distance, pressure, size, and duration features. As shown in Table 1, 21 additional features are computed.

Overall, 55 features are computed based on the touch screen data (Table 1).

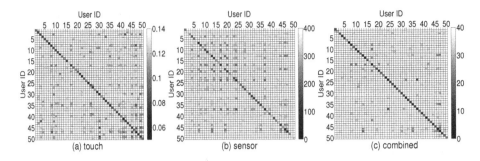

Fig. 4. Difference scores computed across 50 users. Each user performed the 2-hand gesture 30 times, for a total of 1500 gestures. Each small block corresponds to a pair of a test user and a true user, and contains the score between 30 test user gesture instances and the true user's gesture instances. Ideally, all the scores across the diagonal should be much lower (darker color) compared to the rest, indicating that gesture instances from the same user differ significantly less than gesture instances across users. True users are on the x-axis, and test users are on the y-axis.

3.2 Comparing Sensor Fingerprints

When comparing sensor fingerprints across gestures, different techniques are used to quantify the difference of the touch features and that of the sensor patterns.

Touch Features. Let F^1 and F^2 be the set of the 55 touch features recorded across two gesture instances. We quantify the difference D_{touch} between these feature sets as the weighted average difference across all features:

$$D_{touch} = \sum_{i=1}^{55} W_i D_{F^1(i),F^2(i)} \tag{1}$$

where W_i is the weight for feature i, and $D_{F^1(i),F^2(i)}$ is the difference between the values recorded for feature i at the two gesture instances.

The distance between feature values $F^1(i)$ and $F^2(i)$ is defined by their normalized numerical difference:

$$D_{F^1(i),F^2(i)} = min\{\frac{|F^1(i) - F^2(i)|}{|F^1(i)|}, 2\} \tag{2}$$

When the two feature values are identical, the difference score becomes 0. In general, the higher the difference of the feature values across the gesture instances, the higher the distance for that feature will be. However, to prevent a single feature from biasing the result of Equation 1, we limit the maximum value of the distance to 2. This can be particularly useful when most feature values across two gesture instances match closely, but one of them is significantly off (i.e., outlier or faulty measurement). Even though the two gesture instances are almost identical, when an upper bound is not used, this feature can significantly bias the distance score computed in Equation 1.

The weight W_i of the feature i represents the importance of the feature for a given user. In general when users repeat gestures, they can accurately repeat feature values with varying degrees of success. The role of the weight is to emphasize on those features that a specific user can accurately reproduce across gesture instances. Given a set of enrolled gestures from a user, the weight for feature i is defined as:

$$W_i = exp\{-\frac{\sigma_{F(i)}}{\mu_{F(i)}}\} \tag{3}$$

where σ_{F_i} and μ_{F_i} is the variance and mean of the values for feature i across all the enrolled gestures from the true user. When the deviation σ_{F_i} for feature i is 0, the weight takes the maximum value of 1, indicating that this feature is accurately repeatable across gesture instances. Otherwise, a positive weight less than 1 is assigned to the feature that is determined by the ratio of σ_{F_i} and μ_{F_i}.

Figure 4(a) shows the distance scores computed by Equation 1 between every pair of 2-hand gestures recorded from 50 different subjects. Note that the scores recorded along the diagonal are much lower than the rest. This means that gestures from the same user differ less than gestures across users, indicating that touch features have enough discriminating power to differentiate users.

Sensor Patterns. Each sensor fingerprint is comprised of 6 time series signals, each representing the acceleration and rotation of the device across the x, y, and z dimensions ($S_{accel_x}, S_{accel_y}, S_{accel_z}, S_{gyro_x}, S_{gyro_y}, S_{gyro_z}$). Even though a straightforward approach to comparing these signals across gestures would be to simply compute the distance between them, such a method fails due to the noise in the sensor data. For instance, the total time to perform a gesture and the exact timing between finger taps inherently varies across gesture instances even for the same user. These variations can artificially increase the distance between the recorded traces.

Instead, we quantify the difference of these signals across gestures by combining two well known techniques for comparing time series data: dynamic time warping and cross-correlation. Instead of comparing each corresponding sample between the recorded signals, the two signals are slightly shifted to enable the best possible match. This allows us to take into account variations across gesture instances.

Before comparing two signals, each signal is normalized to zero mean and one energy to avoid favoring low energy over high energy signal pairs. Then, each signal is further normalized by its length to avoid favoring short signals over long signals. In particular, each time-series data $S(i)$ in the sensor fingerprint is normalized as follows:

$$S(i) = \frac{S(i) - \mu_S}{\sum_{i=1}^{L}(S(i) - \mu_S)^2 L} \tag{4}$$

where L is the length of the signal, and μ_S is the mean value of all signal samples.

Dynamic Time Warping

Let $S_{accel_x}^1$ and $S_{accel_x}^2$ be the normalized accelerometer signals over the x axis that were recorded across two different gesture instances. Since they are recorded at different times, they might have different lengths, say $L_{accel_x}^1$ and $L_{accel_x}^2$. To compare these two signals, we first compute the direct distance between every pair of samples in $S^1_{accel_x}$ and $S^2_{accel_x}$. In that way, a distance matrix D_{accel_x} with $L^1_{accel_x}$ rows and $L^2_{accel_x}$ columns is computed, where each element takes the following values:

$$D^{ij}_{accel_x} = |S^1_{accel_x}(i) - S^2_{accel_x}(j)|, 1 \le i \le L^1_{accel_x}, 1 \le j \le L^2_{accel_x} \tag{5}$$

In a similar way, distance matrices D_{accel_y} and D_{accel_z} are computed and then added together to form a single distance matrix D_{accel}.

Note that even though the range of acceleration values across different axis might differ, this addition is meaningful given the normalization of all sensor signals according to Equation 4. The exact same process is applied to the gyro data to generate a single distance matrix D_{gyro} that encodes the difference in the gyro sensor data across the x, y, and z dimensions. At the end, accelerometer and gyro distance matrices are added to form a single distance matrix $D = D_{accel} + D_{gyro}$:

Note that the number of samples in the accelerometer and gyro streams might be different depending on the sampling rates the hardware supports for these sensors. As a result, matrices D_{accel} and D_{gyro} might have different dimensions. In this case, we up-sample the lower frequency signal to ensure that both D_{accel} and D_{gyro} have the same dimensions and can be properly added.

Simply adding up the diagonal elements in matrix D, corresponds to the direct distance between the sensor fingerprints across the two gestures. In order to address the variability in the way users perform the gesture (slightly different timing etc.), we define a search space across the diagonal defined by C_{DTW}:

$$D_{ij} = \infty \quad (|i - j| \ge C_{DTW}) \tag{6}$$

where C_{DTW} is the Dynamic Time Warping constraint.By setting distances to infinity, we limit the search space along the diagonal, therefore limiting how much each signal is shifted. The distance between the two signals is now defined as the shortest warping path between the two diagonal points in matrix D:

$$D_{DTW} = \underset{p}{\mathrm{argmin}} \sum_{(i,j) \in p} D_{ij} \tag{7}$$

where p is a warping path between the two diagonal points in the matrix.

When C_{DTW} is equal to 1, the direct distance is calculated as the sum of all the diagonal elements in matrix D. As the value of C_{DTW} increases, more shifting of the two signals is allowed. In Section 4, we study the effect of the C_{DTW} value.

Cross-Correlation

Similarly to Dynamic Time Warping, we combine the accelerometer and gyro data across the x, y, and z dimensions to compute a single cross-correlation value as:

$$Corr = \underset{n \in [-C_{Corr}, C_{Corr}]}{\mathrm{argmax}} \sum_{k=1}^{P} \sum_{m=max\{-n+1,1\}}^{min\{L_{1k}-n, L_{2k}\}} S_{1k}(m+n) S_{2k}(m) \tag{8}$$

where C_{Corr} is a constraint on the permitted shift amount of the signals.

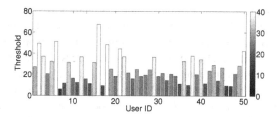

Fig. 5. The computed threshold values for 50 users (2-hand gesture). Values can differ by an order of magnitude indicating the need for a personalized threshold.

The scores produced by the Dynamic Time Warping and Cross-correlation techniques are combined together to quantify the overall distance between gestures in the sensor pattern domain:

$$D_{sensor} = D_{DTW} * (1 - Corr) \tag{9}$$

Figure 4(b) shows the score computed by Equation 9 between every pair of gestures recorded from 50 different subjects. Sensor pattern information appears to be stable across different gesture instances from a given user. All scores across the diagonal (gestures corresponding to the same users) have consistently low distance scores. When compared to Figure 4(a), sensor pattern information appears to have more discriminative power with respect to the touch features.

Combining Touch Features and Sensor Patterns. We combine touch features and sensor patterns by multiplying the corresponding difference scores:

$$D_{combined} = D_{touch} * D_{sensor} \tag{10}$$

Figure 4(c) shows the score computed by Equation 10 between every pair of gestures recorded from 50 different subjects. When compared to Figure 4(a), and Figure 4(b), it is clear that the combination of sensor and touch data helps to better distinguish users. The distance score matrix contains low values (black lines in Figure 4(c)) primarily for gesture instances that belong to the same user.

3.3   Personalized Threshold

Equation 10 quantifies the difference between any pair of gesture instances, but it is not enough to make a decision whether or not a gesture belongs to the same user. Some users can very accurately reproduce the touch and sensor fingerprints across gesture instances, while others might exhibit higher variability. As a result, a low or high score from Equation 10 can be interpreted differently across users.

We deal with this variability by defining a personalized threshold P_{Th} for deciding when the difference between gestures is low enough to assume they belong to the same user. Given N enrolled gestures from a user, we define P_{Th} for this user as:

$$P_{Th} = \mu_{D^{ij}_{combined}} + 3\sigma_{D^{ij}_{combined}}, 1 \leq i, j \leq N, i \neq j \tag{11}$$

where the first term represents the median distance (Equation 10) of all pairs of gestures that belong to the user, and the second term represents the standard deviation of these distances. These two values quantify the variability in the sensor fingerprints across gesture instances for a user. The threshold value for users that accurately reproduce sensor fingerprints across gesture instances will have a low P_{Th} value, and vice versa.

Note that the personalized threshold value P_{Th} (Equation 11) is computed based on positive only data from the true user. This is highly desirable given the lack of negative data on each user's device. As we show in Section 4.1, even a small number of gestures (≈ 10) from the true user is sufficient to generate a reliable P_{Th} value.

Figure 5 shows the P_{Th} values for 50 different users. The range of threshold values is quite large. Even though there are several users that can accurately reproduce their gestures across multiple instances and hence have low threshold values (i.e., value 5 for User 8), there are also many users for which the threshold values are an order of magnitude higher (i.e., value 70 for User 16). This indicates the need for properly computing different thresholds across users.

4 Evaluation

To evaluate the proposed approach we conducted two separate user studies. First, we asked 50 users (12 females and 38 males) to perform each of the proposed unlock gestures 30 times. All users were volunteers and were not compensated for this study. We first explained and demonstrated the proposed gestures to the users, and then allowed them to perform the gesture several times until they became comfortable with it. Each user then repeated each of the two gestures 30 times.

During data collection, several measures were taken to avoid biasing the dataset and artificially increasing the accuracy results. First, all users performed the gesture while standing up. In that way repeatability across gesture instances was not biased by the users' having their arms supported by a desk or a chair. Second, each user had to "reset" the position of his arms in between gesture instances, and pause for several seconds. In that way, data collection was able to capture the variations of how the user holds the device and taps the finger across gesture instances. In this experiment, a total of 3000 gesture instances were collected across all users and gestures. We leverage this dataset to study how different the sensor fingerprints across users are, and what parts of the sensor fingerprints have the most discriminative power.

The second user study focused on simulating an actual attack scenario. A separate set of 20 users (5 females, 15 males) posed as attackers aiming to falsely authenticate as the true user. For each attacker we randomly chose 5 users from the initial 50-subject user study, and gave the opportunity to the attacker to attack each of the 5 users 10 times. Overall, 2000 attack gestures were collected, 1000 for each of the proposed gestures. Right before the attackers attempted to falsely authenticate, they were shown a closeup video of the true user they were attacking. In this video, the attackers could observe, for as much time as they wanted, the true user repeatedly authenticating on the device. In addition, we allowed the attackers to spend as much time as they wanted to perfectly recreate the exact holding position of the device from the true user. Note that in practice, an attacker will rarely, if ever, be able to closely observe all this information, and then try to *immediately* attack the authentication mechanism.

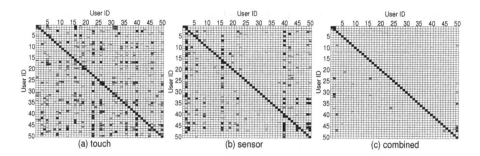

Fig. 6. User classification accuracy for the 50-subject user study when the 2-hand gesture is used. Each block corresponds to a pair of a true user and a test user, containing the classification result for 30 gesture instances from the test user. The black color indicates that the gesture instance is classified as the true user, and the white color the opposite. Ideally only the diagonal boxes should be black. The true users are on the x-axis, and the test users are on the y-axis.

In all cases, we use False Accept Rate (FAR) and False Reject Rate (FRR) to quantify the effectiveness of the proposed approach. The former represents the percentage of gesture instances that belong to users other than the true user, but are erroneously classified as belonging to the true user. The latter represents the percentage of gesture instances that belong to the true user, but are erroneously classified as belonging to a different user.

During both user studies, a single mobile device was used by all users. Specifically, a Google Nexus 4 device running Android 4.3 and a custom data collection application we built, was used to collect the touch, accelerometer and gyro data.

4.1 Differentiating Users

In this section, we leverage the data collected from the 50-subject user study to understand the discriminative power of the proposed unlock gestures in differentiating users. Using the 30 gesture instances from each user, we calculated the personalized threshold for each user. We then used this threshold to classify every single gesture instance recorded across all users as belonging or not to the user. The classification results for the 2-hand gesture are shown in Figure 6.

Ideally, only the diagonal of the classification matrices in Figure 6 should be black, indicating that only the true gesture instances are classified as belonging to the user. When touch data is only used, the classification matrix appears to be noisy. Even though the true user's gesture instances are always classified correctly, there are specific users that are hard to differentiate solely based on the touch fingerprints. When sensor patterns are only used for classification, the classification matrix is noticeably cleaner (only a few users are now hard to differentiate), indicating that the discriminative power of the sensor patterns is superior to that of touch sensor data. However, the combination of touch, accelerometer, and gyro data provides almost perfect classification accuracy, indicating the complementary nature of the different sensors in the classification process.

Table 2 shows the FAR and FRR values achieved by the 2-hand gesture. Overall, approximately 2.5% of the gesture instances that belong to the true user are falsely

Table 2. False accept and reject rates for the 2-hand and 1-hand gestures when different sensor data is used. We also report the FRR of the 4-digit pin as measured in [7].

Mode	2-hand Gesture		1-hand Gesture		Pin
	FRR	FAR	FRR	FAR	FRR
Touch	2.40%	5.28%	1.8%	8.93%	10%
Sensor	2.48%	3.49%	2.61%	18.85	10%
Both	2.48%	0.41%	2.34%	2.40%	10%

rejected. Note that even in the case of traditional 4-digit pins, FRR values as high as 10% have been reported [7]. As users try to quickly enter their 4-digit pin, they accidentally mistype it 1 in 10 times [7]. As a result, the achieved FRR rate of 2.5% is on par with the current pin-based authentication techniques. Depending on the data used in the sensor fingerprint, FAR rates are anywhere between 0.41% and 5.28%.

In the case of the 1-hand gesture, the classification accuracy degrades when touch or sensor data is only used. This is expected as the 1-hand gesture was designed to allow single-hand handling of the mobile device at the expense of quality in the data recorded. However, when touch data and sensor data is combined, the classification accuracy increases, indicating that the 1-hand gesture can be a viable unlock gesture.

Feature Sensitivity Analysis. To understand the importance of individual features in the user authentication process we performed an exhaustive analysis by recomputing the classification matrices shown in Figure 6 for every possible combination of features. In addition to the 57 features available (55 touch features and 2 sensor patterns), we also experimented with two important parameters: the feature weight introduced in Equation 3, and the permitted shift amount of the raw sensor patterns as described in Equations 6, and 8. Specifically, we examined permitted shift amounts of the raw sensor patterns ranging from 0% all the way to 100% at increments of 10%. In the case of feature weights, we exploited the case where feature weights are computed using Equation 3, and when no weights are used (all the weights for all features are set to 1).

Table 3 shows the feature combinations that achieve the best results for both gestures. Consistently, across all combinations and gestures, the feature sets that achieve the best FAR and FRR results leverage feature weights. This verifies our initial intuition that individual users can accurately reproduce different parts of the sensor fingerprint across gesture instances. Feature weights are able to account for the user's variability across gesture instances, and improve the overall accuracy.

In the case of the 2-hand gesture, both accelerometer and gyro sensor patterns appear to be important for ensuring successful authentication. However, for the 1-hand gesture, the value of acceleration data seems to be less important.

For both gestures, though, sensor patterns need to be properly shifted to enable accurate comparison across gesture instances. According to Table 3, accelerometer and gyro patterns provide the best results when shifted anywhere between 30% and 50% depending on the gesture used.

Size of Training Data. So far, all 30 gesture instances for each user were used in the authentication process. Figure 7 shows the impact of the number of gesture instances

Table 3. Feature combinations and parameter values achieving the best FAR and FRR values

Mode	2-hand Gesture			1-hand Gesture		
	Features	FRR	FAR	Features	FRR	FAR
Touch	Distance, Angle, Size, Pressure, Duration,Distance/Pressure Ratio, Feature Weights: Yes	2.40%	5.28%	Distance, Angle, Size, Pressure, Duration Feature Weights: Yes	1.8%	8.93%
Sensor	$gyro_{xyz}$, $accel_{xyz}$ Shift: 40%	2.48%	3.49%	$gyro_{xyz}$ Shift: 30%	2.61%	18.85%
Both	Distance, Angle, Size, Pressure Feature Weights: Yes $gyro_{xyz}$, $accel_{xyz}$, Shift: 40%	2.48%	0.41%	Distance, Angle, Size, Pressure Feature Weights: Yes $gyro_{xyz}$, Shift: 50%	2.34%	2.40%

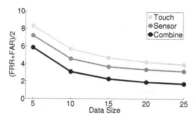

Fig. 7. Accuracy as a function of the number of available gestures per user in the case of the 2-hand gesture. Trends are similar for the 1-hand gesture.

used on both the false accept, and false reject rates achieved. Intuitively, FAR and FRR are reduced as the number of gesture instances increases, but they quickly saturate, eliminating the need for 30 gestures. Anywhere between 10 and 15 gesture instances are enough to achieve FAR and FRR values that are within 0.5% of the values achieved when all 30 gesture instances are used.

4.2 Resilience to Attacks

In this section, we leverage the dataset collected by 20 subjects posing as attackers to study the resilience of the proposed authentication mechanism to an actual attack. To study the resilience of the sensor fingerprints to attacks, we compared all of attacker's sensor fingerprints to the ones of the true users and classified them as belonging to the true user or not in the same way as before. During this process, we leveraged the feature set that achieved the best FAR and FRR values in the previous section.

Table 4 shows the FAR and FRR values for the attacker sensor fingerprints. When compared to the results in Table 3, FAR values are significantly higher when touch or sensor patterns are only used as the sensor fingerprint. This is expected as the attacker was able to directly observe the true user authenticating on the mobile device, and attempted to closely resemble the process. However, when touch and sensor patterns are combined into a single sensor fingerprint, the false accept and reject rates only slightly increase and remain well below 3%. This is surprisingly low given that the attacker was able to closely monitor the true user authentication process right before the attack.

Table 4. FAR and FRR values for the attack scenarios and for both 2-hand and 1-hand gestures

Mode	2-hand Gesture		1-hand Gesture	
	FAR	(FRR+FAR)/2	FAR	(FRR+FAR)/2
Touch	12.99%	7.69%	15.9%	8.85%
Sensor	11.2%	6.87%	20.8%	11.71%
Both	2.86%	2.67%	5.9%	4.12%

In contrast, an attacker that was able to closely observe the true user entering a 4-digit pin, would be able to get 100% false accept rates.

In the case of the single hand gesture, the trends are similar, but now the FAR value increases to reach 6% when both touch and sensor patterns are combined. However, even in this case, the FAR and FRR values remain well below 6% indicating that the 1-hand gesture can still provide reasonable protection from attackers.

4.3   Computation Overhead

On a Google Nexus 4 device running Android 4.3, processing the touch data takes only $6.7ms$. However, processing the accelerometer and gyro data on the same device takes 3.1 seconds. Such a delay is prohibitive for any realistic use of the proposed approach.

This 3 second delay is mainly caused by two factors. First, every candidate sensor fingerprint is currently compared to all 30 enrolled gestures from the true user. Second, for each comparison between a candidate sensor fingerprint and an enrolled sensor fingerprint, the cross-correlation and dynamic time wrap is computed for both the accelerometer and gyro data. This operation is time consuming when the sensors are sampled at very high data rates such as 200Hz.

Figure 8(a) and Figure 8(b) show the processing time as a function of the number of enrolled gestures per user, and the sensor down-sampling rate. Simply down-sampling accelerometer and gyro data by a factor of 2, reduces the processing time to approximately half a second. In addition, when only 15 enrolled gestures are used per user, the overall processing time becomes approximately 200ms. This delay is practically unnoticeable by the user, resulting into an instant authentication user experience. The small processing time also implies a low energy overhead, preventing our method from draining the battery.

As Figure 8(c) and Figure 8(d) show, when sensor data is down-sampled by a factor of 2, and the number of enrolled gestures is 15, the mean FAR and FRR values remain practically unchanged. As a result, the proposed technique can provide an instant authentication experience without sacrificing accuracy and robustness to attacks.

5   Related Work

To address the susceptibility of current authentication techniques to shoulder surfing attacks [14], researchers have already proposed to understand *how* a user performs the gesture, and to leverage this information to strengthen the authentication process while maintaining its simplicity [9,3,4,5,10,12,8,13].

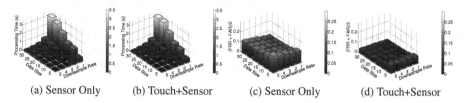

(a) Sensor Only   (b) Touch+Sensor   (c) Sensor Only   (d) Touch+Sensor

Fig. 8. Processing time ((a),(b)) and accuracy ((c),(d)) as a function of the number of enrolled gestures per user, and the sensor down-sampling rate

Specifically, the work in [3] expanded the typical gesture unlock techniques employed by Android devices, to incorporate the timing of the user's gesture. The work in [9] expanded on this idea by incorporating additional information such as pressure, and size of the finger taps during the gesture. In contrast, our work focuses on designing new unlock gestures with the goal of capturing the geometry of the user hand through the touch screen, and the embedded accelerometer and gyro sensors. Even though valuable, timing, size and pressure information does not provide enough discriminating power to accurately differentiate users, resulting into 2-3 times higher false accept and false reject values compared to the approach presented in this paper.

More recently, Shahzad et al. [12] studied various touch screen gestures to understand the feasibility of combining touch screen data with accelerometer signatures to authenticate users. Even though the same sensing modalities were used, the gestures proposed and analyzed in [12] do not focus on, and were not designed to, capture the geometry of the user's hand. Instead, they mainly focus on capturing the velocity at which finger taps take place. However, capturing the geometry of the user's hand through the unlock gesture is a key parameter in terms of accuracy. Evident of this, is the fact that the work in [12] achieves the same FAR and FRR values as the 2-hand gesture proposed in this paper, only when the user performs 3 different 2-hand gestures sequentially. Asking users to perform 3 different gestures in a row increases the cognitive overhead for the user and the time it takes to unlock the device, raising usability concerns. The work in [13] proposed to design user-generated free-form gestures for authentication. However, it was only evaluated on tablets and the effectiveness of the method on devices with smaller screens such as smartphones was not demonstrated.

The closest to our work is the one proposed by Sae-Bae et al. [10] where new multi-touch gestures were proposed to capture the geometry of the user's hand to enable reliable user authentication. In particular, multiple 5-finger gestures were proposed targeting devices with large screens such as tablets. In their approach, only touch sensor data were used to differentiate users. Even though 5-finger gestures can provide even richer information about the user's hand geometry, they can only be applied on tablet-like devices. Not only do smaller devices, such as phones, lack the physical space required by these gestures, but they can only support up to 4 simultaneous touch points.

User authentication techniques have also been proposed outside the context of touch screens, accelerometer and gyro sensors. For instance, Jain et al. [6] proposed to extract a detailed description of the user's hand geometry by taking a picture of the user's hand. Even though this is a more accurate way to capture the hand geometry, asking users to properly place their hands in front of the phone's camera can be awkward, time-consuming, and also susceptible to environmental lighting conditions. Sato et al. [11] proposed a capacitive fingerprinting approach where a small electric current is injected into the user's body through the touch screen, enabling the measurement of user's bio-impedance. However, bio-impedance measurements are inherently noisy due to grounding issues, and variability in the body's fat and water throughout the day.

6   Discussion and Limitations

Our experimental evaluation shows that carefully designed gestures can enable sensor fingerprints to accurately differentiate users and protect against attackers. Note that the goal of this work is not to achieve recognition rates that are similar to fingerprint sensors, nor to replace them. Instead, our goal is to propose an alternative authentication mechanism for mobile devices that is both intuitive and easy for users to perform, and at the same time hard for attackers to bypass. Sensor fingerprints can be significantly more secure compared to pins, picture passwords, and simple unlock gestures, but definitely not as accurate as fingerprint sensors. However, as physical buttons on mobile devices are eliminated in favor of edge-to-edge displays, and given the lack of technology to properly embed fingerprint sensors into touch screen displays, the use of fingerprint sensors becomes challenging. With this in mind, we believe that sensor fingerprints can be a viable alternative to user authentication on mobile devices.

In practice, the use of sensor fingerprints can be rather tricky. When the user is actively moving (i.e., walking, driving, etc.), the accelerometer and gyro recordings will capture the user's motion rather than the displacement of the phone due to the gesture. However, mobile devices already enable continuous sampling of sensors to recognize higher level activities such as sitting, walking, and driving. When these activities are detected, the acceleration and gyro data could be removed from the sensor fingerprint (or the device could fall back to the 4-digit pin). As Table 2 shows, even when only touch data is used, the FAR achieved is still reasonable.

References

1. 1-hand gesture, https://dl.dropboxusercontent.com/u/64756732/gestures/1-hand-gesture.avi
2. 2-hand gesture, https://dl.dropboxusercontent.com/u/64756732/gestures/2-hand-gesture.avi
3. Angulo, J., Wästlund, E.: Exploring touch-screen biometrics for user identification on smart phones. In: Camenisch, J., Crispo, B., Fischer-Hübner, S., Leenes, R., Russello, G. (eds.) Privacy and Identity Management for Life. IFIP AICT, vol. 375, pp. 130–143. Springer, Heidelberg (2012)
4. Feng, T., Liu, Z., Kwon, K., Shi, W., Carbunar, B., Jiang, Y., Nguyen, N.: Continuous mobile authentication using touchscreen gestures. In: HST 2012 (2012)
5. Frank, M., Biedert, R., Ma, E., Martinovic, I., Song, D.: Touchalytics: On the applicability of touchscreen input as a behavioral biometric for continuous authentication. IEEE Transactions on Information Forensics and Security (2013)
6. Jain, A., Ross, A., Pankanti, S.: A prototype hand geometry-based verification system. In: AVBPA 1999 (1999)

7. Jakobsson, M., Shi, E., Golle, P., Chow, R.: Implicit authentication for mobile devices. In: HotSec 2009 (2009)
8. Kolly, S.M., Wattenhofer, R., Welten, S.: A personal touch: Recognizing users based on touch screen behavior. In: PhoneSense (2012)
9. Luca, A.D., Hang, A., Brudy, F., Lindner, C., Hussmann, H.: Implicit authentication based on touch screen patterns. In: CHI 2012 (2012)
10. Sae-Bae, N., Ahmed, K., Isbister, K., Memon, N.: Biometric-rich gestures: A novel approach to authentication on multi-touch devices. In: CHI 2012 (2012)
11. Sato, M., Poupyrev, I., Harrison, C.: Touche: Enhancing touch interaction on humans, screens, liquids, and everyday objects. In: CHI 2012 (2012)
12. Shahzad, M., Liu, A.X., Samuel, A.: Secure unlocking of mobile touch screen devices by simple gestures: you can see it but you can not do it. In: MobiCom 2013 (2013)
13. Sherman, M., Clark, G., Yang, Y., Sugrim, S., Modig, A., Lindqvist, J., Oulasvirta, A.: User-generated free-form gestures for authentication: security and memorability. In: MobiSys 2014 (2014)
14. Wiedenbeck, S., Waters, J., Sobrado, L., Birget, J.: Design and evaluation of a shoulder-surfing resistant graphical password scheme. In: ACM AVI 2006 (2006)

Improving the Performance of Trickle-Based Data Dissemination in Low-Power Networks

Milosh Stolikj, Thomas M.M. Meyfroyt, Pieter J.L. Cuijpers,
and Johan J. Lukkien

Dept. of Mathematics and Computer Science, Eindhoven University of Technology,
P.O. Box 513, 5600 MB, Eindhoven, The Netherlands

Abstract. Trickle is a polite gossip algorithm for managing communication traffic. It is of particular interest in low-power wireless networks for reducing the amount of control traffic, as in routing protocols (RPL), or reducing network congestion, as in multicast protocols (MPL). Trickle is used at the network or application level, and relies on up-to-date information on the activity of neighbors. This makes it vulnerable to interference from the media access control layer, which we explore in this paper. We present several scenarios how the MAC layer in low-power radios violates Trickle timing. As a case study, we analyze the impact of CSMA/CA with ContikiMAC on Trickle's performance. Additionally, we propose a solution called Cleansing that resolves these issues.

1 Introduction

Low-power wireless networks, such as networks of ubiquitous sensors, are being built with the aim to be available for extended periods of time, while using as little energy as possible. This includes wireless sensor networks in forests for detecting fires, in pipelines for detecting leaks, on light poles along streets to control luminosity etc [1]. In such resource-constrained devices, wireless transmissions are the largest source of power consumption. Therefore, networking protocols for low-power wireless networks are designed to avoid unnecessary traffic, such as redundant control information, or to prevent broadcast storms.

Trickle [15] has been proposed as an efficient algorithm for controlling traffic flow. It is being used in routing protocols for reducing the amount of control traffic [8,24], in multicast protocols for reducing redundant repetitions of data packets [9] and in software update algorithms for managing the propagation of updates [15]. Trickle uses two premises to achieve fast propagation and reduced traffic: (1) suppressed transmissions when consistent information has been recently propagated by neighboring nodes, and (2) dynamic transmission rates depending on the consistency of information in the network. The concept of consistency is left to the application layer, which allows the Trickle algorithm to be implemented in different protocols.

The Trickle algorithm relies on accurate timing information in order to work as designed. However, various factors can influence this timing and can cause inconsistencies within the protocol. External disturbances can come from the radio

T. Abdelzaher et al. (Eds.): EWSN 2015, LNCS 8965, pp. 186–201, 2015.

medium (packet loss), network (congestion) and locally (data link layer). In this work, we analyze how the media access control (MAC) layer of low-power radios influences broadcast-based data dissemination using Trickle. As a case study, we consider a MAC layer comprised unslotted Carrier Sense Multiple Access with Collision Avoidance (CSMA/CA) and radio duty cycling. We show that due to contended media and CSMA/CA introduced back-offs, nodes can be starved from Trickle updates. This results in large propagation delays and inefficient messaging, making Trickle unsuitable for deadline-critical applications.

We discuss and analyze two common scenarios where there is a large discrepancy between the measured and expected update delay of Trickle, caused by the MAC layer. To resolve this, we propose a modification to the MAC layer to support dropping of queued Trickle packets based on incoming Trickle packets, called *Cleansing*. Using simulations and experiments we show that the Cleansing MAC modification drastically improves the update delay in bottleneck topologies, and helps reduce the number of transmissions in grid-like topologies.

The paper is structured as follows. First, we cover related work on Trickle in Section 2. Then, we introduce the Trickle algorithm and the low-power protocols at the MAC layer in Section 3. Next, in Section 4, we describe how the MAC layer violates Trickle timing, and analyze this unwanted behaviour in two topologies. Section 5 introduces the Cleansing improvements to the MAC layer. Finally, we compare simulation and experimental results of Trickle with and without Cleansing support in Section 6 and give concluding remarks in Section 7.

2   Related Work

The Trickle algorithm has been initially designed as an efficient method to disseminate software updates in low-power networks [15]. However, since it only specifies *when* messages should be sent, and not *how*, it has been accommodated in many other protocols [14], such as network reprogramming [16], routing [8,24] and data dissemination [11]. Trickle was recently standardized [13] and used as a basis for the Multicast Protocol for Low power and Lossy Networks (MPL) [9].

Various aspects of the Trickle algorithm have been studied so far. For example, in [6,23], Trickle has been observed as unfair in terms of load share - certain nodes transmit more often than others. Trickle in absence of a MAC layer has previously been analyzed, e.g., [2,12,17]. Similarly, CSMA/CA for low-power networks has been analyzed without considering the upper layers, e.g., [4,7]. Finally, the potential problematic interaction between Trickle-based data dissemination and radio duty cycling has been sketched in [20], along with potential energy efficiency improvements by reducing the scope of single-hop broadcasts. However, to the best of the authors' knowledge, a detailed analysis on the interaction between Trickle and the MAC layer, consisting of both CSMA/CA and radio duty cycling, their combined performance and potential problems in specific topologies, has not yet been conducted, which is what this paper aims to do. The analysis and the results presented in this paper explain the simulation results for MPL in [3,18], and the poor performance for small Trickle interval lengths.

3   Trickle-Based Protocols

The Trickle algorithm is used mostly by communication protocols at the network or the application layer. Trickle essentially controls the generation of packets within these protocols. The lower layers are responsible for the actual transmission of the data packets sent by Trickle (Figure 1).

The data link layer of low-power radios as IEEE 802.15.4 [10], which is the focus in this work, is built of two components - media access control (MAC) and a radio handling protocol. The MAC protocol handles the allocation of the shared medium among nodes and covers retransmissions in case of collisions or packet loss. The radio handling protocol determines the efficient use of the radio during the periods allocated by the MAC protocol.

We will now give a detailed description of the Trickle algorithm and the underlying MAC layer protocols.

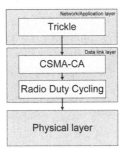

Fig. 1. Flow of Trickle packets in the Contiki operating system [5]

3.1   Trickle Algorithm

Trickle has two main goals. Firstly, whenever new information becomes available in the network, it must be propagated quickly to all nodes. Secondly, when there is no update, communication overhead has to be kept to a minimum. The Trickle algorithm achieves this by moderating the number of packets that nodes generate with a "polite gossip" policy.

We now provide a precise description of Trickle as it is given in [17] (see also [15]). The algorithm has four global parameters, which are the same at every node in the network: a threshold value k, called the redundancy constant, minimum ($I_{\min}$) and maximum interval size ($I_{\max}$), and a listen-only parameter (η), which defines the size of a listen-only period. By default, $\eta = 1/2$. Furthermore, each node in the network has its own timer and keeps track of three local variables: the size of the current interval (I), a counter (c) of the number of consistent data packets received during the current interval, and the transmission time (t) in the current interval.

The behavior of each node is described by the following set of rules. At the start of a new interval a node resets its timer and counter c and sets t to a value in $[\eta I, I]$ at random. When a node receives a new data packet that is consistent with the information it has, it increments c by 1. When a node's timer reaches time t and if $c < k$, it sends a data packet to its MAC layer queue. When a node's interval ends, it sets its interval size to $\min(2I, I_{\max})$ and starts a new interval. When a node receives a data packet that is inconsistent with its own information, then if $I > I_{\min}$ it sets I to $I_{\min}$ and starts a new interval.

Trickle only determines when nodes should transmit; the nature of the transmission (broadcast/unicast), the structure of the message, and the exact definition of what is a consistent transmission is given by the upper layers, i.e. the protocols where Trickle is used. For instance, in dissemination protocols, as multicast, transmissions are always broadcasts; a node receives a consistent transmission when a known data packet is received from another node, and an inconsistent transmission is received when a new, unseen data packet is received.

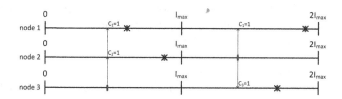

Fig. 2. Example of three synchronized nodes using the Trickle algorithm ($k = 1$, $I = I_{\max}$). In the first interval, the transmissions by nodes 1 and 2 are suppressed by the transmission of node 3, while in the second interval, node 2 suppresses nodes 1 and 3.

In Figure 2 an example is depicted of a network consisting of three nodes using the Trickle algorithm with $k = 1$ and $I = I_{\max}$ for all nodes. Note that while in the example the intervals of the three nodes are synchronized, in general, the times at which nodes start their intervals need not be synchronized. In practice, networks will generally not be synchronized, since synchronization requires additional communication and consequently imposes energy overhead. Furthermore, as nodes get updated and start new intervals, they automatically lose synchronicity.

The four Trickle parameters can be used to tweak the algorithm behavior according to specific scenarios, giving option for trading between redundancy, speed of propagation and risk of collisions. For instance, $I_{\min}$ provides a trade-off between speed of propagation and number of packets: lower values of $I_{\min}$ will make nodes transmit sooner, though with an increased risk of collisions, and therefore, additional transmissions. To prevent such scenarios, the Trickle RFC recommends setting $I_{\min}$ to a multiple of the worst-case link layer latency, defined as the time until the first link-layer transmission of a frame, assuming an idle channel. Typical values of the Trickle parameters for various protocols are given in Table 1. In the remainder of this paper, we will focus on broadcast-based data dissemination as the Trickle application protocol, similar to the MPL protocol, with the recommended value for the redundancy constant ($k = 1$).

Table 1. Default values of Trickle parameters in different protocols

Protocol	k		$I_{\min}$	$I_{\max}$
MPL (control traffic) [9]	1	10 times worst-case link-layer latency		300 s
MPL (data traffic)	1	10 times expected link-layer latency		$I_{\min}$
RPL (DIO) [24]	10		8 ms	8.280 s
CTP [8]	$\infty(0)$		125 ms	500 s

3.2 CSMA/CA Protocol

The actual transmission of packets generated by Trickle is left to the MAC layer. Protocols at this layer handle the allocation of the shared media among nodes and cover retransmissions in case of collisions or packet loss. The IEEE 802.15.4 MAC defines two flavors of the CSMA/CA protocol, depending on the operational mode in use: slotted CSMA/CA, used in beacon-enabled modes, where beacons are sent to synchronize nodes to a super-frame structure; and unslotted CSMA/CA, used in non beacon-enabled modes, where no beacons are sent out and there is no synchronization between nodes. In this paper, we focus on unslotted CSMA/CA, but the same concepts apply to slotted CSMA/CA.

In unslotted CSMA/CA, the basic time unit is the back-off period BP, which is related to the transmission time of a frame. Every node maintains two variables for each frame it wants to send: a back-off exponent BE, and a counter for the number of back-offs for the current transmission NB. These variables are controlled by three parameters: the minimum back-off exponent $BE_{\min}$, the maximum back-off exponent $BE_{\max}$ and the maximum number of back-offs $NB_{\max}$.

Initially, $NB = 0$ and $BE = BE_{\min}$. Before each transmission, each node first waits for a random number of BPs ranging from 0 to $2^{BE} - 1$. After the initial back-off, the node performs a clear-channel assessment (CCA) to determine whether the channel is free. If the channel is free, the node proceeds with the transmission. Otherwise, it increases NB by one, and sets BE to $\min(BE + 1, BE_{\max})$. If $NB \leq NB_{\max}$, the entire procedure is repeated. After $NB_{\max} + 1$ failed attempts, the frame is dropped from the MAC queue.

3.3 Radio Duty Cycling

The MAC layer of low-power radios often includes a second component next to the CSMA/CA protocol - the radio handling protocol. Radio transceivers are among the biggest sources of energy consumption in low-power wireless devices. Therefore, low-power wireless devices must trade-off between keeping the radio transceiver off, to save energy, and periodically wake up to be able to receive data from their neighbors. During the years, many radio duty cycling (RDC) protocols have been proposed. They can be categorized into synchronous, where nodes are synchronized with their neighbouring nodes, and asynchronous, where no pre-synchronization is required. Asynchronous RDCs can be further categorized into sender initiated and receiver initiated protocols. Sender initiated RDC protocols give the transmission incentive to the senders: senders wake up receivers to receive a transmission. Receiver initiated protocols give the incentive to the receivers: receivers inform senders when they are prepared to receive a transmission. Finally, hybrid approaches have been developed, which combine features from any of the given categories.

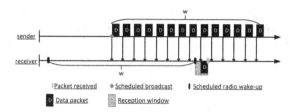

Fig. 3. In ContikiMAC, broadcast transmissions are sent with repeated frames for the full wake-up interval. This illustration is reproduced based on [4].

In this work, we consider ContikiMAC [4], a sender initiated RDC. It is similar to the Coordinated Sampled Listening protocol (CSL), introduced in the IEEE 802.15.4e standard [10]. A brief description of ContikiMAC follows.

By default, every node has its radio turned off. Periodically, at regular intervals of w time units, each node turns its radio on to check for incoming traffic. If a transmission is detected, the radio is kept on until the frame is received. Transmissions are non-periodic, originating from the upper layer(s). When they arrive, a CCA is done to see if the medium is free. If it is free, the node starts transmitting immediately. Broadcast transmissions should be received by all nodes, irrespective of their wake up intervals. Therefore, a broadcast transmission will always be repeated for w time units (Figure 3), so that each node will at least once turn on its radio during the transmission. Hence, assuming an idle channel, the worst-case latency as defined in the Trickle RFC, is w. However, this makes broadcasts expensive both in terms of delay and consumed energy.

The main configuration parameter for ContikiMAC is the radio wake-up frequency $1/w$, i.e. how often each node samples the radio. This parameter also dictates the maximum duration for each individual transmission w. Typically, the wake-up frequencies is set to 4Hz, 8Hz or 16Hz, giving wake up intervals of $250ms$, $125ms$ and $62.5ms$, respectively. Reducing the wake-up frequency reduces the energy usage in the network, at the expense of a higher delay.

4 Interference Scenario

A common feature of both sender initiated and receiver initiated RDC protocols is that transmissions are not instantaneous, and there is a variable delay between the intent to start a transmission and the actual receipt. In sender initiated RDC protocols as ContikiMAC, the transmission starts almost immediately after it is received from the upper layers, but it is not completed until the receiver performs its periodic wake up to sample the channel. Similarly, in receiver initiated RDC protocols, the transmission is delayed until the sender receives a request from the receiver, which is again periodically scheduled. Finally, in case of collisions, in both cases, CSMA/CA will re-schedule transmissions after a certain back-off period. The delayed completion of a transmission creates a window where upper layer protocols may think that a transmission has been completed, while in fact, it is not. This causes unintended and inefficient messaging, as the transmission delay and retransmissions may move from one to another Trickle interval.

For example, consider a network consisting of two nodes (Figure 4). They use unslotted CSMA/CA in combination with radio duty cycling at the MAC layer. Packet transmission is regulated by the Trickle algorithm ($k = 1$, $\eta = 1/2$). Both nodes start a Trickle process at the same time, with consistent information for dissemination. They choose transmission times t_1 and t_2, respectively, such that $t_1 < t_2$. Both counters are initially set to zero ($c_1 = c_2 = 0$). At time t_1, since $c_1 < k$, node 1 sends a packet to its MAC layer. Then, it does a successful CCA and starts transmitting the packet. Node 2 has its next wake-up scheduled at time $t_r > t_2$. Consequently, at time t_2 node 2 has not yet received node 1's broadcast and will decide to transmit itself, sending a Trickle packet to its MAC layer. Since at this time the channel is busy, CSMA/CA will delay this transmission until $t_2 + bo$, where bo is the back-off time. At time t_r, node 2 receives the transmission from node 1, setting $c_2 = 1$, making the queued packet in the MAC layer obsolete. However, since there is no link between the MAC queue and the application layer, the packet will be sent at $t_2 + bo$. This effect can be cascaded if multiple nodes exhibit the same behavior. Moreover, it is possible that node 2's broadcast is delayed into its next Trickle interval (Figure 4), causing node 1 to suppress its next broadcast, further disrupting the Trickle process.

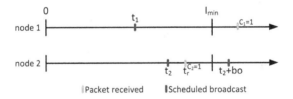

Fig. 4. MAC layer interference on Trickle timing. Nodes 1 and 2 get updated at the same time, and they select transmission times at t_1 and t_2, respectively. If the reception for node 2 (t_r) is scheduled to be after t_2, node 2 will queue a Trickle packet at t_2, even though there is a packet in the air from node 1. Due to CSMA/CA, this packet will be transmitted after the back-off, at time $t_2 + bo$.

4.1   Case Study: CSMA/CA and ContikiMAC

We will now use the Contiki operating system for a case study on the impact of MAC interference on Trickle timing. Contiki 2.7 utilizes the ContikiMAC RDC protocol with a radio wake-up interval length of w, together with a slightly modified version of the unslotted CSMA/CA protocol. Firstly, the default parameters $BE_{\min} = 0$, $BE_{\max} = 3$ and $NB_{\max} = 3$, force CSMA/CA to skip the first back-off. Secondly, the back-off period is equal to the length of the wake-up interval of ContikiMAC ($BP = w$). As w is the worst-case transmission time for ContikiMAC, this ensures that any retransmissions are attempted after the current transmission has finished. Thirdly, the CCA check is delegated to the RDC layer. Finally, the back-off exponent BE is increased only when no acknowledgment is received for sent unicast frames. Since Trickle-based data dissemination uses only broadcast packets, for which no acknowledgment is needed, a back-off can only occur due to a failed CCA or a detected collision. In both cases, BE remains one, causing the back-off for broadcasts to remain $BP = w$.

Scenario 1: Single-Hop Network. We now analyze the likelihood that the scenario discussed at the beginning of this section occurs under ContikiMAC. Denote by $\mathbb{P}_2^{bo}$ the probability that a CSMA back-off takes place in a network of two nodes. For simplicity, we assume the nodes to be synchronized, which would be the case if they got updated simultaneously. We assume that packets are received at radio wake-up and $I_{min} = m \cdot w$, where $m \geq 2$ is a constant and w is the radio wake-up interval. We require $m \geq 2$, since otherwise a node will never be able to finish a transmission within the same Trickle interval as it was scheduled. Furthermore, assume that the Trickle process has $k = 1$ and $\eta = 1/2$. A CSMA back-off will take place if either node 1 or 2 pick their transmission time during a broadcast of the other node and before their radio wake-up and reception. Hence, we can write

$$\mathbb{P}_2^{bo} := 2\mathbb{P}[t_1 \leq t_2 \leq t_r \leq t_1 + w] = 2 \int_{I_{min}/2}^{I_{min}} \mathbb{P}[t_2 \in [t_1, t_r] \mid t_1 = t]\, d\mathbb{P}[t_1 \leq t]. \quad (1)$$

Since both t_1 and t_2 are chosen uniformly in $[I_{min}/2, I_{min}]$ and a broadcast starting at time t is received by the non-transmitting node uniformly at $t_r \in [t, t + w]$, some calculus gives

$$\mathbb{P}_2^{bo} = \frac{2}{m} - \frac{4}{3m^2}. \quad (2)$$

Note that this probability only depends on m, the ratio between the length of an interval I_{min} and the length of a broadcast w. For the MPL standard $I_{min} = 10w$, this implies $\mathbb{P}_2^{bo} = 0.1925$, which is relatively large.

Extending these calculations and noting that nodes choose their timers independently, the probability that b CSMA back-offs occur and $b + 1$ transmissions are scheduled during an interval in a single-hop network consisting of n nodes is given by

$$\mathbb{P}_{n,b}^{bo} := n\binom{n-1}{b}\mathbb{P}[t_2 \in [t_1, t_r]]^b\,\mathbb{P}[t_r \leq t_2]^{n-b-1}. \quad (3)$$

Like (1), this expression can be evaluated analytically and allows us to calculate the probability $\mathbb{P}_n^{bo}$ that at least one CSMA back-off ($b > 0$) takes place during a single interval in a single-hop network consisting of n nodes:

$$\mathbb{P}_n^{bo} := 1 - \mathbb{P}_{n,0}^{bo} = 1 - \frac{1}{m^n}\left((m-1)^n + \frac{1}{2n-1}\right). \tag{4}$$

Moreover, calculating the expected number of redundant transmissions per interval due to poor interaction between Trickle and the CSMA protocol gives:

$$\mathbb{E}[N_n^r] := \sum_{i=0}^{n-1} i\mathbb{P}_{n,i}^{bo} = \frac{n}{m} - \frac{1}{n+1}\left(\frac{2}{m}\right)^n. \tag{5}$$

Hence, the expected number of obsolete broadcasts per interval due to timing issues grows linearly with the size of the single-hop broadcast range. This is intuitive, since every node has the same probability of scheduling a back-off. If Trickle worked as designed, there would be only one packet per interval [1].

Scenario 2: A Bottleneck Network. Consider now a network of four nodes, with connectivity as in Figure 5. This type of connectivity, where part of the network is reachable only through a single bridge node, is common, for example, in street lighting networks. Again all nodes use CSMA/CA in combination with ContikiMAC and run a Trickle dissemination process. The Trickle process has $k = 1$, $\eta = 1/2$ and $I_{min} = m \cdot w$, where $m \geq 2$ is a given constant. Initially, all nodes have consistent information and $I = I_{max}$.

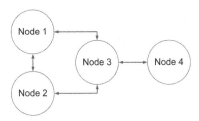

Fig. 5. A network consisting of 4 nodes, where node 3 is a bottleneck node

Suppose at time 0 nodes 1 and 2 receive an update simultaneously from a close-by source, set $I = I_{min}$ and start a new interval (Figure 6). Node 1 is the first node to schedule a broadcast, which it starts to transmit at time t_1. As we have seen in the previous scenario, node 2 will schedule a broadcast before receiving node 1's broadcast with probability $\mathbb{P}_2^{bo}$. If this happens, the MAC protocol will cause node 2 to delay its transmission until time $t_2 + w$. Before this time, however, node 3 will have been updated by node 1's transmission, and will start a new interval of length I_{min} and schedule a transmission at time t_3. Now node 2's transmission follows, suppressing node 3's transmission at time $t_3 > t_2 + w$ and consequently delaying the time that node 4 is updated. In its

---

[1] For a complete calculation of Equations (1-5), see Appendix A of [22].

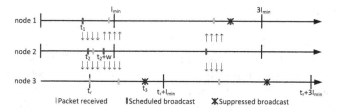

Fig. 6. Suppression of Trickle updates due to MAC layer interference. Nodes 1 and 2 get updated at the same time, and select transmission times at t_1 and t_2, respectively, with the periodic channel check for node 2 (t_r) scheduled to be after t_2. Node 2 queues a Trickle packet at t_2. Due to busy media, CSMA/CA re-schedules the packet for $t_2 + w$. In the mean time, node 3 gets updated and starts a new Trickle interval. The re-transmission at $t_2 + w$ causes node 3 to suppress its transmission in the first interval (t_3). As node 1 and 2 started the second interval earlier than node 3, there is a high probability that they will suppress any future transmissions from node 3.

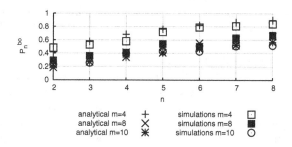

Fig. 7. Analytical and simulation results of the probability that node 4 is updated after the second Trickle interval, for different values of m ($I_{\min} = m \cdot w$)

next interval, node 3 will broadcast only if it starts transmitting before it receives a broadcast by nodes 1 and 2. However, due to the synchronization caused by the Trickle protocol, this has a small probability, as can be seen in Figure 6. In the following intervals the same problem occurs. Only when node 4 eventually transmits its old information, which potentially could take a long time, it will reset node 3's Trickle process and an update will follow.

In general, if node 3 is connected with n synchronized nodes trying to update it, the previously described scenario occurs with probability $\mathbb{P}_n^{bo}$ (see (4)). We have plotted this probability and compared it with simulations for different values of m and n in Figure 7. From the plot it is clear that such an event is not rare. Given that such an event occurs, the probability that node 3 will ever broadcast in the following intervals before being suppressed by its neighbors is small, even for $n = 2$. Therefore, in such an event, with high probability node 4's update is delayed until it advertises its own old information, resetting the Trickle process of node 3. This gives an expected delay of approximately $\frac{1}{2}I_{\max} + \frac{3}{4}I_{\min}$, which is possibly very large since $I_{\max}$ is generally large. If node 4 has neighbors suppressing its own transmissions, then the expected delay will be even larger.

5   Cleansing MAC

In order to reduce the interference of the data link layer on Trickle timing, we propose adding a *Cleansing* mechanism to the MAC layer. If Trickle is treated as a network primitive, as suggested in [14], known at both the network and data link layer, then some decision making can be done at the data link layer. Assuming that the MAC layer maintains separate queues per destination, whenever a new Trickle packet arrives from the network, the Cleansing MAC will purge any queued outgoing Trickle packets. This will lead to less redundant packets in the network, and will minimize the bottleneck problem from the previous section.

In most cases, purging outgoing Trickle packets improves Trickle performance in terms of messaging and delay, and does not lead to functional incorrectness. It remains consistent with the software design of low-power networks, as any purged packet can be seen as a message loss, and applications are already able to handle that situation. However, we can identify two scenarios where performance-wise, purging can be considered to be harmful.

The first scenario is when $k > 1$, a purged Trickle message might not be obsolete. However, this should have minimal impact on the network, since only a small fraction of messages within each single-hop broadcast domain will be purged. Moreover, other nodes in reach will make up for the purged transmission.

The second scenario is when a Trickle message with an old value arrives, and the Cleansing MAC protocol purges an outgoing Trickle message with a new value, increasing the overall propagation delay. However, the effect of the purge is minimal, as due to the old message, the Trickle interval of the node with the new value will be set at I_{min}, which would give a second opportunity for broadcast relatively soon.

6   Evaluation

To confirm the analytical results and to evaluate the performance of the Cleansing MAC modifications, we conducted several experiments in simulation and on a physical test bed. We used one application - dissemination of an update using Trickle, implemented in Contiki 2.7. Each experiment starts by injecting an update in the network. As the update is propagated, nodes increase their Trickle interval. The experiment ends when all nodes have reached their maximum Trickle interval $I_{max} = 10 \cdot I_{min}$. We measured the delay, i.e. the time required to update all nodes, the total number of sent packets, the number of MAC layer retransmissions, and the mean waiting time in the MAC layer queue.

6.1   Simulation Results

The simulations were carried out in the cross-level simulator Cooja [19]. Cooja internally uses the MSPsim device emulator for cycle accurate Tmote Sky emulation [21], as well as a symbol accurate emulation of the IEEE 802.15.4 CC2420 radio chip. We used the Unit Disk Graph Radio Medium propagation model, with no loss. All nodes use unslotted CSMA/CA with the default parameters ($BE_{\min} = 0$, $BE_{\max} = 3$, $NB_{\max} = 3$), and the ContikiMAC RDC protocol, with a wake-up frequency of 8Hz ($w = 125ms$). $I_{\min}$ varies from 250ms to 1.75s, at 250ms steps ($m = 2, 4, ..., 14$), well beyond MPL's recommendation of $m = 10$.

6.2   Bottleneck Topology

The first scenario follows the bottleneck topology, as shown in Figure 5. An update is inserted at the same time at nodes 1 and 2, and is propagated to the rest of the network using Trickle. Each configuration was simulated 1.000 times.

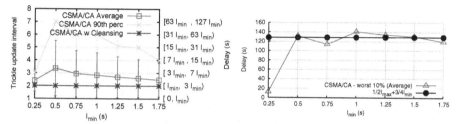

(a) Trickle update interval and update delay   (b) Average update delay - worst 10%

Fig. 8. Update delay in the bottleneck scenario ($I_{\max} = 256s$, $k = 1$, $\eta = 1/2$). a) shows the Trickle interval in which node 4 gets updated, with and without Cleansing MAC improvements. The left y axis shows the Trickle doubling interval, and the right y axis the actual time. b) shows the average delay of the largest 10% of the measurements, and the analytical expected delay. The error bars correspond to the standard deviation.

As expected, without Cleansing, due to the large number of collisions, the update delay of node 4 is highly variable (Figure 8a). Both the mean and the standard deviation peak at $I_{\min} = 0.5s$, and gradually decrease as $I_{\min}$ increases. Surprisingly, the update delay at $I_{\min} = 0.25s$ is stable. This anomaly occurs because at $I_{\min} = 0.25s = 2 \cdot w$, the contention window of nodes 1 and 2 is equal to the broadcast duration (w). This practically guarantees collisions, and a retransmission from one of the nodes. However, node 3's listen-only period will be finished before the retransmission starts, and there is a chance that node 3 will schedule its own transmission before it receives the retransmission. Even if the transmission from node 3 is delayed, it will be sent within one or two broadcast periods. However, with $I_{\min} = 0.5s$, nodes 1 and 2's contention window is still small, giving high probability for collisions. Then, retransmissions will always fall in node 3's listen-only period, forcing it to suppress its own transmission.

Figure 8b depicts the average measured delay of the worst 10% of the observations. This is a clear indication that harmful back-offs due to CSMA/CA are not uncommon, and that their effects can be detrimental to Trickle's performance. The update delay then becomes significantly high, in line with the analytical expected delay of $\frac{3}{4}I_{\min} + \frac{1}{2}I_{\max}$.

Finally, the interference is completely resolved with MAC Cleansing. In that case, updates are always completed in the second interval, as expected.

6.3   Grid Topology

The second scenario consists of 100 nodes, arranged in a 10x10 grid, with 10 meters between two nodes in each axis. A new Trickle event is generated at the top left node. We simulate 100 executions of Trickle with different values for I_{min}. Furthermore, we varied the connectivity range of each node. Each node has a circular coverage area with radius $2 + 10R$ meters, with $1 \leq R \leq 5$.

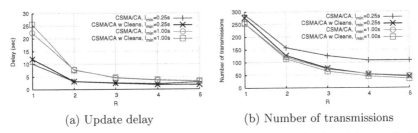

(a) Update delay   (b) Number of transmissions

Fig. 9. Average delay and average number of transmissions in the grid scenario. Using CSMA/CA with Cleansing with $I_{min} = 0.25s$ requires a similar number of transmissions as regular CSMA/CA with $I_{min} = 1.00s$, while the update delay is halved.

Figure 9a shows the update delay when using CSMA/CA with and without Cleansing. Since there are no bottlenecks in this scenario, these are comparable. However, the reduction in the number of sent packets is visible in Figure 9b. We can see that the number of transmissions with Cleansing is significantly lower than without Cleansing, while the average update delays are the same.

Figure 10 shows the average number of transmissions and retransmissions during the entire simulation. As the range of each node grows, fewer messages are required to cover the entire network. Trickle then performs well, suppressing many transmissions (Figure 10a). However, many of the messages are actual retransmissions from the MAC layer (Figure 10b). Since $k = 1$, these are obsolete messages. Furthermore, due to the congested media, frames are left in the queue for a longer time (Figure 10c), often leading to chained attempts for retransmission and further back-offs.

Figures 10d-10f show the impact of using Cleansing. CSMA/CA with Cleansing is aggressive with cleaning the MAC queue, as is visible in Figure 10e. This makes Trickle work as intended even for small values of I_{min}. Additionally, the average queue time is considerably lower compared to the original CSMA/CA.

6.4   Hardware Experiments

To confirm the simulation results, we ran the same application on a physical test bed provided by FIT IoT-LAB [2]. The test bed consists of 119 STM32 (ARM Cortex M3) based nodes, with the AT86RF231 IEEE 802.15.4 radio chip, arranged as in Figure 11a. As before, all nodes use the ContikiMAC RDC protocol with a wake-up frequency of 8 Hz. The redundancy constant was fixed to $k = 1$,

---

[2] http://www.iot-lab.info

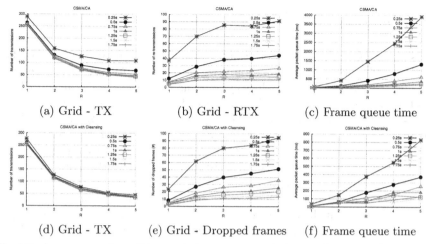

(a) Grid - TX   (b) Grid - RTX   (c) Frame queue time

(d) Grid - TX   (e) Grid - Dropped frames   (f) Frame queue time

Fig. 10. Average number of transmissions, retransmissions and average frame queue time in the grid scenario, with (d-f) and without (a-c) MAC Cleansing, for different values of I_{min}, $k = 1$ and $\eta = 1/2$

with I_{min} set to 0.25s, 0.5s and 1.0s. For each setting, we ran 100 executions of Trickle dissemination of one update, injected at the bottom-right node.

Figure 11d shows that using CSMA/CA, low values of I_{min} introduce a lot of collisions, which force retransmissions by the MAC layer. Increasing I_{min} helps reduce the number of transmissions (Figure 11c), but at the expense of a higher delay (Figure 11b). On the other hand, CSMA/CA with Cleansing has consistent performance using all three different values of I_{min}. Due to the proactive purging policy, the number of messages remains comparable with different values of I_{min}. As expected, the delay increases together with I_{min}, but it is still in the same range as with the original CSMA/CA.

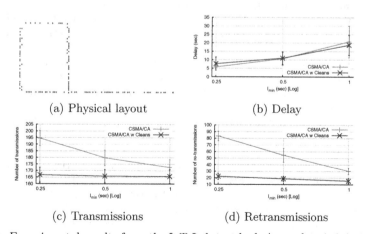

(a) Physical layout   (b) Delay

(c) Transmissions   (d) Retransmissions

Fig. 11. Experimental results from the IoT-Lab test bed. An update is injected at the bottom-right node, and is propagated using Trickle. The entire network is reachable in 12 hops. We show the averages and standard deviations over 100 executions.

7 Conclusion

In this paper we analyzed the performance of the Trickle algorithm for data dissemination when used in combination with low-power MAC protocols. We analyzed how the interplay of radio duty cycling and CSMA back-offs can contribute to bad Trickle performance. Analytically, we showed the MAC layer introduces inconsistencies, which lead to redundant transmissions and large update delays.

In order to resolve these issues, we proposed a small modification to the MAC layer, called *Cleansing*. The Cleansing MAC modification purges obsolete Trickle messages that are sent due to the inconsistencies caused by the MAC layer.

Through a simulation study, and then confirmed with experiments on a large physical test bed, we showed that the Cleansing MAC indeed improves performance. We found that the number of redundant transmissions in dense topologies is decreased greatly and that the update speed in networks with bottlenecks is improved drastically.

As future work, we plan to extend the analysis to environments where the redundancy constant is greater than one. Additionally, we want to generalize the impact of the data link layer to Trickle timing, regardless of the combination of MAC protocol and radio duty cycling protocol.

Acknowledgments. The authors would like to thank Onno J. Boxma for the many useful comments during the writing of this text. This work is supported in part by the Dutch P08 SenSafety Project, as part of the COMMIT program.

References

1. Akyildiz, I., Su, W., Sankarasubramaniam, Y., Cayirci, E.: Wireless sensor networks: a survey. Computer Networks 38(4), 393–422 (2002)
2. Becker, M., Kuladinithi, K., Görg, C.: Modelling and Simulating the Trickle Algorithm. In: Conf. on Mobile Networks and Management (MONAMI), pp. 135–144 (2011)
3. Clausen, T., de Verdiere, A., Yi, J.: Performance Analysis of Trickle as a Flooding Mechanism. In: Conf. on Communication Technology (ICCT) (2013)
4. Dunkels, A.: The ContikiMAC Radio Duty Cycling Protocol. Tech. rep., SICS T2011:13 (2011)
5. Dunkels, A., Grönvall, B., Voigt, T.: Contiki - a Lightweight and Flexible Operating System for Tiny Networked Sensors. In: Workshop on Embedded Networked Sensors (Emnets-I) (2004)
6. Eriksson, J., Gnawali, O.: Poster Abstract: Synchronizing Trickle Intervals. In: European Conf. on Wireless Sensor Networks (EWSN) (2014)
7. Farooq, M.O., Kunz, T.: Contiki-based IEEE 802.15.4 Node's Throughput and Wireless Channel Utilization Analysis. In: Wireless Days (WD), pp. 1–3 (2012)
8. Gnawali, O., Fonseca, R., Jamieson, K., Moss, D., Levis, P.: Collection Tree Protocol. In: Conf. on Embedded Networked Sensor Systems, SenSys (2009)
9. Hui, J., Kelsey, R.: Multicast Protocol for Low power and Lossy Networks, MPL (2014), http://tools.ietf.org/html/draft-ietf-roll-trickle-mcast-09

10. IEEE: Standard for Local and metropolitan area networks Part 15.4: Low-Rate Wireless Personal Area Networks (LR-WPANs), Amendment 1: MAC sublayer. IEEE Std. 802.15.4e-2012 (2012)

11. dos Santos Ribeiro Júnior, N., Vieira, M.A.M., Vieira, L.F.M., Gnawali, O.: CodeDrip: Data dissemination protocol with network coding for wireless sensor networks. In: Krishnamachari, B., Murphy, A.L., Trigoni, N. (eds.) EWSN 2014. LNCS, vol. 8354, pp. 34–49. Springer, Heidelberg (2014)

12. Kermajani, H., Gomez, C., Arshad, M.H.: Modeling the Message Count of the Trickle Algorithm in a Steady-State, Static Wireless Sensor Network. IEEE Communications Letters 16(12), 1960–1963 (2012)

13. Levis, P., Clausen, T., Hui, J., Gnawali, O., Ko, J.: The Trickle Algorithm. RFC 6206 (March 2011), http://www.ietf.org/rfc/rfc6206.txt

14. Levis, P., Brewer, E., Culler, D., Gay, D., Madden, S., Patel, N., Polastre, J., Shenker, S., Szewczyk, R., Woo, A.: The Emergence of a Networking Primitive in Wireless Sensor Networks. Commun. ACM 51(7), 99–106 (2008)

15. Levis, P., Patel, N., Culler, D., Shenker, S.: Trickle: A Self-Regulating Algorithm for Code Propagation and Maintenance in Wireless Sensor Networks. In: Symp. on Networked Systems Design and Implementation (NSDI), pp. 15–28 (2004)

16. Lin, K., Levis, P.: Data Discovery and Dissemination with DIP. In: Conf. on Information Processing in Sensor Networks (IPSN), pp. 433–444 (2008)

17. Meyfroyt, T.M.M., Borst, S.C., Boxma, O.J., Denteneer, D.: Data Dissemination Performance in Large-scale Sensor Networks. SIGMETRICS Performance Evaluation Review 42(1), 395–406 (2014)

18. Oikonomou, G., Phillips, I., Tryfonas, T.: IPv6 Multicast Forwarding in RPL-Based Wireless Sensor Networks. Wireless Personal Communications 73(3), 1089–1116 (2013)

19. Osterlind, F., Dunkels, A., Eriksson, J., Finne, N., Voigt, T.: Cross-Level Sensor Network Simulation with COOJA. In: Conf. on Local Computer Networks (LCN), pp. 641–648 (2006)

20. Pazurkiewicz, T., Gregorczyk, M., Iwanicki, K.: NarrowCast: A New Link-Layer Primitive for Gossip-Based Sensornet Protocols. In: Krishnamachari, B., Murphy, A.L., Trigoni, N. (eds.) EWSN 2014. LNCS, vol. 8354, pp. 1–16. Springer, Heidelberg (2014)

21. Polastre, J., Szewczyk, R., Culler, D.: Telos: Enabling Ultra-Low Power Wireless Research. In: Symp. on Information Processing in Sensor Networks (IPSN) (2005)

22. Stolikj, M., Meyfroyt, T.M.M., Cuijpers, P.J.L., Lukkien, J.J.: Improving the Performance of Trickle-Based Data Dissemination in Low-Power Networks. Tech. rep., TU/e CS-14-10 (2014)

23. Vallati, C., Mingozzi, E.: Trickle-F: Fair Broadcast Suppression to Improve Energy-Efficient Route Formation with the RPL Routing Protocol. In: Sustainable Internet and ICT for Sustainability (SustainIT), pp. 1–9 (2013)

24. Winter, T., Thubert, P., Brandt, A., Hui, J., Kelsey, R., Levis, P., Pister, K., Struik, R., Vasseur, J., Alexander, R.: RPL: IPv6 Routing Protocol for Low-Power and Lossy Networks. RFC 6550 (2012), http://www.ietf.org/rfc/rfc6550.txt

Featurecast: Lightweight Data-Centric Communications for Wireless Sensor Networks

Michał Król, Franck Rousseau, and Andrzej Duda

Grenoble Institute of Technology
CNRS Grenoble Informatics Laboratory UMR 5217
681, rue de la Passerelle, 38402 Saint Martin d'Hères, France
{firstname.lastname}@imag.fr

Abstract. We introduce the concept of *Featurecast* with addressing and routing based on node features defined as predicates. For instance, we can send a packet to the address composed of features {temperature and Room D} to reach all nodes with a temperature sensor located in Room D. Each node constructs its address from the set of its features and disseminates it in the network so that intermediate nodes can build routing tables. In this way, a node can send a packet to a set of nodes matching given features. Our experiments and evaluation of this scheme show very good performance compared to Logical Neighborhoods (LN) and IP multicast with respect to the memory footprint and message overhead.

Keywords: wireless sensor networks, data-centric routing, multicast, IPv6.

1 Introduction

Wireless sensor networks need to support specific traffic patterns related to sensor applications. One of their most important goals is to forward collected data to one or several sinks. They also have to support downward traffic from a sink to all or some sensor nodes. This traffic pattern results from the need for configuring nodes, querying sensors, or transmitting commands to actuators. Sensor nodes may require communication with other nodes, for instance for aggregating data or collaborating on a common reaction to local events.

In addition to the standard unicast communication, many sensor network applications may benefit from *multicasting* to forward packets to a group of nodes or report data to multiple sinks [1,2,3]. Multicasting results in a reduced number of packets forwarded in the network, which in turn limits energy consumption—compared to unicast, nodes transmit less packets when using multicast, because packets are only replicated when needed.

Unicast and multicast are *address-centric* communication modes in which source and destination addresses identify endpoint nodes. Such modes are suitable for structured addresses that result in small routing tables. *Data or content-centric* routing focuses on the packet content instead of communication endpoints. In the

T. Abdelzaher et al. (Eds.): EWSN 2015, LNCS 8965, pp. 202–217, 2015.

context of sensor networks, Directed Diffusion was one of the first proposals for sensor data dissemination based on this approach [4,5]: sensor nodes attach *attributes* (name-value pairs) to generated data, consumers specify interests for sensor data in terms of attributes, and sensors send unicast data packets to consumers. The data-centric paradigm is appealing for sensor networks, because it fits very well their data-oriented nature, however the approach incurs significant overhead by attaching attributes to data, which is prohibitive in energy constrained networks. Directed Diffusion uses flooding to disseminate interests for sensor data, which is inefficient in wireless networks. Moreover, it does not scale well in networks with many sinks that transmit many different queries [6].

In this paper, we propose *Featurecast*, a network layer communication mode well suited for sensor networks. One of our main design goals was to create a system able to cooperate with already existing IPv6 networks. Unlike Directed Diffusion, Featurecast is address-centric, but it uses a data-centric approach to create addresses and operate routing: addresses correspond to a set of features characterizing sensor nodes. Features are predicates, not attributes, which allows us to represent them in a compact way in address fields of packets and in routing tables.

Nodes disseminate Featurecast addresses in the network following a structure usually constructed for routing standard unicast packets such as a Collection Tree (CT) [7] or a DODAG (Destination Oriented Directed Acyclic Graph) [8]. Intermediate nodes merge the features of nodes reachable on a given link and construct a compact routing table for further packet forwarding. Based on the routing tables, a packet can reach all nodes characterized by a given set of features. Our proposal does not define any specific grammar for features, which makes it extremely flexible and easy to use. We propose a specific compact encoding allowing for fitting a Featurecast address into the standard multicast IPv6 address field. To the best of our knowledge, Featurecast is the only protocol able to take advantage of a data-centric approach in traditional IPv6 networks.

We have implemented Featurecast and the proposed scheme for routing in Contiki OS [9] and integrated them within its uIPv6 (micro Internet Protocol) stack. The implementation provides Featurecast at the network layer unlike other proposals that use application layer overlays. To evaluate Featurecast, we have simulated in Cooja an application scenario developed for CoAP group communications [10] with several sensors placed across buildings, wings, and rooms. We have compared Featurecast with Logical Neighborhoods (LN) [11] and IP multicast with respect to the memory footprint and message overhead. Featurecast results in a significantly smaller memory footprint and a lower average number of messages for updating routing tables compared to other schemes.

2   Featurecast

We want to provide a new communication mode for wireless sensor networks to designate relevant sensor nodes or data destinations by means of their characteristics and not with some low level identifiers or node addresses. For instance, we may want to get the *"average temperature on the 1st floor"* or *"turn off all the lights in the building"*. Such reasoning is close to applications that take advantage of sensors and actuators. Obviously, we could support such messages by associating a multicast group with each query, however, the number of such groups may quickly become too large, because of all possible combinations of characteristics.

We introduce below the notion of Featurecast addresses, present the construction of routing tables, and the forwarding process.

2.1 Featurecast Addresses

We assume that each sensor defines a set of its features, for instance its capability of sensing the environment (`temperature`, `humidity`), location (`sector 5`, `1st floor`), state (`low-energy`), or some other custom features (`my favorite nodes`). Features are *predicates*, i.e., statements that may be true or false (in the previous examples, we explicitly state features that are true). Predicates are commonly used to represent the properties of objects and we use them here to represent the properties of sensors: if f is a predicate on sensor X, we say that f is a property of sensor X. Note that features are not attributes (i.e., `name:value` pairs), which allows us to represent them in a much more compact way without loosing any flexibility. We assume that there is no coordination in defining features, but all features are known and each node can define its features at will.

A sensor node derives its Featurecast address from its features—more formally, a node address is the set:

$$A = \{f_1, f_2, ..., f_n\}, f_i \in \mathcal{F}, \tag{1}$$

where f_i is a feature predicate and $\mathcal{F}$ is the set of all possible features with cardinality of N. Features in the network may evolve in time and nodes may change their features, for instance the location of a node may change when it moves or a sensor may define a state of high temperature when exceeding a given threshold. Note that N, the total number of features in the network does not depend on the number of nodes, but rather on applications that define node characteristics.

The destination address may contain a subset of features—we say that it *matches* a node address, if the node address contains the destination address:

$$D = \{f_1, f_2, ..., f_k\}, f_i \in \mathcal{F}, D \text{ matches } A, \text{ if } D \subset A$$

For instance, a packet to `temperature, 1st floor` will match nodes defining both `temperature` and `1st floor` in their addresses. The conjunction seems the right way of representing nodes of interest for most sensor network applications. In the real world, somebody can describe an object with a set observed features. Such an approach is thus a very natural way of designating objects.

We can consider the node address as a representative of all possible multicast groups that would be created based on the node features to make it reachable

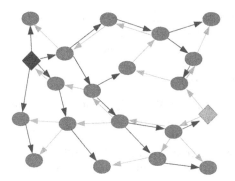

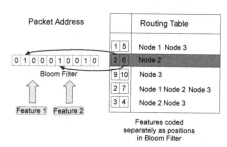

Fig. 1. Multiple DODAGs deployed in the same network for better connectivity.

Fig. 2. Proposed compact representation of features: Bloom filter in the destination address and a bit position list in the routing table.

for any combination of features using the traditional multicast groups, which gives $\sum_{k=0}^{n} C_n^k = 2^n$ addresses for n features.

Note that such an addressing schemes allows other useful communication patterns, for example, a node addressing a packet using its own location can reach all sensor in the same room/floor/building without creating any dedicated multicast group.

2.2   Constructing Routing Tables

Forwarding packets based on Featurecast addresses requires the construction of routing tables that contain the features reachable through a given neighbor. To create routing tables, nodes can advertise features along an existing routing structure for unicast such as a DODAG or a Collection Tree. However, in our implementation, we have used our proper way of constructing a DODAG described below (Featurecast can also operate along any protocol that creates such a structure, e.g. RPL).

Creating a Routing Structure. Using only one routing structure may be inefficient, because two nodes on different branches need to communicate by passing through the root. We can alleviate this problem by deploying multiple DODAGs or Collection Trees in the network (cf. Figure 1). Each node stores the information about all DODAGs present in the network, but to send a packet, it uses only one DODAG, the one with the root closest to the node. Multiple DODAGs deployed in the network result in nodes that are close to any root, which improves communication efficiency.

We also propose to construct each DODAG in a way similar to RPL, but with a modified metric that takes Featurecast into account. The root starts the DODAG construction process by broadcasting route advertisements with the distance set to 0. Each node receiving such a message checks if it knows a node closer to the root. If not, it sets the message sender as its preferred parent and rebroadcast the message with a modified distance d that takes into account the similarity of nodes—a node receiving a route advertisement from a neighbor compares a set of features with its own adds the result to the advertised metric:

$$d = h - (|F_n \cap F_s|)/(|F_n| + 1), \tag{2}$$

where h is the hop count (original metric of RPL OF0), F_n is the set of node features, and F_s is the set of the sender features. Note that $h + 1 > d$.

By grouping similar sensors, we decrease the overall cost of forwarding Featurecast messages, because a packet addressed to a given group of nodes will be duplicated less often. Moreover, nodes are much more likely to find a common ancestor thus reducing communication overhead. In the rest of the paper, we will refer to this routing structure as the Featurecast DODAG.

Advertising Features. The process of advertising features starts at leaf nodes that send their features to their preferred parent. Parents obtain the features from their children nodes, add their own features, and forward the list of features reachable through them to their own parent. The process continues up to the root of the DODAG. Finally, the root node obtains the list of all features in the network and it can use it to forward packets to relevant neighbors. The sink can also initialize the process in the reverse direction by sending its features to children nodes, which speeds up machine-to-machine communication.

When a node receives a feature already in its routing table, it does not forward it to its neighbors and ignores subsequent advertisements, so most of the changes in features will only result in localized transmissions, as shown in Section 4. Even if a single node fails, other nodes may have defined the same feature and the routing tables may remain valid.

2.3   Forwarding

When nodes have created routing tables, they can send packets with the destination addresses containing set of features that intermediate nodes match against the routing tables and forward to all neighbors having the matching entry.

2.4   Topology Maintenance

It is possible that some neighbors of a sensor node disconnect due to topology changes, node failures, or battery depletion. For detecting disconnected peers and maintain a valid topology, Featurecast relies on hello messages and RPL local and global repair mechanisms. In case of neighbor disconnection, a node checks the set of features advertised by other connected neighbors—if they provide all the features advertised by the disconnected node, there is no need for an update. Otherwise, the node informs its parent node about the absence of the features available through the disconnected neighbor. The parent node will do the same with respect to its neighbors and the process continues until the root node if necessary.

It is also possible to delay sending the advertisement about missing features until the node receives a packet using them. A node changing its parent node or changing its set of features, advertises the change as explained in Sect. 2.2.

3   Compact Representation of Features

We have followed several design guidelines for the compact representation. First, we want an open network able to accept any feature defined on nodes. Second, the addressing scheme should not depend on the number of features defined in the network—we do not want to force the user to define a hierarchy of features. Most of data-centric approaches use a grammar exchanged in a text form. Such an approach is often a problem while integrating such solutions into real life scenarios. We want our solution to still use user-friendly addresses, while being easily stored and processed by nodes. We then need fixed-size addresses for efficient forwarding and possibility to integrate Featurecast within the standard IPv6 addressing scheme with 112 bits in the multicast IPv6 address. Such integration will show that a data-centric approach may have the same overhead as address-centric solutions and lead to easy integration with existing networks. A part of such an IPv6 address can be used for a global prefix and routed in the Internet. Finally, we want to take into account resource constraints (memory size) of sensor nodes for storing routing tables.

We also want to avoid global synchronization mechanisms disseminating a mapping between features and their binary representation. Such a solution would result in a significantly higher volume of communications and could delay packet forwarding during the feature update. For these reasons, we have decided to use hash functions and a structure allowing to efficiently store many hashes—a Bloom filter.

3.1   Bloom Filters

A Bloom filter is a probabilistic structure allowing for efficient storage of a set of elements. A typical filter contains an array of m bits. At the beginning all bits are set to 0. There are k hash functions that map an element to a bit position in the array. When inserting an element into a filter, we compute k hash functions on the element and set all the resulting bits to 1. If a bit was already set to 1, we do not change it. To check whether an element belongs to a set, we compute the same hash functions on the element and check if all corresponding bit positions are set to 1. If not, we are sure that the element does not belong to the set.

False positives may occur in Bloom filters: it is possible that all bits corresponding to the hash functions on a tested element are set to 1 by other stored elements, even if the element does not belong to the set. The probability of false positives depends on the number of stored elements n and the size of the filter (m and k):

$$p \approx (1 - e^{-km/n})^k. \tag{3}$$

To maintain the same false positive rate with a growing number of elements, we need to increase the number of bits and hash functions, which results in larger memory consumption and increased computational overhead.

3.2   Naive Bloom Filter Solution

A possible solution is to use Bloom filters of the same size to represent a set of features in the destination address and in the routing table entry for each neighbor. To decide where to forward the packet, we only have to verify if all bits set in the address are also set in the routing entry for a given neighbor. However, such a solution limits the number of possible features to store in the routing tables. If n is the number of elements in the filter (features in our case) and p is the required probability of false positives, the minimum number of bits m for the filter is $m \geq n \log_2(e) \times \log_2(1/p)$. To achieve the probability of 2%, we need 5 bits per feature. To fit 112 bits available in IPv6 address, we would be able to store only 22 features with 2% of false positives, the value we consider as sufficient for the packet destination address (as we store features for only one sensor or a group of sensor), but insufficient for routing tables in which we would need to store all features defined in the network in the worst case.

3.3   Bloom Filter in Addresses and a Bit Position List in the Routing Table

We describe the proposed compact representation of features that satisfies our requirements: being able to represent around 10 features in a destination address limited to 112 bits with a small false positive probability and representing potentially all features in the network in routing tables with a small memory footprint.

The proposed solution consists of using a different feature representation in the routing tables: nodes represent a single feature in the routing table as the positions of bits set in the Bloom filter. For example, we represent a feature that sets bits on positions 5 and 76 in the Bloom Filter with the two numbers in the routing table (cf. Fig. 2). Nodes use a Bloom filter in the address field as described above.

The probability of two different features having the same representation in the routing table is: $p_N = N/m^k$, where N is the number of features in the network and m is the size in bits of the Bloom filter. The size of each represented feature in an address depends on the Bloom filter size and the number of hash functions: $s = k \log_2(m)$.

Taking into account Eq. 3, this solution allows supporting 200 different features in the routing table with the probability of false positives less than 2%, which satisfies our requirements. As we want to use a 112 bit long Bloom filter and 2 hash functions, we only need 2 bytes to store a feature in the routing table, which results in the routing table of only 400 bytes for 200 features.

Routing Entry Aggregation. As Featurecast may operate over multiple DODAGs, we aggregate the same routing entries from multiple DODAGs: for features defined on the same set of neighbors in different DODAGs, we keep only a single entry, which results in a reduced amount of memory without introducing any computational overhead during forwarding.

Computational Overhead. Our representation of routing tables requires iterating through all present features to forward a packet, which makes the operation limited by $O(n)$, where n is the number of features. However, with n features, we are able to construct $g = 2^n$ groups, which means that in a well constructed system, the computational complexity in terms of the number of groups g is $O(\log(g))$. As nodes already store features in a hashed form, each comparison only requires few bitwise operations to check the corresponding bit in the source address Bloom filter, which does not introduce a significant computational overhead, especially by contrast with text comparisons used in many data centric solutions.

To further speed up the forwarding process, we have developed several optimization techniques. First of all, we do not have to iterate through features present at every neighbor. This modification significantly reduces the overhead especially at nodes close to the root, which have many such features. Secondly we start the forwarding process from features being present at only one neighbor. If any of them is present in the source address, we just need to check if this neighbor defines all required features without iterating through the whole table.

4   Implementation and Evaluation

We have implemented Featurecast in Contiki OS (ver. 2.6) [9]. For performance evaluation, we have run simulations in Cooja, a simulator that emulates both the software and hardware of sensor nodes. As an execution platform, we have used Sky Motes with CC2420 2.4 GHz radio and ContikiMAC at Layer 2.

Contiki supports the RPL routing protocol to build a DODAG that takes into account the distance to the sink in terms of the number of hops, the metric defined by Objective Function Zero (OF0). We have modified the metric for constructing the Featurecast DODAG to reflect similarity of stored features (cf. Sect. 2.2).

4.1   Evaluation Setup

We have compared Featurecast with Logical Neighborhoods (LN) [11], which proposes a similar abstraction, but at the application layer, and the traditional IP Multicast as it is the recommended solution for group communications in WSN [10]. We have set the parameters of LN (exploration parameter E and the number of credits) to the values used in the LN evaluation [11]. Note that LN does not guarantee packet delivery for a small amount of credits, so we have used the LN recommended values [11].

As there is no implementation of any multicast routing protocol in Contiki (ver. 2.6), we have implemented a simple routing protocol in which nodes willing to join a multicast group just send a message towards their parents in the RPL DODAG using UDP. Each sensor, after receiving the message, waits for an advertisement from its children, adds its own advertisement, and sends it up through the DODAG. We use the number of control messages exchanged for maintaining Featurecast or multicast routing as the main comparison index. They directly influence the energy consumption of nodes and the network lifetime.

4.2   Scenarios

We consider two scenarios: i) the building control application developed for CoAP group communication [10] and ii) a random topology of nodes with random features.

Building Control. The building control scenario uses a deployment scheme in which sensor nodes are placed in several buildings across multiple floors, wings, and rooms. The scenario considers sensor nodes of multiple types (e.g. measuring temperature, humidity, luminosity, etc.). CoAP clients communicate with sensor nodes by means of URLs with a hierarchical structure that encodes the node location and its capabilities using the following format: node_type.room.wing.-floor.building. If q_i is a number of elements on each level, then to be able to access any set of nodes, we need to define a label for each feature at each level (u being the number of levels in the URL): $\sum_{i=1}^{u} q_i$.

We need the same amount of features for LN expressed in the form of attributes. If we use IP multicast in the same scenario, we have to define a multicast group for each combination, which results in $\prod_{i=1}^{u} q_i$. If we want to use the URLs that do not contain all the defined levels (e.g. bldg1.all_nodes), the number of multicast groups is even higher: $\prod_{i=1}^{u} (q_i + 1)$.

Random Topology. In the second scenario, we evaluate communication performance in a random topology. Each node chooses its address as a set of 10 random features. After establishing the routing infrastructure, we choose a random node to send a packet to a randomly chosen group. We vary the network size from 50 to 500 nodes and average the results from 100 different runs. A UDP packet with 100B payload is generated every 30s.

4.3   Results: Memory Footprint in Building Control Scenario

First, we perform our evaluation in the building control scenario with 128 sensor nodes across 2 buildings (Building 1 and 2), 2 floors in each building (Floor 1 and 2), 2 wings (East, West), 4 rooms in each wing (Room 1 to 4), and 2 sensor types (light, temperature). We place 2 temperature and 2 light sensors in each room. We place nodes at regular intervals on a 16x8 matrix and assign the right features simulating the given scenario. Featurecast and LN require 12 features or attributes to in this scenario, while with IP multicast, we need 405 groups. We place the sink in the center of the network. We also evaluate Featurecast with 2 and 3 DODAGs (Featurecast2 and Featurecast3 respectively).

We can note that in this scenario, Featurecast is extremely scalable. If we want to connect another building with a similar infrastructure, we need to add only

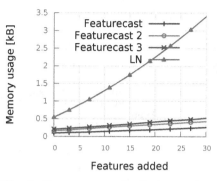

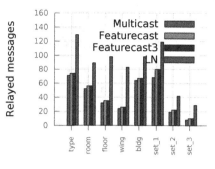

Fig. 3. Memory usage for Featurecast (1, 2, 3 DODAGs) and LN

Fig. 4. Number of relayed messages needed by the sink to access all nodes in a given group

one new feature (e.g. Building 3), while with IP multicast, we need to add 135 new groups. LN maintains associations between attributes, so with every new added attribute, the amount of memory per item increases. Fig. 3 presents the routing table memory usage for Featurecast and LN. We reduce x axis to 30 new features for better readability. We also omit the results for IP Multicast: because of an extremely large number of the required groups and high memory usage per address, IP Multicast needs 6480 B (over 67 times more then Featurecast) with only 12 unique features.

Then, we add features at each level of the hierarchy defined in the scenario [10] (one building, one floor etc.). Featurecast performs more then 5 times better (96 B vs. 544 B) than in our original scenario. Each new item in LN adds some new information to all existing entries, which requires much larger amount of memory per item. With 100 new features added to the network, Featurecast requires more then 26 times less memory (654B vs 17044B). Note that even the topologies with multiple DODAGs (Featurecast 2, Featurecast 3) consume much less memory than LN due to entry aggregation (1064B and 1323B, respectively, for 100 added features).

4.4 Results: Message Overhead in Building Control Scenario

To establish the forwarding topology and guarantee connectivity, Featurecast needed to exchange only 248 messages per DODAG. In comparison, IP Multicast used 4992 messages to construct a DODAG for each multicast group. LN requires 226 messages, which is slightly better then Featurecast. However, the LN messages are on the average 5 times bigger than the ones of Featurecast, so even for 3 DODAGs, our system requires 2 times less bandwidth.

To evaluate routing performance after constructing the forwarding structure, we consider two cases: i) the sink sends packets to a given group of sensors, ii) a node communicates with another node. Fig. 4 presents the results of the first case: the average number of relayed messages (how many times intermediate nodes forward a message before it reaches the destination). We also present the results for 3 different sets of features: Set1 (type, floor), Set2 (building,

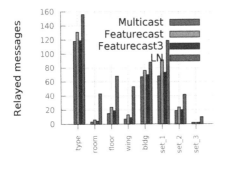

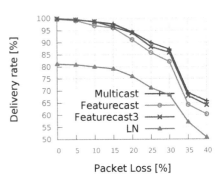

Fig. 5. Number of relayed messages needed by a member node to access all nodes in a given group

Fig. 6. Delivery rate for different packet loss rates

wing, floor), and Set3 (building, wing, floor, room, type). IP Multicast creates a minimal spanning tree for each destination group, which gives a bound for this type of traffic. Featurecast only creates one common Featurecast DODAG for all possible groups, but performs only slightly worse. The version with 3 DODAGs achieves almost the same performance as the optimal solution. LN requires however much more messages on the average to reach all destination nodes. It explores routes not present in the routing tables trying to quit local minima, which introduces an additional overhead.

Fig. 5 shows the results of the second case (node-to-node communication). Multicast IP exhibits the best performance that sets a theoretical bound. We can observe that Featurecast also requires a small number of messages. The Featurecast DODAG connects similar nodes thus allowing to find a common nearby ancestor. Introducing additional DODAGs decreases the gap even more. A LN node is never sure if a minimum is local or global, so even after reaching all target nodes, it performs a search of external paths thus increasing the number of messages.

To evaluate the cost of maintaining routing tables, we progressively disconnect random nodes from the network and compare the performance of Featurecast, IP Multicast, and LN. A LN node broadcasts a complete node description every 15s. However, if the underlying MAC layer is duty cycled such as ContikiMAC, the node needs to transmit each broadcast message separately to all neighbors (or it may use ContikiMAC broadcast, but it requires sending a frame during the whole check interval, which consumes a lot of energy). In both Featurecast and IP Multicast, we rely on small hello messages to check the connectivity between neighbors and send the required route update only if it is necessary. IP Multicast and Featurecast try to repair the topology only when detecting a neighbor failure. Without any topology changes, LN sends a constant amount of 507 messages every 15s with the average size of 106B. Our implementation of IP Multicast and Featurecast sends on the average 384 hello messages of 4B each. The lower number of messages results from maintaining connectivity only with

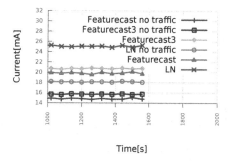

Time[s]

Fig. 7. Energy consumption, with and without traffic

Discon- nected	FC	FC 3	Mcast	LN
type	3	4	240	4
room	6	7	672	6
wing	18	18	1239	19
floor	12	15	2991	14
building	13	13	2721	13

Fig. 8. Number of relayed control messages after disconnecting different groups of nodes

neighbors in the DODAG. In total, LN transfers 53742B while Featurecast and IP Multicast only 1536B, which is more than 34 times less.

To analyze the behaviour of all solutions in a dynamic configuration, we shut down a single node placed further from the sink, then 2 nodes of the same type in the same room, a group of nodes in one room, all nodes in a wing, all nodes on a floor, and finally all nodes in a building. Table 8 presents the average number of additional messages needed to update the routing tables. When disconnecting single nodes, all approaches do not send any messages, because there is another node belonging to the same group that allows maintaining the DODAG. Disconnecting both nodes of a given type in a room only causes a small number of message exchanges in both Featurecast and LN, as there are other nodes defining the same features in the neighborhood. In IP Multicast, disconnecting the same nodes causes changes in several multicast groups (`bldg1.floor1.west.room4.temperature`, `bldg1.floor1.west.room4.*`, `bldg1.floor1.west.*.temperature`, etc.), and some part of this information needs to be transmitted to the sink causing a lot of traffic. Disconnecting a larger number of nodes causes more multicast group deletions and more control traffic. Shutting down the whole floor or building deletes a lot of multicast groups, but nodes responsible for sending the updates are directly connected to the sink, which lowers the number of exchanged messages.

In all cases, IP Multicast results in a large amount of control traffic due to a much larger number of groups and no group aggregation, which makes it unsuitable for implementation in sensor networks. Featurecast and LN send a much smaller number of messages in all considered scenarios. However, Featurecast messages are on the average 5 times smaller due to the compact feature representation.

4.5 Results: Random Topology Scenario

We have evaluated communication performance in the random topology scenario. Fig. 9 presents the number of relayed messages. Featurecast with a common DODAG has almost the same performance as LN. We have also tested

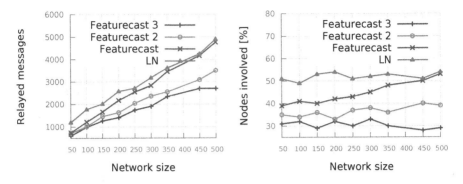

Fig. 9. Number of relayed messages for random communications

Fig. 10. Number of nodes involved in the communication process

Featurecast over 2 and 3 DODAGs in the network. To send packets, a node uses a DODAG with the closest root. Both cases with 2 and 3 DODAGs, significantly outperform other approaches.

We have also evaluated the number of nodes involved in communication in the random topology scenario (cf. Fig. 10). We consider a node involved in communication if it receives or sends a message at the MAC layer. We can observe that Featurecast with only one DODAG performs better than LN for a small number of nodes and involves the same number of nodes in larger networks. However, Featurecast with 2 or 3 DODAGs performs significantly better for all tested network sizes. Note that such a scenario is equivalent to having many sinks in the network. The results show that we do not need one DODAG per sink and several sinks can share one DODAG with only slight drop of performance.

Fig. 7 presents energy consumption measured every 60s using PowerTrace. Featurecast consumes significantly less energy, due to smaller messages and maintaining communication only with neighbors in the DODAGs and not with all nodes in the radio range. Note that Featurecast does not send hello messages separately for each DODAG, but only once for each neighbor present in any deployed DODAG.

To evaluate protocol robustness, we have measured the packet delivery rate for different packet loss rates in a network with 300 nodes. We have performed 1000 random transmissions for each rate. Figure 6 presents the results: with small packet loss rates, the MAC layer can retransmit packets if necessary, so almost all protocols are close to 100% delivery rate. LN even without packet loss cannot find all destination nodes because of the limited number of credits. Featurecast constructs slightly longer paths between destination and performs slightly worse than the optimal solution, however during the tests with 3 DODAGs, the difference is less than 1%. For packet loss rates greater than 15%, the performance of all protocols significantly decreases. Table. 1 summarizes all results.

Table 1. Summary of results: the gain of Featurecast compared to other solutions

Aspect	Featurecast	Featurecast-3	LN	Multicast
Memory (12 features)	1x (96B)	2.15x (206B)	5.67x (544B)	67.5x (6480B)
Memory (100 features)	1x (654B)	2.02x (1323B)	26.06x (17KB)	1711156x (111MB)
sink→nodes	1x (345)	1x (345)	1.99x (687)	0.96x (331)
node→node	1x (367)	0.86x (316)	1.58x (579)	0.82 (299)
hello (msgs)	1x (384)	1.1x (422)	1.32x (507)	1x (384)
hello (B)	1x (1536B)	1.1x (1688B)	34.99x (53742B)	1x (1536B)
after disconnection (msgs)	1x (52)	1.56x 81	1.08x 56	151.21x (7863)
after disconnection (B)	1x (624B)	1.56x (972B)	5.41x (3374B)	252x (157KB)
energy, no traffic	1x (15.1mA)	1.05x (15.9mA)	1.2x (18.2mA)	—
energy, with traffic	1x (19.9mA)	1.04x (20.7mA)	1.27x (25.3mA)	—
random (msgs)	1x (23557)	0.67x (15668)	1.11x (26227)	—
random (nodes)	1x (401)	0.59x 235	1.17x 468	—

4.6   Discussion of Packet Drops Due to Inexistent Addresses

Finally, we have investigated packet drops due to non-existent conjunction of features. The drops result from the aggregation of features in routing tables and not keeping more information about their compositions. If S_a is a set of features in an address, S_t^i a set of features in the routing table for neighbor i, and S_n a set of features defined by a node, the packet drop occurs when: $S_a \subset S_t^i \wedge \nexists S_n$, $S_a \subset S_n$.

In our scenario, the packet drop may occur if an address contains a combination of features that are not defined by any node, for example Building 1 and Building 2. In this case, the packet can be routed through nodes that may have both features available through the same neighbor. Eventually, it will be dropped by a sensor node that routes packets to this group through different nodes. Creating an invalid address with the location feature usually will not cause a lot of unnecessary traffic, however putting for instance only temperature and light into an address will cause global network flooding even if there is no node defining both features.

To alleviate this problem, a packet drop may be signaled by an ICMP packet, so that the user can avoid sending packets with the address in the future. Another problem arises if there are nodes defining for instance both temperature and light, but the rest of nodes defines only one of them. In such a case, a new feature temperature_light shall be defined allowing to efficiently query both types of nodes. However, the problem heavily depends on applications and will not occur in well configured network (as indicated above).

5   Related Work

Huang et al. proposed a spatio-temporal multicast protocol called *mobicast* that distributes a message to nodes in a delivery zone that evolves over time in some predictable manner [1]. Flury et al. focused on efficient algorithms for routing: they provide close to optimal unicasting and constant approximations to anycast and multicast with small routing tables of a bounded size [2]. Su et al. described oCast, an energy-optimal multicast routing protocol for wireless sensor networks [3]. The authors take into account networks operating under intermittent connectivity resulting from duty-cycling and consider small multicast groups. All three solutions focus more on constructing the minimal spanning tree than proposing an addressing scheme, which gives an opportunity to apply them in our future work.

As mentioned earlier, Directed Diffusion [4,5] is a data dissemination protocol in which sensor nodes attach *attributes* (name-value pairs) to generated data. Nodes interested in some attributes send interests that propagate in the network and in response, sensors send unicast packets to the interested nodes. The approach is similar to ours, but Directed Diffusion uses attributes for the sensed data and not for sensor nodes, focusing more on a publish/subscribe approach. Moreover, Directed Diffusion uses the packet payload and not addresses to convey attributes. The routing approach is also completely different from ours. To contact nodes, Directed Diffusion performs global flooding every time, later establishing a path between the sender and the recipient, which in our case would be inefficient.

Content-Centric Networking (CCN) focuses on content considered as a communication primitive [12]. It is designed for dissemination of data objects in the Internet and basically operates as a Publish-Subscribe system: each data object has a name and are sent to a subscriber in response to interests sent to publishers. Caching content is one important aspect that contributes to speed up the delivery of objects.

6   Conclusion and Future Work

We have presented Featurecast, a one-to-many communication primitive designed for Wireless Sensor Networks. In our proposal, nodes can create addresses representing some properties of nodes without any coordination or without an external name server. To support routing to Featurecast addresses, nodes disseminate features in the network so that intermediate nodes can merge the features of nodes reachable on a given link for further packet forwarding.

Our comparisons with LN and IP Multicast show very good performance of Featurecast. The application of Featurecast to the building control scenario supports our view that such a primitive can greatly simplify the process of sensor application development—it is possible to introduce already existing applications into a completely new environment without any changes to the code or relying on external systems like DNS or DHCP.

Featurecast defines a simple abstraction based on predicates that enables the reuse of IPv6 addresses and results in efficient memory usage and simple processing at nodes. We believe that such ability can be crucial for integration with existing systems. Even if our implementation is dedicated to wireless sensor networks and the Contiki IPv6 stack, it remains generic and flexible so it may adapt to other use cases.

Acknowledgements. This work was partially supported by the French National Research Agency (ANR) project IRIS under contract ANR-11-INFR-016 and the European Commission FP7 project CALIPSO under contract 288879.

References

1. Huang, Q., Lu, C., Roman, G.C.: Spatiotemporal Multicast in Sensor Networks. In: Proc. ACM SenSys, pp. 205–217. ACM, New York (2003)
2. Flury, R., Wattenhofer, R.: Routing, Anycast, and Multicast for Mesh and Sensor Networks. In: IEEE INFOCOM (2007)
3. Su, L., Ding, B., Yang, Y., Abdelzaher, T.F., Cao, G., Hou, J.C.: oCast: Optimal Multicast Routing Protocol for Wireless Sensor Networks. In: Proc. of ICNP, pp. 151–160 (2009)
4. Intanagonwiwat, C., Govindan, R., Estrin, D.: Directed Diffusion: a Scalable and Robust Communication Paradigm for Sensor Networks. In: Proc. of MOBICOM, pp. 56–67 (2000)
5. Intanagonwiwat, C., Govindan, R., Estrin, D., Heidemann, J., Silva, F.: Directed Diffusion for Wireless Sensor Networking. IEEE/ACM Trans. Netw. 11, 2–16 (2003)
6. Hebden, P., Pearce, A.: Data-Centric Routing Using Bloom Filters in Wireless Sensor Networks. In: Proc. of ICISIP 2006, pp. 72–78 (2006)
7. Gnawali, O., Fonseca, R., Jamieson, K., Moss, D., Levis, P.: Collection tree protocol. In: Proc. ACM SenSys, Berkeley, CA, USA (2009)
8. Winter, T., et al.: RPL: IPv6 Routing Protocol for Low power and Lossy Networks. RFC 6550, IETF (2012)
9. Dunkels, A., Grönvall, B., Voigt, T.: Contiki—a Lightweight and Flexible Operating System for Tiny Networked Sensors. In: IEEE EMNETS, Tampa, Florida, USA (2004)
10. Rahman, A., Dijk, E.: Group Communication for CoAP. IETF draft-ietf-core-groupcomm-07 (2013)
11. Mottola, L., Picco, G.: Logical Neighborhoods: A Programming Abstraction for Wireless Sensor Networks. In: Proc. IEEE DCOSS (2006)
12. Jacobson, V., Smetters, D.K., Thornton, J.D., Plass, M.F., Briggs, N.H., Braynard, R.L.: Networking Named Content. In: Proceedings of CoNEXT 2009, pp. 1–12. ACM, New York (2009)

RoCoCo: Receiver-Initiated Opportunistic Data Collection and Command Multicasting for WSNs

Andreas Reinhardt[1] and Christian Renner[2]

[1] TU Clausthal, Clausthal-Zellerfeld, Germany
andreas.reinhardt@tu-clausthal.de
[2] Universität zu Lübeck, Lübeck, Germany
renner@iti.uni-luebeck.de

Abstract. Many data collection protocols have been proposed to cater for the energy-efficient flow of sensor data from distributed sources to a sink node. However, the transmission of control commands from the sink to one or only a small set of nodes in the network is generally unsupported by these protocols. Supplementary protocols for packet routing and data dissemination have been developed to this end, although their energy requirements commonly thwart the low-power nature of data collection protocols. We tackle this challenge by presenting RoCoCo in this paper. It combines data collection and dissemination by extending the low-energy ORiNoCo collection protocol by means to reconfigure subsets of nodes during runtime. Synergistically leveraging existing message types, RoCoCo allows for the definition of multicast recipient groups and forwards commands to these groups in an opportunistic fashion. Relying on Bloom filters to define the recipient addresses, RoCoCo only incurs small memory and energy overheads. We confirm its feasibility by evaluating the introduced delays, command success rates, and its energy overhead in comparison to existing collection/dissemination protocols.

1 Introduction

Wireless sensor networks (WSNs) are often used to collect environmental parameters from a range of locations at a single sink node. As the underlying embedded sensing devices are commonly confined in their available energy budget, many energy-efficient data collection protocols have been developed (e.g., [30,9,4]). These protocols are optimized for the predominant traffic type in WSNs, namely data being relayed from sensor nodes towards the sink, and thus allow for increased operational times of such networks. As collection protocols generally do not provide support for the transmission of messages from the sink to one or multiple nodes, however, changing the network configuration during runtime is complicated. If supported by the collection protocol at all, control messages (e.g., to change a node's sampling rate or to temporarily suspend its data collection) can only be flooded to all devices in the network. Besides drastically increasing the network's energy demand, having to flood each control message naïvely through the network also represents a scalability issue.

T. Abdelzaher et al. (Eds.): EWSN 2015, LNCS 8965, pp. 218–233, 2015.

To alleviate this problem, dedicated WSN routing protocols have been devised (e.g., [29,8]). As they mostly focus on low delays while their energy consumption only plays a secondary role, however, they effectively defeat the data collection component's low-power operation when both are combined. Due to the inherent differences between data collection and control command routing, the simple combination of two such solutions is also generally suboptimal in terms of the resulting performance and energy expenditure. In order to overcome these limitations, we present RoCoCo, a sophisticated fusion of data collection and control command multicasting. Based on the low-energy ORiNoCo data collection protocol [27], it follows the primary objective of allowing for enduring operation on a tight energy budget. At the same time, RoCoCo seamlessly integrates commands and routing information into the messages used by the collection protocol in order to transfer packets from the sink to any set of nodes in the network. As a result, reconfiguration and control of individual devices becomes possible during runtime with RoCoCo at a small energy overhead. Our approach is very different from existing routing protocols like RPL [29], where a measurable amount of routing information needs to be stored at the nodes. Instead, RoCoCo relies on probabilistic data structures of constant size to make its routing decisions. We make the following contributions in this paper:

- We briefly revisit the fundamental mechanisms behind ORiNoCo and provide more detail on how destination addresses are specified by RoCoCo.
- We present RoCoCo's underlying design decisions in more detail, and highlight how it opportunistically combines energy-efficient data collection and the possibility to emit control commands to sets of nodes.
- We evaluate our solution in comparison to existing combinations of collection and dissemination protocols by means of testbed experiments as well as high-resolution power measurements.

2   Problem Statement and Background

The collection of data from distributed sensors has manifested itself as the primary application domain of WSNs. A myriad of corresponding deployments have been presented in literature, including the observation of volcanoes [28], glaciers [19], and the spreading of animal species [13]. With batteries representing the predominant energy source for the distributed nodes, however, the sensors are bound to tightly restricted energy budgets. To still achieve reasonable operational times, data collection protocols (e.g., MintRoute [30], CTP [9], Dozer [4]) were designed to forward data to the sink in an energy-efficient manner.

While catering to the transmission of data from the nodes to the sink, sending control commands from the sink to individual nodes or groups of nodes is generally beyond the capabilities of these protocols. In real applications, it may however be necessary to reconfigure a subset of nodes during runtime. Existing protocols to distribute such messages with a high probability of reaching the destination node thus often rely on broadcasting the data through the network, either by means of simple flooding or by using dissemination protocols

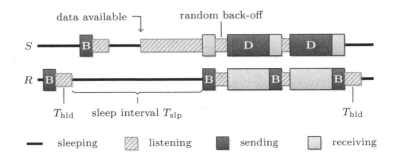

Fig. 1. Fundamental operation principle of ORiNoCo (B: beacon, D: data)

like Trickle [16], Drip [26], or DIP [17]. None of these protocols has, however, been designed to transmit commands to a subset of nodes only, and neither have they been developed with a focus on their seamless integration with existing collection protocols. Instead, dissemination protocols are commonly orthogonal to the underlying data collection protocol, making them easily interchangeable at the price of lower energy efficiency due to the separation of components.

In this paper, we overturn this traditional separation of components by presenting RoCoCo. It combines an energy-efficient data collection protocol with means to control individual nodes or groups of nodes. We show how the fusion of functionalities can lead to a dissemination of control data at little energy overhead. Likewise, due to the use of probabilistic data structures to store the destination set for control commands, only little extra memory is required. Finally, by piggybacking control commands on messages that are sent by the data collection protocol in any case, no extra packet overhead is introduced. RoCoCo represents a novel combination of collection and dissemination protocols, yet it builds on a contribution that we have made in prior work. We thus briefly revisit ORiNoCo as follows to cater for a better understanding.

2.1 ORiNoCo: Opportunistic Data Collection

The opportunistic receiver-initiated no-overhead collection (ORiNoCo) protocol is a data-collection protocol for low-power sensor networks [27]. To achieve low power consumption, ORiNoCo duty-cycles the radio and bases its communications on low-power probing. Figure 1 illustrates a packet forwarding procedure from sender S to receiver R. Both nodes switch on their radio periodically to send short beacons that advertise their readiness to receive a packet. Each of these beacons contains a metric that models the node's path *cost* when forwarding to the sink, e.g., the hop count. If no data packet is received as response to the beacon within a short period T_{hld}, the node switches off its radio again and waits a time T_{slp}, the sleep interval, before transmitting its next beacon.

If a node S has either created a data packet itself or needs to forward data from other nodes, it switches on its radio and waits for beacon messages. Upon reception of a beacon, S decides whether to send its data packet depending on the path cost metric contained in the beacon. If the beacon's sender R offers a suitable cost, i.e., it is closer to the sink, S transmits its data packet after a small random back-off (at most T_{hld}). Successful packet reception is acknowledged by R through a beacon addressed to the data sender. Upon reception of the acknowledging beacon, S switches off its radio, if there are no more packets, or continues transmitting further packets to R. Acknowledging beacons are overheard by all nearby nodes with data to send and thus continue to serve their purpose as invitations to send data. The random back-off before packet transmissions is used to prevent collisions, should there be more than one node with data to send. If S overhears a data packet to R (during its back-off), it aborts its sending process and waits for the next beacon. Finally, acknowledging beacons are also used to maintain the path cost metric of each node. In case the hop count metric is being used to describe the path cost, this means that a node adapts its distance to the lowest value in its vicinity plus one. To cope with link failure and changing network topology, a node resets its distance metric to a large value, if it does not receive an appropriate beacon to forward its data within a predefined time interval. In summary, ORiNoCo builds a tree-like routing structure that relies on a path cost metric to ensure that messages are only relayed towards the sink. Instead of maintaining static routes, however, each node opportunistically forwards data to any node that is closer to the sink. ORiNoCo thus has a better response to changing channel qualities and does not require nodes to maintain routing state information locally.

3 RoCoCo: Combining Opportunistic Data Collection and Control Command Multicasting

Extending a data collection protocol by means to transfer control messages from the sink to data collecting nodes poses a number of challenges. Especially as our primary objective is to retain the collection protocol's low power consumption, avoiding the energy overhead introduced by additional packet transmissions is of utmost importance. We thus present in this section how the newly introduced RoCoCo data fields are symbiotically combined with existing messages.

3.1 Destination Addressing

By convention, the sink is the final destination for all data packets in collection WSNs. Control messages, in contrast, are emitted by the sink and addressed to one or more nodes in the network. A first required step towards the distribution of a control command is thus the specification of its intended recipients. Existing protocols only support addressing a single node [29] or all nodes in the network [16,17]. We, however, argue that subsets of a WSN (e.g., nodes fitted with certain sensor types, boards of a certain hardware revision, or spatially co-located devices) may also be recipients for an emitted control command. We hence specifically design RoCoCo such that control messages can be addressed to a multicast receiver set. Depending on the number of entries, however, the set can potentially grow very large. Additionally, for WSN operating systems without dynamic memory allocation, a worst-case amount of memory must be allocated when growing lists of destination node identifiers need to be accommodated. The usage of a memory structure with constant overhead is thus inevitable to cater for the scalability to networks with a large number of nodes. Hence, we have chosen to store the set of recipient addresses for each control message in a Bloom filter [3]. The use of Bloom filters also represents the major difference to other WSN routing schemes[1], because it eliminates the need to maintain dynamically expanding lists of routable destinations.

Due to the constant memory demand of Bloom filters (BFs), the required buffers can be statically allocated, which strongly contributes to their performance on embedded systems. Because an infinite number of entries can be added to a BF, they also fulfill the requirement for message multicasting. Only the risk of false positives due to their probabilistic nature represents a downside of their usage. This potentially leads to situations in which a node may receive and execute a command although it was not among the intended recipients. As the BF is populated at the sink, where the identities of all data collecting nodes are implicitly known from the data collection, however, false positives can be detected before the command has been emitted. Details about the implementation and dimensioning of the Bloom filters used in RoCoCo are provided in Sec. 4.1, where we also analyze the introduced energy overhead.

3.2 Command Definition

Once a control message has reached its destinations, the action to take must be determined. To achieve fast reaction times, we have decided in favor of storing command identifiers within the control message. For this purpose, a field of one byte has been added to each control message, for which we have defined an initial configuration, including, e.g., commands to change the sampling rate. Please note that RoCoCo is not bound to the one byte limit for the command fields and can easily accommodate larger command definition fields. As a result of mapping the range of commands to internal functions, commands from the defined set can be immediately executed upon reception of a control message. For the transfer of larger command payloads, a reserved command identifier prompts the receiving nodes to fetch the actual command data from the sink.

3.3 Duplicate Detection

Due to the fluctuating channel qualities in WSNs, multicast control messages may reach the same node twice or even more often. However, some commands (e.g., requests to transfer a node's complete history of collected data) should

---

[1] With the exception of our previous work CBFR [21] and Duquennoy et al.'s ORPL [8], neither of which however supports multicast addressing.

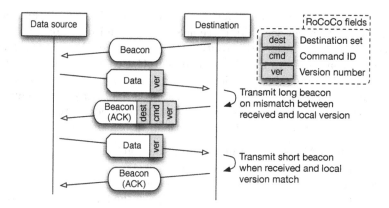

Fig. 2. Visual comparison of ORiNoCo and RoCoCo communication sequences for the transmission of 2 data packets. Fields added by RoCoCo are highlighted.

only be executed once upon the first reception of the control message. In order to avoid the repeated execution of commands, we have thus incorporated a version number into the RoCoCo control messages. This two byte field is incremented whenever the sink has made any changes to at least one of the two aforementioned control fields (destination set and command identifier). As a version number thus inherently relates to a set of destination nodes and the command to execute, it can be used as a shorthand form to refer to these fields. As a result, RoCoCo uses version numbers not only as a means to avoid the duplicate execution of commands, but also to identify if a node in the network holds a newer/older command and thus needs updating. As version numbers are assigned by the sink, their consistency throughout the network is guaranteed.

3.4 RoCoCo Messages

As highlighted above, we assume a WSN in which data collection plays a major role, whereas the dissemination of control commands happens significantly less frequently. Our primary design goal has thus been to integrate the routing information fields described above into ORiNoCo in a way that retained its ultra low-power operation. As a result, RoCoCo leverages ORiNoCo's existing periodic beacon and data messages in a synergetic fashion instead of defining its own message types. As follows, we describe RoCoCo's modifications to the existing packets, that result in no additional overhead on regular beacon transmissions and only a single field added to each data packet.

Extended Beacon Messages. Beacons are being sent by potential packet receivers and both serve as invitations to send as well as acknowledgments for previous data transmissions. We thus leverage them in order to disseminate control messages into the network by means of the three control message fields described above. By default, however, these optional fields are not part of transmitted beacons; beacon sizes thus are unchanged in comparison to ORiNoCo.

Only when sender and receiver of a data message carry different versions of their routing information (cf. Sec. 3.5), these fields are transmitted in order to update the receiving node with the latest routing information. For the sake of clarity, we term the beacon messages that bear none of RoCoCo's newly introduced fields (destination set, command identifier, version number) as *short beacons*. We refer to beacons that contain these three entries as *long beacons*. To enable the receiver to interpret the beacons correctly, a flag was added to the previously existing ORiNoCo beacon flags field to distinguish beacon types.

Extended Data Messages. Similar to the beacons, the main objective when modifying the second-most frequently used message type, i.e., data messages, was to keep the introduced overhead small. In addition to the application-defined payload, RoCoCo thus only relies on the version of the local routing information to be transmitted along with data packets. All data packets have been augmented by the version field that identifies the current routing information version of their sender. The data recipient is thus implicitly able to detect whether its communication partner has outdated routing information. If this is the case, a long acknowledgment beacon can be easily used to update the data source to the current routing version. In case both devices share the same version of the routing information, the data message is acknowledged using a short beacon.

Command Confirmation Messages. Finally, we added a new message type, allowing nodes to acknowledge to the sink that they have received and executed a command. This *confirmation* message is a regular data packet and contains the control message version number.

3.5   Summary: RoCoCo vs. ORiNoCo Communication Flow

In Fig. 2, we visually compare the communication flows of ORiNoCo and RoCoCo. While ORiNoCo would only transmit the contents shown in black and white, the fields newly added by RoCoCo and required for the control command multicasting are highlighted. The operation annotation on the right-hand side represents the comparison between the received and node's local version. After the first data transmission, the destination has detected a mismatch between its local and the received version, such that the returned acknowledgment beacon is augmented by the control command data. Subsequently transmitted data packets reflect the newest version number, thus the destination only transmits short acknowledging beacons for all successive packet transmissions. Direct neighbors of the sink hence receive the updated routing information as soon as they have transmitted a packet (cf. Sec. 2.1). Still, consistent with the opportunistic nature of the data collection, we need to point out at this point that there is no guaranteed time bound for a control command to reach its destination.

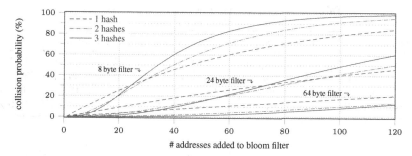

Fig. 3. Collision probability when adding a further node address to the BF

4   Evaluation

We conduct practical evaluations of RoCoCo in order to prove both its ultra low-power operation and its potential to route control messages to sets of nodes.

4.1   Bloom Filter Dimensioning and Beaconing Energy Consumption

In RoCoCo, we calculate the hash functions according to Bob Jenkins' Integer hashing[2]. In case multiple hash functions are being used, the input data is combined with index of the hash function (similar to the notion of a cryptographic salt) prior to hashing. Bob Jenkins' hash has particularly been chosen because of its speed and its minimal resource demand on motes [21]. In order to add a destination address to the BF, we take the output of each hash function modulo the size of the Bloom filter and set the resulting bit offsets in the BF.

As BFs are present in all long beacon messages, their length has an immediate impact on the protocol's energy consumption. Choosing small BF sizes thus seems desirable to minimize the energetic overhead, however, it simultaneously increases the risk of false positives. In contrast, larger BFs increase the size of long beacons and thus inherently incur a higher energy demand for their transmission. We hence analyze the tradeoff between BF size and the energy demand for its transmission. To this end, we determine the likeliness of collisions by inserting 120 sequential 16-bit node addresses into Bloom filters of 8, 24, and 64 bytes in size. In the experiment, we vary the number of hash functions from 1 to 3. The averaged collision results for 50,000 runs of the experiment with different initial addresses are shown in Fig. 3. It can be observed that the usage of a single hash function has a higher probability of collisions when a small number of addresses are inserted into the filter. At the same time, however, a larger number of hash functions leads to more collisions when more elements are inserted into the BF. A tradeoff for both the filter size and the number of hash functions thus needs to be found depending on the application's requirements.

The number of nodes expected in the network and the permitted degree of false positives are, however, not the only criteria used for dimensioning the BF.

---

[2] Available at http://burtleburtle.net/bob/hash/integer.html

Table 1. Energy demand of beacon transmissions

BF size	Energy	Overhead	BF size	Energy	Overhead	BF size	Energy	Overhead
none	155.4 µJ	reference	16 bytes	231.2 µJ	48.7 %	32 bytes	326.5 µJ	110.1 %
4 bytes	181.3 µJ	16.7 %	20 bytes	249.7 µJ	60.6 %	40 bytes	369.2 µJ	137.5 %
8 bytes	199.4 µJ	28.3 %	24 bytes	275.9 µJ	77.5 %	48 bytes	413.2 µJ	165.8 %
12 bytes	224.4 µJ	44.3 %	28 bytes	295.7 µJ	90.3 %	64 bytes	433.5 µJ	179.0 %

Choosing its size also depends on the allowed energy consumption that is incurred by transmitting larger routing information packets. We have thus measured the energy demand to transmit Bloom filters of different sizes, and show the results in Table 1. All measurements were collected by means of a Hitex Power-Scale [12] unit and represent the mean energy consumption as determined from three to five packet transmissions each. The table confirms that the transmission of filters has a direct impact on the energy demand over regular short beacons, with Bloom filters of 64 bytes almost tripling the beaconing energy demand.

4.2 Testbed Evaluation Setup

For all testbed experiments, we have used the following parameter set unless stated otherwise. Each node created collection data packets at an interval of 1 min. The time of the first packet was randomly chosen within the first 1 min after node reboot to simulate the behavior of an asynchronously started and operated network. Buffering queues were installed on each node with a length of 30 packets to cater for intermittent disconnection of nodes in the network due to bad radio conditions, or when incoming packets needed to be buffered before forwarding. Unless congestion occurred, collection data were thus generally sent during the next transmission opportunity. On the data collecting nodes, the mean sleep interval T_{slp} has been set to 750 ms with a random variation of 10 %. In order to achieve higher delivery, the sink has been configured to provide opportunities to receive data (by sending beacons) every 125 ms. For all nodes, we used a waiting time of $T_{hld} = 8$ ms. We employed the hop count as path cost metric and enabled the duplicate detection built into ORiNoCo.

We conducted our experiments on WiseBed (Lübeck site) [6]: This testbed is comprised of 54 TelosB nodes, numbered from 0 to 70, with each fourth address unallocated and 36 functioning nodes at the time of evaluation. Due to the size of this testbed, we have used a Bloom filter of 8 bytes in size. In all experiments, the sink issued a new command every 10 min. In order to study command and confirmation success rates and delays with an equal number of commands sent to each node, the sink always added all nodes to the BF. We conducted three experiments with different transmission powers (0 dBm, −7 dBm, and −15 dBm) to study the impact of connectivity, network depth, and density. Each experiment was run for at least 20 h, equivalent to 120 commands issued by the sink.

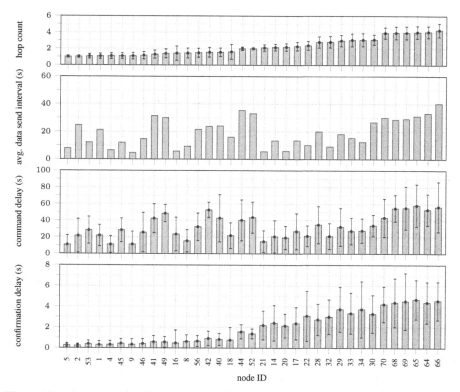

Fig. 4. Command and confirmation delay for $-7\,\mathrm{dBm}$ transmission power. Nodes are ordered by average hop count. The figure also shows the average data (collection data and confirmations) send interval. Error bars indicate the single standard deviation.

4.3 Command and Confirmation Delays

A crucial measure for control systems is the reaction time, or command delay, of a node. By design (of RoCoCo), a node can only receive updated beacons when it has data to send and when (at least one of) its neighbors has already received the update. Therefore, the command delay to a node depends on several factors, of which the most important ones are (1) the data send interval of a node (i.e., its traffic rate), (2) its distance to the sink (in hops), and (3) the command delay to its neighboring nodes that are closer to the sink (i.e., its potential parents).

A detailed study is presented in Fig. 4. It shows the general trend that nodes with a similar data send interval (second row) exhibit a similar command delay (third row). Note that the data send interval may be smaller than 1 min (cf. Sec. 4.2), because nodes also forward (send) remote data. Data send intervals and, hence, command delay are highly topology-dependent. The figure also indicates an impact of the distance to the sink (first row) on the command delay. For nodes close to the sink, however, the data send interval is the dominating factor; e.g., compare nodes 1 and 4. However, the figure reveals exceptional behavior, e.g., nodes 2 and 53 have an equal hop count and a similar command

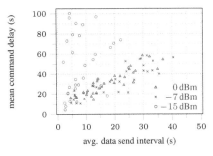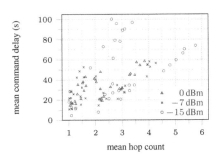

Fig. 5. Effect of network density on the relationship of command delay vs. send interval and hop count, respectively

delay, yet their send intervals differ by a factor of almost two. This is due to asynchronous packet creation among all nodes (cf. Sec. 4.2) and more likely for nodes with low traffic. In contrast, the confirmation delay is mainly affected by the hop count, as confirmations are sent as regular collection data packets. Variations stem from link qualities and the number of neighbors per node. Results for the two experiments with different transmission power settings are similar.

Figure 5 analyzes the impact of network density. For dense networks (0 dBm), hop counts are lower while send intervals are longer, because shorter paths result in less traffic per node. For sparse networks (−15 dBm), hop counts are higher while send intervals are shorter, because longer paths result in more traffic per node. As a consequence, the spread of command delay is higher for sparse networks. However, some nodes (those close to the sink with a high traffic load) achieve extremely low command delays, whereas nodes with high distance to the sink are faced with longer command delays.

Next, we consider the command execution confirmation that is sent whenever a node has received a control message. As this confirmation travels in the usual direction (i.e., where all collected data flows) and represents an individual packet, its collection is considerably faster than the distribution of command messages in many cases. We assessed the round-trip time from the time when the sink issues a new command (i.e., it updates the Bloom filter) and finally receives the confirmation. For dense networks (0 dBm) the round-trip time is very close to the command delay. Due to the low hop count and the high number of potential parents, confirmations are reliably and quickly transported to the sink. On the contrary, the round-trip time may considerably deviate from the command delay in sparse networks, where long paths and few potential parents exist. This is supported by Fig. 6, which portrays the fraction of the round-trip time (RTT) caused by the confirmation. For the dense network setup, this value stayed below 14% in all cases, while it exceeded 56% in ten cases for the sparse network (not shown in the figure).

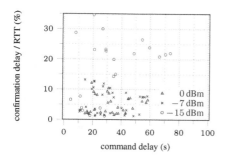
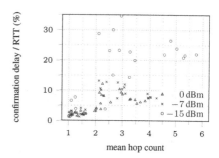

Fig. 6. Effect of network density on round-trip time vs. command delay and hop count

Table 2. Average node power consumption for RoCoCo and existing protocols

TX power	CTP	CTP/Drip	CTP/DIP	CTP/DHV	ORiNoCo	RoCoCo
0 dBm	2.0 mW	3.9 mW	2.0 mW	4.5 mW	1.4 mW	1.4 mW
−15 dBm	1.6 mW	3.8 mW	2.0 mW	4.5 mW	1.4 mW	1.4 mW

4.4   Command Success Rates and Energy Penalty

To assess the quality of command dissemination in RoCoCo, we analyzed the success rates of command and confirmation reception. For the former, we calculated the percentage of received command messages (regardless of their destination) per node. For the testbed experiments with 0 dBm and −7 dBm, all commands and confirmations were received. For the experiment with −15 dBm, the command reception rates of all nodes range from 96% to 100% with the exception of a single node with only 90%. The percentage of command confirmations received at the sink is between 99% and 100%.

We also assessed the energy consumption penalty of RoCoCo vs. ORiNoCo by analyzing the percentile of long beacons compared to the overall number of beacons. The per-node percentile ranges from 0.1% to 1.5%. Across the entire network, the percentile of long beacons is between 0.2% and 0.4%. For a Bloom filter size of 8 bytes this equals an additional energy expenditure of less than 0.11% across the entire WSN and of less than 0.42% per node. We did not analyze the additional energy consumption incurred by the extra version field in data packets, because the impact of data packet length is minor compared to the energy consumption due to waiting for a beacon. This, however, represents the main source of energy consumption of asynchronous low-power MAC protocols.

4.5   Comparison against Existing Protocols

In order to put RoCoCo's energy demand into perspective, we have compared it against a combination of the well-known data collection protocol CTP [9] and the dissemination protocols Drip [26], DIP [17], and DHV [7]. We used the publicly available TinyOS implementations of these protocols and enabled the

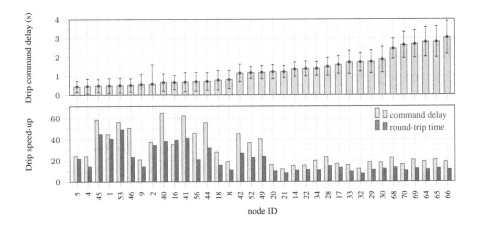

Fig. 7. Speedup of command delay and round-trip time of CTP/Drip vs. RoCoCo (−7 dBm power). Nodes are ordered by command delay (upper row) of Drip.

low-power listening MAC. The protocols were configured to use the same parameters as stated in Sec. 4.2, however with the command creation rate increased to one update per minute. The experiments were run in a one-sink one-node configuration, and the average energy consumption of the data collecting node has been practically determined for each protocol combination. The results are shown in Table 2 for transmission power settings of 0 dBm and −15 dBm. Besides highlighting that RoCoCo does not increase the energy demand of ORiNoCo measurably, the results also confirm that the RoCoCo node requires 30% less energy than the next most energy-efficient approach that combines collection and dissemination (CTP/DIP).

The combination of CTP/Drip was also run on the testbed, and statistics about the success rates plus command and confirmation delays were collected. While success rates of distributed commands are similar, CTP causes a lower success rate of confirmations; e.g., the latter ranges from 83% to 99% for the experiment with 0 dBm. It is even lower in the other experiments. Moreover, Fig. 7 shows the delays for an experiment with a transmission power of −7 dBm. In a few cases, CTP/Drip leads to a speedup factor in excess of 25 for nodes with a low command delay and close distance to the sink (primarily one- and two-hop neighbors). This speedup reduces to a factor of 10 to 25 for nodes farther away from the sink. Round-trip speedups are also around a factor of 10 for these nodes. Results for the other two experiments are similar. While the delay of command confirmations is similar between CTP/Drip and RoCoCo, command delay (and hence round-trip time) is higher for RoCoCo by design. However, note that RoCoCo has deliberately been designed to accept an increased command delay in favor of its low-power operation, while its delays (on the order of seconds) are still practical for many WSNs.

5 Related Work

Data collection in WSNs is predominantly based on static routing trees rooted at the sink (e.g., MintRoute [30]). With the introduction of opportunistic data collection, however, the restriction that each node may at most have one single parent has been removed. This possibility to choose another node for forwarding data has been shown to bear the potential for improving data throughput and reducing energy consumption [20,2]. ORW is an opportunistic data collection algorithm for sensor networks [15] and in some aspects similar to RoCoCo, although there are notable differences. While RoCoCo does not track information about its neighborhood explicitly, ORW relies on estimates such as the number of potential parents and link qualities. Most other approaches also rely on assessing link qualities, a difficult challenge in sensor networks due to the instability and low predictability of low-power wireless links. Alizai et al. hence suggest to exploit unstable, but bursty, links in [1]. Their proposed algorithm improves the performance of multi-hop routing, although an additional energy expenditure for link-quality estimation is still required.

In the domain of multicasting in WSNs, Sheth et al. presented the VLM^2 system in [23], which caters for the routing of multicast messages by maintaining stateful route information on intermediate nodes. Similarly, Chun and Tang proposed a multicasting mechanism in [5] that relies on message flooding and subsequent local matching against existing multicast group IDs. In both solutions, nodes can only subscribe to pre-defined multicast groups; a dynamic composition of multicast groups is not possible. In [24] and [22], the application of multicasting in IPv6-enabled sensor networks has been presented. The primary goal of these works is to enable nodes to join and leave IPv6 multicast groups during system operation. Neither the resulting energy demand nor the incurred routing overhead are discussed in detail, and thus their applicability in WSNs with limited energy budgets is unclear. While aforementioned approaches are primarily based on the composition of multicast groups, a number of contributions have analyzed the optimum structure of the routing tree in order to achieve delivery of messages at the smallest possible overhead ([25,31,14,10]). The papers however exclusively focus on routing when group memberships are known and provide no support for the dynamic creation and adaptation of groups.

Marchiori and Han use Bloom filters in [18] in order to route multicast messages without previous computation of the optimum route. While their PIM-WSN protocol is optimized for fast message delivery, it does not comprise a data collection component. Furthermore, it does not specifically strive for low energy consumption, rendering it inapplicable for energy-constrained data collection applications. Likewise, Heszberger et al. specify routing information by means of BFs [11], but do not combine it with a data collection protocol. Only recently, Duquennoy et al. have also presented an opportunistic point-to-point routing extension to RPL [29] in [8]. Similar to RoCoCo, their solution relies on Bloom filters to individually address nodes in the IPv6 space. In contrast to RoCoCo, however, ORPL does not support addressing a message to multiple recipients.

6   Conclusion

Due to the tightly limited energy budget of WSN nodes, ultra low-power protocols are essential to achieve long operation times. While a number of such protocols have been proposed for data collection, emitting control commands to the network is beyond their capabilities. We have thus presented RoCoCo, a lightweight extension to ultra low-power data collection that allows the sink to route control messages to sets of nodes. The fusion of data collection and control command multicasting enables administrators to configure and control the WSN during runtime. RoCoCo relies on Bloom filters to define the destination set and can thus operate in both small and large networks without any modifications. Despite its opportunistic nature, practical testbed experimentation has shown that RoCoCo achieves command dissemination success rates of 96–100% with command delays in the order of tens of seconds, even in a 36-node setting. While the observed command delays were higher than with CTP/Drip, the additional energy expenditure incurred by its application was below 0.11%. RoCoCo thus offers control command multicasting while maintaining the ultra low-power operation of the underlying ORiNoCo collection protocol.

Acknowledgments. The authors would like to thank Daniel Burgstahler, Till Schmitt, and Daniel Bimschas for their support.

References

1. Alizai, M.H., Landsiedel, O., Bitsch Link, J.A., Götz, S., Wehrle, K.: Bursty Traffic Over Bursty Links. In: SenSys (2009)
2. Biswas, S., Morris, R.: ExOR: Opportunistic Multi-Hop Routing for Wireless Networks. In: SIGCOMM. pp. 133–144 (2005)
3. Bloom, B.H.: Space/Time Trade-offs in Hash Coding with Allowable Errors. Communications of the ACM 13(7) (1970)
4. Burri, N., von Rickenbach, P., Wattenhofer, R.: Dozer: Ultra-Low Power Data Gathering in Sensor Networks. In: IPSN (2007)
5. Chun, W., Tang, W.: Multicasting in Wireless Sensor Networks. In: NGNCON (2006)
6. Coulson, G., Porter, B., Chatzigiannakis, I., Koninis, C., Fischer, S., Pfisterer, D., Bimschas, D., Braun, T., Hurni, P., Anwander, M., Wagenknecht, G., Fekete, S.P., Kröller, A., Baumgartner, T.: Flexible Experimentation in Wireless Sensor Networks. Communications of the ACM 55(1) (2012)
7. Dang, T., Bulusu, N., Feng, W.-c., Park, S.: DHV: A code consistency maintenance protocol for multi-hop wireless sensor networks. In: Roedig, U., Sreenan, C.J. (eds.) EWSN 2009. LNCS, vol. 5432, pp. 327–342. Springer, Heidelberg (2009)
8. Duquennoy, S., Landsiedel, O., Voigt, T.: Let the Tree Bloom: Scalable Opportunistic Routing with ORPL. In: SenSys (2013)
9. Gnawali, O., Fonseca, R., Jamieson, K., Moss, D., Levis, P.: Collection Tree Protocol. In: SenSys (2009)
10. Han, K., Liu, Y., Luo, J.: Duty-Cycle-Aware Minimum-Energy Multicasting in Wireless Sensor Networks. IEEE/ACM Transactions on Networking 21(3) (2013)

11. Heszberger, Z., Tapolcai, J., Gulyas, A., Biro, J., Zahemszky, A., Ho, P.H.: Adaptive Bloom Filters for Multicast Addressing. In: HSN (2011)

12. Hitex Development Tools GmbH: Hitex PowerScale with ACM Probe, http://www.hitex.com/ (last access on September 10, 2014)

13. Hu, W., Tran, V.N., Bulusu, N., Chou, C.T., Jha, S., Taylor, A.: The Design and Evaluation of a Hybrid Sensor Network for Cane-toad Monitoring. In: IPSN (2005)

14. Hwang, S.F., Lu, K.H., Su, Y.Y., Hsien, C.S., Dow, C.R.: Hierarchical Multicast in Wireless Sensor Networks with Mobile Sinks. Wireless Communications and Mobile Computing 12(1) (2012)

15. Landsiedel, O., Ghadimi, E., Duquennoy, S., Johansson, M.: Low Power, Low Delay: Opportunistic Routing meets Duty Cycling. In: IPSN (2012)

16. Levis, P., Patel, N., Culler, D., Shenker, S.: Trickle: A Self-Regulating Algorithm for Code Propagation and Maintenance in Wireless Sensor Networks. In: NSDI (2004)

17. Lin, K., Levis, P.: Data Discovery and Dissemination with DIP. In: IPSN (2008)

18. Marchiori, A., Han, Q.: PIM-WSN: Efficient Multicast for IPv6 Wireless Sensor Networks. In: WoWMoM (2011)

19. Martinez, K., Ong, R., Hart, J.: Glacsweb: A Sensor Network for Hostile Environments. In: SECON (2004)

20. Pasztor, B., Musolesi, M., Mascolo, C.: Opportunistic Mobile Sensor Data Collection with SCAR. In: MASS (2007)

21. Reinhardt, A., Morar, O., Santini, S., Zöller, S., Steinmetz, R.: CBFR: Bloom Filter Routing with Gradual Forgetting for Tree-structured Wireless Sensor Networks with Mobile Nodes. In: WoWMoM (2012)

22. Sá Silva, J., Camilo, T., Pinto, P., Ruivo, R., Rodrigues, A., Gaudêncio, F., Boavida, F.: Multicast and IP Multicast Support in Wireless Sensor Networks. Journal of Networks 3(3) (2008)

23. Sheth, A., Shucker, B., Han, R.: VLM^2: A Very Lightweight Mobile Multicast System for Wireless Sensor Networks. In: WCNC (2003)

24. Silva, R., Sá Silva, J., Simek, M., Boavida, F.: Why Should Multicast be Used in WSNs. In: ISWCS (2008)

25. Su, L., Ding, B., Yang, Y., Abdelzaher, T.F., Cao, G., Hou, J.C.: oCast: Optimal Multicast Routing Protocol for Wireless Sensor Networks. In: ICNP (2009)

26. Tolle, G., Culler, D.: Design of an Application-Cooperative Management System for Wireless Sensor Networks. In: EWSN (2005)

27. Unterschütz, S., Renner, C., Turau, V.: Opportunistic, Receiver-Initiated Data-Collection Protocol. In: EWSN (2012)

28. Werner-Allen, G., Johnson, J., Ruiz, M., Lees, J., Welsh, M.: Monitoring Volcanic Eruptions with a Wireless Sensor Network. In: EWSN (2005)

29. Winter, T., Thubert, P., Brandt, A., Hui, J., Kelsey, R., Levis, P., Pister, K., Struik, R., Vasseur, J., Alexander, R.: RPL: IPv6 Routing Protocol for Low-Power and Lossy Networks. RFC 6550 (2012)

30. Woo, A., Tong, T., Culler, D.: Taming the Underlying Challenges of Reliable Multihop Routing in Sensor Networks. In: SenSys (2003)

31. Wu, S., Candan, K.S.: GMP: Distributed Geographic Multicast Routing in Wireless Sensor Networks. In: ICDCS (2006)

Implementation and Experimentation of Industrial Wireless Sensor-Actuator Network Protocols

Mo Sha[1,2,*], Dolvara Gunatilaka[1,*], Chengjie Wu[1], and Chenyang Lu[1]

[1] Cyber-Physical Systems Laboratory, Washington University in St. Louis,
St. Louis, MO, USA
[2] National Renewable Energy Laboratory, Golden, CO, USA

Abstract. Wireless sensor-actuator networks (WSANs) offer an appealing communication technology for process automation applications. However, such networks pose unique challenges due to their critical demands on reliability and real-time performance. While industrial WSANs have received attention in the research community, most published results to date focused on the theoretical aspects and were evaluated based on simulations. There is a critical need for experimental research on this important class of WSANs. We developed an experimental testbed by implementing several key network protocols of WirelessHART, an open standard for WSANs widely adopted in the process industries, including multi-channel TDMA with shared slots at the MAC layer and reliable graph routing supporting path redundancy. We then performed a comparative study of the two alternative routing approaches adopted by WirelessHART, namely source routing and graph routing. Our study shows that graph routing leads to significant improvement over source routing in term of worst-case reliability, at the cost of longer latency and higher energy consumption. It is therefore important to employ graph routing algorithms specifically designed to optimize latency and energy efficiency.

1 Introduction

Process automation is crucial for process industries such as oil refineries, chemical plants, and factories. Today's industry mainly relies on wired networks to monitor and control their production processes. Cables are used for connecting sensors and forwarding sensor readings to a control room where a controller sends commands to actuators. However, these wired systems have significant drawbacks. It is very costly to deploy and maintain such wired systems, since numerous cables have to be installed and maintained, which often requires laying cables underground in harsh environments. This severely complicates effort to reconfigure systems to accommodate new production process requirements.

---

* Mo Sha started this research project while at Washington University in St. Louis and currently works at National Renewable Energy Laboratory. The first two authors contributed equally to this work.

T. Abdelzaher et al. (Eds.): EWSN 2015, LNCS 8965, pp. 234–241, 2015.

WSAN technology is appealing to process automation applications because it does not require any wired infrastructure. WSANs can be used to easily and inexpensively retrofit existing industrial facilities without the need to run dedicated cabling for communication and power. IEEE 802.15.4 based WSANs are designed to operate at a low data rate and low power, making them a good fit for industrial automation applications where battery life is often important.

Industrial WSANs pose unique challenges due to their critical demands on reliable and real-time communication. Violation of their reliability and real-time requirements may result in plant shutdowns, safety hazard, or economic/environmental impacts.

To meet the stringent requirements on reliability and predictable real-time performance, industrial WSAN standards such as WirelessHART [15] made a set of unique network design choices.

- The network should support both source routing and reliable graph routing: the source routing provides a single route for each data flow, whereas the graph routing provides multiple redundant routes based on a routing graph.
- The network should also adopt a multi-channel Time Division Multiple Access (TDMA), employing both dedicated and shared time slots, at the MAC layer on top of the IEEE 802.15.4 physical layer. Only one transmission is scheduled in a dedicated slot, whereas multiple transmissions can share a same shared slot. The packet transmission occurs immediately in a dedicated slot, while a CSMA/CA scheme is used for transmissions in a shared slot.

Recently, there has been increasing interest in developing new network algorithms and analysis to support industrial applications. However, there is a critical need for experimental testbeds for validating and evaluating network research on industrial WSANs. Without sufficient experimental evaluation, industry consequently has shown a marked reluctance to embrace new solutions.

To meet the need for experimental research on WSANs, we have developed an experimental testbed for studying and evaluating WSAN protocols. Our testbed supports a suite of key network protocols specific to the WirelessHART standard and a set of tools for managing wireless experiments. We then present a comparative study of the two alternative routing approaches adopted by WirelessHART, namely source routing and graph routing. Specifically, we investigate the tradeoff among reliability, latency, and energy consumption under the different routing approaches. This study leads to our insight on the development of resilient industrial WSANs that graph routing leads to significant improvement over source routing in term of worst-case reliability, at the cost of longer latency and higher energy consumption. It is therefore important to employ graph routing algorithms specifically designed to optimize latency and energy efficiency.

The rest of the paper is organized as follows. Section 2 describes our implementation of WirelessHART protocols and Section 3 presents our experimentation of source and graph routing. Section 4 reviews related work and Section 5 concludes the paper.

2   Implementation of WirelessHART Protocols

We have implemented a WSAN system comprising a network manager running on a server and a protocol stack running on TinyOS 2.1.2 and TelosB motes. Our network manager implements a route generator and a schedule generator. The route generator is responsible for generating source routes or graph routes based on the collected network topology. We use Dijkstra's shortest-path algorithm[1] to generate routes for source routing and follow the algorithm proposed in [6] to generate the reliable graphs. The schedule generator uses rate monotonic scheduling algorithm [7] to generate transmission schedules.

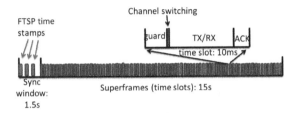

Fig. 1. Time frame format of RT-MAC

Our protocol stack adopts the CC2420x radio driver [2] as the radio core, which provides an open-source implementation of IEEE 802.15.4 physical layer in TinyOS [1] operating over TI CC2420 radios. The CC2420x radio stack takes care of the low-level details of transmitting and receiving packets through the radio hardware. On top of the radio core, we have developed a multi-channel TDMA MAC protocol, *RT-MAC*, which implements the key features of WirelessHART's MAC protocol. As shown in Figure 1, RT-MAC divides the time into 10 ms slots following the WirelessHART standards and reserves a **Sync** window (1.5 s) in every 1650 slots. Flooding Time Synchronization Protocol (FTSP) [8] is executed during the Sync window to synchronize the clocks of all wireless devices over the entire network. Our micro-benchmark experiment shows that a FTSP's time stamp packet can finish the traversing of the entire 55-node testbed within 500 ms. Therefore, RT-MAC configures the FTSP to flood three time stamps with 500 ms intervals over the network in each Sync window to adjust the local clocks of all devices to a global time source, which is the local time of the mote attached to the network manager. The time window following the Sync window consists of recurring superframes (a series of time slots) and idle intervals. We reserve 2 ms of guard time in the beginning of each slot to accommodate the clock synchronization error and channel switching delay, since our micro-benchmark experiments show that more than 95% of field devices over the entire network

---

[1] An alternative is to use expected transmission count (ETX) as the routing metric. In practice, a shortest path is usually close to a minimum-ETX path in a WirelessHART network because of link blacklisting using a high threshold (e.g., 80%).

can be synchronized with errors less than 2 ms and channel switching takes only a few microseconds to write to the registers. The rest of field devices may disconnect from the network due to larger clock synchronization errors, but they will be reconnected in the next Sync window after they catch the new time stamps generated by FTSP. RT-MAC supports both dedicated and shared slots. In a dedicated slot, only one sender is allowed to transmit and the packet transmission occurs immediately after the guard time. In a shared slot, more than one sender can attempt to transmit and these senders contend for the channel using CSMA/CA.

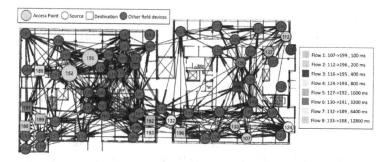

Fig. 2. Locations of access points and field devices. The bigger yellow circles denote the access points which communicate with the network manager running on the server through the wired backbone network. The other circles and squares denote the field devices. The source and destination of a flow are represented as a circle and a square, respectively. The pair of source and destination of a same flow uses the same color. The period of each flow is randomly selected from the range of $2^{0\sim7}$ seconds, which falls within the common range of periods used in process industries.

3   Experimentation of Source and Graph Routing

Our WSAN testbed includes a four-tier hardware architecture that consists of field devices, microservers, a server, and clients. The field devices in the testbed are 55 TelosB motes [4], a widely used wireless embedded platform integrating a TI MSP430 microcontroller and a TI CC2420 radio compatible with the IEEE 802.15.4 standard. A subset of the field devices can be designated as access points in an experiment. The field devices and access points form a multihop wireless mesh network running WSAN protocols. A key capability of our testbed is a wired backplane network that can be used for managing wireless experiments and measurements without interfering with wireless communication. The back-plane network consists of USB cables and hubs connecting the field devices and microservers which are in turn connected to a server through Ethernet. The microservers are Linksys NSLU2 microservers running Linux. Microservers are responsible for forwarding network management traffic between the field devices and the server. The server runs network management processes, gathers statistics on network behavior, and provides information to system users. The server also serves as a gateway and runs the network manager of the WSAN. The clients are regular computers used by users to manage their wireless experiments and collect data from the experiments through the server and the backbone network.

Following the practice of industrial deployment, the routing algorithms used in our study only consider reliable links with PRR higher than 80%. We use 8 data flows in our experiments. We run our experiments long enough such that each flow can deliver at least 500 packets from its source to its destination. Figure 2 shows the network topology along with a set of flows used in our study. We also repeat our experiments with two other network configurations by varying the location of access points, sources, and destinations.

We conduct a comparative study of the two alternative routing approaches adopted by WirelessHART, namely source routing and graph routing. Specifically, we investigate the tradeoff among reliability, latency, and energy consumption under the different routing approaches. We run two sets of experiments, once with the source routing and once with the graph routing. We repeat the experiments under a clean environment, a noisy environment, and a stress testing environments.

1. Clean: we blacklist the four 802.15.4 channels overlapping with our campus Wi-Fi network and run the experiments on the remaining 802.15.4 channels.
2. Noisy: we run the experiments by configuring the network to use channels 16 to 19, which overlap with our campus Wi-Fi network[2].
3. Stress testing: we run the experiments with channels 16 to 19 under controlled interference, in the form of a laptop and an access point generating 1 Mbps UDP traffic over Wi-Fi channel 6, which overlaps with 802.15.4 channels 16 to 19.

We use the packet delivery rate (PDR) as the metric for network reliability. The PDR of a flow is defined as the percentage of packets that are successfully delivered to their destination. Figure 3 compares the network reliability under source routing and graph routing in the three environments. As shown in Figure 3, under the first network configuration, compared to source routing, graph routing improves the median PDR by a margin of 1.0% (from 0.99 to 1.0), 15.9% (from 0.82 to 0.95), and 21.4% (from 0.70 to 0.85) in the clean, noisy, and stress testing environments, respectively. Graph routing shows similar improvement over source routing under the other two network configurations. More importantly, graph routing delivers a significant improvement in min PDR and achieves a smaller variation of PDR than source routing, which represents a significant advantage in industrial applications that demand predictable performance. The improvements in min PDR are 35.5% and 63.5% in noisy and stress testing, respectively. This result shows that graph routing is indeed more resilient to interference due to route diversity. However, as shown in Figure 4, route diversity incurs a cost in term of latency, with graph routing suffers an average

---

[2] Co-existence of WirelessHART devices and WiFi is common in industrial deployments since WiFi is often used as backhauls to connect multiple WSANs.

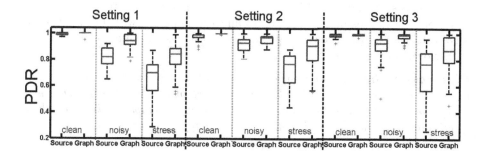

Fig. 3. Box plot of the PDR of source routing and graph routing in the clean, noisy, and stress testing environments. Central mark in box indicates median; bottom and top of box represent the 25th percentile (q_1) and 75th percentile (q_2); crosses indicate outliers ($x > q_2 + 1.5 \cdot (q_2 - q_1)$ or $x < q_1 - 1.5 \cdot (q_2 - q_1)$); whiskers indicate range excluding outliers. Vertical lines delineate three different network configurations.

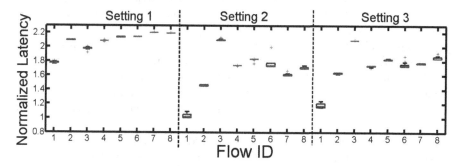

Fig. 4. Box plot of the normalized latency of source routing and graph routing of each flow under graph routing over that under source routing

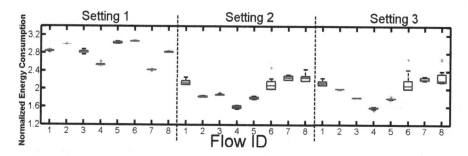

Fig. 5. Box plot of the normalized energy consumption of source routing and graph routing of each flow under graph routing over that under source routing

of 80% increase in end-to-end latency. We also estimate the energy consumption based on timestamps of radio activities and the radio's power consumption in each state. As Figure 5 shows, graph routing consumes an average of 130% more energy over source routing.

Observation: Graph routing leads to significant improvement over source routing in term of worst-case reliability, at the cost of longer latency and higher energy consumption. It is therefore important to employ graph routing algorithms specifically designed to optimize latency and energy efficiency.

4   Related Works

In recent years, there has been increasing interest in studying industrial WSANs. Previous research mostly focused on network algorithms and theoretical analysis. Zhang et al. [17] developed a latency-optimal link scheduling policy and established performance bounds for convergecast in WirelessHART networks. Chraim et al. [3] studied the decentralized sequential hypothesis testing problems for the WirelessHART networks at the theoretical level. Franchino et al. [5] proposed a real-time energy-aware MAC layer protocol. Han et al. [6] presented a graph routing algorithm. Saifullah et al. presented a series of theoretical results on real-time transmission scheduling [13], rate selection for wireless control [12], and delay analysis [14,16]. All these works are based on theoretical analysis and simulation studies. In this paper, we present an experimental study of WSAN protocols on a physical testbed that implements a set of network mechanisms of the WirelessHART standard.

There has been recent work that implemented and evaluated real-time WSN protocols experimentally. Recently, O'donovan et al. [10] developed the GIN-SENG system which uses a WSN to support mission-critical applications in industrial environments. Munir et al. [9] designed a scheduling algorithm that produces latency bounds of the real-time periodic streams and accounts for both link bursts and interference. Pottner et al. [11] designed a scheduling algorithm to meet application requirements in terms of data delivery latency, reliability, and transmission power. While valuable insights can be drawn from those efforts, the novelty of our work lies in its focus on key aspects of the WirelessHART standard such as graph routing that was not studied in earlier work.

5   Conclusion

Industrial WSANs offer a promising technology for process automation while posing unique challenges due to their critical demands on reliable and real-time communication. Complementary to recent research on theoretical aspects of WSAN design, we have implemented a suite of network protocols of the WirelessHART standard in TinyOS and TelosB motes and then empirically studied the tradeoff among reliability, latency, and energy consumption under source and graph routing in a 55-node testbed. Our experimental results show that graph routing leads to significant improvement over source routing in term of worst-case reliability, at the cost of longer latency and higher energy consumption. It is therefore important to employ graph routing algorithms specifically designed to optimize latency and energy efficiency.

Acknowledgments. This work is supported, in part, by NSF through grants 1320921 (NeTS), 1144552 (NeTS) and 1035773 (CPS).

References

1. http://www.tinyos.net/
2. CC2420 radio stack, http://www.tinyos.net/tinyos-2.x/doc/html/tep126.html
3. Chraim, F., Pister, K.: Smart fence: Decentralized sequential hypothesis testing for perimeter security. In: ICST (2013)
4. Crossbow Technology. TelosB mote platform, http://www.xbow.com/Products/Product_pdf_files/Wireless_pdf/TelosB_Datasheet.pdf
5. Franchino, G., Buttazzo, G.: WBuST: A real-time energy-aware MAC layer protocol for wireless embedded systems. In: ETFA (2012)
6. Han, S., Zhu, X., Mok, A., Chen, D., Nixon, M.: Reliable and real-time communication in industrial wireless mesh networks. In: RTAS (2011)
7. Liu, J.W.S.: Real-time systems (2000)
8. Maróti, M., Kusy, B., Simon, G., Lédeczi, Á.: The flooding time synchronization protocol. In: SenSys (2004)
9. Munir, S., Lin, S., Hoque, E., Nirjon, S., Stankovic, J., Whitehouse, K.: Addressing burstiness for reliable communication and latency bound generation in wireless sensor networks. In: IPSN (2010)
10. O'donovan, T., Brown, J., Busching, F., Cardoso, A., Cecilio, J., Do, J., Furtado, P., Gil, P., Jugel, A., Pottner, W.-B., Roedig, U., Silva, J.S., Silva, R., Sreenan, C.J., Vassiliou, V., Wolf, T.V.L., Zinonos, Z.: The ginseng system for wireless monitoring and control: Design and deployment experiences. ACM Transactions on Sensor Networks 10(1) (November 2013)
11. Pottner, W.-B., Seidel, H., Brown, J., Roedig, U., Wolf, L.: Constructing schedules for time-critical data delivery in wireless sensor networks. ACM Transactions on Sensor Networks 10(3) (August 2014)
12. Saifullah, A., Wu, C., Tiwari, P., Xu, Y., Fu, Y., Lu, C., Chen, Y.: Near optimal rate selection for wireless control systems. In: RTAS (2012)
13. Saifullah, A., Xu, Y., Lu, C., Chen, Y.: Real-time scheduling for wirelesshart networks. In: RTSS (2010)
14. Saifullah, A., Xu, Y., Lu, C., Chen, Y.: End-to-end delay analysis for fixed priority scheduling in wirelesshart networks. In: RTAS (2011)
15. WirelessHART (2007), http://www.hartcomm2.org
16. Wu, C., Sha, M., Gunatilaka, D., Saifullah, A., Lu, C., Chen, Y.: Analysis of EDF Scheduling for Wireless Sensor-Actuator Networks. In: IWQoS (2014)
17. Zhang, H., Soldati, P., Johansson, M.: Performance bounds and latency-optimal schedules for convergecast in WirelessHART networks. IEEE Transactions on Wireless Communications 12(6) (June 2013)

Recycling Corrupt Packets over Multiple Hops

Muhammad Hamad Alizai[1], Muhammad Moosa Khattak[1], Dong Han[2], Omprakash Gnawali[2], and Affan A. Syed[3]

[1] University of Engineering and Technology, Peshawar, Pakistan
[2] Department of Computer Science, University of Houston, USA
[3] National University of Computer and Emerging Sciences, Islamabad, Pakistan
{hamad.alizai,moosa.ktk}@uetpeshawar.edu.pk
{donny,gnawali}@cs.uh.edu, affan.syed@nu.edu.pk

Abstract. We propose a Corrupt Packet Recycling (CPR) approach for WSN that processes and forwards partially-corrupt packets over multiple hops without necessitating their complete recovery. We motivate this approach with two insights: address-agnostic routing in WSN can forgive header errors since intermediate nodes know the next hop and the destination; and that payload errors can be either interpolated, due to error-tolerant nature of information in WSN applications, or rectified using spatio-temporal redundancies. CPR, without introducing any transmission overhead, improves information delivery rate by up to $4\times$.

Keywords: error tolerant, multihop wireless, data collection.

1 Introduction

Partially-corrupt packets contain valuable information. Since most corrupt packets have only few symbol-errors [3,11], discarding such packets results in wasteful information loss and reduced network efficiency in terms of reliability, latency, energy and bandwidth. Techniques such as partial-packet recovery [4] and error checksums [5] try to recover corrupt packets at a smaller cost than traditional ARQ but have three limitations: First, they can only repair a small subset of corrupt packets locally (i.e., with multiple copies) [1] discarding others for which bit-by-bit information is not recovered. Second, they introduce undesirable transmission overhead in WSN, e.g., 22-64% for FEC [5] and preamble-header duplication for partial recovery [4]. Third, they operate at PHY and link layers and do not consider the potential for packet recovery over multiple hops.

We propose an error-tolerant approach at the network layer, called CPR (corrupt packet recycling), that *recycles* partially-corrupt packets over multiple hops towards the base station. The term recycling refers to *processing and forwarding corrupt packets without necessitating their complete recovery* at intermediate nodes. CPR achieves this recycling by providing a simple, best-effort service to locally repair header errors while concealing payload errors altogether during multihop communication. As a result, CPR is the first approach (i) that can recycle 100% corrupt data packets[1] received at an intermediate node, (ii) has

---

[1] All network layer data packets that bypass link layer CRC.

T. Abdelzaher et al. (Eds.): EWSN 2015, LNCS 8965, pp. 242–249, 2015.
© Springer International Publishing Switzerland 2015

no transmission overhead, and (iii) and operates at network layer to facilitate multihop operation.

CPR is enabled by two key insights of WSN characteristics: First, *adress-agnostic hierarchical routing* (e.g., collection tree) results in each data packet forwarded to a single or same set of outgoing links. This allows CPR to easily tolerate "header errors" since, once the communication paths are established, each intermediate node antecedently knows the next hop and the destination. Second, we see that the *nature of information in WSN is often error-tolerant*: data bytes are typically a digital quantization of analog signals from potentially inaccurate and heterogeneous sensors. Thus bit-level "payload errors" are often tolerable by WSN applications as compared to TCP/IP based networks where fidelity of content (like files and video) remains essential. For example, in some applications [8, 7, 12], it is useful to receive a packet even if it is corrupt because reception itself could provide information about the sensing activity. Furthermore, base station can utilize state-of-the-art data mining techniques or spatio-temporal redundancies in transmissions (due to dense and overlapping node deployments) to extract meaningful information from erroneous data.

The main goal of CPR is thus to avoid data packet drop "no-matter-what". For this purpose, CPR enables wireless protocols at the network layer to handle corrupt packets in two steps. The first step is *header recovery* using domain knowledge obtained from a history of correct packets from the same source. For example, in a typical collection tree, if the `origin` field in the packet header is undamaged, the packet `sequence-number` can be recovered based on the transmission frequency of previous packets from the same source. The second step is *forwarding* of packet, whose header has been recovered in the first step, to the next hop in the collection tree. However, CPR can also be "stubborn" in the second step, i.e., forward packets even if the header recovery failed to achieve recycling of 100% network-level packets.

Contributions: (i) We motivate and design an error-tolerant approach at the network layer that recycles corrupt packets over multiple hops (Section 2 and 3). (ii) Our preliminary results — up to 4× improvement in information delivery rate — advocate the high utility of CPR for WSN (Section 4).

2   The Need for Recycling Packets in WSN

Figure 1 motivates the need for CPR: the number of partially-corrupt packets varies between < 10% to > 70% on just a single hop, across different deployment conditions. Thus, every recycled packet (i) saves retransmissions and improves latency, energy and bandwidth efficiency, and (ii) delivers valuable information that otherwise is completely lost due to packet drop. We see that a vast majority of WSN applications are indeed tolerant to corruption of individual bytes and thus can benefit from recycling packets over multiple hops. We now argue this breadth of coverage by presenting how the two broad categories of WSN applications benefit from this approach.

Passive Collection Streams is the most common category of WSN applications with a goal to maximize the network lifetime of periodic data collection.

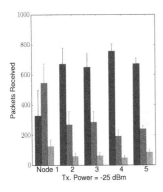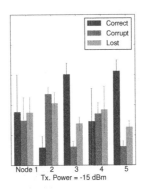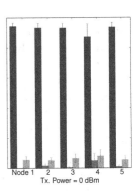

Fig. 1. Average packet reception over five experiments, in each we sent 1000 packets every $128ms$, at five TelosB receiver nodes radially distributed (4.5m) around a sender indoors. The number of corrupt packets (mismatched CRC) vary over different deployment conditions depicted by tx power levels. Lost packets are not notified by the network interface. Error bars represent standard deviation.

However, most practical deployments of WSN, from the Great Duck Island [8] to Volcano deployment [12], report the need to revisit these deployments due to (a) insufficient amount of data collected at sink and (b) reduced network lifetime from excessive radio hardware utilization. CPR can help improve the information delivery rate for these applications while reducing radio activity, thus obviate the need for manual reprovisioning.

Another category of WSN —*Active Event Detection*— actively monitors the environment for an event of interest. These applications mostly remain in a quiescent state, generating none-to-very-little traffic, but have bursts of very critical data generated when an event is detected. We believe that, while the delivery of the actual data (a digitized sensor reading), is important, delivering partially-corrupt packets still conveys meaningful information to the application. Consider a fire-monitoring application that, on event detection, send a much higher rate of packets reporting the intensity of fire at a particular location. From the application perspective, even the increased rate of *possibly corrupt* packet-delivery is a good indication of an alarm condition that can trigger some appropriate response.

An orthogonal benefit in employing an error-tolerant approach becomes evident for WSN deployed in *extreme communication environments*, such as burrows, underwater, and industrial settings. Here, scientists are known to struggle in collecting information [9,7] since most wireless links have poor quality. CPR can utilize such unreliable links which are otherwise rendered useless for packet forwarding. In a DTN based burrow deployment [7], it has been demonstrated that turning off CRC allows efficient neighborhood discovery without imposing correct packet reception.

These examples above motivate the case for recycling corrupt packet in WSN. We now focus on the design of one particular instance of CPR approach to facilitate its implementation in real-world and evaluate its benefits.

3   Designing an Instance of CPR

Using CPR, we can either develop a new routing system or upgrade an existing protocol. Here we focus on the latter to emphasize on the CPR approach itself rather than on protocol development related intricacies. When integrated with existing protocols, the design of CPR is strongly dependent upon the host protocol. Therefore, we first select a host protocol and then detail our customized solution.

3.1   The Host Protocol and Its Header

We use CTP [2], a widely used collection protocol for experimentation, as the host protocol. We revisit each field in the CTP packet header to investigate if it is necessary for each field to be received correctly for successful packet delivery to the collection root. We find that an error in almost all these fields could be ignored or repaired to improve data delivery in the network. In our scheme, a *few* correctly received packets provide enough context to a node to repair these fields in partially-corrupt packets. Unlike single-hop error-tolerant techniques used in protocols such as Refector [10] and UDP Lite [6], our scheme can successfully fix and forward a corrupt packet over multiple wireless hops.

P: Routing pull (1 bit) - *The nodes use the P bit to request routing information from other nodes.* If this bit is flipped 0 to 1, we may have unnecessary control packets. If this bit is flipped 1 to 0, the control information may be delayed until correct reception in the future. In either case, we can continue to forward the data packet. We can use similar argument for the next four header fields — congestion notification (1 bit), reserved (6 bits), THL (1 byte), and ETX (1 byte) — as their integrity may be ignored temporarily to prevent dropping packets that can be successfully forwarded. THL and ETX are used to avoid loops which rarely occur in CTP [2].

Origin (2 bytes) - *The originating address of the packet.* This field is not essential for packet forwarding. An error in this field may cause a duplicate packet cache miss decreasing the effectiveness of duplicate suppression – a small price to pay instead of dropping a multihop packet. It is possible to recover this field in a corrupt packet by correlating its length, ETX, and/or seqno with a sample of correct packets from the same source.

Seqno (1 byte) - *Origin sequence number:* The seqno field is required to uniquely identify packets from the same source. This field can be recovered if the origin field in the packet is undamaged, for example, by observing the transmission frequency of previous packets from the same origin. Moreover, as for the origin field, sampled header information from previous successful packets can be used to recover this field.

Collect_id (1 byte) - *Higher-level protocol identifier:* This field only needs to be recovered if CTP is serving multiple flows, which is not a frequent phenomena in application-centric WSN. Apart from the mechanism advocated for origin and seqno above, this field additionally provides the possibility of manually increasing Hamming distances (i.e., the number of differing bits between two bit

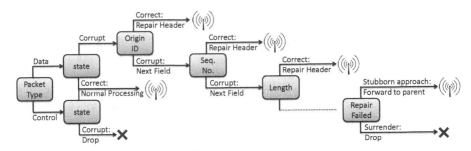

Fig. 2. The decision tree for repairing routing headers

strings) between `collect_id` of different flows. An incoming packet at the base station with a corrupt `collect_id` can be assigned to the flow with minimum hamming distance.

Data (max 128 bytes for IEEE 802.15.4) - *the payload.* This is the *don't care* part of the packet from CPR perspective since our goal is to conceal payload errors until packet reaches its intended destination.

Overall, we can conclude that errors in most header fields of a collection protocol can be repaired with the knowledge of the protocol and application and the tradeoffs we are willing to make. Important fields, such as `origin`, can be recovered if some of the header fields are correctly received.

3.2   Header Recovery Algorithm

Our algorithm is based on *decision tree* classification method which selects a class by descending a tree of possible decisions. Each internal node in the tree corresponds to one of the input variables. While descending the tree, at each node, the corresponding input variable is compared with a threshold value. This threshold value is determined based on training data, which, in our case, is a history of K correct packets from a particular origin. One of the two child nodes is then selected based on the result of the comparison until leaf node, that is the final prediction, is reached. For example, in a corrupt packet, we can determine whether or not the `origin` field (input variable) is corrupt by observing if the node has recently received packets from the same origin (threshold value from training data).

We use decision tree analysis because of its suitability for WSN: it is simple to implement, compute and respond when compared with alternative methods such as neural networks. One possible instance of CPR's decision tree is shown in Figure 2. The position of nodes in this tree can change based on the information gain from the training data, e.g., the `origin` node can be replaced by `length` node and vice versa.

Please note that CPR only targets data packets. Corrupt control packets are immediately dropped as (i) they are typically not retransmitted and (ii) they carry vital information necessary to maintain a robust network topology.

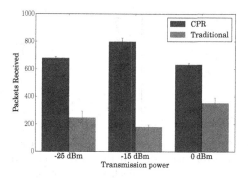

Fig. 3. Average (of three experiments) packets received at sink node, out of 1000 transmitted, by a sender node at one end of a linear five-hop topology with inter-node spacing of $4.5m$. CPR, with corrupt packets being recycled, outperforms the traditional approach. The error bars represent the best and worst of these experiments.

Apart from link layer de-multiplexing, corrupt control and data packets can be differentiated simply by using significantly different packet sizes.

4   Preliminary Results

We now describe the results from experiments that evaluate the benefits of CPR in terms of header recovery and data delivery over traditional, non-recycling, multihop data collection (i.e., CTP [2]). Our comparison focuses on the traditional approach since CPR operates at the network layer and any link layer recovery techniques are orthogonal and will equally improve the performance of routing with and without CPR.

4.1   Multihop Packet Reception Rates

We first evaluate packet reception rates (PRR) over multiple hops to quantify the raw magnitude of improvement achievable with CPR. This implies (i) we use the "stubborn" forwarding mechanism of CPR, i.e., forward packets even if header recovery fails, and (ii) we disabled retransmissions in CTP so we can study the enhancement due to only CPR's mechanisms in a simple multihop protocol. Our experiment setup uses a linear topology of five hops where a sender, at one end of the topology, transmits one thousand packets to the root node at the other end over 5 hops. Figure 3 shows the results both for CPR, with intermediate nodes forwarding corrupt packets, and traditional, where the nodes forward only the packets with valid CRC. With CPR, we see 2-4× improvement in PRR, indicating a significant potential to improve throughput, latency and lifetime (by reducing the need for retransmissions).

It is clear that improvement in PRR due to recycling depends upon the number of corrupt packets in a particular deployment. Hence, to maximize the magnitude of this improvement, the main goal of CPR is to ensure maximum recycling

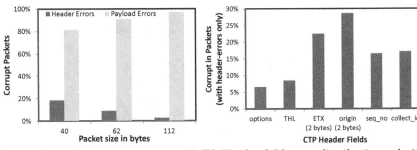

(a) Header vs Payload errors using dif- (b) Header-field error distribution only in
ferent packet sizes   packets with corrupt CTP headers

Fig. 4. Recycling efficiency of CPR

at an intermediate node irrespective of deployment conditions. We next evaluate
this recycling efficiency of CPR.

4.2   Network Layer Recycling and Header Recovery

We estimate the number of corrupt packets that are recycled at an intermediate
node (i) with successful header recovery, and (ii) with header errors (head recovery failed). For this purpose, we first need to determine the number of packets
that are received with only header errors. With symbol-errors frequently reported
as roughly uniformly distributed in corrupt packets [3,11], we can easily estimate
the ratio of header vs payload errors for a particular packet size. However, here
we calculate this ratio through empirical observations.

We place two motes 4.5m apart. For each packet size (see Figure 4(a)), the
sender transmits packets with an interval of $128ms$. We stop the experiment
when the receiver receives 1000 corrupt packets for a particular packet size. Our
results in Figure 4(a) substantiate the roughly uniform distribution of symbol
errors in packets: for 40 bytes packets (with 8 bytes header for CTP), nearly
20% of the packets have corrupt headers. Similarly, the header errors are less
likely as payload size increases. We can thus conclude that for the worst case of
the presented data (size = 40 bytes), 80% of the packets will be automatically
recycled in CPR with correct headers.

We now narrow down our focus on the remaining 20% of packets with only
corrupt headers. Figure 4(b) shows how the corruption is distributed across different header fields for these packets. To understand the worst case performance
of CPR, we assume that only the headers with the correct `origin` field can be
recovered[2]. As shown in the Figure 4(b), 30% of the these packets have corruption in the `origin` field suggesting 70% headers can be recovered in the worst
case.

Overall, in this scenario, CPR recycles two sets of packets with correct headers:
(i) 80% of the total packets with only payload errors (see Figure 4(a)), and (ii)

---

[2] Our estimate is deliberately conservative because we want to do worst case analysis.

14% of the total packets (0.7 × 20% with correct `origin` in Figure 4(b)) whose headers are repaired by CPR algorithm. Hence, in the worst case, CPR recycles 94% of the corrupt packets with no header errors. The remaining 6% can be recycled using "stubborn" forwarding.

5   Conclusions and Future Work

This paper presents a network layer error-tolerant approach for recycling corrupt packets over multiple hops. CPR, by avoiding packet drop, improves information delivery that can benefit error-tolerant WSN applications. Our preliminary evaluation demonstrate the high utility of CPR in terms of information delivery (2-4× improvement) and recycling efficiency per intermediate node (100%).

A complete implementation of header recovery algorithm and thorough evaluation on a widely used testbed is still pending. An important implementation aspect is to enable the link layer to issue acks for corrupt packets to avoid retransmissions. We also plan to extend and explore CPR's utility for 6LoWPAN and multi-radio systems.

References

1. Dubois-ferrière, H., Estrin, D., Vetterli, M.: Packet combining in sensor networks. In: Sensys (2005)
2. Gnawali, O., Fonseca, R., Jamieson, K., Moss, D., Levis, P.: Collection tree protocol. In: Sensys (2009)
3. Hermans, F., Wennerström, H., McNamara, L., Rohner, C., Gunningberg, P.: All is not lost: Understanding and exploiting packet corruption in outdoor sensor networks. In: EWSN (2014)
4. Jamieson, K., Balakrishnan, H.: Ppr: Partial packet recovery for wireless networks. In: SIGCOMM (2007)
5. Jeong, J., Ee, C.-T.: Forward error correction in sensor networks. In: WWSN (2007)
6. Larzon, L.-A., Degermark, M., Pink, S., Jonsson, L.-E., Fairhurst, G.: The Lightweight User Datagram Protocol (UDP-Lite). RFC 3828 (2004)
7. Link, J.Á.B., Fabritius, G., Alizai, M.H., Wehrle, K.: Burrowview - seeing the world through the eyes of rats. In: IEEE PerCom, Workshop Proceedings (2010)
8. Mainwaring, A., Culler, D., Polastre, J., Szewczyk, R., Anderson, J.: Wireless sensor networks for habitat monitoring. In: ACM WSNA (2002)
9. Cattani, M., Zuniga, M.A., Woehrle, M., Langendoen, K.G.: Sofa: Communication in extreme wireless sensor networks. In: EWSN (2014)
10. Schmidt, F., Alizai, M.H., Aktaş, I., Wehrle, K.: Refector: Heuristic header error recovery for error-tolerant transmissions. In: CoNEXT (2011)
11. Schmidt, F., Ceriotti, M., Wehrle, K.: Bit error distribution and mutation patterns of corrupted packets in low-power wireless networks. In: WiNTECH (2013)
12. Werner-Allen, G., Lorincz, K., Welsh, M., Marcillo, O., Johnson, J., Ruiz, M., Lees, J.: Deploying a wireless sensor network on an active volcano. In: IEEE Internet Computing (2006)

On the Scalability of Constructive Interference in Low-Power Wireless Networks

Claro A. Noda[1,2], Carlos M. Pérez-Penichet[2], Balint Seeber[3], Marco Zennaro[4],
Mário Alves[1], and Adriano Moreira[2]

[1] CISTER/INESC-TEC, Polytechnic Institute of Porto (ISEP/IPP), Portugal
{candz,mjf}@isep.ipp.pt
[2] Algoritmi Research Centre, University of Minho, Guimarães, Portugal
{cpp,adriano}@dsi.uminho.pt
[3] Ettus Research, Santa Clara, USA
balint.seeber@ettus.com
[4] Guglielmo Marconi Laboratory, ICTP, Trieste, Italy
mzennaro@ictp.it

Abstract. Constructive baseband interference has been recently introduced in low-power wireless networks as a promising technique enabling low-latency network flooding and sub-μs time synchronisation among network nodes. The scalability of this technique has been questioned in regards to the maximum temporal misalignment among baseband signals, due to the variety of path delays in the network. By contrast, we find that the scalability is compromised, in the first place, by emerging fast fading in the composite channel, which originates in the carrier frequency disparity of the participating repeaters nodes. We investigate the multisource wave problem and show the resulting signal becomes vulnerable in the presence of noise, leading to significant deterioration of the link whenever the carriers have similar amplitudes.

1 Background and Related Work

Constructive Baseband Interference (CBI) exploits the spatial, temporal and spectral diversity exhibited by the wireless channel to introduce link redundancy and increase reliability. This diversity of the wireless channel manifests itself as a given symbol stream reaches across different wireless channels simultaneously and each symbol is unlikely to suffer the same level of distortion, small-scale multipath fading and attenuation in all channels at the same time. Therefore, concurrent transmission of identical packets from several senders can increase the quality of the wireless link towards a receiver.

CBI has been recently introduced in wireless networks by Rahul et al. [15]. Dutta et al. employed CBI to alleviate the acknowledgement implosion problem, using simultaneous transmissions of short acknowledgement packets, in a receiver-initiated low-power Medium Access Control (MAC) protocol [6]. Ferrari et al. devised a communication primitive for low-latency network flooding and sub-μs time synchronization for low-power wireless nodes [9]. In following works, Ferrari et al. also proposed an infrastructure (analogous to a shared bus), which supports mobile nodes in a multi-hop low-power wireless network [8]. Doddavenkatappa et al. further optimise network flooding enabling a multichannel packet pipeline across the network [3,4].

However, some limitations in the efficacy and scalability of CBI have been studied by Wang et al. [17]. They investigate the worst case scenario in a multihop network

T. Abdelzaher et al. (Eds.): EWSN 2015, LNCS 8965, pp. 250–257, 2015.

showing that cumulative non-deterministic delays in the system cause the temporal displacement between concurrent transmissions to exceed the symbol boundaries, leading to poor packet reception rate. We take a different perspective on this matter by analysing the superposition of carrier waves. The main contribution of this paper is that the scalability of CBI is not only limited by the variety of temporal delays as investigated by Wang et al. but, firstly, by specific properties of the composite signal.

The scalability of CBI is relevant because the disposition of wireless sensor nodes in a deployment should follow application needs. Consider the plausible scenario where a large number of fixed sensor nodes may be required in a given location, while sparse nodes suffice in other areas. Also mobile sensors attached to humans, animals or robots impose a dynamic spatial density. In such scenarios, bulk data transfer with high-throughput, low-latency and low-power are important system features. For example, the time window to transfer data might be limited in railway-bridge monitoring, as data is uploaded to passing trains [2]. CBI enhances link performance, radio coverage and enables node mobility. Nevertheless, we reveal a critical lack of link quality scalability with the number of concurrent repeaters.

We present the multisource wave problem (Section 2) and investigate the error rate and the envelope of the composite signal, which results from the superposition of all repeater signals. Our experiments (described in Section 3) show an acute signal vulnerability in the presence of noise and the consequent deterioration of the link quality for a power imbalance among two or more repeater signals smaller than 5 dB (Section 4). We discuss the results and reach conclusions in Section 5.

2   Constructive Interference

Constructive Baseband Interference occurs when multiple-source carriers, modulated with identical information and adequate time synchronization, add up in the receiver antenna. The time synchronization error plus the wave propagation delay difference among these signals must remain within symbol boundaries, to avoid intersymbol interference [5]. In the case of the IEEE 802.15.4 physical layer (PHY), half the symbol time corresponds to 0.5 µs [6,9].

Since the modulated carrier of each transmitter traverses distinct wireless channels towards the receiver, we refer to them as *individual channels* as they are, in general, statistically independent. Furthermore, the composite signal that results from the superposition of waves can be interpreted as if it traverses a *composite channel* characterised by the resulting sum of multisource carriers, in addition to the overall multipath effect of the individual channels.

2.1   Carrier Waves

Let us now look into wave properties to understand CBI. Without losing generality, we restrict this analysis to unmodulated carriers. The reader is referred to [17] for a detailed discussion on the baseband signal and carrier modulation. Let the composite unmodulated signal A_c from n sources be expressed as:

$$A_c = \sum_{i=1}^{n} A_i \sin(w_i t + \phi_i) \tag{1}$$

Also let A_i, w_i and ϕ_i represent the amplitude, angular frequency and phase of the individual sources respectively. Note that the multisource problem in equation (1) is similar to the multipath problem, where all frequencies are equal since they originate at a single source. On the other hand, multiple sources implies small disparities in the carrier frequencies, as there is always a limit in the frequency accuracy of the quartz-crystal based oscillators used to synthesize the carrier. Section 2.2 elaborates on this.

The properties of the probability density function (*pdf*) of the resultant amplitude or envelope of equation (1) are important for the performance evaluation of wireless systems. The modelling of fading and shadowing in the multipath problem (all w_i are equal) has been widely studied and an expression for the *pdf* can be found in [18].

To the best of our knowledge, an exact expression for the *pdf* of the envelope in equation (1) remains an open mathematical problem. Thus, for the sake of simplicity, let us consider the case of two sources ($n = 2$). Let the envelope E_c of equation (1) be:

$$E_c = \left[A_1^2 + A_2^2 + 2A_1A_2 \cos\left((\omega_1 - \omega_2)t + \varphi\right)\right]^{1/2} \tag{2}$$

Equation (2) reveals a harmonic function with angular frequency $w_c = w_1 - w_2$ which leads to periodic depressions in the amplitude of the composite signal. This is known as the beating effect. It is important to note that these depressions can be quite numerous during the packet duration, depending on w_c. As the amplitude decreases, the signal which is blurred by noise in the wireless channel, gets closer to the decision boundary making it increasingly vulnerable. With more sources, the peak to average ratio of the composite signal envelope increases and the problem gets worse, as we will see in Section 4.

2.2 Hardware

The oscillator's frequency accuracy of IEEE 802.15.4 compliant radios is mandated below ± 40 ppm [12]. This accuracy ensures tight bounds on the transmitter carrier frequency and allows the receiver to use a narrow channel filter to attenuate out-of-band noise power. However, a frequency discrepancy of up to 200 kHz is possible between two radios operating in the same channel of the 2.4 GHz band. We examine the carrier frequency dispersion for TelosB sensor nodes [14] employing a Software Defined Radio (SDR) from Ettus Research [7] for spectrum analysis, and an Agilent 8648C Signal Generator as a reference (10 Hz accuracy and time-base stability below ± 0.1 ppm typical). We verify such a frequency offset among nodes and observe no perceptible time variation in the frequencies, provided a constant room temperature is maintained.

The IEEE 802.15.4 standard also specifies the receiver sensitivity must be measured at a packet error rate (PER) of 1% for 52-symbol packets [12]. Thus, the required SER results near 10^{-4}, which we use as the reference threshold for minimal link performance. Note that a corresponding CER value, assuming chip errors are i.i.d., is not applicable since errors are more probable during envelope depressions. Hence, we measure both chip and symbol errors rates (CER and SER).

2.3 The Composite Channel

The signals traversing the wireless channel reach the receiver with amplitudes that depend on the path loss of the individual channels. Since the baseband signals are time synchronised, the receiver always locks with the preamble of the strongest signal (to decode the symbols). Therefore, when the amplitude imbalance is sufficiently large there

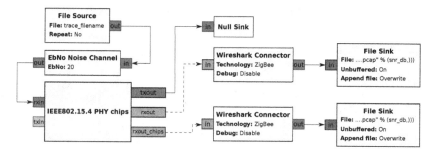

Fig. 1. GNU Radio flow graph used to measure SER and CER in the composite channel by adding synthetic noise in an AWGN channel

is always *capture*. However, when the magnitudes of the carriers are similar, intrinsic properties of the composite channel emerge.

The indoor multipath wireless channel is a time-invariant channel whose Channel Impulse Response (CIR) is considered quasistationary with a typical *rms delay spread* $\sigma_\tau < 100$ ns (see Saleh and Valenzuela [16]). Thus, the time dispersive nature of the channel is minimal and the coherence bandwidth is larger than the IEEE 802.15.4 Direct Sequence Spread Spectrum (DSSS) signal bandwidth. Also the individual channel is very slow time varying [16], with a coherence time much larger than the symbol duration, $T_{ci} \gg T_s$. This regime is known as *flat* and *slow* fading [11].

On the other hand, according to equation 2, the worst-case coherence time of the composite channel can be expressed as $T_{cc} = \pi/2w_c$ and results in $1\,\mathrm{ms} \geq T_{cc} \geq 5\,\mu\mathrm{s}$ with high probability, which is orders of magnitude shorter than what would be observed due to the Doppler spread. Thus, the composite channel one observes under CBI displays *fast* fading, which originates in the carrier frequency disparity of the participating repeater nodes.

3   Experimental Setup

We design our experiments to analyse the IEEE 802.15.4 PHY signals. This analysis benefits from an SDR platform as one can tap into the digital signal processing chain with ease. Our setup is designed around the Ettus USRP B210 board [7] and an SDR transceiver implementation in GNU Radio by Bloessl et al., which interoperates with IEEE 802.15.4 radios [1].

We employ a set of TelosB sensor nodes running Glossy [9] in a one-hop network composed of the initiator and at most eight repeaters. We then record low-noise complex baseband signals, at least 40 dB over the noise floor. We use an example application (rx_sample_to_file) from the USRP Hardware Driver (UHD) package running in an overdimensioned Linux workstation to avoid buffer overflows when recording the signal at 4 Msps. The initiator sends 15 packets per second, which are retransmitted 16 and 8 times for the wired and wireless experiments, respectively. Our 480-second-long baseband traces contain at least 1.6×10^5 symbols for our error-rate study. Note that failure to detect the PHY header invalidates the packet, thus we use payloads smaller than 16 byte to maintain robust statistics under high noise levels.

Our first configuration requires all antenna ports (from nodes and SDR) be wired through a 5-port 40 dB T-Network resistive power attenuator which acts as an ideal

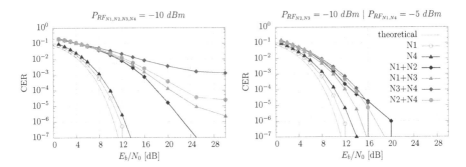

Fig. 2. The CER for pairs of nodes decreases for a 5-dB RF power imbalance. Each point in the graph is computed from 9.4×10^4 frames, 16 byte each. A 40-dB power attenuator fixes path loss to resemble a non-delay and non-multipath channel. Some curves were removed for clarity.

wireless channel without multipath distortions nor external interference. One node functions as the flooding initiator, transmitting at an RF power of $P_{RF} = -15$ dBm. Its signal runs through an additional 30-dB attenuator, thus reaching the SDR at -85 dBm. The repeater operates up to $P_{RF} = -5$ dBm, hence it reaches the SDR at -45 dBm. This power allocation is intended to guarantee the repeaters get the initiator packets with high probability but also forces its signal below the noise floor at the SDR.

Our second configuration involves a setup of sensor nodes fastened to an external glass wall, and the B210 SDR board with a 12-dBi YAGI antenna (ANT2400Y12WRU) fixed to a mast on the other end of the office, approximately 7 meters apart. In this case the initiator antenna is replaced with a dummy load to attenuate its signal.

The rest of our experiments are conducted off-line, in the computer, employing the rich component tool set in GNU Radio [10]. Using predefined payloads in Glossy, which are not altered by repeaters, we compute CER and SER by comparing the received frame content from the traces with the expected payload.

We extend the SDR transceiver by Bloessl et al. to export frames containing received chips, prior to decoding DSSS symbols. We generate two separate *packet capture* (pcap) files with frames containing chips and symbols respectively. In order to study link performance, we develop a channel module suitable to add controlled noise quantities to match a desired SNR value. This module requires specifying the energy-per-bit (E_b) to spectral noise density (N_0) ratio E_b/N_0 (in dB) and simulates an Additive White Gaussian Noise (AWGN) channel. The variance values σ^2 are internally computed based on the signal's peak amplitude, the bandwidth of the IEEE 802.15.4 channel and the specified E_b/N_0. By adding synthetic noise we can study a wide range of SNR ratios in a controlled and repeatable experiment. The GNU Radio flow graph used for the error-rate study is shown in figure 1. The flow graph consists of a file source, containing the complex baseband signal, our channel module to add Gaussian noise, and the extended transceiver. Frames containing decoded chips and symbols are stored in their respective pcap files for further processing.

4   Experimental Results

The IEEE 802.15.4 PHY coding scheme for the 2.4 GHz band uses pseudo-orthogonal codes where $k = 4$ bits are encoded together into an $n = 32$ chip sequence. The raw

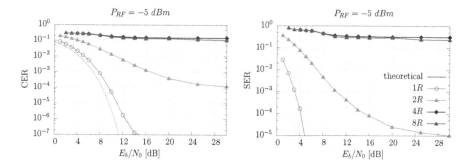

Fig. 3. CBI among up to eight repeater nodes after symbols traverse a highly correlated indoor wireless channel. Each point in the graph is computed from 4.8×10^4 frames, 8 byte each. The theoretical curve, as derived in [11, Section 6.1.2], is shown for CER only.

signalling is carried out using Offset-Quadrature-Phase-Shift-Keying with half-sine-shaping (OQPSK-HSS) at a rate of 2 Mchip/s. The code rate $r = k/n = 1/8$ then results in a throughput of 250 kbps. Thus, DSSS processing gain is $P_G = 10 \log(\frac{1}{r}) \approx 9$ dB.

Since symbols are encoded in phase, magnitude variations of the signal do not directly impact detection reliability. However, as intersymbol distances in the constellation diagram diminish with the carrier amplitude, the envelope depressions lead to errors (Section 2.1). A brief summary of the most significant experimental results we have accumulated follows, illustrating the limits of the link performance under CBI.

4.1   Wired Configuration

We use a combination of up to three nodes directly *wired* to the SDR. This guarantees controlled and repeatable settings, as well as very similar power levels from repeaters. Additionally, the attenuator introduces a constant power loss across the signal bandwidth and proper impedance matching avoids reflections.

Figure 2 shows CER curves for single- and two-repeater combinations. All three-node combinations produce error rates well above 10^{-1} and are not shown. For pairs of nodes, we obtain a family of curves with varied and generally poor link performance. We observe a correlation between error rate and power (P_{RF}) imbalance. We show two power configurations: (i) all repeaters use $P_{RF} = -5$ dBm and (ii) decrease one repeater to $P_{RF} = -10$ dBm. As we raise the power imbalance by 5 dB, the link performance increases. Note that 5 dBm is the minimum power step the nodes allow.

The figure also shows that power imbalance moves the curves towards the minimum theoretically attainable error rate and near the single-repeater curve. We can relate this result with the ameliorated beating effect brought about by power imbalances. Note that having different amplitudes in equation (2) is better than having similar ones.

4.2   Wireless Configuration

We assess to what extent channel diversity could help reduce error rates. Figure 3 shows CER and SER for up to eight repeaters. For the two-node curve an E_b/N_0 of 16 dB is needed to maintain a minimum SER of 10^{-4}, a 12 dB difference relative to one repeater. For the cases of four and eight repeaters, both error rates remain above 10^{-1}.

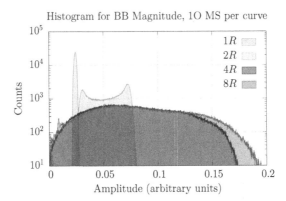

Fig. 4. Amplitude observations in the magnitude of the signal spread as the number of repeaters increases. Although the magnitude contains no information, the lower-end observations become vulnerable to noise, compromising link quality.

This experimental result indicates the channel diversity gain is limited for highly correlated indoor wireless channels. Unfortunately, these are very common settings for wireless sensor network deployments.

Furthermore, we estimate the *pdf* of the baseband signal's envelope. The results are shown in figure 4. As the number of repeaters increases, the envelope's histogram spreads, showing a large range of amplitude observations. Besides making the signal vulnerable to noise as previously discussed, the composite signal demands a high dynamic range on the receiver. As there is not an automatic gain control (AGC) on the B210 board, signal clipping may occur as more repeaters are added. We make sure the SDR operates in linear mode, hence the large error rates in figure 3 are exclusively due to the depressions in the composite signal. Note that the two-repeater curve in figure 4 recreates the behaviour described by equation (2). The rate of change of the cosine function that describes the envelope's undulations is lower on the extreme values, which explains the two peaks in the histogram.

5   Discussion and Conclusion

We have shown that link quality under CBI does not scale with the number of repeaters due to lack of coherence among multisource carriers. Specifically, the link layer reliability is affected by emerging fast fading in the composite channel, wherever capture effect is absent. Thus, we find a fundamental limitation that potentially impacts all concurrent transmissions and puts a high demand for dynamic range in the receivers. Commercial transceiver chip implementations feature greater receiver sensitivity than the SDR board used in these experiments, and use an AGC that reacts to (not very fast) envelope depressions by increasing the gain in the receiver's signal chain. Combined, these attributes can improve the apparent link quality, e.g. [9, figure 12]. However, we suspect this is effective for a low-noise channel only, since amplification cannot improve SNR.

Doddavenkatappa et al. orchestrate multichannel transmissions to sustain a packet pipeline while flooding the network [3,4]. Multichannel operation expands the degrees of freedom and time diversity increases probability of reception, but open questions remain in regard to suitable repeater selection for effective network flooding, i.e., guaranteeing power imbalance in all receivers, for enhanced performance. An alternative solution is to introduce channel diversity gain in the PHY layer, using space-time codes [13] which would be suitable for low-power design.

Acknowledgements. This work was partially supported by National Funds through FCT (Portuguese Foundation for Science and Technology) and by ERDF (European Regional Development Fund) through COMPETE (Operational Programme 'Thematic Factors of Competitiveness'); within projects PEst-OE/EEI/UI0319/2014, FCOMP-01-0124-FEDER-014922 (MASQOTS) and FCOMP-01-0124-FEDER-037281 (CISTER). We wish to thank Fernando A. Miranda Bonomi (National University of Tucumán, Argentina), for fruitful discussions and early contributions to this work during the ICTP School on Applications of Open Spectrum and White Spaces Technologies.

References

1. Bloessl, B., Leitner, C., Dressler, F., Sommer, C.: A GNU Radio-based IEEE 802.15. 4 Testbed. 12. GI/ITG FACHGESPRÄCH SENSORNETZE (2013)
2. Chebrolu, K., Raman, B., Mishra, N., Valiveti, P.K., Kumar, R.: Brimon: A sensor network system for railway bridge monitoring. In: ACM MobiSys, NY, USA (2008)
3. Doddavenkatappa, M., Chan, M.C., Leong, B.: Splash: Fast data dissemination with constructive interference in wireless sensor networks. In: USENIX NSDI 2013, Lombard, IL (2013)
4. Doddavenkatappa, M., Choon, M.: P3: A practical packet pipeline using synchronous transmissions for sensor networks. In: ACM/IEEE IPSN (2014)
5. Dutta, A., Saha, D., Grunwald, D., Sicker, D.: SMACK: A SMart ACKnowledgment scheme for broadcast messages in WLANs. In: ACM SIGCOMM, NY, USA (2009)
6. Dutta, P., Dawson-Haggerty, S., Chen, Y., Liang, C.J.M., Terzis, A.: Design and evaluation of a versatile and efficient receiver-initiated link layer for low-power wireless. In: ACM SenSys, Zurich, Switzerland (2010)
7. Ettus Research: USRP B200/B210 Bus Series Product Overview, http://goo.gl/W0YLmQ, (accessed: September 22, 2014)
8. Ferrari, F., Zimmerling, M., Mottola, L., Thiele, L.: Low-power wireless bus. In: SenSys. ACM, New York (2012)
9. Ferrari, F., Zimmerling, M., Thiele, L., Saukh, O.: Efficient Network Flooding and Time Synchronization with Glossy. In: ACM/IEEE IPSN, Chicago, IL, USA (April 2011)
10. GNU Radio Website, http://www.gnuradio.org (accessed September 2014)
11. Goldsmith, A.: Wireless Communications. Cambridge Univ. Press, NY (2005)
12. IEEE 802.15.4 Working Group: Wireless MAC and PHY Specs for Low-Rate WPANs, rev. 802.15.4-2011 edn. (September 2011)
13. Jafarkhani, H.: A quasi-orthogonal space-time block code. IEEE Transactions on Communications 49(1) (January 2001)
14. Polastre, J., Szewczyk, R., Culler, D.: Telos: Enabling ultra-low power wireless research. In: ACM/IEEE IPSN, Piscataway, NJ, USA (2005)
15. Rahul, H., Hassanieh, H., Katabi, D.: SourceSync: A Distributed Wireless Architecture for Exploiting Sender Diversity. In: ACM SIGCOMM 2010, New Delhi, India (August 2010)
16. Saleh, A.A.M., Valenzuela, R.: A statistical model for indoor multipath propagation. IEEE Journal on Selected Areas in Communications 5(2), 128–137 (1987)
17. Wang, Y., He, Y., Mao, X., Liu, Y., Huang, Z., Li, X.Y.: Exploiting Constructive Interference for Scalable Flooding in Wireless Networks. In: IEEE INFOCOM, Orlando, FL, USA (2012)
18. Maghsoodi, Y., Exact, S.A.: amplitude distributions of sums of stochastic sinusoidals (2008)

LibReplay: Deterministic Replay
for Bug Hunting in Sensor Networks

Olaf Landsiedel, Elad Michael Schiller, and Salvatore Tomaselli

Chalmers University of Technology, Sweden
{olafl,elad}@chalmers.se, tiposchi@tiscali.it

Abstract. Bug hunting in sensor networks is challenging: Bugs are often prompted by a particular, complex concatenation of events. Moreover, dynamic interactions between nodes and with the environment make it time-consuming to track and reproduce a bug. We introduce LibReplay to ease bug hunting in sensor networks: it provides (1) lightweight and flexible logging and (2) deterministic replay. LibReplay logs function calls to and from the application or another code of interest. It enables deterministic replay of execution traces in a controlled environment such as a full-system simulator. This allows the user to benefit from well-established debugging tools such as stepping through code, breakpoints, or watchpoints. We show that the lightweight architecture of LibReplay provides the benefits of replay debugging at an efficiency that is comparable to traditional logging tools, which commonly do not allow replay debugging.

Keywords: Cyber Physical Systems, Internet of Things, Wireless Sensor Networks, Debugging, Replay, Tracing, Logging, Simulation.

1 Introduction

Bug hunting in sensor networks is challenging: (1) sensor networks are distributed and deeply embedded into a non-deterministic environment. (2) The non-determinism of both the wireless network and the physical environment makes it time-consuming to track and reproduce bugs. (3) Bugs are often prompted by a particular, complex concatenation of events. Source-level debugging capabilities as common in sequential programming, i.e., local and non-distributed applications, would significantly ease the debugging process. For example, stepping through code, breakpoints, and watchpoints are well-established tools to debug sequential code. However, the distributed and embedded nature prevents us from pausing program execution on a node to examine its state.

Large-scale distributed systems on the Internet solve this issue by employing logging and replay capabilities [5,8,9]. These log all interaction between the code of interest and the system itself, e.g., function calls to and from a part of an application that is suspected to malfunction. Next, they replay the execution of the code of interest accordingly to the logged function calls and their parameters. As a result, the local replay can be debugged using well-established debugging tools such as GDB and allows for stepping through code, breakpoints,

T. Abdelzaher et al. (Eds.): EWSN 2015, LNCS 8965, pp. 258–265, 2015.

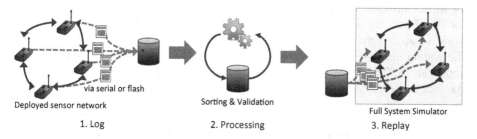

via serial or flash

Deployed sensor network

Sorting & Validation

Full System Simulator

1. Log   2. Processing   3. Replay

Fig. 1. LibReplay in a nutshell: (1) Distributed logging via serial or flash, (2) sorting and validation of logs, and (3) replay in a full-system simulator

and watchpoints. While this technique is well-known in large-scale distributed systems, we see limited application in the area of sensor networks due to the resource limitations of sensor nodes.

This paper closes this gap and provides LibReplay, a lightweight and deterministic solutions for distributed logging and source-level replay (see Figure 1). It allows debugging of sensor network applications and protocols with source-level debuggers, such as GDB.We achieve this by replaying execution traces in a full-system simulator, such as Cooja [10], MspSim [4], Avrora [16], or QEMU [1]. This paper makes three contributions:

- **Lightweight, Distributed Logging:** we introduce a system architecture for distributed, lightweight logging that is customizable to code regions of interest. It employs a two-phase logging to reflect resource constraints and to minimize the side effects of logging on program execution.
- **Deterministic Replaying:** From the logs we replay all input events to the code of interest. Using full-system simulators we enable deterministic, high fidelity replay. Utilizing the debugging capabilities of these platforms, one can now step through source-code and employ breakpoints and watchpoints.
- **Implementation and Performance Evaluation:** We demonstrate a working implementation of LibReplay with an efficiency that is on par with traditional logging tools, which commonly do not provide replay capabilities. We evaluate LibReplay's performance with respect to MCU and memory before showing that its overhead is similar to today's logging approaches, which cannot provide the same functionality.

Next, we discuss the limitations of traditional debugging tools and outline the differences of LibReplay to the state of the art (Section 2). We then introduce LibReplay in detail (Section 3) and compare the performance of LibReplay with the state of the art (Section 4) before addressing future directions and concluding (Section 5).

2   Limitations of the State of the Art

Logging and tracing are two common approaches for hunting bugs in sensor networks. Logging tools [2,6,11] record execution details. Commonly, they store the log in the flash memory for off-line collection or feed them to the host system via the serial port. In practice, bug hunting with such logging tools often follows an iterative approach: (a) adding or refining logging statements, (b) re-executing the system until the bug is triggered, and (c) analyzing the log and spotting bug appearances. The developers have to repeat these steps until they understand the bug causes, try to fix them and then check whether all bugs were removed by again repeating these steps. Moreover, the non-deterministic and dynamic nature of the wireless network and interactions with the environment make it time consuming to reproduce a bug sufficiently often for this repetitive approach. In contrast, LibReplay logs function calls and their parameters to and from the code of interest, such as a malfunctioning routing protocol. As a result, LibReplay collects sufficient information to replay program execution deterministically allowing one to employ source-level debuggers for bug hunting. In our experience, this limits the need for repeated testing, and in most cases a single logging run is sufficient to fix the bug in replay debugging, because analysis and bug spotting is mainly carried out off-line using an iterative debugger that replays the log.

Tracing tools [12,14,15,17,18] follow a different approach: They trace the program execution by logging function calls. For example, a tracer logs each function and its parameters that a packet takes on its path through the protocol stack from the application to the radio driver. A key challenge is that tracing program execution leads to large traces when compared to traditional logging [13]. Some approaches [12,15] address this challenge with additional hardware on the nodes. For example, Minerva [12] connects a dedicated debugging-board to the JTAG adapter of the sensor node. Controlling multiple debugging-boards over Ethernet, Minerva can examine network-wide state. LibReplay, in contrast, merely logs function calls and their parameters to and from the code of interest, limiting its intrusiveness while not requiring additional hardware.

3   LibReplay: Design and System Architecture

We start the discussion of LibReplay by illustrating its basic idea before introducing LibReplay in detail.

3.1   Basic Idea: Flexible Logging and Deterministic Replay

With LibReplay, we log function calls to and from a user-specified code-region of interest, such as a malfunctioning routing protocol. In the replay, we feed the calls back to the code of interest in the same order as they were logged on the real system (see Figure 2). Thus, in the replay every event happens in the same order as on the real system and with the same function parameters. Using cycle-accurate simulation of the entire system, each event will also take the same number of cycles as on the real system. Thus, a complete log that includes all functions to the code of interest generates a complete replay with all local states equaling to the ones of the real-system. We note that due to

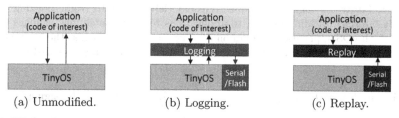

(a) Unmodified.   (b) Logging.   (c) Replay.

Fig. 2. We log function calls to and from the code of interest, such as a malfunctioning routing protocol. For replay, we feed the logs back to the code of interest. Replay in a full-system simulator, such as Cooja, provides us with well-established debugging tools such as stepping through code, breakpoints and watchpoints.

the run-to-completion semantics, e.g., tasks in TinyOS, of many OSs for Cyber-Physical Systems (CPS) and Internet of Things (IoT) we do not have to log the OS scheduler itself.

3.2   Lightweight and Flexible Logging

The first building block of LibReplay is its lightweight, flexible logging-architecture. It has three design goals: (1) to reduce the overhead of logging to limit potential side-effects on program execution, (2) to provide distributed logging of events across multiple nodes, and (3) to ease integration into user-defined applications and components.

Deferred Logging to Limit Side-Effects on Applications: Whenever a function to or from the code-region of interest is called, LibReplay logs the function, its parameters, the return value, and a logical timestamp, i.e., an event sequence-number. To limit run-time overhead, LibReplay employs a two-phase approach to logging: As a first step, any log data is merely buffered in RAM and the execution can continue with only minimal delay. As second step, a deferred, background process – only scheduled if no other process is to be scheduled – handles the storage itself: it moves the log buffers to flash or the serial port for storage.

Distributed Logging of Events across Multiple Nodes: When testing and debugging distributed systems, we experienced it as essential that we can trace events and messages across multiple nodes. For example, we often needed to trace how a single message travels through the network and which state changes it triggered along its path, such as timeouts and re-transmissions. To trace events across multiple nodes, LibReplay adds a logical timestamp to each outgoing radio message, which is send by the code of interest. This allows to create a globally valid order of the events for replay. Optionally, LibReplay can also re-use sequence numbers and source addresses that most protocols already provide to identify messages and their order uniquely. This avoids overhead, as no additional timestamps need to be added to messages.

Easy to Integrate into User-Defined Applications and Components: When designing LibReplay, we put a special focus on its ease and flexibility of use.

Table 1. LibReplay logging example: Without (left) and with (right) logging of the `Receive` interface. Adding logging to applications requires merely few changes to the wiring of TinyOS applications. Common logging components, such as the `ReceiveLogC` component used in this example to log the `Receive` interface, are provided by LibReplay.

Listing 1.1. Without logging	**Listing 1.2.** With logging

```
[...]


App.Receive -> AMReceiverC;


[...]
```

```
[...]
components new ReceiveLogC() as Log;
App.Receive -> Log;
Log.Receive -> AMReceiverC;
[...]
```

For example, LibReplay can be easily integrated into own applications and tailored by adding own logging interfaces. LibReplay places a logging component between each interface of the code of interest and the OS, see Table 1. LibReplay provides logging components for common interfaces of TinyOS.

3.3 Processing the Logs: Globally-Ordered Replay

Once events are collected from the individual nodes, we utilize the logical timestamps to construct a globally-ordered replay. Events such as radio events have (or can have) a counterpart on the other nodes, such as a transmit and receive event. This guides LibReplay to obtain a global order of events [7].

3.4 Deterministic Replay

For replay, we replace each logging component with its counterpart replay-component. Similar to the logging components, we have one replay component per interface and LibReplay provides these for the common interfaces in TinyOS. Thus, we replay the code of interest and feed it the events we previously logged.

Compared to the logging components, the data flow is now reversed and replay components feed events to the application (see Figure 2c). Bug hunting can now utilize the advanced debugging capabilities of modern system simulators such as monitoring of individual variables and stepping through code fragments. Note that when performing such tasks on the deployed systems directly, they cause high overhead and significant side effects. Additionally, we use the recorded output to detect deviations between the log and the replay, which can indicate subtle system bugs such as buffer overflows, etc. Note that the main replay-target of LibReplay are full-system simulators, as these can replay multiple nodes, and we can analyze their interaction. However, LibReplay can also replay the execution on a real node and we can connect and debug via JTAG, for example.

3.5 Discussion: Generic Design

In TinyOS, modules are the natural integration points for logging. They encapsulate local state, and state changes are only triggered via their interfaces.

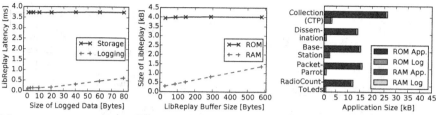

(a) MCU load when a logging a function call: Logging is completed within 1ms. The low-priority background task handles the heavy lifting.

(b) The RAM footprint of LibReplay mainly depends on the size of the logging buffers. ROM remains constant independent of buffer size.

(c) The overall memory footprint of LibReplay is small when compared to the application itself (default setting, 300 bytes buffer).

Fig. 3. MCU and memory overhead of LibReplay

Nonetheless, the design of LibReplay is generic and is not bound to TinyOS. For example, instead of interfaces we can log traditional function calls to and from a block of code. This, for example, matches the design of other common OS in CPS and IoT such as Contiki [3] or FreeRTOS.

4 Evaluation

After introducing LibReplay and its architecture, we evaluate its performance. We begin with a set of micro benchmarks to determine MCU and memory efficiency. Next, we compare LibReplay to the state of art and show that its overhead is similar to today's approaches to logging while these commonly do not log sufficient information for providing replay capabilities. We implemented LibReplay in TinyOS 2.1.2 and evaluate using TelosB nodes.

4.1 MCU and Memory Efficiency of LibReplay

In LibReplay, logging consists of two steps: the fast logging itself to an in-memory buffer and a second low-priority background process that handles the heavy lifting to external storage. As a result, the logging itself has only minimal impact on the program execution (see Figure 3a). The RAM footprint of LibReplay strongly depends on the buffer size chosen (see Figure 3b). ROM is stable independent of the buffer size chosen. For the following, we use the default value of 300 bytes for the buffer. Our experience shows that this is sufficient for most application scenarios, and it is similar to the default setting in the state of the art. Nonetheless, when compared to the overall memory footprint of the application, the footprint of LibReplay stays small (see Figure 3c), leaving sufficient space for complex applications.

4.2 LibReplay and Traditional Approaches to Logging

We compare the efficiency of LibReplay to traditional logging approaches: printf, TinyLTS [11], and the customized logging layer of the Collection Tree Protocol

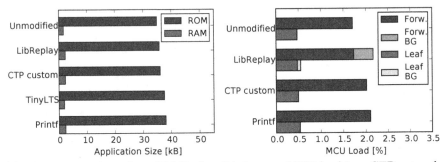

(a) The memory footprint of LibReplay is similar to traditional logging systems. The footprint of TinyLTS is taken from its publication [11], as the source code is not available to us.

(b) Average MCU load in a CTP network of 25 nodes. We distinguish leaf nodes and forwarders. For LibReplay we also distinguish between logging and the background (BG) process.

Fig. 4. The memory footprint of LibReplay and its MCU load are similar to traditional logging approaches.The benchmark application is CTP routing (**TestNetwork**), we use the default buffer size of all loggers.

(CTP) [6]. Our results show that both the memory footprint and the MCU load of logging with LibReplay is comparable to these traditional approaches to logging (see Figure 4). We note that these, in contrast to LibReplay, commonly do not log sufficient information to enable replay debugging.

5   Conclusion

We introduced LibReplay, a lightweight architecture for flexible logging and deterministic replay in sensor networks. LibReplay enables (1) event logging with only a small intrusion of the system, and (2) deterministic event replay in controlled environments such as system simulators. As a result, we can exploit the debugging capabilities of modern system simulators. Overall, LibReplay simplifies bug hunting in deployed sensor networks and provides a debugging experience similar to debugging (local and non-distributed) sequential programs. We discuss the architecture of LibReplay and our performance evaluations show that the efficiency of LibReplay is similar to the state of the art, which commonly does not log sufficient information to provide replay capabilities. We have made the source code of LibReplay publicly available at https://github.com/olafland/LibReplay.

Acknowledgments. This work was partially supported by the EC, through project FP7-STREP-288195, KARYON (Kernel-based ARchitecture for safetY-critical cONtrol), and by the Swedish Energy Agency under the program Energy, IT and Design.

References

1. Bellard, F.: QEMU, a Fast and Portable Dynamic Translator. In: ATEC: Proc. of the Annual Conf. on USENIX Annual Technical Conference (2005)
2. Dong, W., et al.: Dynamic Logging with Dylog for Networked Embedded Systems. In: SECON: Proc. of the IEEE Int. Conf. on Sensing, Communication, and Networking (2014)
3. Dunkels, A., Gronvall, B., Voigt, T.: Contiki - A Lightweight and Flexible Operating System for Tiny Networked Sensors. In: LCN: Proc. of the IEEE Conf. on Local Computer Networks (2004)
4. Eriksson, J., et al.: Towards Interoperability Testing for Wireless Sensor Networks with COOJA/MSPSim. In: EWSN: Proc. of the European Conf. on Wireless Sensor Networks (2009)
5. Geels, D., et al.: Replay Debugging for Distributed Applications. In: ATEC: Proc. of the Annual Conf. on USENIX Annual Technical Conference (2006)
6. Gnawali, O., et al.: Collection Tree Protocol. In: SenSys: Proc. of the ACM Conf. on Embedded Networked Sensor Systems (2009)
7. Lamport, L.: Time, Clocks, and the Ordering of Events in a Distributed System. Commun. ACM 21(7) (1978)
8. Narayanasamy, S., et al.: BugNet: Continuously Recording Program Execution for Deterministic Replay Debugging. In: ISCA: Proc. of the Annual Int. Symposium on Computer Architecture (2005)
9. Netzer, R.H.B., Miller, B.P.: Optimal Tracing and Replay for Debugging Message-passing Parallel Programs. In: Supercomputing: Proc. of the ACM/IEEE Conf. on Supercomputing (1992)
10. Österlind, F., et al.: Cross-Level Sensor Network Simulation with COOJA. In: LCN: Proc. of the IEEE Conf. on Local Computer Networks (2006)
11. Sauter, R., et al.: TinyLTS: Efficient Network-Wide Logging and Tracing System for TinyOS. In: INFOCOM: Proc. of the IEEE Int. Conf. on Computer Communications (2011)
12. Sommer, P., Kusy, B.: Minerva: Distributed Tracing and Debugging in Wireless Sensor Networks. In: SenSys: Proc. of the ACM Conf. on Embedded Networked Sensor Systems (2013)
13. Sundaram, V., Eugster, P., Zhang, X.: Prius: Generic Hybrid Trace Compression for Wireless Sensor Networks. In: SenSys: Proc. of the ACM Conf. on Embedded Networked Sensor Systems (2012)
14. Sundaram, V., et al.: Diagnostic Tracing for Wireless Sensor Networks. ACM Trans. Sen. Netw. 9(4) (2013)
15. Tancreti, M., et al.: Aveksha: A Hardware-software Approach for Non-intrusive Tracing and Profiling of Wireless Embedded Systems. In: SenSys: Proc. of the ACM Conf. on Embedded Networked Sensor Systems (2011)
16. Titzer, B.L., Lee, D.K., Palsberg, J.: Avrora: Scalable Sensor Network Simulation with Precise Timing. In: IPSN: Proc. of the ACM/IEEE Int. Conf. on Information Processing in Sensor Networks (2005)
17. Wan, L., Cao, Q.: Towards Instruction Level Record and Replay of Sensor Network Applications. In: MASCOTS: Proc. of the IEEE Int. Symp. on Modeling, Analysis Simulation of Computer and Telecommunication Systems (2013)
18. Wang, M.O.: Dependence-based Multi-level Tracing and Replay for Wireless Sensor Networks Debugging. In: LCTES: Proc. of the SIGPLAN/SIGBED Conference on Languages, Compilers and Tools for Embedded Systems (2011)

If You Can't Take the Heat: Temperature Effects on Low-Power Wireless Networks and How to Mitigate Them

Florian Schmidt[1], Matteo Ceriotti[2], Niklas Hauser[1], and Klaus Wehrle[1]

[1] Communication and Distrib. Systems Group, RWTH Aachen University, Germany
{schmidt,wehrle}@comsys.rwth-aachen.de, niklas.hauser@rwth-aachen.de
[2] Networked Embedded Systems Group, University of Duisburg–Essen, Germany
matteo.ceriotti@uni-due.de

Abstract. Low-power wireless networks, especially in outdoor deployments, are exposed to a wide range of temperatures. The detrimental effect of high temperatures on communication quality is well known. In this paper, we use a testbed with self-made temperature control devices to investigate the effects of temperature on several communication-relevant metrics. The analyses both confirm some previously published results and demonstrate deviations from others. Based on these results, we propose a Reed–Solomon-based FEC scheme to mitigate the negative effects of temperature and provide results suggesting that such a scheme is both feasible and advantageous.

Keywords: wireless sensor networks, measurements, packet corruption, bit errors, reliability, forward error correction, temperature effects.

1 Introduction

Low-power wireless networked devices are seeing more and more uses, enabling monitoring of areas both remote and inaccessible, and within our own homes, from any point on Earth. Depending on the deployment scenario, those devices can be exposed to strongly varying environmental effects. In recent publications, it has been shown that temperature has a strong effect on communication quality [2,3,4,5]: as temperature rises, communication becomes more challenging, up to an eventual complete breakdown. To further investigate these effects, we designed "HotBox", a solution to exactly control temperature and spatial orientation of sensor nodes. While our experiments confirm the influence of temperature, they also highlight some deviations. In particular, we observe a more marked link quality decrease in the case of a heated receiver, in contrast to the more significant impact of a heated transmitter demonstrated in the literature.

Based on the gathered measurements, we propose a solution to offset the effect that temperature has on the wireless communication by using an adaptive Reed–Solomon-based FEC mechanism, and discuss preliminary results. This paper presents our investigation and paves the way for both gathering further knowledge about the interplay between temperature and low-power wireless communication, as well as possible counteractions to preserve system reliability.

T. Abdelzaher et al. (Eds.): EWSN 2015, LNCS 8965, pp. 266–273, 2015.
© Springer International Publishing Switzerland 2015

2   Related Work

We first turn our attention to the current knowledge about the impact of temperature on the reliability of low-power wireless communication. Then, we survey FEC schemes proposed for low-power wireless networks.

Bannister et al. [2] were one of the first to analyze the impact of temperature on the performance of the CC2420 radio, the one employed in our study. The results demonstrated a reduction of RSSI with an increase of temperature, more marked with a heated transmitter. In [3], this behavior was also identified, again with larger differences when the transmitter was heated than when the receiver was. Both studies identify the cause in the loss of gain in the CC2420 Low Noise Amplifier. The asymmetry was confirmed by Boano et al. [4] for Noise Floor, PLR and LQI in a comprehensive study on the effects of temperature. Their Temp-Lab [5] setup is based on remotely-controlled IR light bulbs, polystyrene foam enclosures, and Peltier elements to build cheap and small temperature chambers. In our work, we develop a similar solution to experiment with temperature and spatial orientation of devices, which we make available for everybody to reproduce [9]. Using this testbed, we extend the available knowledge by demonstrating deviations from the previously reported behavior, in particular showing a greater impact of a heated receiver on the decrease in link quality.

FEC increases transmission reliability by recovering corrupted payloads by using correction information added to transmitted messages. The additional per-message overhead is justified by the reduced number of retransmissions required for a successfully delivery, reducing overall energy consumption. Reed–Solomon (RS) codes [7], a popular choice for FEC, can be very efficient in correcting corrupted messages while maintaining energy efficiency. Moreover, changing the code rate dynamically [1] at run time based on link quality outperforms static RS codes. Finally, Hermans et al. [6] exploit knowledge about mutation patterns caused by the CC2420's MSK demodulator used to receive OQPSK modulated signals. They build probability distributions to infer the most likely transmitted symbol and reconstruct the original data. In our work, we propose an adaptive FEC scheme that exploits the knowledge about error distributions inside corrupted packets and the impact of temperature on the reception probability.

3   Influence of Temperature on Communication

In the following, we present results from our experimental setup investigating the influence of temperature on the communication quality between sensor nodes.

3.1   Experimental Setup

For our experiments, we used TelosB sensor nodes from different manufacturers as well as production runs and ages. The TelosB is a widely-used platform that employs a CC2420 radio chip for communication which implements the IEEE 802.15.4 standard. At the physical layer, the standard defines a DSSS OQPSK modulation in the 2.4 GHz ISM band, with a nominal data rate of 250 kbps. All experiments were conducted in a room that witnesses little interference from surrounding IEEE 802.11 (WiFi) networks; furthermore, we used channel 26 of the 802.15.4 standard, which is outside the band allocated to 802.11 in Europe.

For temperature control during the experiments, we designed a system we termed "HotBox". Its design stems from the need to accurately control the influence of temperature on sensor motes. One of our goals with HotBox was to design a highly accurate control system (less than 0.5 °C deviation) which can be produced relatively quickly and cheaply. Thus, all hardware elements are off-the-shelf items, while all manufacturing can be done with a soldering iron, a PCB mill, and a laser cutter, which are often available via the rapidly-spreading FabLab concept. For reasons of brevity, we refrain from an in-depth description and performance evaluation of HotBox and refer to [9] for further information.

Experiments used direct (single-hop) connections between links. Each experiment comprised two boxes with one node each. Both nodes were connected to a PC via USB; the PC created the packets and sent them via USB to one node (alternating the sender role between the two nodes every packet); the node would then send the packet via the CC2420 radio. If the other node received the packet, it forwarded the received version to the PC via USB, which then compared the original and the received version for bit errors. Otherwise, a timeout would be triggered at the PC to identify the missed reception. Each run comprised 180 000 packets, spread out over approximately 3.5 hours, during which we gradually increased the temperature in one of the boxes from 30 °C to 80 °C, while keeping the other at 30 °C. We exchanged the nodes between experimental runs to account for potential performance differences between production runs and different models of the TelosB nodes. However, for the metrics presented in this paper, we could not find any noticeable performance differences.

3.2 Packet Error Dependency on Temperature

First, we aimed to reproduce the results from previous work [2, 3, 4, 5] in our setup. We started with a temperature of 30 °C and gradually increased the temperature in 5 or 10 °C increments, spending 20 minutes at each target temperature. Results for each node were saved separately, thereby creating two separate datasets from heating the transmitter and from heating the receiver, respectively. We recorded the RSSI, the Link Quality Indicator (LQI), and bit error rate (BER) as well as packet reception rate (PRR). We split the latter into three cases: a packet could be received without errors; received, but with errors; or not received at all (completely lost). Figure 1 shows a typical result from one of our experiments. All presented results are values as witnessed by the receiving mote. Thus, the temperature shown in Figure 1b shows temperature changes throughout the experiment. Conversely, Figure 1a does not show any changes in the temperature, because it was the transmitter which was heated, while the receiver, whose values are shown, was kept at a constant temperature.

Overall, it can be seen that all metrics are negatively influenced by temperature. However, the amount as to which they are influenced differs, and heating

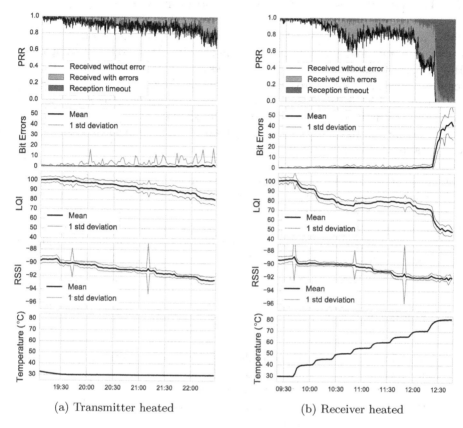

(a) Transmitter heated   (b) Receiver heated

Fig. 1. Influence of temperature on several key communication metrics. Note that all results are collected at the receiver, hence temperature in Fig. 1a stays stable because only the transmitter is heated. While temperature has a negative effect on all metrics, the effect is generally much stronger if the receiver is heated.

the transmitter and the receiver has different magnitudes of effect for most metrics. The only metric that is largely independent of this fact is the RSSI. All other metrics show a much higher negative influence when the receiver is heated. Heating the transmitter to 80 °C still allows communication, albeit with a packet error rate of more than 20%. In contrast, communication completely breaks if that temperature is applied at the receiver's side, and even at 70 °C, PER is much higher at above 50%. This is reflected in the BER, which explodes at receiver temperature above 70 °C. At the same time, LQI significantly decreases.

Summarizing, our results reinforce the notion of temperature as a significant influence on the communication quality in low-power networks. However, we were not able to reproduce the results in [4], which showed transmitter heating as the larger influence on quality metrics. In our experiments, heating the receiver produces a larger impact. This has repercussions that we will discuss later.

4   Temperature-Based FEC for Sensor Nodes

These results show that, while bit error rate increases with temperature, it typically does not do so massively until the point the connection collapses completely. However, even those relatively small increases already lead to steadily and significantly increasing packet error rates. Considering these results, we investigated the use of an FEC scheme that introduces redundancy into the sent messages in challenging link conditions. Such a system should (1) be adaptable so that an optimum tradeoff between reliability and overhead can be chosen, and (2) be computationally simple enough to work well on constrained devices. These requirements suggest the use of Reed–Solomon (RS) codes. Moreover, readily available implementations for constrained devices already exist, e.g., TinyRS [7].

A Reed–Solomon code [8] is parameterized with a tuple (m, n, k), where m is the size of a block in bits, and the code transforms k blocks into n blocks with $n > k$ (which gives a so-called *code rate* of k/n), being able to correct up to $\lfloor (n - k + 1)/2 \rfloor$ erroneous blocks (that is, blocks with at least one flipped bit) in the resulting message. We decided to use 8-bit blocks because byte-level operations are efficient to use on microcontrollers.

4.1   Simulator

To investigate the effects of RS-based FEC on reception quality, we need to exactly reproduce the environmental effects during each experiment. Otherwise, the differences in channel quality impair the comparability of results in different runs, because the effects of channel conditions mix with those of different FEC strengths. However, repeatability of wireless testbed results is a well-known hard problem. To abstract from channel conditions, we created a simple trace-based simulator. In such a simulator, a trace (i.e., a recording of a real-world communication that contains bit errors, environmental conditions, etc.) is used to translate bit errors that occurred in the real world onto a simulated connection.

The simplest way to use such a trace would be to mark which bits were corrupted, and overlay this pattern 1:1 onto another message, regardless of length and contents of both messages. This, however, would discount the differences in relative errors depending on message content. It has been shown [6, 10] that different nibbles (4-bit blocks) of data have different error rates. Hence, we first extracted from the trace the relative BER for each nibble. The simulator would then compute 16 values, one for each nibble, and normalize them to an average of 0 (resulting in some negative and some positive values). During the experiment, whenever a packet was prepared for sending by the PC, instead of forwarding it to the mote via USB, we handed it to the simulator. The simulator took the next packet in the trace, counted its bit errors and calculated the BER for that packet. It then added the relative per-nibble values to that rate, and finally applied, for each nibble in the simulated message, the corresponding per-nibble BER to its 4 bits. The resulting (potentially corrupted) packet was then handed back to the PC application, which would compare it to the original version.

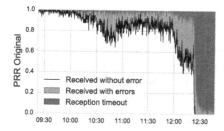
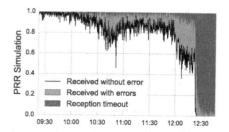

Fig. 2. Comparison of packet reception rates between the real-world experiment presented in Figure 1b and a simulation run based on that experiment's trace. The simulator closely follows the real-world results.

Figure 2 shows a comparison of a real-world measurement and the trace-based simulation of random packet contents of the same size. The simulation models the real-world results well; it only slightly overestimates packet error and loss rates. This means that results produced with the simulator will potentially underestimate the efficacy of our FEC scheme, but not overestimate it.

4.2   Evaluation Setup

To minimize the differences between the packets in the trace and simulated packets, we required all packets to have the same size. For our experiments, we used 80 bytes of payload. However, different robustnesses of RS codes mean that for a fixed k, n has to be increased. Due to the fixed packet size, we decided to do the opposite: for the baseline experiment without any FEC, we sent 80-byte payloads. As robustness increased, code length n stayed the same, but data length k was reduced accordingly. Thus, at a code rate of $1/2$, the packet length was still 80 byte, but it only carried 40 bytes of data, plus 40 bytes of redundancy.

Under these circumstances, packet reception rate is not a meaningful metric any more. Normally, if the amount of data is kept static, the packet size increases with stronger FEC to accommodate the additional code bytes. This serves as a trade-off in itself, since as the packets grow in size, the chance of having more bit errors within a packet increases, too. If packet size is kept static, packet reception rate will only increase with increasing FEC robustness, as more and more errors can be repaired. We therefore account for the amount of data bytes in each packet by calculating a *normalized throughput* metric: $T(80, k) = \frac{k}{80} \cdot \frac{PRR_{decoded}}{PRR_{received}}$, where k is the number of data bytes in the 80-byte payload, and $PRR_{received}$ and $PRR_{decoded}$ are the rate of packet with errors before and after Reed–Solomon error correction, respectively. Thus, T yields a value of 1 for an unencoded connection without packet losses. As robustness increases (and therefore the amount of data bytes in the 80-byte packet decreases), $k/80$ decreases: the potential maximum throughput is reduced due to coding. The code can offset this by repairing corrupted packets and therefore increasing $PRR_{decoded}/PRR_{received}$.

4.3   Evaluation Results

We then used traces from the experiments described in Section 3 to drive our simulator. To investigate the effects of different Reed–Solomon code robustnesses, we repeated the experiments with different settings of data length k. The results presented in Figure 3 are based on the trace of the measurement shown in Figure 1b; hence, the packet reception rates follow the same general behavior.

The figure clearly shows that the performance of FEC strongly depends on the channel conditions. At low temperatures, channel conditions are unproblematic, so the unencoded connection shows the highest throughput. As temperature rises, however, FEC shows its advantages: while each message can transport less information, the information is more robust and more rarely lost. At the very high end, when communication breaks down almost completely, higher and higher code rates are needed to keep at least some messages uncorrupted.

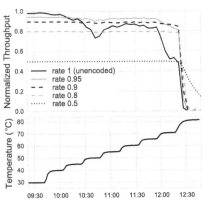

Fig. 3. Reed–Solomon FEC increases effective throughput in challenging conditions by significantly reducing packet loss. This simulation is based on the results presented in Figure 1b. Even using as little as 5% of the message for FEC (rate 0.95) produces a large benefit as soon as temperatures rise above 40 °C.

Interestingly, even under conditions that are common and not especially challenging (40 °C are easily reached in watertight containers under sunshine), FEC can already provide noticeably fewer packet losses with a small overhead, keeping communication both more stable and reliable, and often also increasing the throughput. We therefore suggest to always consider whether adding FEC will provide beneficial effects to your low-power wireless connectivity, especially if challenging conditions cannot be ruled out or can even be expected at least intermittently.

5   Discussion and Future Work

We originally devised the presented FEC scheme in the hope that we could reproduce previous results [4], which showed that the sender's temperature has a larger effect on communication quality than the receiver's. This would allow for a temperature-driven adaptive FEC, where the robustness of the Reed–Solomon code is increased as temperature at the sender rises. That decision would stem from purely locally available information: the temperature of the mote itself.

However, we could not reproduce this effect in our experiments. Instead, the receiver's temperature always had a larger influence on quality metrics such as packet reception rate or LQI than the sender's temperature. Therefore, the temperature that produces the larger effect is not available locally to the sender, and cannot be used to decide on code rate before sending of the message.

We envision several possibilities that warrant further scrutiny. An adaptive FEC scheme could nevertheless solely rely on sender temperature, which does have some impact on the communication; such an adaptation would therefore be merely suboptimal. When mote temperatures correlate strongly, for example, inside rooms or on flat terrain, purely local information may already be sufficient. Alternatively, a system of feedback should also be investigated. For example, motes could inform their neighborhood about their temperature by piggybacking this information onto other messages. However, if we already consider feedback, we should not only focus on temperature. In the end, high communication performance always depends on low packet loss rates. Instead of feeding back information about an influence factor on packet loss (temperature), information about packet loss rate itself could be fed back from the receiver to the sender. If the communication already uses acknowledgments, this information can be effectively inferred by the sender "for free" from the number of received acknowledgments. It can then be used to adapt the code rate to minimize packet losses. At this point, such an FEC scheme closely resembles rate adaptation schemes as found in WiFi networks. We consider the investigation whether and in what fashion the myriad of contributions in the field of WiFi rate adaptation can be applied to low-power wireless networks an exciting field for future work.

Acknowledgments. This research was partially funded by the Alexander von Humboldt Foundation.

References

1. Ahn, J.S., Hong, S.W., Heidemann, J.: An adaptive fec code control algorithm for mobile wireless sensor networks. J. Comm. Netw. 7(4), 489–498 (2005)
2. Bannister, K., Giorgetti, G., Gupta, S.K.S.: Wireless sensor networking for "hot" applications: Effects of temperature on signal strength, data collection and localization. In: Proc. HotEmNets. ACM (2008)
3. Boano, C.A., et al.: The impact of temperature on outdoor industrial sensornet applications. IEEE Trans. Ind. Informat. 6(3), 451–459 (2010)
4. Boano, C.A., et al.: Hot Packets: A systematic evaluation of the effect of temperature on low power wireless transceivers. In: Proc. ExtremeCom. ACM (2013)
5. Boano, C.A., et al.: Templab: A testbed infrastructure to study the impact of temperature on wireless sensor networks. In: Proc. IPSN. IEEE Press (2014)
6. Hermans, F., Wennerström, H., McNamara, L., Rohner, C., Gunningberg, P.: All is not lost: Understanding and exploiting packet corruption in outdoor sensor networks. In: Krishnamachari, B., Murphy, A.L., Trigoni, N. (eds.) EWSN 2014. LNCS, vol. 8354, pp. 116–132. Springer, Heidelberg (2014)
7. Liang, C.J.M., Priyantha, N.B., Liu, J., Terzis, A.: Surviving Wi-fi Interference in Low Power ZigBee Networks. In: Proc. SenSys, pp. 309–322. ACM (2010)
8. Reed, I.S., Solomon, G.: Polynomial codes over certain finite fields. Journal of the Society for Industrial and Applied Mathematics 8(2), 300–304 (1960)
9. Schmidt, F., Ceriotti, M., Hauser, N., Wehrle, K.: Hotbox: Testing temperature effects in sensor networks. Tech. Rep. AIB-2014-14, RWTH Aachen (2014)
10. Schmidt, F., Ceriotti, M., Wehrle, K.: Bit error distribution and mutation patterns of corrupted packets in low-power wireless networks. In: ACM WiNTECH (2013)

A Software Approach to Protecting Embedded System Memory from Single Event Upsets

Jiannan Zhai, Yangyang He, Fred S. Switzer, and Jason O. Hallstrom

Clemson Univeristy, Clemson, South Carolina, USA
{jzhai,yyhe,skyler,jasonoh}@clemson.edu

Abstract. Radiation from radioactive environments, such as those encountered during space flight, can cause damage to embedded systems. One of the most common examples is the *single event upset* (SEU), which occurs when a high-energy ionizing particle passes through an integrated circuit, changing the value of a single bit by releasing its charge. The SEU could cause damage and potentially fatal failures to spacecraft and satellites. In this paper, we present an approach that extends the AVR-GCC compiler to protect the system stack from SEUs through duplication, validation, and recovery. Three applications are used to verify our approach, and the time and space overhead characteristics are evaluated.

1 Introduction

One high-energy ionizing particle passing through an integrated circuit can release enough charge to change the state of a binary digit, causing a stored bit to change to its opposite value (i.e., a 0-bit can become a 1-bit, and vice-versa [18]). The results can range from system malfunction to system crash.

Modern approaches used to prevent and correct SEU errors often introduce additional hardware to the target system. In this paper, we present a *software-only* approach that detects and corrects SEUs in RAM. The paper focuses on the system stack, which is the most important and dynamic region in memory. The system stack is protected by injecting code into the target assembly generated by AVR-GCC. Our approach does not introduce additional hardware, and since it operates at the assembly level, it is language and application neutral.

2 Related Work

One of the primary hardware-level radiation hardening approaches is Silicon-on-Insulator (SoI) technology, used in microprocessor fabrication [1]. The design improves the circuit's tolerance to highly-charged particles, reducing the chance of SEU occurrence. Irom et al. [7] compare SEU error rates in SoI microprocessors to conventional microprocessors. SEU rates were observably lower in SoI microprocessors. Though SoI technology protects systems from SEUs, it prevents developers from using commercial off-the-shelf (COTS) devices, increasing system cost due to the high price of SoI circuits.

T. Abdelzaher et al. (Eds.): EWSN 2015, LNCS 8965, pp. 274–282, 2015.
© Springer International Publishing Switzerland 2015

Redundancy is a widely used fault-tolerance technique, both via hardware and software. The Triple Modular Redundancy (TMR) [8] approach executes instructions on three unique systems. A voting module is used to compare the results and choose the common result. Due to the low probability that more than one SEU will occur simultaneously at the same geographic location in more than one device [16], TMR is a popular SEU protection technique and allows the use of COTS components. However, hardware-based TMR introduces significant hardware overhead and power consumption, which can present concerns for weight-limited and power-critical systems.

Time Redundancy [2] is a software-only redundancy technique which runs each instruction three times on a single processor. The results are stored, and a voting module is invoked to yield the (most) common result. Error Detection by Duplicated Instructions (EDDI) [11], a variation on Time Redundancy, duplicates each instruction during the compilation phase and assigns each different registers and memory space. As a result, EDDI is able to protect systems from not only data SEUs, but also instruction SEUs. Time Triple Modular Redundancy [2] is a combination of time redundancy and hardware-based TMR. Each instruction is executed by three unique systems, as in standard TMR, but the systems execute the instruction in different clock cycles in a time-redundant fashion. This allows more instructions to be executed in parallel.

A watchdog timer (WDT) [6] is a timer used to detect and recover from system crashes by repeatedly querying the protected system and resetting the system if no response is received. A software-based WDT is straightforward to implement and introduces little overhead. However, it suffers the risk that an SEU may cause the WDT itself to malfunction. Despite increased cost, hardware-based WDT provides a reliable solution. Note, however, that WDT is typically used with other techniques since it only detects severe system faults.

Shirvani et al. [13] examine a set of Error Detection and Correction (EDAC) methods used to detect and correct errors in memory, such as those caused by SEUs. The authors find that the reliability of software-based methods tends to decrease over time more rapidly than hardware-based methods. However, the loss rate is low enough that software-based methods are still more cost effective than hardware-based methods.

3   System Design

We focus on the protection of the runtime stack under the following assumptions: (i) Flash memory and registers are not affected by SEUs. (ii) Only one SEU will occur during a given function execution. It is rare for more than one bit to be upset simultaneously; this occurs in only 5 to 6 percent of bit flip errors [17].

Our approach is designed to align with the NASA coding standards for C applied in space projects [10]: First, dynamic memory allocation is not allowed, so the heap section in RAM is not used. However, for the sake of completeness, we consider the possibility of a non-empty heap in our approach. Second, the goto statement is not allowed. Finally, each function should have fewer than 60 lines of code, making the execution time of each function relatively short.

Our approach protects the system stack by introducing auxiliary assembly code. The new code is injected at both the beginning and end of each function or interrupt handler. When a function is called, the code injected at the beginning of the call calculates the CRC of the caller's stack frame and saves both the CRC and the stack frame. Before the callee returns, the code injected at the end calculates the CRC of the caller's stack frame again, compares it with the saved CRC, and restores the caller's stack frame if the CRCs do not match.

3.1   Supporting Memory Sections

To store stack frame replicas, two new sections are created in SRAM just after the `.bss` section by modifying the linker script [14]. The new `md` section is used to store stack frame replicas, which are referred to as *Stack Frame Snapshots* (SFSs). The new `sp` section is used to store the address of the next available memory space in `md`, similar to the stack pointer. This address is referred to as the *Snapshot Top Pointer* (STP). To protect the STP from SEUs, the size of the `sp` section is set to 6 bytes, and 3 STP duplicates are stored in this section. Given that we assume only one SEU will occur during the execution of a given function, only one STP replica could be altered by a flipped bit. The altered STP is easily identified and corrected by comparing the values of the three STP replicas.

3.2   Injected Code Segments

The injected code segments are designed to use only registers, reducing their dependence on RAM. *CRC Calculate* is used to calculate the CRC of a memory region. In our implementation, CRC16-CCITT is used [5]. *CRC Save* is used to save the CRC to the stack. *CRC Compare* is used to compare two CRCs. The comparison result indicates whether an SEU is detected. *Frame Copy* is used to copy a stack frame to a given destination, and to save and restore stack frames. *Frame Size Save* is used to save the size of the stack frame for the current function. *STP Initialize* is used to initialize the STP so it points to the lowest address of the `md` section. *STP Update* is used to update the STP. First, it obtains the correct STP value by comparing the three STP replicas. The replicas are then updated to reflect the addition or removal of a stack frame.

3.3   Modified Function Execution Process

Modified Function Invocation Process. The code segments injected at the beginning of each function are used to calculate a CRC over the caller's stack frame, and to save a duplicate of the caller's stack frame, as shown in Figure 1. Each rectangle represents two stack bytes. The "starred" steps denote stack changes caused by the injected code. SP denotes the stack pointer, and Y denotes the stack frame pointer.

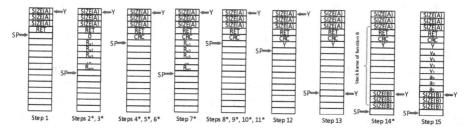

Fig. 1. Modified Function Invocation Process

When a function B is called by a function A, the return address is pushed onto the stack automatically by the function call instruction (step 1). To calculate the CRC of the caller's stack frame, multiple registers are used, so they must be saved before the CRC calculation process and restored when the process is finished. To prevent the calculated CRC from being overwritten when the registers are restored, two bytes are pushed onto the stack as a placeholder (step 2) for the CRC result before the registers used to calculate the CRC are saved (step 3). After the CRC of function A's stack frame is calculated (step 4), the CRC result is saved to the placeholder location (step 5). The registers used to calculate the CRC are then restored (step 6).

Next, the stack frame of the caller, function A, has to be saved. The registers used to save the frame are pushed (step 7). Next, the correct STP is selected by comparing the values of the three STP copies (step 8). Using the correct STP, the specified memory is then copied and saved in the SFS (step 9). After the STP copies are updated (step 10), the CRC registers are restored (step 11).

After the stack frame pointer of function B is saved (step 12), and the stack frame is established (step 13), three copies of the callee's frame size are pushed onto the stack (step 14), which is a key operation in the injected code.

When a function is called, the callee does not have sufficient context regarding its caller, including the caller's stack frame address and size. It is impossible for a callee to calculate the CRC of it's caller's frame and to duplicate the frame without this information. To solve this problem, each function saves its frame size in the stack, which is used by its callee to perform the CRC calculation and frame copy. To ensure the correctness of the frame size, three copies are saved. Comparison is used to yield the correct value.

Modified Function Return Process. The code segments injected at the end of each function are used to verify the stack frame of the caller, and to restore the stack frame if an SEU is detected, as shown in Figure 2. When function B returns, it first pops its stack frame size (step 1). After the space used to store the arguments and local variables is released (step 2), the stack frame pointer is restored (step 3). The CRC of function A's stack frame is then calculated and temporarily stored in two registers (steps 4-6). The values stored in these registers are saved before the function return process. Next, the calculated CRC is compared with the CRC saved in the stack (step 7). If the two CRCs do not match, the saved stack frame of A is restored, and the STP is updated to release the space used to store the stack frame of A (steps 8-12). Again, the stack frame size of function A saved in the stack is used to support the CRC comparison and stack frame restoration (if needed). If the two CRCs match, the STP is updated (steps 13-14). After verification of A's stack frame is complete, the CRC is popped from the stack (step 15). Finally, function B returns, and the return address is popped automatically (step 16).

4   Evaluation

To evaluate our approach under varying stack conditions and SEU injection rates, three AVR applications are considered. The stack usage pattern of each application is shown in Figure 3.

4.1   Validation

We first validate our approach and consider the SEU protection efficacy it affords. In our analysis, we ignore both the .data and the .bss sections, as well as the heap section. Data stored in the .data, .bss, and heap sections can be protected using well-known techniques based on cloning and comparison. We focus our analysis on stack frame protection. We first assume that the currently executing

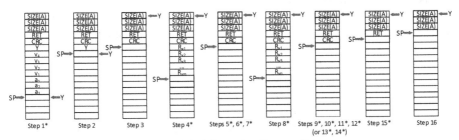

Fig. 2. Modified Function Return Process

function's frame, which includes the return address of the injected code segment, is not affected by SEUs. The stack frames of callers and callees are guaranteed to be correct, so the stack is guaranteed to be correct. To verify this claim, the AVR Simulator IDE [12] was used to manually inject SEUs, and to observe execution results. The results showed that each function is able to detect and fix SEUs introduced "beneath" the topmost stack frame.

However, if the stack frame of the current function is affected by an SEU, protection is not guaranteed. If the SEU changes key data, such as the return

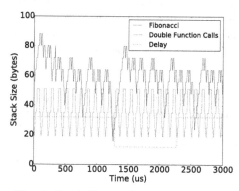

Fig. 3. Stack Usage of Test Applications

address or stack frame size, the current function will not execute as expected. We assume that only one SEU will occur during a given function execution, and that the SEU is uniformly likely to affect all bits in RAM. The probability of successful SEU protection can be expressed as $p = 1 - c/(2s + e - c + 6)$. Where p is the probability of successful protection, s is the stack size, e is the size of the unused space in RAM, 6 is the size of the three STP copies, and c is the average size of a stack frame. Since the return address of the injected code segment is stored in the current stack frame, the two bytes for the return address are included in c. The total size of protected memory is $s + e + (s - c) + 6$, where $s - c$ is the size of the stack frame copies stored in the md section.

We extend our analysis to cases where more than one SEU may occur during a given function execution. Due to lack of space, we omit the derivation details. The (conservative) probability of successful protection can be expressed as:

$$
\begin{aligned}
p = & \left(1 - \frac{c}{2s + e - c + 6}\right)^n * \left(1 - \frac{6}{2s + e - 2c + 6}\right)^n \\
& * \left(1 - \frac{6}{2s + e - 2c}\right)^n * \left\{\left(1 - \frac{2c}{2s + e - 2c - 6}\right)^n\right. \\
& + C_2^1 * \left(1 - \frac{c}{2s + e - 2c - 6}\right)^n * \left[1 - \left(1 - \frac{c}{2s + e - 3c - 6}\right)^n\right]\right\}
\end{aligned}
\tag{1}
$$

Where p is the probability of success, s is the size of the stack, e is the size of the unused space in RAM, 6 is the size of the three stack frame size copies or the three STP copies, c is the average size of the stack frame (including the return address of the injected code segment), and n is the number of SEUs that occur during a function's execution. In equation 1, the number of SEUs that occur, n, can be expressed as $n = y * l * f/m$, where y is the number of clock cycles used to execute each instruction, m is the frequency of the microprocessor, l is the average number of function instructions, and f is the SEU injection rate. Most AVR instructions require 2 clock cycles to execute, and the frequency of our ATmega644 is set to 10MHz.

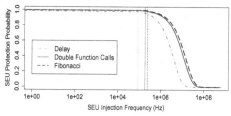

Fig. 4. SEU Protection Probability

We now consider the relationship between SEU protection probability and SEU occurrence rate. To demonstrate the relationship, we collect the corresponding parameters for the three test applications using AVR Simulator IDE. Figure 4 plots the change in SEU protection probability as a function of SEU injection rate.

The x-axis represents the rate at which SEUs are injected, and the y-axis represents the corresponding SEU protection probability. Each vertical line marks where the number of SEUs begins to exceed 1 (for each application). When only one SEU occurs during a given function execution (left side of the vertical line), the SEU protection probability is constant (Delay: 99.48%, Double Function Calls: 99.71%, Fibonacci: 99.68%) because the only case the approach cannot handle is when the current frame is affected. When more than one SEU occurs during a given function execution (right side of the vertical line), the SEU protection probability increases. As the SEU occurrence rate increases, the SEU protection probability decreases, until it approaches 0. The lower the stack dynamism, the longer the function execution time, which increases the probability of SEU occurrence in the current stack frame.

4.2   Performance

Since the same code is injected for every function, the execution overhead is similar for all functions, varying only when an SEU is detected. The execution overhead depends on the size of the (recovered) stack frame. The *CRC Calculate* code segment and *STP Update* code segment execute twice for each function, and the *Frame Copy* code segment executes either once or twice, depending on whether an SEU is detected. Each of the other code segments executes once for each function execution. The minimum overhead introduced in terms of number of clock cycles is $62 * S + 304$, when an SEU is not detected. The worst case is $70 * S + 432$ clock cycles, when an SEU is detected.

We next evaluate space overhead using the three test applications. The ROM space data was collected using *avr-size*. The results are summarized in Figure 5. The y-axis represents ROM size, in bytes. Delay and Fibonacci involve two functions, and Double Function Calls involves four. From Figure 5, we can see that the ROM overhead for the Double Function Calls application is twice the Delay and Fibonacci applications. ROM overhead is related only to the number of functions in the program.

4.3   Physical Hardware

To validate our approach on physical hardware, we emulate the occurrence of SEUs by flipping random bits in the target SRAM area. To perform auditable test runs, we developed an AVR application which continuously generates an increasing integer sequence, which is then sent to the UART interface at a controllable speed. A Python program running on a desktop is used to receive the sequence and observe the impact of flipped bits by monitoring the continuity of the sequence. A timer interrupt is used to trigger the occurrence of SEUs. The interrupt service routine generates a random address within the range of the top of the stack and the end of RAM space, excluding the stack frame of the current interrupt, and then flips the bit at this location.

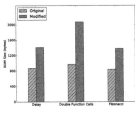

Fig. 5. ROM Overhead

We declare (observable) failure when one of the following two situations occurs: (i) The AVR application stops generating integers; or (ii) the integer sequence received by the Python program becomes discontinuous. We monitor the integer sequence and record the maximum count before failure. The experimental results are summarized in Figure 6. The x-axis represents SEU injection frequency, and the y-axis represents the maximum count received by the Python program. The figure shows that as SEU injection frequency increases, running time to failure decreases. This is explained as follows: As SEU injection frequency increases, the probability that an SEU occurs in a critical area increases. When the frequency is extremely high (e.g. approximately 10 MHz), the program can hardly send any values. However, the observed SEU occurrence rate in outer space is approximately $10^{-6} SEU/bit\text{-}Day$ [16]. Given that the total RAM size of an Atmega644 is 4K Bytes, the expected SEU occurrence rate for an Atmega644 is 0.0032 SEU/day, which is significantly lower than the lowest frequency (9765.625 SEU/second) that we used. This situation would be extremely rare in real scenarios.

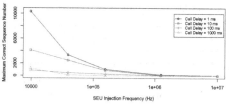

Fig. 6. Physical Hardware Results

5   Conclusion

The single event upset is among the most common types of system faults introduced by radiation, posing significant risk to spacecraft embedded systems. Modern approaches to guarding against such faults typically introduce additional hardware to detect and correct SEU errors in target systems. In this paper, we present a software-only approach to protecting embedded system memory from SEUs, focused on the system stack. The stack is protected by injecting auxiliary assembly code within the target program. The prototype implementation is based on the AVR architecture, but is easily adapted to other architectures. Analytical and experimental results show that our approach detects and corrects SEU errors as expected.

Acknowledgments. This work is supported by the National Science Foundation through awards CNS-0745846 and CNS-1126344, and the City of Aiken, SC.

References

1. Celler, G.K., Cristoloveanu, S.: Frontiers of silicon-on-insulator. Journal of Applied Physics 93(9), 4955–4978 (2003)
2. Czajkowski, D., McCartha, M.: Ultra low-power space computer leveraging embedded seu mitigation. In: IEEE Aerospace Conf., vol. 5, pp. 2315–2328 (2003)

3. Darling, P.: Intel to Invest More than 5 Billion to Build New Factory in Arizona (October 2013), http://newsroom.intel.com/community/intel_newsroom/blog/2011/02/18/intel-to-invest-more-than-5-billion-to-build-new-factory-in-arizona

4. Dutton, B.F., Stroud, C.E.: Single Event Upset Detection and Correction in Virtex-4 and Virtex-5 FPGAs. In: CATA (09), W. L. 0025, Ed., ISCA, pp. 57–62

5. Geluso, J.: CRC16-CCITT (January 2014), http://srecord.sourceforge.net/crc16-ccitt.html

6. Huang, L., Selman, J.J.: Watchdog timer. US Patent 4,627,060 (December 2, 1986)

7. Irom, F., Farmanesh, F., Johnston, A., Swift, G., Millward, D.: Single-event upset in commercial silicon-on-insulator PowerPC microprocessors. IEEE Transactions on Nuclear Science 49(6), 3148–3155 (2002)

8. Lyons, R., Vanderkulk, W.: The Use of Triple-Modular Redundancy to Improve Computer Reliability. IBM JRD 6(2), 200–209 (1962)

9. NASA. Space Shuttle Era Facts (October 2013)

10. NASA. JPL Institutional Coding Standard for the C Programming Language (April 2014), http://lars-lab.jpl.nasa.gov/JPL_Coding_Standard_C.pdf

11. Oh, N., et al.: Error detection by duplicated instructions in super-scalar processors. IEEE Transactions on Reliability 51(1), 63–75 (2002)

12. OshonSoft. AVR SIMULATOR IDE (January 2014), http://www.oshonsoft.com/avr.html

13. Shirvani, P., Saxena, N., McCluskey, E.: Software-implemented EDAC protection against SEUs. IEEE Transactions on Reliability 49(3), 273–284 (2001)

14. sourceware. Linker Scripts, 10 13, http://sourceware.org/binutils/docs/ld/Scripts.html

15. ucsusa. USC Satellite Database (October 2013), http://www.ucsusa.org/nuclear_weapons_and_global_security/space_weapons/technical_issues/ucs-satellite-database.html

16. Underwood, C., Ward, J., Dyer, C., Sims, A.: Observations of single-event upsets in non-hardened high-density srams in sun-synchronous orbit. IEEE Transactions on Nuclear Science 39(6), 1817–1827 (1992)

17. Underwood, C., Ward, J., Dyer, C., Sims, A.: Observations of single-event upsets in non-hardened high-density SRAMs in Sun-synchronous orbit. IEEE Transactions on Nuclear Science 39(6), 1817–1827 (1992)

18. Vincent, L., Pisacane, H.K.U.: Embedded Software Systems. In: Fundamentals of Space Systems, 2nd edn., Oxford University Press, New York (2005)

Revealing Protocol Information and Activity from Energy Instrumentation in Wireless Sensor Network

Dong Han[1], Omprakash Gnawali[1], and Abhishek B. Sharma[2]

[1] University of Houston, USA
{donny,gnawali}@cs.uh.edu
[2] NEC Laboratories America, Inc.
absharma@nec-labs.com

Abstract. In this paper, we present a novel approach to study and reveal network and protocol information from energy instrumentation in wireless sensor network. Unlike prior approaches which focused on analyzing the aggregate statistics of energy efficiency of a network or a protocol, our approach aims at revealing network protocols, application workloads, and topology information by fine-grained energy instrumentation on the nodes. We design a set of features based on various aspects of energy data and use those features to classify and reveal network activity. Results from experiments on three testbeds indicate that our approach can achieve 97% accuracy to identify the routing protocols, and infer the network topology with 98% accuracy.

Keywords: Power Measurements, Wireless Sensor Networks, Protocols.

1 Introduction

Energy instrumentation has a long history of research in wireless sensor network. Energy efficient protocols and applications are one of the objectives of Wireless Sensor Network (WSN) research. Energy instrumentation and analysis allows us to determine if the proposed protocol is better than the state-of-the-art. Various hardware-based energy instrumentation, simulation based study of energy footprint, and using radio activity as a proxy for energy has found widespread adoption in the community.

In this paper, we argue that despite the long history of energy instrumentation in WSN, we have not fully understood the implications of energy instrumentation in WSNs. Other communities have found that instrumentation of any type must be performed with care. Otherwise, there can be privacy and security implications. Existing work has indicated that power measurements can also act as side channel with the potential to compromise private information about the users [9]. We study these issues and implications in the context of sensor networks: could the energy instrumentation we collect in almost every sensor network deployment serve as side a channel to reveal unintended information?

We motivate the possibilities with one example from real-world devices. Monster powercontrol is a commercially available smart plug. We measure the power

T. Abdelzaher et al. (Eds.): EWSN 2015, LNCS 8965, pp. 283–290, 2015.

used by the plugs to reveal four properties of the system without any source code. First, we can tell the power state (On/Off) of plug outlet from the energy draw. Second, the current draw gives hints about the periodic communication between the plug and base station. Third, we can verify that the devices query the base station for new commands rather than the base station pushing messages to the devices: the periodic current crests continue even when we turn off the base station. Fourth, the current draw can also give hints about the wireless connectivity between the user devices and the base station.

We evaluate the design of our energy instrumentation and classification accuracy of the features based on energy data by doing extensive experiments on three WSN testbeds. Our results from analyzing four-million energy data and radio activity points, indicate that energy instrumentation and carefully designed features can not only reveal information about the network protocol but also some information about the application and the workload.

In this paper, we make three contributions:

- Design of classification features based on energy data with the goal of revealing protocol, network, and application information.
- Experimental evaluation of those features on three testbeds across multiple protocols, network topologies, and application workloads. We find that classification with those features can identify the routing protocol with more than 97% accuracy and application workloads with 85% accuracy.
- Demonstrate how we revealed the routing topology in the network, including next hop for each node, with just energy instrumentation, with 98% accuracy.

2   Related Work

In this section, we will give an overview of research related to energy measurement, profiling, and their applications in sensor networks and beyond.

Energy Instrumentation: Energy consumption is a significant concern in the design and development of WSN, hence, much progress and various measurement methods have been designed to measure the energy used by the nodes. Flock-Lab [8] has power meters attached to motes so the researchers could understand energy footprint of their protocols and applications. LEAP2 [11] provides unprecedented capabilities for directly observing energy usage for wireless sensor nodes in real-time, with microsecond-scale time resolution enables power profiling for each hardware subsystem. Researchers proposed a software based on-line code-level energy estimation model, the mechanism uses the current draw of each component during different period and aggregate them together to produce the total energy consumption [4].

Applications of Energy Measurement: While the primary reason for energy measurement is to understand the energy used by a sensor network system, researchers have found other use for energy data. Power Trace Testing is presented in [14], which designed a methodology to automatically investigate the correctness of a WSN system by utilizing non-intrusive power measurement. In the testcase the system was able to detect an unexpected use of hardware component, which is not as scheduled. Dunkels et al. [3] use power state tracking to estimate the wireless network power consumption on network-level. Their approach even can break down the power consumption into individual activities on each node, enable the power profiling the pre-activity energy cost.

Revealing Privacy and Security Information: Researchers proposed a technique that use link-layer header data to infer network topology, de-anonymize servers present in anonymized network, to break their anonymization[10]. Researchers demonstrated even without priori-knowledge of household activities, it is still possible to extract complex usage patterns and privacy information from the household smart meter [9].

3 Features Design

In this section, we describe two novel features that we designed to reveal information about the network.

Radio Awake Length Counter (RALC): We define Radio Awake Length (RAL) as the total time that a node stayed in awake mode during each awake-sleep cycles. The RAL is not a fixed value, it depends on the packet size, the time before a node receives acknowledgment, etc. We used the threshold values 25ms, and half of the LPL settings 100ms to divide the RAL into three categories corresponding to a node only performing CCA check, receiving packets and transmitting packets, respectively. We name these three ranges as T_1, T_2 and T_3 as defined below, where T presents the RAL of each time:

$$T_1 : T \leq 25ms \tag{1}$$
$$T_2 : 25ms < T \leq 100ms \tag{2}$$
$$T_3 : 100ms < T \tag{3}$$

Within 10s disjoint window size, we count the amount of RAL in each of these ranges, and use these three counters are the feature, named Radio Awake Length Counter, i.e., $RALC = [m1, m2, m3]$, where m1 is the number of RALs that satisfy the predicate T_1. m2 and m3 are defined analogously. On Indriya and Twonet without energy meters, we measure RAL using software instrumentation.

Radio Awake Overlap Counter (RAOC): When a node successfully transmits a packet, the intersection of their radio awake time must not be empty. We count the times of two nodes have their radio awake time overlapped during a given period of time, and call it Radio Awake Overlap Counter. We use this feature to help us to infer the network topology in section 5.2.

4 Instrumentation Design

Protocols: A Collection Protocol is designed to reliably collect the data packets generated from every node in the network. In our experiments, we use Collection Tree Protocol (CTP) [5] and MultiHopLQI (LQI) [13]. A Dissemination Protocol is designed to reliably deliver data packet from the base station to every node in the network. In our experiments, we use Drip [12] and DHV [1].

Testbed and Motes: We instrument the power uses and radio chips activities on three testbeds. FlockLab provides high-resolution power measurement profiling and precise time synchronization on 30 nodes. Indriya [2] has over 100 wireless sensor nodes. Twonet [7] is a testbed with 100 dual-radio nodes, which can operate in 2.4 GHz and 900 MHz. We set the Twonet nodes to run on 900 MHz to verify that our proposed approach works with 900 MHz as well. We use TinyOS for our experiments.

Low Power Listening (LPL): When using LPL, the node wakes up periodically to perform Clear Channel Assessment (CCA) to save energy. The node stays awake until the packet is received if it detects any preamble on the wireless medium. Otherwise it turns off its radio and switches back to sleep mode to save energy. In this study, we set LPL sleep interval to 200ms.

Experiment Configurations: Each experiment runs for an hour. Though it is impossible to ensure exactly the same workload across collection and dissemination protocols, we tried out best to make the workload similar across protocols by matching the packet sending interval, using the similar payload size with same sink node for all of the four experiments in each set.

Classifier Training: We use a 10s disjoint window to extract the RALC. Hence, for an one hour experiment, we have 360 feature vectors. In each set, four experiments generate 1440 feature vectors. We test four classifiers, J48, Logistic, Bagging and NaiveBayes. These are implemented in Weka [6], which has a collection of machine learning algorithms for data mining tasks. We also perform 10-fold cross-validation.

5   Experiment Settings and Evaluations

In this section we describe results on how accurately we are able to infer network and application aspects using features derived from energy instrumentation.

5.1   Identify Routing Protocols

Classify Network Protocols: We plot the classification accuracy results by using RALC across three testbeds in figure 1(a). The first group in figure shows all of four algorithms on FlockLab can achieve similar accuracy, and the average accuracy to classify the network protocol from RALC is more than 90%. The 2nd and 3rd group in figure 1(a) show the classification accuracy of using software measured RALC on Indriya and Twonet, where the average accuracy above 97% and 98%, respectively. This experiment show two highlights of RALC: It gives a robust results over the four classifiers. It generates a stable accuracy results over three testbeds, with different network layout and different radio bands.

To test the performance of RALC with external Wi-Fi interference, we repeat same experiments using two different channels, which one is overlapped with Wi-Fi, the other one is not. The results show the feature RALC can tolerant Wi-Fi

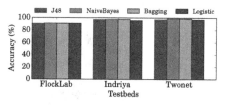

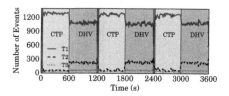

(a) Classification accuracy using RALC across three testbeds.

(b) Unsupervised clustering of two alternative network protocols.

Fig. 1. comparison of accuracy by using different features over 4 algorithms

interference and achieve similar classifier accuracy. We also evaluate RALC by training it on sample sets from one experiment configuration and then testing it on data from another experiment configuration. We have 7 such cases and RALC's accuracy was between 82-97%.

The reason why RALC gives a high classification results is because it can capture the unique patterns between the protocols. The control messages of each protocol is designed uniquely, e.g. the time interval between transmit control packets and number of control packets. While the workloads from the application layer are the same, using RALC makes it feasible to distinguish the protocols by looking at the patterns in radio activities triggered by transmit and receive packets, including data packets and control packets.

Cluster Analysis of Alternating Protocols: Next, we evaluate the effectiveness of RALC for clustering two protocols running during different periods. We switch back and forth between CTP and DHV protocols during a one-hour experiment. We use a general non-parametric cluster algorithm, MeanShift to cluster the RALC from the measurements. In figure 1(b), yellow and green backgrounds show the periods with correct clustering, while red shows the mis-clustered period. Out of 360 snapshots, only 18 of them were mis-clustered; thus, the percentage of correctly clustered snapshots is 95%. All of mis-clustered periods happen right after CTP starts. During the warm up period of CTP, the nodes exchange a lot of control packets to setup routing paths compared to the stable period. This causes the algorithm to mis-cluster CTP as DHV. This experiment shows that RALC can correctly identify the protocols running during different periods, and can also detect the moment when the protocol changes. Because RALC can capture the change in control overhead caused by a protocol switch. Hence, we expect our proposed approach can also cluster three or more protocols.

5.2 Infer Network Topology

Next, we study the effectiveness of RAOC in revealing information about the network topology and routing path for each node.

Parent Node and Routing Path: The RAOC across two nodes can be used to estimate the parent-child relationship across the network running multi-hop collection protocol . We remove the radio overlap length that are too short

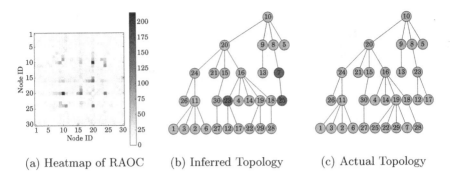

(a) Heatmap of RAOC   (b) Inferred Topology   (c) Actual Topology

Fig. 2. Use RAOC to find the parent node for each node, and reveal the topology of whole network. Red circles indicate the node with wrong parent node.

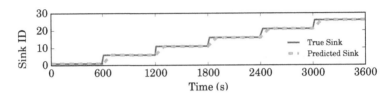

Fig. 3. The detected sink node by only using RALC compare to the ground truth

(less than 0.025s) to focus on significant overlaps in our analysis. Figure 2(a) shows the heatmap of RAOC across every node-pair during a 200s window size. The darker color represents those two nodes having larger overlapped times. A heuristic to find the parent for a node is to simply designate the node with which a node has the largest overlap as its parent. For example, for y=20, the pixel at x=10 is darkest. Hence, we guess that node 10 is the parent of node 20. If multiple nodes have same overlap length, we use overlap information from adjacent time window. We use this heuristic for each node in the heatmap and construct the routing topology, which is shown in figure 2(b). We found that this inferred topology based on the heatmap is surprisingly close to the actual routing topology shown in figure 2(c). Only the nodes marked red had the wrong estimate of routing parent. We ran CTP and LQI multiple times on testbed and used the heuristics above to estimate the routing topology. The estimation accuracy across the experiments was 97.8% and 90.2% for CTP and LQI protocol, respectively.

Sink Node: Next we study how to identify the sink with RALC. During each 100s window period, the nodes with the maximum number of T_2 had the highest possibility to be the sink node, since the T_2 could reflect the number of receive events. We ran CTP for one hour, where the sink node changed every 600s. The red curve in figure 3 shows the true sink node ID while the blue curve shows the predicted sink node ID. The result shows that identifying the sink using RALC is accurate and feasible. The slight lag between predicted and actual sink is due to the 100s window when we calculate RALC.

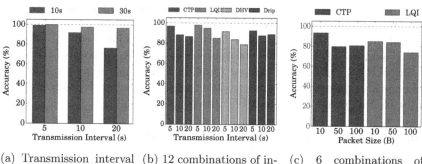

(a) Transmission interval 5s, 10s, 20s on CTP.

(b) 12 combinations of intervals and protocols.

(c) 6 combinations of packet size and protocols.

Fig. 4. True Positive Rate when using RALC to detect application workloads

5.3 Determine Application Workloads

In this section, we evaluate the effectiveness of RALC to distinguish different application workloads, including application layer packet transmission interval and payload size. In this section all of the experiments were run on FlockLab. We used J48 algorithm to perform the classification test.

Packet Transmission Interval on Same Protocol: We first run CTP with data being generated at three different intervals: 5s, 10s, and 20s. We calculate the True Positive Rate (TPR) when classifying each interval from the mixed dataset. We use 10s as the window size to calculate the RALC, and its corresponding TPRs are plotted with blue color in figure 4(a). The TPR is 99.2% to classify 5s interval, then TPR decreases to 91.9%, even drops to 76.5% for interval 10s and 20s, respectively. The drop is due to the packet transmission interval becoming larger than the RALC window. Thus, TPR increases with a larger RALC window size (30s), significantly improved the classification accuracy, as showed in the same figure with red color.

Packet Transmission Interval over Various Protocols: In Figure 4(b), we plot the results from determining packet intervals across four protocols using 30s window size. The average accuracy to classify one of the instance from all of the 12 combinations of 4 protocol and 3 intervals is 87.5%.

Packet Size: We vary the data packet size sent with CTP and LQI from 10 to 50 to 100 bytes. The dataset includes a total 6 distinct types of instances, which are the combination of two protocols and three packet sizes. Figure 4(c) shows the average accuracy to classify one instance from 6 combinations is 82.8%.

6   Conclusions

In this paper, we demonstrated that energy instrumentation can be a powerful tool to study and reveal information about the network, protocol, or workload. We designed features for classification and analysis based on energy instrumentation. We found that the feature called Radio Awake Length Counter is especially versatile in revealing information across protocols and application workloads, such as 97% accurate for classify protocols, and average 87.5% accurate for classify workloads. Furthermore, another feature named Radio Awake Overlapped Counter could reveal the parent node for each node, even to disclose the actual network topology with 98% accuracy. Our extensive experimental results performed on three different testbeds over 100 test cases suggest that our proposed features are robust across the testbeds, frequency bands.

Acknowledgments. This work was partially supported by the National Science Foundation under grant no. IIS-1111507.

References

1. Dang, T., Bulusu, N., Feng, W.C., Park, S.: Dhv: A code consistency maintenance protocol for multi-hop wireless sensor networks. In: Wireless Sensor Networks, pp. 327–342 (2009)
2. Doddavenkatappa, M., Chan, M.C., Ananda, A.L.: Indriya: A low-cost, 3D wireless sensor network testbed. In: Korakis, T., Li, H., Tran-Gia, P., Park, H.-S. (eds.) TridentCom 2011. LNICST, vol. 90, pp. 302–316. Springer, Heidelberg (2012)
3. Dunkels, A., Eriksson, J., Finne, N., Tsiftes, N.: Powertrace: Network-level power profiling for low-power wireless networks (2011)
4. Dunkels, A., Osterlind, F., Tsiftes, N., He, Z.: Software-based on-line energy estimation for sensor nodes. In: EmNets, pp. 28–32 (2007)
5. Gnawali, O., Fonseca, R., Jamieson, K., Moss, D., Levis, P.: Collection tree protocol. In: ACM SenSys (2009)
6. Hall, M., Frank, E., Holmes, G., Pfahringer, B., Reutemann, P., Witten, I.H.: The weka data mining software: an update. ACM SIGKDD Explorations Newsletter 11(1), 10–18 (2009)
7. Li, Q., Han, D., Gnawali, O., Sommer, P., Kusy, B.: Twonet: Large-scale wireless sensor network testbed with dual-radio nodes. In: ACM SenSys (2013)
8. Lim, R., Ferrari, F., Zimmerling, M., Walser, C., Sommer, P., Beutel, J.: Flocklab: A testbed for distributed, synchronized tracing and profiling of wireless embedded systems. In: ACM/IEEE IPSN (2013)
9. Molina-Markham, A., Shenoy, P., Fu, K., Cecchet, E., Irwin, D.: Private memoirs of a smart meter. In: ACM BuildSys (2010)
10. Pang, R., Allman, M., Paxson, V., Lee, J.: The devil and packet trace anonymization. ACM SIGCOMM Computer Communication Review 36(1), 29–38 (2006)
11. Stathopoulos, T., McIntire, D., Kaiser, W.J.: The energy endoscope: Real-time detailed energy accounting for wireless sensor nodes. In: ACM/IEEE IPSN (2008)
12. TinyOS: The drip protocol, https://github.com/tinyos/tinyos-main/tree/master/tos/lib/net/drip
13. TinyOS: Multihoplqi collection protocol, https://github.com/tinyos-main/tree/master/tos/lib/net/lqi
14. Woehrle, M., Lampka, K., Thiele, L.: Exploiting timed automata for conformance testing of power measurements. In: Ouaknine, J., Vaandrager, F.W. (eds.) FORMATS 2009. LNCS, vol. 5813, pp. 275–290. Springer, Heidelberg (2009)

Is RPL Ready for Actuation?
A Comparative Evaluation in a Smart City Scenario

Timofei Istomin[1], Csaba Kiraly[2], and Gian Pietro Picco[1]

[1] DISI – University of Trento, 38123 Povo, Trento, Italy
{timofei.istomin,gianpietro.picco}@unitn.it
[2] Bruno Kessler Foundation, 38123 Povo, Trento, Italy
kiraly@fbk.eu

Abstract. Low-power wireless actuation is attracting interest in many domains, yet it is significantly less investigated than its sensing counterpart, especially in large-scale scenarios. As a consequence, guidelines about which protocol, among the few existing ones, is best suited to a given scenario are generally lacking.

In this paper, we investigate the relative performance of simple dissemination-based solutions against the standard, state-of-the-art RPL protocol. These choices of protocols are motivated concretely by our involvement in the deployment of a large-scale infrastructure for smart city applications, which directly informs our evaluation, where we use the actual network topology.

Our findings, albeit in a specific scenario, suggest that RPL still leaves much to be desired w.r.t. actuation. Two out of the three RPL implementations we considered exhibited unacceptable performance when used out-of-the-box. Even after some tuning and debugging, simple, dissemination-based solutions perform surprisingly better under several conditions. These findings motivate further research on the topic of large-scale low-power wireless actuation.

1 Introduction

The growing importance of cyber-physical systems, where the target environment is augmented with small devices able to sense and actuate according to the application logic, has brought low-power wireless networks to the forefront as an enabling technology. Nevertheless, although wireless *sensing* has been a popular research topic in the last decade, wireless *actuation* has received considerably less attention. As a result, not only there are fewer proposals in this latter realm, but also noticeably less common knowledge about the protocol tradeoffs, especially when applied to a real scenario.

Goal and Motivation. The work we present here stems from this observation, and was prompted by a concrete necessity. Our research team was sought after for collaboration by a company deploying in Trento, Italy, a large-scale wireless infrastructure of 860+ IEEE 802.15.4 nodes, for monitoring and control of public lighting and other "smart city" applications. Our task was to improve the current network stack which is based on simple *flooding*, by identifying an existing solution providing better performance, to be used in the final deployment. *"Beating flooding: that's going to be a piece of cake"* we thought cockily—a thought probably shared by many readers. This paper shows instead

T. Abdelzaher et al. (Eds.): EWSN 2015, LNCS 8965, pp. 291–299, 2015.

that the winner is not so clear. As our study is based on the deployment topology and scale for a smart city—a scenario at the forefront of today's technological trends—our findings raise questions about the state of the art of low-power wireless actuation.

Protocols under Study. We chose RPL [13] as the main candidate because it is a standard and provides interoperability with mainstream Internet technology. Moreover, it is designed to support both the many-to-one traffic typical of sensing and the unicast or multicast one-to-many necessary to large-scale actuation. Several implementations of the standard exist, which bear significant differences [9]. We focused on TinyRPL [16] and ContikiRPL [15], arguably the most popular implementations available. We include also ORPL [3], which aims to improve the scalability of downward routing of RPL.

The baseline for our comparison is the flooding protocol currently operational in our reference smart city deployment. It implements a simple scheme, in which nodes repeat incoming messages once, after a small random delay, using link-level broadcast. A history of seen messages and time-to-live (TTL) are used to filter duplicates and avoid loops. We also included Trickle in our comparison as another representative of *dissemination* protocols. In fact, protocol complexity was an issue for the company, therefore, Trickle constitutes an alternative to flooding less radical than RPL.

Scenario and Methodology. We cast our comparison in the real-world scenario above, leveraging the first-hand information we can obtain from it. The planned deployment comprises 864 nodes on lampposts, divided into 13 clusters whose size is 25 to 134 nodes, each with a dedicated gateway to the Internet. Peculiar network topologies determined by the urban structure and radio interference properties make this scenario different from the indoor testbeds typically employed to evaluate protocol performance. Since nodes on lampposts are mains-connected, a duty-cycling MAC is not necessary.

Nevertheless, we do not have access to the actual infrastructure deployment, and cannot perform protocol experiments directly on it. Simulation is essentially the only option to perform our comparison. The use of simulation has well-known drawbacks, e.g., the approximations made w.r.t. the radio channel. In our study, in the absence of radio models or experimental traces expressly targeting a smart city environment, we resort to the MRM model provided by the Cooja emulator and commonly used by the literature. However, we also aim to reproduce the interference and background noise present in diverse urban environments, based on noise measurements we acquired in several locations, described in Section 2 along with simulation settings.

Related Work. Most experimental studies of RPL explore its data collection performance and topology stability [5, 7, 9, 12]; only a few deal with one-to-many traffic required for actuation. Authors of [8] study downward routing of TinyRPL in a 30 node indoor testbed and report results matching our observations for small clusters under low noise. The design of RPL downward routing is criticized in [1], although experiments are limited to many-to-one routing in an indoor testbed. The one-to-many routing of ORPL is shown to outperform RPL in an indoor environment [3], using ContikiMAC.

Other protocols like WirelessHART, ISA100.11a [11] and LWB [4], although in principle relevant to our study, were excluded due to lack of support by simulators.

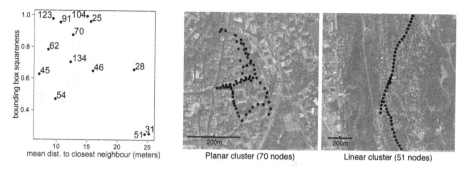

Fig. 1. Summary statistics about the geometry of the topology of all the 13 clusters (left) and topology of two representative clusters (right). Note the different scale of the maps.

Findings. Section 3 presents the results of our study, which is geared towards answering a very simple question: *"Is RPL ready for actuation?"* Based on the results, Section 4 formulates an answer, which is not a positive one. Finally, we end the paper with brief concluding remarks, including opportunities for future work on the topic.

2   Simulation Settings

We base our study on Cooja [10], which supports both Contiki [15] based implementatations and others (e.g., TinyRPL) thanks to its hardware emulation feature.

Topologies. The left side of Fig. 1 shows a comparison of cluster geometries, characterized by three metrics: *i)* number of nodes in the cluster (point label); *ii)* distance to the closest neighbor, averaged over all nodes (x-axis); *iii)* aspect ratio of a bounding box aligned with the largest span, indicating how "linear" a cluster is (y-axis). The right side of Fig. 1 shows the topology of two representative clusters.

Signal Propagation Model. We base our simulation on Cooja's multi-path ray tracing model (MRM). It models radio hardware properties, background noise and interference through signal-to-interference-and-noise ratio (SINR), the capture and multi-path effects; however, its simplistic obstacle model is not sufficient to define the complex architecture of a city. We configure MRM based on the popular CC2420 radio chip.

Modeling Noise. The background radio noise (including ambient and man-generated effects) directly influences signal-to-interference-and-noise ratio (SINR), thus also radio reception range and protocol performance. The noise floor in a dense urban environment can be relatively high and with high short-term variations.

This is in contrast with works assuming a noise-free environment (e.g., [14]), and with the conditions found in the testbeds commonly used in experiments. To verify this statement we performed measurements on all IEEE 802.15.4 channels in the Indriya [2] and TWIST [6] testbeds as well as in several places of Trento and Moscow, including suburbs, densely inhabited areas and the university campus. The testbed measurements show a mean noise floor of −90 to −98 dBm and a standard deviation of 2–4 dBm,

Table 1. Layer 3 parameters

Protocol	L3 parameters	L2
Flooding	rebroadcast delay: 8–80ms	
Trickle	I_{min}=1/32s, I_{max}=1/2s, K=1	CSMA 1
ContikiRPL	routing table size: 70, routing	
TinyRPL	metric: ETX	CSMA 2
ORPL	routing metric: EDC	RDC

Table 2. Layer 2 parameters

Parameter	CSMA 1	CSMA 2	RDC
CCA backoff	128ms–1.2s	0.3–10ms	125–500ms
backoff increase	exponential	none	linear
no-ACK retry delay	as backoff	103ms	as backoff
duty-cycle interval		—	125ms
no-ACK TX attempts		5	
neighbour table size		20	60

depending on the node and channel. In the cities, the mean noise floor is usually -85 to -95 dBm (occasionally up to -75 dBm), and the standard deviation is 0–10 dBm.

We use the notation $MRM(N_{avg}, N_{sd})$ to indicate an MRM model with noise floor N_{avg} and standard deviation N_{sd}. We also consider the *theoretical radio reception range*, an estimate calculated using Friis transmission equation based on N_{avg}, the parameters of the radio subsystem, and a transmission power of 0 dBm.

Protocol Settings. All the protocols under study are highly customizable through parameters such as buffer sizes, timeouts, retries and hop count. Wherever possible, we used the default values, as these are likely to be first choice in a deployment and the ones tested the most. We did, however, include tuned and modified versions of ContikiRPL and ORPL, since their initial results showed clear discrepancies w.r.t. expectations. The most important protocol parameters used in our study are summarized in Tables 1 and 2.

Application Setup and Performance Metrics. We test protocol performance in sending commands from the gateway to other nodes in the cluster, as in the current infrastructure. Messages have a 6 B payload, enough to fit a command code and 1–2 parameters. As actuation commands are issued sparingly, we focus on the reliability and timeliness of delivering isolated commands, rather than scalability in terms of traffic load.

In each experiment, after a warm-up time needed to stabilize logical topology, the gateway sends $B = 2000$ isolated commands, each destined to a node chosen with uniform random selection, with an inter-command interval (ICI) of 5 s. For statistical relevance, simulations are run 5 times per set of parameters; the plots report the average value along with error bars denoting the minimum and maximum values. Reliability and timeliness are quantified by measuring the *packet delivery ratio (PDR)* and average *delivery delay* for each destination and further averaging over all nodes of the cluster.

We also consider the *network utilization per actuation command*, expressed in bytes sent over the radio. To compute it we sum up the data and control traffic transmitted after the warm up and normalize w.r.t. the number of actuation commands sent.

3 Results

We compare the selected protocols in different radio propagation environments and network topologies. Space limitations force us to show the effect of noise floor only for the two distinctive clusters presented in Fig. 1: a 70-node "planar" one and a 51-node "linear" one. The noise variance was set to $N_{sd} = 1$ dBm. We then focus on two

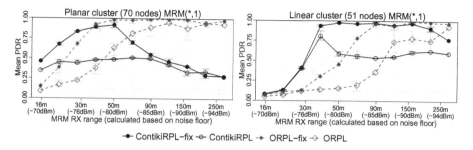

Fig. 2. PDR achieved by ContikiRPL, ORPL, and their debugged variants

interesting noise configurations, and analyze the impact of topology and scale, showing results for all the clusters.

Debugging ContikiRPL and ORPL. In our first trials, ContikiRPL showed lower performance than expected. Log inspection identified routing table management as the culprit. When a node rejoins through another DODAG branch, the next-hop entry at the branching point is not updated until it expires. Traffic along the stale path causes routing errors, triggering unnecessary DODAG reconstructions through version increase. A vicious circle is formed: version increase causes churn, churn brings routing errors and version increase. Our fix to this issue has been merged into the Contiki code base.

The default ORPL configuration also performed poorly. A custom one, with bitmap filters and a 125 ms ContikiMAC period showed better performance, though degrading over time. The so-called false positive mechanism stalled nodes; we disabled it, as it is anyway useless with bitmap filters. We also disabled the bitmap ageing mechanism and modified the input filters in the reception path to solve occasional memory corruptions.

The effect of our modifications is evident in Fig. 2, showing PDR as a function of radio range (noise floor) on our reference clusters. Our modified implementations match or outperform the original ones on all clusters and for all the metrics, often with remarkable performance gains. Therefore, hereafter they are the only ones we report.

Impact of Noise Floor. Fig. 3 shows the protocol performance as a function of noise floor, similarly to Fig. 2 but this time with all metrics and for all studied protocols.

From a reliability perspective, only Trickle performs well in all cases where the graph is still connected. This is expected, since it is the only protocol enjoying unlimited retransmissions; in case of an isolated message, sooner or later Trickle delivers.

On the planar cluster, ContikiRPL-fix handles high noise better than flooding. In this situation, the radio range is so small that nodes have only few neighbors with weak links; the L2 retransmissions of ContikiRPL-fix are more effective than the multipath properties of flooding. Nevertheless, below −75 dBm, as the improved range and link quality makes link-local broadcasts more efficient, flooding takes the lead. On the linear cluster, ContikiRPL-fix provides good results below −77 dBm, against the −80 dBm of flooding. However, ContikiRPL-fix never reaches $PDR = 100\%$, even in medium-noise scenarios where its competitors do, and shows poor performance at low noise, especially on the planar cluster. The increased radio range makes the network

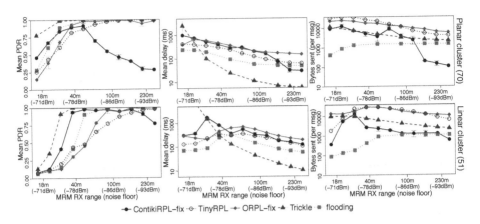

Fig. 3. Effect of noise floor on protocol performance: PDR, delay, and network utilization (columns) on the two selected clusters (rows)

denser, overfilling the neighbor tables; further, when the next-hop node is not found among the neighbors, a global DODAG repair is triggered. ORPL-fix delivers less than ContikiRPL-fix at high noise, but it does not suffer from higher density, and performs in line with dissemination protocols when noise is −80 dBm in the planar cluster, and −85 dBm in the linear one. TinyRPL follows in the ranking, consistently on both clusters. It is not affected by high network density since it does not rely on the neighbor table to resolve the next-hop link-local address for a given target. Instead, the address is obtained directly as the last two octets of the link-local IPv6 address of the neighbor.

Regarding the *average delay* of packet delivery, differences were so significant that we had to resort to a logarithmic scale. Trickle achieves best performance in low-noise situations. At high noise, it is the only protocol with high PDR values, which makes its seemingly larger average delay non-comparable to other protocols. Flooding and TinyRPL follow with a significant increase in delivery times. ContikiRPL-fix and ORPL-fix close the ranking, with delays between 500 and 800 ms. For ORPL-fix this higher delay is partly justified by the use of the duty-cycling MAC.

For evaluating *network utilization*, a logarithmic scale was again required. For flooding, the metric is simply proportional to the cluster-level average PDR, since each node that receives a packet repeats it exactly once. Trickle is heavier than flooding due to its retransmissions. Although flooding involves the whole network when delivering a single packet, its network utilization is still less than RPL variants under most conditions, except for very low noise situations. Indeed, RPL cannot amortize the topology maintenance cost under the (realistic) traffic properties used in our tests.

All Clusters: Trends and Effects of Topology. After exploring the influence of the noise floor, we demonstrate the effects of topology characteristics under typical low and high noise scenarios, $MRM(-90, 2)$ and $MRM(-85, 3)$ respectively. Fig. 4 shows the results for all clusters. Note that we use the number of nodes to identify them.

Both ContikiRPL-fix and TinyRPL show scalability issues as the number of nodes grows. Moreover, the selected radio model values fall outside the "comfort area" of

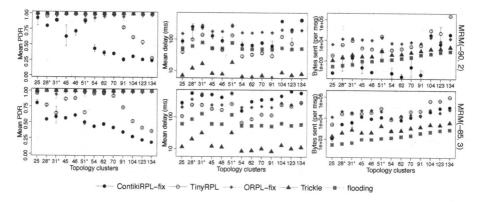

Fig. 4. Results for all the clusters. PDR, delay and network utilization (columns); low noise and high noise scenarios (rows).

ContikiRPL-fix, triggering its node density issues, for which it provides the worst PDR of all protocols. ORPL-fix, on the other hand, reaches high PDR, thanks to the noise level below -85 dBm. Other trends are the high PDR and almost flat delay recorded for flooding and Trickle regardless the number of nodes. Network utilization instead increases almost linearly with the number of nodes for all protocols.

There are, however, outliers from the above trends; some are correlated to topology characteristics, as in the case of the three clusters marked by asterisks which have "special" topologies. Clusters 31 and 51 are sparse and long, while cluster 28 is U-shaped with the two long branches behaving like the linear topologies. In these clusters, delays are increased for all protocols due to larger hop-counts in paths. Trickle and TinyRPL also shows increased network utilization, while flooding is not affected. The performance of TinyRPL is decreased in these special clusters (can only be seen in high noise), but it is not clear whether larger node distances or longer multi-hop paths are to blame. ContikiRPL-fix instead shows a performance increase but only at lower noise, and in this case we know it is due to the decreased neighborhoods.

4   Discussion, Conclusions, and Future Work

Our involvement in the design of the network stack for a smart city infrastructure was the opportunity to study the applicability of RPL and its variants to the problem of large-scale low-power wireless actuation. We performed our study by simulation, borrowing the actual placement of nodes to experiment with a real network scale and topology.

We were convinced that flooding was going to be left in the dust by RPL; our results tell a different story. The RPL variants were outperformed by flooding (and Trickle) especially in low-noise conditions (or high range and therefore neighbor density), where RPL suffered from various reasons, including scalability issues and topology reconstructions leading to increased packet losses. ContikiRPL-fix outperforms flooding, thanks to link-level retransmissions, in situations with high noise (low density) where long multi-hop paths are required to deliver messages, e.g., on linear topologies.

However, in these cases the other RPL variants are outperformed by flooding, with significant differences among the various implementations. Further, the simple dissemination scheme of Trickle outperforms ContikiRPL-fix, and appears to be the best choice.

Trickle is also the fastest protocol, while flooding is the one with the lowest network utilization, leaving few reasons to choose RPL over our dissemination baseline. To be fair to RPL, the overhead of maintaining its topology is expected to be amortized by the many-to-one data collection traffic (not considered here) for which it is optimized, and "reused" for actuation. Our results, however, show that this reuse falls short of expectation, suggesting that a dedicated and complementary solution, possibly dissemination-based, should be used for the relatively lower-traffic of actuation.

These RPL shortcomings are exacerbated by implementation considerations, beyond the difficulties we encountered in using ContikiRPL and ORPL out of the box. The superior performance of dissemination protocols is complemented by their simplicity, yielding less demands in terms of memory consumption. In fact, the studied RPL implementations occupied almost all RAM and Flash memory of the popular TMote Sky.

In summary, the verdict is against RPL. Aside from relatively immature RPL implementations, it is hard to beat the simplicity and robustness of dissemination protocols.

There are obvious opportunities for future work on the topic of this paper: our findings are specific to our smart city target scenario, and should be validated in other kinds of large-scale actuation scenarios, possibly through real-world experiments. Finally, this paper poses a research question, namely, whether low-power wireless actuation really needs the complexity of maintaining a routing topology, or instead dissemination protocols should be the foundation to be optimized towards this functionality.

Acknowledgments. This work was partially funded by EIT ICT Labs (Activity 12149) and by Algorab S.r.l., which also provided information about the smart city deployment.

References

1. Clausen, T., Herberg, U., Philipp, M.: A critical evaluation of the IPv6 Routing Protocol for Low Power and Lossy Networks (RPL). In: Proc. of WiMob (2011)
2. Doddavenkatappa, M., Chan, M.C., Ananda, A.L.: Indriya: A Low-Cost, 3D Wireless Sensor Network Testbed. In: Korakis, T., Li, H., Tran-Gia, P., Park, H.-S. (eds.) TridentCom 2011. LNICST, vol. 90, pp. 302–316. Springer, Heidelberg (2012)
3. Duquennoy, S., Landsiedel, O., Voigt, T.: Let the Tree Bloom: Scalable Opportunistic Routing with ORPL. In: Proc. of SenSys (2013)
4. Ferrari, F., Zimmerling, M., Thiele, L., Mottola, L.: The low-power wireless bus. In: Proc. of IPSN (2012)
5. Gaddour, O., Koubâa, A.: RPL in a nutshell: A survey. Computer Networks 56(14) (2012)
6. Handziski, V., Köpke, A., Willig, A., Wolisz, A.: TWIST. In: Proc. of REALMAN (2006)
7. Iova, O., Theoleyre, F., Noel, T.: Stability and efficiency of RPL under realistic conditions in wireless sensor networks. In: Proc. of PIMRC (2013)
8. Ko, J., Dawson-Haggerty, S., Gnawali, O., Culler, D., Terzis, A.: Evaluating the Performance of RPL and 6LoWPAN in TinyOS. In: Proc. of the IP+SN Workshop (2011)
9. Ko, J., Eriksson, J., Tsiftes, N., Dawson-Haggerty, S., Terzis, A., Dunkels, A., Culler, D.: ContikiRPL and TinyRPL: Happy together. In: Proc. of the IP+SN Workshop (2011)
10. Osterlind, F., Dunkels, A., Eriksson, J., Finne, N., Voigt, T.: Cross-Level Sensor Network Simulation with COOJA. In: Proc. of LCN (2006)

11. Petersen, S., Carlsen, S.: WirelessHART versus ISA100.11a: the format war hits the factory floor. IEEE Industrial Electronics 5(4) (2011)
12. Radoi, I., Shenoy, A., Arvind, D.: Evaluation of Routing Protocols for Internet-Enabled Wireless Sensor Networks. In: Proc. of ICWMC (2012)
13. Winter, T., et al.: RPL: IPv6 routing protocol for low-power and lossy networks. RFC 6550
14. Zamalloa, M.Z., Krishnamachari, B.: An analysis of unreliability and asymmetry in low-power wireless links. ACM Trans. on Sensor Networks (TOSN) 3(2), 7 (2007)
15. Contiki operating system official website, http://contiki-os.org
16. TinyOS official website, http://tinyos.net

Adaptive Packet Size Control
for Bulk Data Transmission in IPv6
over Networks of Resource Constrained Nodes

Yang Deng, Zhonghong Ou, and Antti Ylä-Jääski

Aalto University, Espoo, Finland
{yang.deng,zhonghong.ou,antti.yla-jaaski}@aalto.fi

Abstract. Conventional transmission in IPv6 over Networks of Resource
Constrained Nodes (6lo) favours fixed-size packets and results in low network performance when bulk data transmission is required by applications, for example firmware updating. To tackle this problem, we first
investigate performance of bulk data transmission through large packets and make two important observations. Then we propose an adaptive
mechanism at IP layer to dynamically adjust packet size in 6lo. We implemented the mechanism on Contiki OS and evaluated it through a series of experiments in Cooja. Experimental results demonstrate that our
mechanism outperforms Contiki standard implementation significantly
from both reliability and goodput under various network conditions.

Keywords: 6lo, Bulk Data Transmission, Packet Size Control.

1 Introduction

IPv6 over Networks of Resource-constrained Nodes (6lo) is a network that provides IPv6 connectivity over constrained nodes such as sensors or actuators. It
introduces an adaptation layer to deal with the mapping between IPv6 packets
and link frames (hereafter referred to as `packet` and `frame` respectively). Con-
ventionally, when data are transmitted in 6lo, they are firstly encapsulated into
a fixed-size packet and then header compression is applied to reduce the packet
size. If the compressed packet fits into a single frame then it will be sent out
instantly; otherwise fragmentation-reassembly mechanism (hereafter referred to
as `6lo fragmentation`) is invoked. The value of the fixed-size is preconfigured
empirically (e.g. 140 bytes for IEEE 802.15.4 in Contiki). As RFC4944 [6] points
out, in links with a small maximum transmission unit (MTU), the conventional
transmission works but with two assumptions: (i) most applications will not
use large packets and (ii) application payload is relatively small. Nevertheless,
there are application scenarios where these conditions do not hold. Considering
firmware updating on-the-fly or massive data exchanging between nodes, both
of them involve bulk data transmission for which 6lo conventional transmission
is not suitable due to low network performance.

In order to improve 6lo performance of bulk data transmission, we present
an adaptive mechanism that adjusts packet size dynamically based on network

T. Abdelzaher et al. (Eds.): EWSN 2015, LNCS 8965, pp. 300–307, 2015.
© Springer International Publishing Switzerland 2015

conditions and utilizes 6lo fragmentation (different from IP fragmentation) to send large packets. Unlike other adaptive mechanisms [2, 3, 7], our mechanism works at IP layer whereas others only work at link layer. Link layer mechanisms highly rely on the link of a specific type. For example the mechanism designed for IEEE 802.15.4 might not be feasible for Bluetooth Low Energy (BLE) or Near Field Communication (NFC), both are documented by 6lo working group. As 6lo operates over links of different types, an upper-layer mechanism is therefore much more desirable. Furthermore, even if frame size can be dynamically controlled by link layer mechanisms, there remains a need for determining IP packet size in 6lo. Unfortunately, to the best of our knowledge, such a mechanism is still missing so far. Our work fills in this gap and in summary it makes three key contributions as follows:

- We investigate performance of bulk data transmission in 6lo through large packets and make two important observations.
- We present design, implementation, and evaluation of IP layer adaptive mechanism suitable for bulk data transmission in 6lo.
- We demonstrate that our adaptive mechanism is able to provide better reliability and higher goodput than Contiki standard implementation under various network conditions.

2   Related Work

Before IPv6 is introduced to Wireless Sensor Network (WSN), frame size optimization for WSN has been studied extensively in literature. Modiano et al. [5] developed a Markov chain model to analyse the channel then performed a maximum likelihood approach to estimate frame size. Sankarasubramaniam et al. [8] used energy-efficiency as the optimization object to determine the best frame size based on a set of radio and channel parameters. The work from [9] discussed the cross-layer solutions to set frame size for different environments like underwater and underground networks. All of these studies focus on finding an optimal fixed size. Another thread of research work suggests using adaptive approaches. Jelenković et al. [3] designed an algorithm to divide the frame into several small chunks to fit available channel periods. Dong's work [2] followed a similar idea that small chunks can be reassembled into a bigger frame. Nonetheless, these solutions work only at link layer. Because 6lo has a wide diversity of links, a solution working at IP layer is beneficial, which is the main contribution of this paper.

3   Mechanism

3.1   Overview

Our motivation comes from the assumption (justified in section 4.2) that bulk data transmission in 6lo by using large packets (invoking 6lo fragmentation if necessary) can improve network performance significantly. Nodes in 6lo usually suffer from intra-path interference [4], which means that when the successor node forwards the packet at the same time it will prevent the reception of following packet coming from the predecessor node. Employing pipeline mechanisms to send packets might mitigate this problem; however, a poorly-designed scheduling policy can cause traffic congestion and lead to an even worse situation. Thus, stop-and-wait Automatic Repeat reQuest (ARQ) is the widely-used protocol to transmit bulk data in 6lo. One good example is Contiki TCP implementation where the window size is 1. In stop-and-wait ARQ, transmission time decreases as packet size increases. Nonetheless, the desire for large packets is limited by network conditions because the whole packet has to be retransmitted if any of the fragments gets lost. To tackle this problem, we propose an adaptive mechanism to adjust packet size based on network conditions; if network condition becomes better the packet size is increased, otherwise it is decreased.

For simplicity and practicality, network conditions are indicated by packet loss rate (PLR) [1]. Through empirical experiments, we make two important **observations**: (1) PLR of large packets is mainly impacted by the number of fragments that the packet is divided into; (2) if frame length is relatively small (approximately 100 octets), it has a trivial influence on the PLR. Due to space limit, we omit the analysis here. Inspired by these two observations, we propose an adaptive mechanism by following two rules:

Rule 1. Adjust packet size by fragments rather than octets, which is deduced from observation (1).

Rule 2. Given the number of fragments, make sure each fragment fills the frame as fully as possible, which is deduced from observation (2).

Based on these two rules, we design two modules, i.e., *Unit Discovery Module* and *Packet Adjustment Module*, to enable the adaptive mechanism.

3.2 Unit Discovery Module

Unit Discovery Module is responsible for finding the unit value by which packet size is increased/decreased in the mechanism. Considering a multi-hop 6lo, the unit value should be the *maximum* size of packet that will not be fragmented by any node along the path from the sender to the receiver. Note that given a packet, the decision on whether it should be fragmented or not is different at different nodes along the path. For example, by default 6lo employs Routing Protocol for Low power and Lossy Networks (RPL) as its routing protocol, the intermediate nodes between the sender and the receiver might insert RPL options into the packet. As a consequence, the packet without need of fragmentation at the sender might be fragmented at an intermediate router. To tackle this problem, we introduce a discovery procedure similar to Path MTU Discovery (PMTUD). Before bulk data transmission starts, the sender pings the receiver using an Internet Control Message Protocol (ICMP) Echo Request message whose size is the current unit value. After an intermediate node receives this message it checks whether 6lo fragmentation is needed or not. If yes, the node drops the message and sends back an ICMP Packet Too Big message containing the new appropriate unit value to the sender. Upon receiving ICMP Packet Too Big message, the sender re-pings the receiver by a new ICMP Echo Request message whose size is the updated unit value. The discovery procedure continues until the sender receives an ICMP Echo Reply message from the target receiver. The unit value corresponding to the receiver is saved in a cache and ready for use in *Packet Adjustment Module*.

3.3 Packet Adjustment Module

Once the unit value is discovered, *Packet Adjustment Module* uses it to adjust packet size according to network conditions, assuming that the routing information is not changed throughout the course of bulk data transmission. Packet size is adjusted by the following equation (note that 6lo fragmentation cuts the packets into 8-octet units):

$$S(n) = \begin{cases} U & n = 1 \\ \lfloor \frac{U-L_{F1}}{8} \rfloor \times 8 + \lfloor \frac{M-L_{FN}}{8} \rfloor \times 8 \times (n-2) + (M - L_{FN}) & n \geq 2 \end{cases} \quad (1)$$

where U is the unit value and M is the link MTU, L_{F1} and L_{FN} (4 and 5 in 6lo) are the length of initial fragment header and non-initial fragment header. It is important to note here that n should be less than 10 as (i) PLR increases significantly as n grows, and (ii) constrained nodes do not have enough memory to collect many fragments.

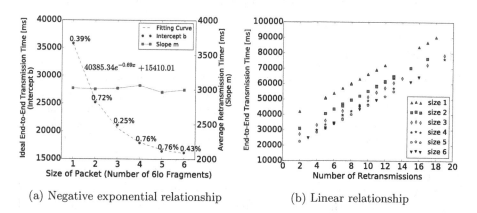

(a) Negative exponential relationship   (b) Linear relationship

Fig. 1. Transmitting bulk data (16KiB) in medium traffic (10s) network with link FER(15%)

Another function of *Packet Adjustment Module* is to adjust packet size efficiently. When running the experiments in section 4.2, we find out that there exists a linear relationship between the end-to-end transmission time and the number of retransmissions, as shown in Fig. 1b. For each packet size we use least squares method to fit the scatters by a linear function $y = mx + b$, and the fitted parameters (slope m and intercept b) with normalized root-mean-square deviation (NRMSD) are plotted in Fig. 1a. Both m and b have practical meaning: m is the average value of retransmission timer (3 seconds in our experiments); whereas b implies the end-to-end transmission time in ideal situation where no retransmission occurs. From Fig. 1a it is clear to see that intercept b against packet size follows a negative exponential function (dashed line in the figure), which means that the performance gain achievable by increasing packet size is significant when packet size is small; as packet size increases, the gain becomes less significant. With this observation, we set up a threshold value (represented as the number of fragments) in our mechanism. When increasing packet size, if the threshold is not reached, we increase it by one fragment every time; and if the threshold is passed, we increase packet size by its current number of fragments, i.e. doubling the size. Conversely, when decreasing packet size, we half the size if the threshold is not reached; and decrease by one fragment if the threshold is passed.

4   Evaluation

We implemented our mechanism on Contiki OS. For the configuration of network stack in Contiki, we chose 6lowpan as the adaptation layer and employed CSMA at the link layer to provide media access control. As applications usually require bulk data to be transmitted as fast as possible, we used maximum power to transmit the data. To minimize the latency caused by wake-up synchronization among nodes, we switched *contikimac* to *nullrdc*, in which nodes do not sleep. In practice, nodes can switch back to *contikimac* after bulk data transmission completes if necessary.

4.1   Simulation Environment

We simulated a network containing 20 nodes in Cooja, the standard simulator for Contiki. Each node has a transmission range and a larger interference range. Within transmission range, the frame error rate (FER) is able to be configured and it increases as the transmission distance becomes larger; while in interference range, FER is 100% and other nodes are interfered accordingly. We chose one node as the sender (located at one edge of the network) and another node as the receiver (located at the other edge); there were 4 or 5 hops between the sender and the receiver. Moreover, to increase simulation fidelity, we generated background traffic in the network by making each node (except the sender and the receiver) send small packets to random nodes randomly within an interval. If the interval was set to 0, then no background traffic was generated.

4.2   Performance through Large Packets

In section 3.1 we claimed that bulk data transmission in 6lo through large packets can improve network performance significantly. This subsection quantifies this claim. To start with, we consider experiments of medium traffic network (the interval is set to 10 seconds) with different FERs (0%, 15%, 30%, and 45%) where the bulk data (16KiB) are transmitted in different packet sizes. Each experiment was performed 20 times and we use two metrics to compare network performance: end-to-end transmission time, and total transmitted octets by all the nodes along the path from the sender to the receiver. The result from $FER = 15\%$ is shown in Fig. 2. Results from other FER values are similar, thus, are omitted for brevity. The exceptional outputs (represented as outliers) are mainly caused by network congestion resulting from the background traffic. Note that the outliers are excluded when calculating the mean value in the figure. Fig. 2a illustrates that as the packet size increases the end-to-end transmission time decreases accordingly; however, when the packet size exceeds a specific value, the transmission time increases again. The same trend occurs for the total transmitted octets, as shown in Fig. 2b. The reasons for this are explained in section 3.1. From Fig. 2, we can see that if large packets are used, the end-to-end transmission time is improved by 38% (from $\sim$ 65s to $\sim$ 40s), and total transmitted octets are reduced by 20% (from $\sim$ 200KiB to $\sim$ 160KiB).

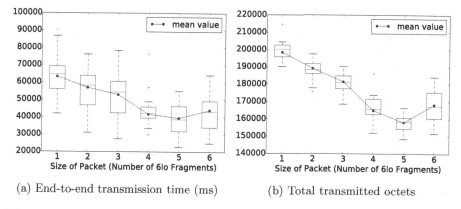

(a) End-to-end transmission time (ms)   (b) Total transmitted octets

Fig. 2. Network performance with $FER = 15\%$ for different sizes of packet (represented by number of fragments)

4.3 Mechanism Effectiveness

To evaluate the effectiveness of our adaptive mechanism in terms of reliability and goodput, we investigate a series of experiments similar to those in section 4.2 except two more types of background traffic are introduced: low traffic (the interval is set to 0) and high traffic (the interval is set to 5 seconds). Instead of calculating PLR continuously (cf. section 3.1) to determine network conditions, we simply define network conditions as bad (if retransmission occurs) or good (if the payload is successfully acknowledged). The threshold value introduced in section 3.3 is set to 3, which means that the possible number of fragments is 1, 2, 3, or 6. Again, each experiment was performed 20 times.

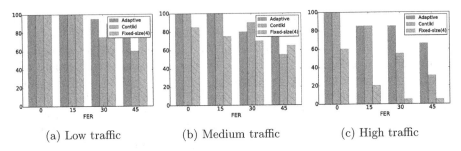

(a) Low traffic   (b) Medium traffic   (c) High traffic

Fig. 3. Percentage of successful transmissions [%], the higher the better

We compare our adaptive mechanism (referred to as Adaptive) with the Contiki standard implementation (referred to as Contiki), as well as the approach using a fixed-size packet (referred to as Fixed-size). Firstly, we focus on the percentage of successful transmissions (i.e. how many tests are completed successfully within the 20 tests), which is an indicator of reliability and robustness. The results are shown in Fig. 3. From the figure, we can see that when network traffic is low and link condition is good, all of the three mechanisms complete 100% of tests. When network traffic increases or link condition becomes worse, the percentage of both Adaptive and Contiki decrease slightly, while Fixed-size drops dramatically. We have discussed the reasons for this behaviour in section 3.1. It is worth mentioning that even in high network traffic with the worst link condition, Adaptive can still complete around 70% of tests, which is significantly higher than that of Contiki. The reason is that the *Unit Discovery Module* in our mechanism ensures that in the worst cases there is no 6lo fragmentation invoked at any node along the path; while in Contiki, intermediate nodes are still possible to trigger 6lo fragmentation that might lead to packet loss in bad network conditions.

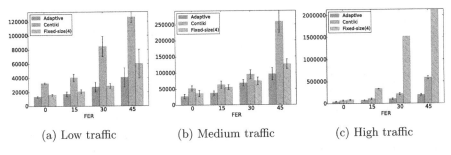

(a) Low traffic   (b) Medium traffic   (c) High traffic

Fig. 4. Estimated end-to-end transmission time [ms], the less the better

Secondly, we evaluate network goodput using end-to-end transmission time because network goodput is inversely proportional to end-to-end transmission time. Note that if the test gets failed, it is not possible to acquire the output data. Thus, it is unfair to compare only successful results and exclude the failed cases. To make up for this, we introduce a penalty function, which is defined as $1/percentage$. We then compute the estimated results by successful results times penalty function. We present the estimated results in Fig. 4. From the figure, it is clear that regardless of network traffic, overall transmission time for the three mechanisms increases as link conditions get worse. Compared with Contiki and Fixed-size, Adaptive outperforms them in all three network traffic environments. It is also worth noting that despite the decent performance of Fixed-size for low and medium traffic, the transmission time of it for high traffic is extremely high, which demonstrates its severe weakness in such environments. In summary, our adaptive mechanism is able to provide better reliability and higher goodput than the current state-of-the-art approaches in various network conditions.

5 Conclusion

In this paper, we justified the momentum of adjusting packet size adaptively for bulk data transmission in 6lo. Through an empirical study, we made two important observations that inspired the adaptive mechanism design. By evaluating a series of carefully-designed experiments in Cooja, we demonstrated the effectiveness of our mechanism from both reliability and goodput. In the future, we will conduct a systematic study on real devices. Furthermore, power consumption and duty cycles will also be investigated.

References

1. Baccour, N., Koubâa, A., Mottola, L., Zúñiga, M.A., Youssef, H., Boano, C.A., Alves, M.: Radio link quality estimation in wireless sensor networks: A survey. ACM Transactions on Sensor Networks 8(4), 34:1–34:33 (2012)
2. Dong, W., Liu, X., Chen, C., He, Y., Chen, G., Liu, Y., Bu, J.: DPLC: Dynamic Packet Length Control in Wireless Sensor Networks. In: Proceedings of IEEE INFOCOM 2010, pp. 1–9 (2010)
3. Jelenković, P.R., Tan, J.: Dynamic Packet Fragmentation for Wireless Channels with Failures. In: Proceedings of ACM MobiHoc 2008, pp. 73–82 (2008)
4. Kim, S., Fonseca, R., Dutta, P., Tavakoli, A., Culler, D., Levis, P., Shenker, S., Stoica, I.: Flush: A Reliable Bulk Transport Protocol for Multihop Wireless Networks. In: Proceedings of ACM SenSys 2007, pp. 351–365 (2007)
5. Modiano, E.: An Adaptive Algorithm for Optimizing the Packet Size Used in Wireless ARQ Protocols. Wireless Networks 5(4), 279–286 (1999)
6. Montenegro, G., Kushalnagar, N., Hui, J., Culler, D.: Transmission of IPv6 Packets over IEEE 802.15.4 Networks. RFC 4944 (Proposed Standard) (September 2007)
7. Ou, Z., Harjula, E., Ylianttila, M.: Effects of different churn models on the performance of structured peer-to-peer networks. In: Proceedings of IEEE PIMRC 2009, pp. 2856–2860 (2009)
8. Sankarasubramaniam, Y., Akyildiz, I., McLaughlin, S.W.: Energy efficiency based packet size optimization in wireless sensor networks. In: Proceedings of the First IEEE International Workshop on Sensor Network Protocols and Applications, pp. 1–8 (2003)
9. Vuran, M.C., Akyildiz, I.: Cross-Layer Packet Size Optimization for Wireless Terrestrial, Underwater, and Underground Sensor Networks. In: Proceedings of IEEE INFOCOM 2008, pp. 780–788 (2008)

Author Index

Ahmed, Mohsin Y.   68
Alhamoud, Alaa   52
Ali, Falah   151
Alizai, Muhammad Hamad   242
Alves, Mário   250

Basu, Prithwish   84
Bocchino, Stefano   1
Boehnstedt, Doreen   52

Ceriotti, Matteo   266
Cobârzan, Cosmin   135
Cuijpers, Pieter J.L.   186
Cuspinera, Luis Ponce   151

Deb, Budhaditya   84
Deng, Yang   300
Duda, Andrzej   202

Englert, Frank   52

Fedor, Szymon   1

Gnawali, Omprakash   242, 283
Grinnemo, Karl-Johan   104
Gunatilaka, Dolvara   234

Hallstrom, Jason O.   274
Han, Dong   242, 283
Hauser, Niklas   266
He, Yangyang   274
Hermans, Frederik   35
Hidell, Markus   104

Istomin, Timofei   291
Iyer, Venkatraman   35

Kenkeremath, Sean   68
Khattak, Muhammad Moosa   242
Kiraly, Csaba   291
Król, Michał   202

Landsiedel, Olaf   258
Li, Tongyang   19
Liu, Jie   168

Lu, Chenyang   234
Lukkien, Johan J.   186
Lymberopoulos, Dimitrios   168

Meyfroyt, Thomas M.M.   186
Montavont, Julien   135
Moreira, Adriano   250

Nguyen-Dinh, Long-Van   151
Noda, Claro A.   250
Noel, Thomas   135

Ou, Zhonghong   300

Pérez-Penichet, Carlos M.   250
Petracca, Matteo   1
Picco, Gian Pietro   291
Pombo, Guilherme   151

Reinhardt, Andreas   52, 218
Renner, Christian   218
Roggen, Daniel   151
Rousseau, Franck   202

Schiller, Elad Michael   258
Schmidt, Florian   266
Scholl, Philipp   52
Seeber, Balint   250
Sha, Mo   234
Sharma, Abhishek B.   283
Sjödin, Peter   104
Söderman, Pehr   104
Song, Lei   19
Stankovic, John   68
Steinmetz, Ralf   52
Stolikj, Milosh   186
Switzer, Fred S.   274
Syed, Affan A.   242

Tan, Haisheng   19
Tomaselli, Salvatore   258

Voigt, Thiemo   35

Wang, En   120
Wang, He   168

Wang, Yongcai   19
Wehrle, Klaus   266
Wu, Chengjie   234
Wu, Jie   120

Xu, Pei   52

Yang, Yongjian   120
Ylä-Jääski, Antti   300

Zennaro, Marco   250
Zhai, Jiannan   274